Human Performance Enhancement in High-Risk Environments

Recent Title in
Technology, Psychology, and Health

The PSI Handbook of Virtual Environments for Training and Education:
Developments for the Military and Beyond
Dylan Schmorrow, Joseph Cohn, and Denise Nicholson, editors

Human Performance Enhancement in High-Risk Environments

INSIGHTS, DEVELOPMENTS, AND FUTURE DIRECTIONS FROM MILITARY RESEARCH

Paul E. O'Connor and
Joseph V. Cohn, Editors

Technology, Psychology, and Health
Dylan Schmorrow and Denise Nicholson, Series Editors

PRAEGER SECURITY INTERNATIONAL
An Imprint of ABC-CLIO, LLC

Santa Barbara, California • Denver, Colorado • Oxford, England

Library of Congress Cataloging-in-Publication Data

Human performance enhancement in high-risk environments : insights, developments, and future
    directions from military research / Paul E. O'Connor and Joseph V. Cohn, editors.
        p. cm. — (Technology, psychology, and health)
    Includes bibliographical references and index.
    ISBN 978–0–313–35983–5 (hbk. : alk. paper) — ISBN 978–0–313–35984–2 (ebook)
1. Hazardous occupations. 2. Situational awareness. 3. Human engineering. 4. Performance
technology. I. O'Connor, Paul E. II. Cohn, Joseph V.
HD7262.H86   2010
658.3'14—dc22   2009038247

14 13 12 11 10   1 2 3 4 5

This book is also available on the World Wide Web as an eBook.
Visit www.abc-clio.com for details.

ABC-CLIO, LLC
130 Cremona Drive, P.O. Box 1911
Santa Barbara, California 93116-1911

This book is printed on acid-free paper ∞

Manufactured in the United States of America

CONTENTS

FOREWORD

As the military and other organizations work to optimize technology-enhanced human performance in increasingly dangerous high-risk situations, the need for a comprehensive collection of best practices has emerged. In response to that need, the editors of this volume have compiled recommendations from military and civilian researchers that include: (1) field-tested strategies and practices to maximize safety, (2) processes for selection of team members to achieve the most effective function, and (3) design of efficient training to prepare team members to perform highly complex tasks. The intention of this volume, as part of the Praeger *Technology, Psychology, and Health* series, is to provide examples of how these human performance issues are being addressed in the military and to describe how lessons learned can be applied to other, nonmilitary, high-reliability organizations (HROs).

With contributions from the brightest researchers working on human performance issues, the *Technology, Psychology, and Health* series was established to showcase the remarkable advances being achieved through the integration of research from diverse disciplines, where unified approaches to psychology, engineering, training, and practice result in more effective human systems applications. The volumes in the series address the general themes of requisite foundational knowledge, emergent scientific discoveries, and practical lessons learned, as well as cross-disciplinary standards, methodologies, metrics, techniques, practices, and visionary perspectives and developments. As part of this ongoing series, this volume explores the critical area of human performance enhancements in high-risk environments with the hope that these narratives will advance the general understanding of these challenges, providing solutions that increase opportunities for success while minimizing risk.

The chapters in this volume are arranged in four sections, each focusing on a key enabler of HROs: team selection, training, safety, and design. Although each chapter in the section emphasizes lessons learned from the military, the examples included offer applications beyond the military domain and are intended to benefit all organizations in which highly trained personnel interact with complex machinery while facing high consequences of error. For example, the discussions of stress among military aviators (Chapter 11) and the research on cockpit design (Chapter 15) might be equally useful for pilots and aircraft designers in general. In addition, the principles of use-inspired science (chapters 2 and 16) offer a wide range of present and future applications, such as the examination of the linkages between brain, body, and environment that challenge some aspects of traditional cognitive models. Discussions of these developing ideas serve as a bridge to new discoveries, innovations, and outcomes.

Like the three-volume *PSI Handbook of Virtual Environments for Training and Education* (Schmorrow et al., 2008), this text includes contributions from cross-disciplinary teams in order to consolidate and disseminate cutting-edge research and to forecast future human systems capabilities. All volumes in the series are uniquely designed to advance both the theory and the practice of emerging science and technology solutions in military and commercial applications. We offer this collection as an opportunity for additional collaboration and research, and we encourage interested researchers to contact the editors with comments, questions, and/or suggestions for further study.

Dylan Schmorrow and Denise Nicholson
Series Editors

Part I: Introduction and Overview

Chapter 1

ENHANCING HUMAN PERFORMANCE IN HIGH-RELIABILITY ORGANIZATIONS: LEARNING FROM THE MILITARY

Paul E. O'Connor and Joseph V. Cohn

SUCCESSFULLY MANAGING RISK: HIGH-RISK INDUSTRIES AND HIGH-RELIABILITY ORGANIZATIONS

Today's increasingly interconnected, diverse, and distributed work environments, with their growing reliance on integrated human–technology systems (HTSs), represent a distinct shift in the work roles assumed by the human operators and their partner technologies. Whereas in the past, the human operator may have played a more active and decisive role in guiding the outcome of these systems, today, the role of the human in these HTSs is limited to one of supervisory control, with many of the more complex analyses and actions being delegated to the partner technologies. Current HTS control paradigms continue to enforce this parsing of tasks, increasingly emphasizing the important role of technology, at the expense of the human operator. One important consequence of this shift in roles is that failures in these technologies often lead to catastrophic and unrecoverable accidents.

Organizations whose performance may be catastrophically impacted by failures in these complex HTSs are known as high-risk industries (Shrivastava, 1986). Those organizations that succeed in avoiding catastrophes in high-risk environments are known as high-reliability organizations (HROs; Roberts & Rousseau, 1989) and provide excellent use-cases for understanding the principles underlying risk management in these complex environments. HROs are found in many different domains, from petrochemical industries to nuclear power generation to the military and are formed from the need for effective performance in high-risk environments. The common factor underlying these diverse HROs is that, while a failure of reliability has the potential for death, loss, damage to assets, or ecological disaster, these organizations have developed unique properties that enable them to quickly and effectively adapt to unexpected events before they lead to catastrophic failures, by placing increasing importance on understanding and leveraging the role of the human operator.

Roberts and Rousseau (1989) identify eight primary characteristics of HROs:

- *Hypercomplexity.* It is necessary for personnel to interact with a number of different components, systems, and levels. Each operational unit has its own procedures, training, and command hierarchy.
- *Tight coupling.* There is reciprocal interdependence across many different units and levels. There are many time-dependent processes, invariant processes, goals, which can only be met in one way, and there is little slack in the system.
- *Extreme hierarchy differentiation.* The structure of the personnel in the organizations is very hierarchical.
- *Large number of decision makers in complex communication networks.* Along with extreme hierarchical differentiation, there are numerous interdependent individuals making decisions simultaneously while employing highly redundant communication systems.
- *Degree of accountability that does not exist in most organizations.* Substandard performance or deviations from standard procedures have severe adverse consequences.
- *High frequency of immediate feedback about decisions.* Quick decision making and feedback are characteristics of operational decisions.
- *Compressed time factors.* Cycles of major activities are measured in seconds.
- *More than one critical outcome that must happen simultaneously.* Simultaneity signifies both the complexity of operations and the inability to withdraw or modify operational decisions.

This list of factors suggests that the role of the human operator is much more than simply the often-assumed "supervisor." Despite the constant risk of failure, it is the collective efforts of personnel working in these organizations that result in remarkable levels of safety (Weick & Sutcliffe, 2001). From studies of military HROs (e.g., aircraft carriers, Weick & Roberts, 1993; and nuclear submarines, Bierly & Spender, 1995) and civilian HROs (e.g., petrochemical plants, civil aviation, and maritime industry, Perrow, 1999), it has been found that the personnel operating in these complex HTSs have distinctive social properties, including collective mindfulness (shared, intense vigilance against error) and heedful interrelating (member interactions characterized by care and attentiveness; Weick & Roberts, 1993), that give rise to these eight factors.

It is important to note that HROs are not immune to problems or errors. The high-risk nature of the industries in which HROs arise dictates that such organizations will always be exposed to such challenges. Rather, the personnel comprising HROs are able to synergize in different ways, developing unique solutions to new problems, solving them before they lead to catastrophes. Simply put, HRO personnel are good at recovery (Weick & Sutcliffe, 2001).

However, to ensure that these personnel are able to perform effectively, HRO leaders must ensure that four processes are in place:

1. *Selection*: To ensure that only members with the desired attributes are hired;
2. *Training*: To ensure that processes are in place to provide these members with the appropriate knowledge, skills, and abilities;
3. *Safety*: To develop and implement policies and procedures for ensuring safe performance; and
4. *Design*: To develop and integrate into the workplace only technologies (equipment) that are well designed, with easy-to-use interfaces, from the user's perspective.

In short, despite their high reliance on complex technologies, HROs are able to effectively manage risk precisely because of the high value they place on their human resources, and the steps they take to ensure that these resources are afforded every opportunity to succeed.

THE U.S. MILITARY AS A UNIQUE HIGH-RELIABILITY ORGANIZATION

In many ways, today's military is the ultimate HRO. Like other HROs the same factors that contribute to successful HROs may be found in the military:

- There is a growing need for military personnel to interact across many layers of command (*hypercomplexity*).
- These interactions oftentimes occur with short turnaround, real-time decision making, and resultant feedback, occurring between senior commanders and their more junior officers, who may be distributed across vast geographical locations (*tight coupling, large number of decision makers, high frequency of immediate feedback, compressed time factors*).
- The interdependence between different personnel across the military is extremely hierarchical, with decision makers present at most, if not all, levels of the organizational structure (*extreme hierarchy*).
- Throughout the military there is typically a "zero error" tolerance policy in place, holding decision makers directly accountable for the consequences of bad decisions (*accountability*).
- Many, if not all, missions typically involve a range of interdependent outcomes, making any mission a very complex affair to plan and manage (*more than one critical outcome*).

Unlike HROs, the military is multifaceted and works in many different domains simultaneously—covering a wide range of operational environments with an extremely diverse workforce (e.g., Army, Navy, Air Force, and Marines). In this way, the military may be more like a meta-HRO. This makes the challenge of enabling the military to perform effectively all the more acute. Adding to the challenge, unlike its commercial equivalents, where unsafe, unpredictable, and unstable environments are meant to be avoided at all costs, the military routinely works in precisely these kinds of environments with the expectation that its human resources will ensure high reliability in the face of these pressures, in parallel to continued improvements in the reliability of their associated technologies.

Clearly, the military has made great strides in improving the reliability of the hardware and software of these complex HTSs, resulting in dramatic decreases in the number of technology-based failures over the last century. To illustrate, in U.S. Naval aviation, 776 aircraft were destroyed due to accidents in 1954 compared to only 24 in 2000 (Wiegmann & Shappell, 2003). These significant improvements are directly attributable to enhanced design methods and more effective technologies. However, concurrent with this reduction in the absolute accident rate, the human contribution to accidents has become more acute. In U.S. Naval aviation, human error is causal in more than 80 percent of mishaps (Naval Safety Centre, 2006). This finding is not unique to naval aviation; between 80 percent and 90 percent of all work-related accidents and incidents can be attributed to human error (Health and Safety Executive, 2002; Hollnagel, 1993; Reason, 1990). Stark illustrations of the effects of failings in human performance are provided by high-profile military accidents such as the shooting down of an Iranian airliner by the *USS Vincennes* in 1988 and the collision between the U.S. nuclear submarine *USS Greeneville* and the Japanese fishing training ship *Ehime Maru* in 2001. Thus, even as the capability to design more reliable systems continues to grow, throughout the military there is a renewed interest in understanding the newly emerging kinds of challenges that such systems may reveal to ensure that the overall reliability of HTSs remains at as high a level as possible.

Learning Lessons from the U.S. Military

The military places a premium on its human resources (cf. Navy, 2006) and continues to focus significant resources on linking four key human resources processes—selection, training, safety, and design—into a single "value chain" so that shifts in one process can be leveraged to find efficiencies in other processes (Department of Defense Instruction, 2008). The purpose of this book is to use examples of how human performance issues are being addressed in the military and to describe how these lessons learned can be applied to other nonmilitary HROs. Arguably, military aviation has made some of the most significant investments to ensure that human performance issues do not interfere with mission performance, and that human performance is not sacrificed as new technologies are brought online, and many of the examples in the book are provided from this domain. Other domains, including the Submarine and Surface Navy as well as the Army and Marine Corps Infantry, are included to provide additional real-world examples.

THE BOOK'S ORGANIZATION

The book is divided into six parts. Chapter 2 completes Part I, presenting an overview of the state of the art in human performance research by our Distinguished Contributors Dr. Eduardo Salas (Pegasus Professor and University Trustee Chair at the University of Central Florida), Dr. Steve Fiore (Director, Cognitive Sciences Laboratory at the Institute for Simulation and Training, University of Central Florida), and Davin Pavlas (University of Central Florida). This is followed by four distinct parts, each focusing on a key enabler of HROs (selection, training, safety, and design), with each chapter in a part emphasizing lessons learned from the military. Importantly, despite the military flavor of each chapter, the chapter discussions have been written to highlight implications for other domains in which highly trained personnel are operating complex machinery with high consequences of error. A final chapter on Future Directions in Enhancing Human Performance, also by our Distinguished Contributors, rounds out the book. A brief summary of each of the four HRO enabler sections is provided below.

Part II: Selection

Any effective HRO begins by selecting the right kind of personnel to perform specific tasks. When done correctly, selection will be optimized in terms of other HRO enablers like training and design. Of course, there is a limit to how much savings on training and design an HRO can expect from specific selection procedures. Thus, it is crucial to have dynamic, adaptive policies in place for making changes in selection based on current events. *Chapter 3* provides an overview of how selection policy has been developed in the Navy, and how this policy flexes with improvements in other HRO enablers, such as system design, providing a prime example of the benefits of a flexible human resources value chain. As the Navy's mission evolves, and as new technologies become available, different metrics have been used to determine suitable selection criteria. *Chapter 4* provides a detailed discussion of how naval aviation selection works and how the outcome is used to ensure that the screened applicants are assigned to the right type of training, for the right kind of platform. The last chapter in this section, *Chapter 5*, describes the selection test that is used by the submarine force to identify suitable personnel for that unique operating environment.

Part III: Training

Effective selection processes alone will not guarantee effective HROs; the new and emerging demands that HROs must meet, and the technologies they use to successfully do so, are complex and generally involve knowledge that must be acquired over time, through training. Consequently, training programs are critical to making up this difference. HROs present specific knowledge requirements, which demand unique instructional strategies and implementation policies. *Chapter 6* provides some key examples of the types of high-risk environments for which training efforts must prepare individuals with the necessary knowledge. *Chapter 7* describes the development and implementation of crew resource management (CRM) training to develop training strategies to manage risk in one such environment, naval aviation. The implementation of the training in the U.S. Navy is outlined, and recommendations for how to maximize the effectiveness of CRM within the Navy, and other HROs, are delineated. Effectiveness may be quantified in many ways, and *Chapter 8* provides a novel framework for determining effectiveness at the highest levels. It focuses on what Don Kirkpatrick has called the fourth level of training effectiveness evaluation (Kirkpatrick, 1976, 1998)— the organizational measure of return on investment of providing training. Finally, any attempt to perform such determinations relies heavily on performance metrics. In the spirit of new measurements for evaluating training effectiveness, *Chapter 9* provides insights into developing physiology-based measures of training effectiveness.

Part IV: Safety

Organizations that successfully manage high risk do so by concentrating, in part, on enabling safe operations to reduce human error. The focus of this section is on the identification and reduction of the human contribution to accidents by developing and implementing safety policies and procedures. *Chapter 10* describes how such policies and procedures may be designed, using a risk reduction strategy called Operational Risk Management (ORM), and how it is being applied in U.S. military aviation. While it is recognized that risk cannot be avoided in military operation, the purpose of ORM is to manage risk such that unnecessary risks are avoided. Managing risk includes understanding not only how to prevent it but also how to cope with it and mitigate it when its performance degrading effects become realized. *Chapter 11* discusses how military personnel, working in high-risk environments, cope with the daily stress such environments engender to ensure sustained, effective, performance. It is suggested that the papers reviewed in this chapter have implications for coping with stress in other high-risk environments. Prevention is, of course, the best cure, and *Chapter 12* provides a set of tools for identifying the human factors causes of accidents utilizing the Human Factors

Analysis and Classification System (HFACS) and for identifying accident mitigation measures using a system called the Human Factors Intervention Matrix (HFIX). With such information in hand, it is possible to develop approaches for managing these human challenges to safety.

Part V: Design

The interface between the human and the machine is critical to ensuring effective performance in any high-risk environment that uses HTSs. Interface designs that support the unique abilities of humans are more likely to reduce errors, increase productivity, enhance safety, and enhance comfort (Wickens, Lee, Liu, Becker, & Sallie, 2004). Further, to fully reap the benefits of effective design, man–machine interface development must be considered early on in the design process (Wiener, 1988). If an evaluation of how a human interacts with a piece of equipment is not considered prior to "bending metal," it can be costly, or impossible, to make changes to address this issue. *Chapter 13* focuses on the many benefits of implementing user-centered design, and Human System Integration (HSI) for managing risk in complex HTSs such as those present aboard Naval ships, and how these principles can be written into policy. It also provides examples of where HSI has resulted in safety improvements, performance enhancements, increased quality of life, and reductions in manpower. *Chapter 14* outlines methods that can be used to conduct user-centered design to identify potential issues that can be addressed prior to building interfaces. The last chapter in this section, *Chapter 15*, reviews cognitive, behavioral, and psycho-physiological measures of workload and situation awareness. The purpose is to evaluate whether human factors engineers have the tools to allow them to make informed design decisions.

REFERENCES

Bierly, P. E., & Spender, J. C. (1995). Culture and high reliability organizations: The case of the nuclear submarine. *Journal of Management*, 21 (4), 639–656.

Department of Defense Instruction. (2008). *Operation of the Defense Acquisition System*. Retrieved from http://www.dtic.mil/whs/directives/corres/pdf/500002p.pdf, February 16, 2009.

Health and Safety Executive. (2002). *Strategies to promote safe behavior as part of a health and safety management system*. London, UK: HSE.

Hollnagel, E. (1993). *Human reliability analysis: Context and control*. London, UK: Harcourt Brace.

Kirkpatrick, D. L. (1976). Evaluation of training. In R. L. Craig & L. R. Bittel (Eds.), *Training and development handbook* (pp. 18.1–18.27). New York: McGraw Hill.

———. (1998). *Evaluation training programs*. San Francisco: Berrett-Koehler.

Naval Safety Centre. (2006). *Aviation 3750*. Norfolk, VA: Naval Safety Center.

Navy. (2006). *MPT&E Strategic Vision*. Retrieved from http://www.nps.edu/ Research/HCS/Docs/MPTE_Strategic_Vision.pdf, February 16, 2009.

Perrow, C. (1999). *Normal accidents: Living with high-risk technologies*. Princeton, NJ: Princeton University Press.

Reason, J. (1990). *Human error*. New York: Cambridge University Press.

Roberts, K. H., & Rousseau, D. M. (1989). Research in nearly failure-free, high-reliability organizations: Having the bubble. *IEEE Transactions on Engineering Management*, 36 (2), 132–139.

Shrivastava, P. (1986). *Bhopal*. New York: Basic Books.

Weick, K., & Roberts, K. H. (1993). Collective mind and organizations: The case of flight operations on an aircraft carrier deck. *Administrative Science Quarterly*, 38 (3), 357–381.

Weick, K., & Sutcliffe, K. M. (2001). *Managing the unexpected: Assuring high performance in an age of complexity*. San Francisco, CA: Jose-Bass.

Wickens, C. D., Lee, J. D., Liu, Y., Becker, G., & Sallie, E. (2004). *An introduction to human factors engineering*. Upper Saddle River, NJ: Pearson Prentice Hall.

Wiegmann, D. A., & Shappell, S. A. (2003). *A human error approach to aviation accident analysis*. Aldershot, UK: Ashgate.

Wiener, E. L. (1988). Management of human error by design. In *Human error avoidance techniques conference proceedings*, Society of Automotive Engineers, Inc.

Chapter 2

A VIEW ON THE HISTORY OF USE-INSPIRED SCIENCE IN HUMAN PERFORMANCE RESEARCH

Stephen M. Fiore, Eduardo Salas, and Davin Pavlas

The twentieth century saw enormous growth in the disciplines seeking to understand human performance. Concomitant with this was a tremendous increase in the integration of theory and methods with tools and technologies to support human performance in both individuals and in teams. This field reaches far beyond the halls of a single department—linking psychology and engineering as well as neuroscience and physiology. These efforts have produced important advancements in human system integration, resulting from a sophisticated understanding of human performance and how humans interact with technology in high-risk settings.

Research on human performance in high-risk environments is by necessity a largely applied science in that examination of a specific behavior or task is driven by the need to remedy an existing real-world problem. But what is important to recognize is that research in human performance has often bridged the divide between basic and applied research. By focusing on specific needs in particular contexts, yet pursuing a fundamental understanding of human behavior, the field has implicitly operated in a mode of research currently described as "use-inspired" science. This notion arose out of the more general dichotomy that categorizes research—the split between basic research (i.e., research for understanding) and applied research (i.e., research toward a practical goal). Basic research works toward increasing scientific knowledge, while applied research harnesses knowledge by instantiating it in technology, techniques, and procedures.

This précis on "use-inspired science" highlights the scientific considerations that set human performance research apart from so much of psychological science. Stokes (1997) noted that the basic–applied dichotomy fails to consider research that exists both to advance scientific understanding and produce a beneficial outcome—what he labeled use-inspired basic science. A prominent example of use-inspired basic research was the work of

Louis Pasteur, which not only provided a better understanding of microbiology but also produced techniques for disease prevention (Stokes, 1997). Essentially, concomitant with the process of seeking a useful end scientific knowledge is provided, eliminating the misguided gap separating knowledge and use.

But this concept of use-inspired science is also necessary not only to understand the history of this field but to help guide future developments as well. Thus, in this chapter, we use this concept to contextualize key points in the history of research in human performance.

DEVELOPMENTS IN THE HISTORY OF HUMAN PERFORMANCE RESEARCH

Although the stakes in high-risk environments have never been as high as in complex contemporary roles, the need to improve performance in high-risk environments is nothing new. The roughly 100-year history of human performance research provides numerous lessons in the benefits of use-inspired science. Understanding the evolution of the field can only come from an examination of the interdisciplinary efforts that constituted its beginnings. What follows is a brief review of human performance research, not meant to be an exhaustive, but rather, meant to provide context in which to situate the discussion of how this field has long crossed disciplinary boundaries.

The Birth of Applied Psychological Research

Scholars of the history of psychology suggest that the origin of applied psychological research can largely be attributed to the efforts of Hugo Münsterberg (e.g., Moskowitz, 1977). His work in examining the reliability of courtroom testimony marked a shift from a field focused largely on introspection and his approach resulted in the formation of the applied psychology research laboratory at Harvard in 1908 (Moskowitz, 1977). In his book on witness testimony, Münsterberg noted the intrinsically interdisciplinary nature of applied psychology: "The time for ... Applied Psychology is surely near, and work has been started from most various sides. Those fields of practical life which come first in question may be said to be education, medicine, art, economics, and law" (Münsterberg, 1908, p. 9). But, illustrating the beginnings of the tension that exists to this day from the clash of basic and applied research, Münsterberg was confronted with disapproval from the psychological establishment. Despite such confrontations, Münsterberg's research branched out in various directions and helped to create numerous applied areas of scientific inquiry such as industrial efficiency (Moskowitz, 1977).

Nonetheless, despite a desire by many to see applied psychology develop, throughout the beginnings of this field, there existed significant conflict between academic purists who championed studying the mind solely for understanding and the contingent of applied psychologists who believed psychology should result in something of practical use (Moskowitz, 1977). Purists believed applied psychology "debased" the scientific pursuit of psychology, while applied psychologists felt pure psychology offered nothing of practical value. Academia was almost entirely composed of purists, so the force for applied research came from the actual areas that needed its potential products and interventions. For example, Binet's intelligence testing work conducted for the French Ministry of Public Instruction (Hoffman & Deffenbacher, 1992) and Carnegie-Mellon's business consortium-funded research conducted by the Bureau of Salesmanship Research (Katzell & Austin, 1992), both applied psychological science to real-world problems. Similarly, the Life Insurance Management Agency Association at various times employed pioneering psychologists such as Arthur Kornhauser, Albert Kurtz, and Rensis Likert (see Koppes, Thayer, Vinchur, & Salas, 2007). Out of such applied research came important theoretical gains in our understanding of, for example, intelligence, motivation, and critical early work in aptitude tests. However, it is unclear how accepted applied psychological research and its importance to understanding human performance would be had the early twentieth century not experienced the massive global conflicts of the world wars.

Enhancing Performance during the World Wars

Once the world was cast into the turmoil of World War I (WWI), applied psychology had already gained a foothold in Britain and the United States (Koppes et al., 2007). The advent of complicated new combat machinery vastly increased the performance requirement of human operators, and applied psychology offered ways to ensure that soldiers were able to meet these needs. For example, Watson and Dunlap studied the effects of fatigue and oxygen deprivation on the new class of operators known as aviators (Hoffman & Deffenbacher, 1992). The high risk experienced by pilots of combat aircraft combined with their newfound importance on the battlefield made efforts to improve the performance of these pilots especially meaningful to the military, and work on aviation flourished during both world wars. Dunlap's development of psychological tests to determine which individuals were fit to withstand the effects of high-altitude combat was one of the earliest nonmedical testing procedures employed by the military (Meister, 1999). Despite the highly applied nature of such research, theoretical contributions continued to emerge. For example, Thorndike's examination of cadet ratings of trainers and supervisors led to the discovery of the halo effect in addition to providing useful information for the military (Thorndike, 1920). The halo effect is still discussed in contemporary research (e.g., Coombs & Holladay, 2006) and is a prime example of how applied research can further theoretical science.

One of the most significant advances in applied psychology during the two world wars was the vastly increased use of psychological measures for selection. At the dawn of WWI, members of the American Psychological Association quickly formed the Psychological Committee of the National Research Council (led by Yerkes) as well as a psychological program in the Adjutant General's Office called the Committee on Classification of Personnel (led by Scotts & Bingham; Katzell & Austin, 1992). Though these two groups differed in opinion on how their efforts should be organized within the hierarchy of the military, their goals remained the same: to create selection procedures that would direct talent in military branches appropriately. The success of the Army Alpha and Beta mental ability examinations created by Yerkes's group furthered the widespread acceptance of psychological testing in government and private ventures (Hale, 1982). Indeed, the massive enlistment rate resulted in more than 1.7 million inductees being administered newly developed intelligence tests (Uhlaner, 1977). The use of such selection techniques ensured that individuals were suited to the tasks they would be required to perform, which was particularly important given the military context of these new tests. After WWI, military applications of applied psychology waned. However, by the time World War II (WWII) began, psychological testing had matured through use in nonmilitary settings (e.g., Vietele's work on industrial psychology; Katzell & Austin, 1992) and was once again employed en masse by the military to select individuals and inform policy decisions (Driskell & Olmstead, 1989). After such widespread use, the role of applied psychology in selection as well as training and human factors became firmly entrenched with the military. Since WWII, selection testing has been consistently employed by military organizations around the world. However, selection was not a solely military requirement. The burgeoning use of psychological selection techniques branched into the emerging field of industrial/organizational psychology, and this domain would largely carry the field after WWII (Katzell & Austin, 1992).

A critical point to recognize from this brief review is how the growing demand for useful insight into human performance led applied psychology to partner with other scientific disciplines. Thus, "need-driven" multidisciplinary research led to numerous productive collaborations. We see engineering, biology, and psychology each playing roles in improving how human beings perform in high-stakes situations (Katzell & Austin, 1992). The aviation research performed by Watson and Dunlap required not only their psychological expertise but also collaboration with military medical officers and physiologists (Meister, 1999). After the end of WWII, human performance research was bolstered by contributions from fields ranging from computer science to cognitive psychology (Katzell & Austin, 1992). Any science that could contribute to understanding human behavior in the context of the human, the system, or the task was meaningful to this burgeoning effort.

Growth of Applied Research to Enhance Performance

As the use of research on performance progressed, a basic taxonomy of the approaches that could be used to enhance performance began to form. The three main arms of such applied research were selection techniques, training, and enhancing systems through design (Katzell & Austin, 1992). As noted, selection and design were particularly well-represented in the wartime research efforts, but the science of training required more time to reach maturity. Indeed, even to this day, understanding the myriad components inherent to successful training requires effort from the global science community rather than efforts from only a single field (cf. Fiore, 2008). Over the past two decades, the growth of the science of training has been driven by the contributions of cognitive science, team science, organizational science, simulation and gaming, interaction science, and many other specialized fields (Salas & Cannon-Bowers, 2001). This broad range of inquiry has, piece by piece, produced a science of training approaching true maturity. Today, the need for a science of training is widely accepted and integrated into organizational culture (Salas & Cannon-Bowers, 2001). The global implications of this acceptance is visible on a wide scale, from the way school curricula are designed, to the prevalence of large-scale corporate training efforts, to the highly standardized training approaches employed by militaries around the world.

But it is the merging of psychology and engineering that is perhaps the most significant contributor to the field's ability to enhance performance. Specifically, human system integration provides not only an inclusive theoretical look at contextual performance but also an immediate outlet for findings. Because human–system integration and human–computer interaction research is highly use-inspired, examples of its influence on human performance in high-risk environments are readily available.

Two developments in the latter portions of the twentieth century exemplify this merging. First, due to the devastating costs of nuclear power plant failure, research on improving the performance of operators began to draw on numerous fields to ensure success. Automation, computer-based cognitive aids, effective training, and human-centered design all contribute to the success of modern nuclear power plant operators (e.g., Hollnagel, Woods, & Leveson, 2006; Moray & Huey, 1988). By examining the highly contextualized nature of this complex work, researchers began to develop multilevel theoretical accounts of human performance. Such research helped us come to understand, for example, how an operator's ability to successfully resolve a crisis in the control room may depend on the controls available to him or her, the nature of the work environment (e.g., changing shifts to deal with fatigue), or even the ability of the system to remain useful while the operator is under stress (Moray & Huey, 1988).

The medical field encounters similar multilevel problems, where doctors, nurses, and oftentimes administrators are faced with high-impact and high-consequence decisions. For example, medical error is a pervasive problem for the world's health care organizations, with the United States alone suffering over 98,000 deaths per year attributable to error (Kohn, Corrigan, & Donaldson, 1999). These errors can take place in time-stressed environments or unfold over the course of hours and days. For example, errors can happen because of lapses in judgment or memory, failures in communication, or broader systemic problems within an organization's culture (Alonso et al., 2006). Reducing the impact of such errors has become the focus of much effort from the psychological community, with training (Alonso et al., 2006) and design (Zhang, 2005) being the primary focus for enhancing medical performance. With military and civilian institutions recognizing the need for applied research in solving issues of human performance, it falls to researchers to answer the call and provide the means by which to do so.

ACKNOWLEDGMENTS

The writing of this paper was partially supported by Grant N000140610118 and Grant N0001408C0186 from the Office of Naval Research. The views, opinions, and findings contained in this article are the authors' and should not be construed as official or as reflecting the views of the University of Central Florida or the Department of Defense.

REFERENCES

Alonso, A., Baker, D. P., Holtzman, A., Day, R., King, H., Toomey, L., & Salas, E. (2006). Reducing medical error in the military health system: How can team training help? *Human Resource Management Review*, 16, 396–415.

Coombs, W. T., & Holladay, S. J. (2006). Unpacking the halo effect: Reputation and crisis management. *Journal of Communication Management*, 10 (2), 123–137.

Driskell, J. E., & Olmstead, B. (1989). Psychology and the military: Research applications and trends. *American Psychologist*, 44, 43–54.

Fiore, S. M. (2008). Interdisciplinarity as teamwork: How the science of teams can inform team science. *Small Group Research*, 39, 251–277.

Hale, M., Jr. (1982). History of employment testing. In A. K. Wigdor & W. R. Garner (Eds.), *Ability testing: Uses, consequences, and controversies* (pp. 3–38). Washington, D.C.: National Academy Press.

Hoffman, R. R., & Deffenbacher, K. A. (1992). A brief history of applied cognitive psychology. *Applied Cognitive Psychology*, 6, 1–48.

Hollnagel, E., Woods, D. D., & Leveson, N. (Eds.). (2006). *Resilience engineering: Concepts and precepts*. Aldershot, UK: Ashgate.

Katzell, R. A., & Austin, J. T. (1992). From then to now: The development of industrial-organizational psychology in the United States. *Journal of Applied Psychology*, 77 (6), 803–835.

Kohn, L. T., Corrigan, J. M., & Donaldson, M. S. (1999). *To err is human: Building a safer health care system.* Washington, D.C.: National Academy Press.

Koppes, L. L., Thayer, P. W., Vinchur, A. J., & Salas, E. (2007). *Historical perspectives in industrial and organizational psychology.* London: Routledge.

Meister, D. (1999). *The history of human factors and ergonomics.* Mahwah, NJ: Lawrence Erlbaum and Associates.

Moray, N., & Huey, B. (1988). *Human factors research and nuclear safety.* Washington, D.C.: National Academies Press.

Moskowitz, M. J. (1977). Hugo Münsterberg: A study in the history of applied psychology. *American Psychologist*, 32, 824–842.

Münsterberg, H. (1908). *On the witness stand.* New York: Doubleday Page.

Salas, E., & Cannon-Bowers, J. A. (2001). The science of training: A decade of progress. *Annual Reviews in Psychology*, 52, 471–499.

Stokes, D. E. (1997). *Pasteur's quadrant: Basic science and technological innovation.* Washington, D.C.: Brookings Institution Press.

Thorndike, E. L. (1920). A constant error in psychological ratings. *Journal of Applied Psychology*, 4, 25–29.

Uhlaner, J. E. (1977). *The research psychologist in the army: 1917 to 1977* (Report No. 1155). Washington, D.C.: U.S. Army Research Institute for the Behavioral and Social Sciences.

Zhang, J. (2005). Human-centered computing in health information systems. Part 1: Analysis and design. *Journal of Biomedical Informatics*, 38, 1–3.

Part II: Selection

Chapter 3

TESTING, VALIDATING, AND APPLYING AN EMPIRICAL MODEL OF HUMAN PERFORMANCE IN A HIGH-PERFORMANCE ORGANIZATION

Steve Watson

Organizations whose performance may be catastrophically degraded by failures are known as high-risk organizations (Shrivastava, 1986). Given the extreme mission requirements, the autonomy of command, and the highly industrial and technological nature of the workplace, a Navy ship at sea is an inherently high-risk environment from stem to stern. Whether at war, during peace keeping missions, or while performing humanitarian relief efforts, the external risks of an unpredictable environment loom. Additionally, the internal risks of working and living (24 hours per day while deployed) in an industrial environment which has a high reliance on team coordination and human–machine interfaces compound the risk to personnel and equipment. To mitigate these risks, the Navy must ensure that we have correctly trained personnel in appropriate numbers assigned to each ship, submarine, and squadron.

Although there are many ways to characterize risk aboard a Navy vessel, one effective way is to consider these many risks in terms of a composite risk, such as workload. When workload is excessive, fatigue occurs, resulting in compromise of safety and performance (Johnson, 2007). Assuming that the required workload aboard a ship to fulfill anticipated mission requirements is relatively constant, personnel processes which result in understaffing conditions naturally result in additional workload to individuals aboard that ship. Fiscal constraints mandate that each ship is manned at the most efficient levels, so there is little (if any) planned excess labor availability. When required workload exceeds available personnel resources, a higher risk of failure occurs at the individual (sailor) and unit (ship) level. To protect against inherent danger in an understaffed condition, each ship must maintain the correct level of manning and readiness prior to deploying.

It is not only important to have the right number of personnel on board, but the highest possible proficiency levels for each sailor, both in specific technical skill and general seamanship, is imperative. Assuming an enlisted force of 320,000 with 40,000 successful new accessions per year, the U.S. Navy (USN) experiences a turnover rate of roughly one-eighth of the workforce every year. Projecting out, this means that approximately a quarter of the workforce has less than two years' experience. Subtracting an average of six months spent in basic and initial skills training results in an estimate closer to 18 months of shipboard experience for one-fourth of our workforce.

Considering the high-risk nature of Navy work, the goal is to have all positions manned at the appropriate level; this level matches the correctly trained and available workforce to the work requirements. To achieve this goal, we must have strong manpower models which enable us to correctly match personnel to training and work requirements. We must also have strong enabling technologies to deliver these decision support services to a fleet that is deployed worldwide. The focus of our efforts in this area is to provide a real-time decision support system for decision makers, analysts, recruiters, and in-service career counselors to assist in matching our available personnel inventories to the real work requirements, both in aggregate numbers and with appropriate skill sets. The work described here captures our efforts to match in-service personnel resources to USN requirements, by providing one of the first-ever demonstrations of the effective application of a composite measure of performance and arousal trade-offs.

BACKGROUND

In-Service Enlisted Community Management

In order to supply each command with the right mix of enlisted personnel, an appropriate pool of personnel for each enlisted specialty, referred to by the Navy as an enlisted rating (or simply "rating"), must exist. In a completely stable manpower and personnel environment, accession planning would account for planned personnel losses and we could readily maintain a close match between rating inventory and billet requirements. However, unplanned events result in substantial mismatches between distributable inventory and requirements for in-service personnel. On the personnel side, unplanned losses due to attrition and rating disqualification create deviations from planned inventories. On the manpower side, when ships are decommissioned or manning requirements change, the billet requirement changes as well. Additionally, changes in rating structure such as combining two related ratings or simply eliminating a rating add to the churn.

Since manning requirements and rating inventory can vary unpredictably from planned requirements, there is frequently a mismatch between rating and billet requirements. If the personnel inventory is not within 5 percent of the derived target, an overstaffed or understaffed condition exists (Watson,

Mills, & Arendt, 2004). Overstaffed conditions result in excessive inventory beyond actual billet requirements, whereas understaffed conditions reflect depleted inventory, unable to satisfy workforce requirements.

Our overarching goal for this effort is to provide a "matchmaking" system for Navy counselors and enlisted community managers. This effort is concerned with both the initial job assignment in recruiting (classification) and the movement of in-service personnel from overstaffed to understaffed ratings. To do both of these effectively, we must guide personnel to ratings where we have a need and anticipate they will succeed. Improvements must focus on filling vacancies while maximizing measures of performance, such as training success.

The Rating Identification versus How It Is Done Today

The Navy has established the Rating Identification Engine (RIDE) as the corporate model and technology for sailor-rating matchmaking. Originally designed for use in recruiting, RIDE has recently (2009) been established as a reusable Web service, making it available to provide this functionality for all Navy personnel classification events. RIDE is scheduled to replace existing Navy recruiting algorithms over the next few years.

Historical Precedence

In the course of a single year, the Navy matches tens of thousands of newly enlisted sailors to initial technical training programs. Classroom curricula, size, and schedule are developed to fulfill known rating requirements in quality and in quantity. The goal of this accession process, which includes recruiting, training, and initial assignment, can best be summed up in the Navy mantra: "Right Sailor, Right Place, Right Time."

For the accession process to flow efficiently, Sailors must complete their chosen course of instruction within established time limits and be able to demonstrate required levels of technical proficiency and knowledge. If the sailor-rating match is done poorly, training failures and setbacks occur, resulting in process inefficiency and increased cost. Moreover, failures and setbacks disrupt planned distributable rating inventories and can result in manning shortfalls in the fleet.

Beginning in 1973, the Navy's Personalized Recruiting for Immediate and Delayed Enlistment (PRIDE) computer system enabled enlisted job counselors (Classifiers) to reserve training seats for new enlistees on a first-come, first-served basis (Kroeker & Rafacz, 1983). In 1981, the Navy implemented a new job assignment composite model entitled Classification and Assignment within PRIDE (CLASP). Kroeker and Rafacz (1983) developed this optimal-sequential assignment process to assign personnel to "optimal" ratings while filling school seats evenly across ratings and maintaining demographic fill targets. While the CLASP algorithms represent a historic advance in sailor accession processing and sailor-rating matchmaking, thorough review of these processes indicated a need to revamp this portion of the USN's personnel system.

Ward, Haney, Hendrix, and Pina (1978) established some key design criteria for personnel systems:

1. Acceptance by managers and members of the organization;
2. evolutionary (incremental) adjustments leading to continued improvement; and
3. ease of incorporating new human resources research findings into the operational personnel system.

As described above, the CLASP algorithms match sailors to ratings while simultaneously considering a variety of policy concerns. Although this is a laudable goal, interpretation and maintenance of this complex set of algorithms have proven extremely difficult for a variety of reasons. Waters (in Eitelberg, 1984) describes complications for analysts in interpreting CLASP due to difficult-to-interpret weighing procedures. Eitelberg (1984, 78) interpreted: "the individual elements of the system [CLASP] are far from simple to pinpoint or evaluate from an outsider's perspective."

The inherently abstract and complex nature of the instantiation of the CLASP algorithms makes understanding, explaining, and predicting outcomes uncertain, resulting in failure of all three of Ward and colleagues' criteria. In 1999, a program assessments report indicated low acceptance by managers, no appreciable evolutionary improvement, and no concept or support for including new instruments (e.g., a measure of vocational interest) into the model.

Development of New Algorithms

Responding to the number of challenges experienced with the CLASP algorithms, researchers initiated efforts to develop a new process for optimizing sailor-rating matchmaking. To avoid some of the pitfalls experienced with previous efforts, researchers focused on developing optimization processes utilizing well-established, generally understood concepts. It was anticipated that if valid optimization algorithms could be produced from some established "building blocks," the resultant matchmaking process was more likely to acquire management acceptance and allow incremental improvement in optimization and incorporation of new techniques and instruments.

Detangling Goodness of Fit and Management Decisions

As a starting point, it was decided to decouple management policies and training performance concerns. Ward (1977) discussed two types of information to be considered in the estimation of person-job matching value estimates. Management-related value involves filling overall and demographic-based quotas, whereas quality-of-assignment-related value involves person-job matching based on anticipated performance.

While it may first appear elegant to combine management-related values and quality-of-assignment-related values into a single composite value for use by the job counselor, the complications which arise can severely challenge the usefulness of this approach. For example, CLASP algorithms contain a fraction fill component which attempts to maintain a balanced fill rate for all ratings. Since the CLASP composite utility is thereby dependent on scheduling factors (e.g., date of counseling session, scheduling of classes, and size of classes), it can no longer be interpreted as representing the goodness of fit between the sailor's aptitude and the rating's requirements (e.g., training). Amplifying the problem from an operational perspective, ratings with very small class sizes and infrequent start dates (e.g., as few as twice a year for a lithographer) have an erratic effect on the utility values.

To avoid these complications, RIDE algorithm development focused on developing a composite score indicating the goodness of fit between sailor aptitudes and rating requirements, with a focus on maximizing job performance. Managerial concerns regarding class size, scheduling, and fill rates are more appropriately handled directly through training reservation systems.

School Success Criteria

Beyond the difficulty of decoupling policy concerns and ability matching within the CLASP algorithms were challenges to assumptions made in the development of the School Success Component of CLASP. First, these utility functions were based on final A-School (technical training received by recruits on completion of initial training) performance grades. Although utilization of these scores may have been valid during the development of the CLASP, a year-long review of corporate data identified varying performance standards, testing practices, and data entry standards, making comparisons across training programs very difficult to interpret. Second, maintenance procedures used scores from A-Schools only. Instead, sailors are matched to training pipelines, where pipelines can be any combination of pre-schools, A-Schools, C-Schools, and other follow-on training. Focusing on A-School performance alone does not consider the extent of training actually attended by the newly accessed sailors.

Understanding these limitations, the author reviewed available training data from over 100 course pipelines and multiple corporate data systems. From this year-long analysis, it was determined that the most reliable and interpretable performance data should be captured in a single variable, entitled First Pass Pipeline Success (FPPS). This binary variable captures whether or not sailors completed their entire training pipeline without failure or setback (remediation).

Performance Curves

Finally, and perhaps most interesting from a scientific perspective, is that CLASP algorithms assumed a monotonic linear relationship between selection composite and school performance. That is, as test scores on a relevant selection composite increased, the algorithms implied that school performance, and utility for that sailor-rating match, would also increase. Observations of real data from 75,000 enlisted sailors across 90 ratings from 1996 to 1998, as well as some well-known theories of human performance (e.g., Yerkes & Dodson, 1908), directly challenged this assumption.

A NEW APPROACH: RECONSIDERING YERKES-DODSON

One of the most generally accepted laws in psychology is the inverted-U human performance curve. As a descendent of seminal research by Drs. Robert Yerkes and John Dodson (1908), this curve (frequently referred to as the Yerkes-Dodson law, but see Winton, 1987) has been broadly interpreted to describe how measures of human performance increase in positive relation to cognitive arousal, then decrease continually after an optimal level of arousal is exceeded. Although this law has come under a variety of criticisms (e.g., Lacey, 1967), the inverted-U curve, like the depiction in Figure 3.1, continues to be a widely accepted description of human performance related to factors such as stress and motivation.

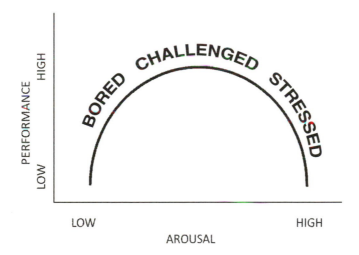

Figure 3.1.   Inverted-U relating human performance and arousal.

Given the strong historic precedence, and ease of understanding, the Yerkes-Dodson curves were selected to guide the development of the RIDE models. The challenge was to develop a human performance curve relating some measurable predictor of human performance to a criterion variable meaningful to Navy job fit. As discussed above, our selected criterion was FPPS. We investigated means to construct these curves relating established tests of human ability to FPPS, in a form mimicking the Yerkes-Dodson inverted-U performance function. In particular, we undertook to determine the degree to which metrics derived from current assessments could be leveraged to build these curves.

Armed Services Vocational Aptitude Battery

The Armed Services Vocational Aptitude Battery (ASVAB) is the principal device for selection and classification in the U.S. Armed Services. In 1974, the Department of Defense (DoD) directed that all services use a single test battery for selection (qualification for military service) and classification (qualifying individuals for specific military occupations; Eitelberg, 1988). The ASVAB consists of 10 subtests which are used in various combinations to perform selection and classification screening.

The selection composite is referred to as the Armed Forces Qualification Test (AFQT) and is computed from the ASVAB subtests Arithmetic Reasoning (AR), Word Knowledge (WK), Paragraph Comprehension (PC), and Mathematics Knowledge (MK). These subtests are frequently referred to as the "scholastic knowledge" subtests, and the AFQT can be readily understood as an indicator of learning ability. Each service sets minimum AFQT scores for selection; the current Navy minimum is 35 on a percentile scale from 1 to 99.

The classification composites are formed from various linear combinations of ASVAB subtests. The "technical subtests" such as Electronic Information (EI) and General Science (GS) can be included in these composites, which may or may not also include the scholastic knowledge subtests from the AFQT. Classification composites comprising technical knowledge tests have proven to be (moderately) useful in the prediction of success in technical training for specific military jobs.

In the Navy, jobs for enlisted personnel are referred to as "ratings." Each Navy rating has a specified cut score (CS) on the classification composite, and each applicant has a derived qualification score (QS) for each Navy rating. An applicant's QS must be above the specific CS to be classified into that rating.

The idea of a single test battery serving two functions is an attractive one, but not without its problems. A number of empirical studies over the years have supported a Spearman-Holzinger Bi-Factor model for the ASVAB. Two features characterize the ASVAB factor structure:

1. *General factor*. The ASVAB has a dominant general factor accounting for approximately 60 percent of the variance (Kass, Mitchell, Grafton, & Wing, 1983; Welsh, Watson, & Ree, 1990).

2. *Group factors*. In a number of studies, group factors have been identified and could be replicated: verbal ability (Verbal), quantitative ability (Quantitative), Speed, and Technical Knowledge (Kass et al., 1983; Welsh, Kucinkas, & Curran, 1990). While the above studies were done with exploratory factor analysis techniques, Ippel (2006) and Ippel and Watson (2008) used a confirmatory technique to determine the structure of the ASVAB. The best-fitting model was characterized by a general factor with loadings on all ASVAB tests and three group factors: Verbal, Quantitative, and Technical Knowledge.

A problematic consequence of a bi-factor model for any collection of tests is that each of the tests used in a classification composite based on that test collection has a loading of the general factor and a specific factor loading. As a result the classification composites necessarily must be highly correlated (and highly correlated with the AFQT).

While limits in the use and interpretation of the classification composites is an important area of investigation (as in Hunter, 1986), it is important to note that these composites are still mandated by DoD and are a standard practice in all services (Sellman, 2004). Since the RIDE efforts are focused on developing an optimal solution to the sequential multiple assignment problem using existing "building blocks," we used the existing selection and classification composites to develop our models.

RIDE Technical Specifications: Building the Curves

The goal of the RIDE effort is to equip Navy counselors with a decision support system that helps them match sailors to enlisted jobs (ratings) while maximizing predicted job success. To restate this problem, our goal is to build a set of heuristic algorithms, utilizing readily available training success predictors (ASVAB composites) to maximize aggregate values of the criterion variable (FPPS) across multiple sequential assignments (classifications).

Although a variety of heuristic algorithms can be applied to the classification problem (Electronic Data Systems, 2001; Kroeker & Rafacz, 1983), the development of the RIDE algorithm is unique in that it is directly tied to an established model of human performance. Assumptions based on the Yerkes-Dodson inverted-U model are used in conjunction with historic data to establish the shape and parameters of the utility functions.

To develop and test the utility curves, data were assembled using 75,000 records from 1996–1998 Navy recruiting and training databases. These data were organized into two distinct sets of elements (data elements with an asterisk are used for testing and validation purposes and are not required to construct initial utility curves):

1. Applicant (sailor) Data	2. Job (rating) Data
• Applicant ID	• Rating
• AFQT score	• Minimum cut score
• Rating assigned (classification)	• AFQT mean (derived from applicant data)
• Classification composite score (for rating assigned)	• AFQT standard deviation (derived from applicant data)
• FPPS for rating assigned (1 or 0)	• Classification composite formula*
• ASVAB subtest scores*	• Training vacancies available (sum of rating assigned in applicant data)*

From this data we developed and tested two utility functions which combine to form a composite utility which behaves in accordance with a Yerkes-Dodson inverted-U approximation.

School Pipeline Success Utility

The School Pipeline Success Utility (SPSU) estimates the value (or utility) of assigning individual i to rating r (referred to in equation form here as S_{ir}). The S_{ir} curves are developed for each rating using the empirical relationships between FPPS and QS. For each rating, a table is created from the Applicant Data set by calculating the average FPPS value for each value of QS above the minimum CS. The Job Data set is used in this stage to retrieve minimum CS for each rating.

Figure 3.2 illustrates a typical relationship between FPPS and QS. It is critical to note that FPPS does not continue to increase across all values of QS. The Point of Diminished Return (PDR) identifies the point at which an increase in QS is not likely to result in an appreciable increase in FPPS.

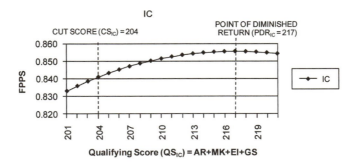

Figure 3.2. **Empirical relationship between FPPS and the Qualifying Score (QS) for the Interior Communication (IC) rating. The CS is the minimum QS required for classification into the IC rating. The PDR is the QS above which we expect no improvement in FPPS.**

The PDR characteristic assumption distinguishes the RIDE models from competing models of this type.

For our initial efforts (and best for illustration purposes here), regression lines for each rating were fit using a logistic regression (for similar procedure see Ippel & Watson, 2008). In an iterative process, the PDR was determined by progressively restricting the maximum QS in the regression analysis until the best fit was determined. The maximum QS from the best-fit logistic regression was used as the PDR.

It must be noted that using this type of procedure would be very expensive in an operational system, as it would require inordinately complex maintenance procedures and very large sample sizes. A simplified automated technique for establishing PDR, using a simple rule of thumb, has been developed during algorithm testing and will be described briefly in that section.

After the minimum FPPS and PDR are determined for each rating, the SPSU curves are developed. Figure 3.3 illustrates how the PDR and CS are used to define the utility value S_{ir} for the IC rating (S_{iIC}). In general, for each individual and rating: when QS is below CS, $S = 0.00$; when QS is at CS, $S = 1.00$; when QS is at or above PDR, $S = 100.00$; for parsimony, a straight line between CS and PDR assigns intermediate values of S.

For our initial efforts, values of S_{ir} varied between 0.00 and 100.00 for all ratings to standardize utility assessment across all ratings, regardless of maximum and minimum FPPS rates for individual ratings. Since many factors influence difficulty levels for our different training pipelines, this standardization process was considered appropriate to ensure that ratings with very high or low average levels of FPPS were not incorrectly over- or undervalued. As with the PDR calculations, this procedure has changed during the testing phase of our efforts, and these changes will be described in that section. The current illustration is historically accurate for this phase of development and makes the most sense in the context of these initial descriptions.

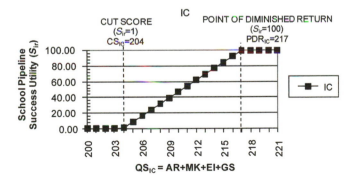

Figure 3.3.   School Pipeline Success Utility for the Interior Communication (IC) rating. Assigns S_{iIC} value linearly from 1 at Qualification Score (QS$_{IC}$) to 100 at the Point of Diminished Return (PDR$_{IC}$).

AFQT Utility

The purpose of this function is to "penalize" the overall utility score when an applicant is overqualified for a rating. The Q_{ir} curves are developed using parameters from the Job Data set. AFQT mean and standard deviation for each of the ratings are used to develop a unique curve for each rating.

When overqualification is large enough, both the Navy's and the applicant's interests are best served by placing the applicant in a rating in which general aptitude more closely matches those of other applicants who are assigned to the rating. This concept is based on the assumption that the AFQT score represents a measure of the applicant's overall general aptitude, while the QS is a measure of the specific aptitudes and skills for the rating. In general, when an applicant's AFQT score is multiple standard deviations above the mean for that rating (represented in function here as $M_r + \delta_r$), AFQT Utility (Q_{ir}) decreases from 100.00 to 0.

The utility function shown in Figure 3.4 demonstrates this concept. Utility is at 100.00 when AFQT is less than or equal to $M_r + \delta_r$, where δ_r is 2 standard deviations. Utility then decreases to zero at θ_r, where θ_r is $M_r + \delta_r + 4$ standard deviations.

RIDE Composite Score

When the RIDE algorithms are run for an individual during a counseling session, a composite score is created for that individual as a function of the SPSU and AFQTU functions. The composite scores are rank ordered, and the individual is guided toward highly ranked ratings.

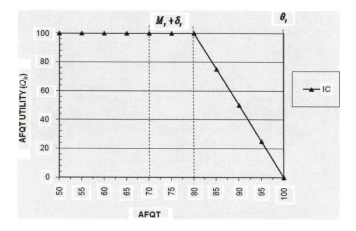

Figure 3.4. The AFQTU "penalty" function. When an individual's AFQT greatly exceeds the average for that rating, assigned AFQT Utility (Q_{ir}) decreases.

The RIDE composite score for individual i and rating r is defined as:

$$C_{ir} = w_S S_{ir} + w_Q I\{S_{ir} = S_{MAX}\} Q_{ir},$$

where $I\{S_{ir} = S_{MAX}\} = 1$ if $S_{ir} = S_{MAX}$ and zero otherwise, and w_S and w_Q are the weights associated with the SPSU and AFQTU functions, respectively.

This specifies a classification policy with the following properties:

1. For a given individual i, all ratings with $S_{ir} = 100$ have a larger Composite Utility than ratings with $S_{ir} < 100$.

2. The composite ranking of all ratings whose S_{ir} is less than 100 is determined by the rank ordering of their S_{ir}.

3. The composite ranking of all ratings whose S_{ir} equals 100 is determined by the rank ordering of their Q_{ir}.

If $w_S = w_Q = 1/2$, the Composite utilities range from a minimum of zero (for individuals whose QS is less than the CS) to 100 (for individuals whose QS is $\geq$PDR$_r$ and whose AFQT score is $\leq M_r + \delta_r$).

Figure 3.5 shows a notional depiction of our Yerkes-Dodson approximation in two dimensions. In order to think of the composite distribution in relation to Yerkes-Dodson, it is necessary to visualize plotting two points (SPSU and AFQTU), where the x-axis indicates high/low ASVAB scores. It is critical to remember that the AFQT data point (overqualification penalty) only becomes relevant when $S_{ir} \geq$ PDR$_r$ (overqualification).

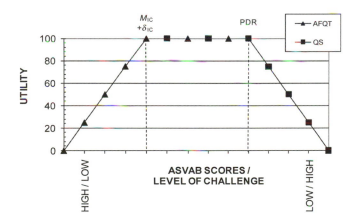

Figure 3.5.   A notional illustration of how the Composite Utility (C_{ir}) approximates the Yerkes-Dodson inverted-U model of human performance. The x-axis is reversed from previous depictions, such that ASVAB scores are decreasing from right to left, so that challenge and arousal increase from left to right, matching other Yerkes-Dodson depictions.

It is also necessary to flip the x-axis, such that the lowest values of ASVAB (AFQT and QS) are to the left and the highest values are to the right. This mimics the Yerkes-Dodson curve, as higher test scores result in lower challenge. As scores decrease (moving to the right), challenge increases to an optimal level. As test scores become too low (continuing to the right), challenge becomes too high, and utility decreases. While some readers may question why a two-dimensional representation is used here, a three-dimensional representation of the Composite Utility becomes inordinately complex and does little to help explain the concept at an introductory level.

In sum, the composite RIDE utility leverages established ASVAB composite scores to match individual aptitude to each Navy rating's training requirements. Using AFQT as a measure of general cognitive ability, and classification composite QS as the measure of specific aptitude for each rating, we were able to rapidly construct composite functions to mimic the Yerkes-Dodson inverted-U human performance curves. Since all of the key components of the RIDE algorithm had extensive validation in multiple decades of work, the RIDE efforts progressed with high efficiency and low risk.

VALIDATION RESEARCH

Early Validation Research

In trying to recount the earliest phases of Fleet RIDE development (years 1998–1999), a strong enough distinction cannot be made between development and validation to present results here as being true validation efforts. That is, procedures historically used to validate models were used iteratively throughout the process as ideas were clarified and tested. Therefore, our earliest efforts are presented here briefly (and only to a level of detail that can be stated with certainty). More formal and well-documented validation efforts are referenced, which compare the model developed to other possible multiple sequential assignment (classification) heuristics.

As described in the Technical Specifications section, two data sets were constructed to develop and test the utility and composite functions. Actual recruiting and training databases were used to create two sets of data: the Applicant Data set and the Job Data set. In these data sets, the Training Assignments Available field in the Job Data set for each rating is equal to the sum of the Rating Assigned field in the Applicant Data. Since we have no way to go back and calculate the actual training opportunities available, we simply count the training opportunities that were actually used and this became the "demand signal" in the Job Data set.

Simulations from our initial validation efforts compared the classifications actually made in our data set to simulated classifications using combinations of the RIDE utility functions. In these types of simulations, the training vacancies for each rating are filled using a sequential assignment process, which mimics the way that applicants appear in the classification process. Rather than using actual rating assigned, the assignment algorithms use the existing ASVAB subtests and AFQT score to reassign this record according to the specified heuristic. The goal of the heuristic process was to maximize average FPPS across all classifications and minimize unused training assignments.

Existing classifications in the 1996–1998 databases indicated an average FPPS of 88 percent, with (by definition) no vacant training assignments. FPPS was remarkably stable within 0.5 percent across all three years. Using only SPSU as the assignment heuristic, multiple simulations resulted in a stabilized average FPPS of 97 percent; however, percent unassigned repeatedly averaged roughly 30 percent, and occasionally as high as 40 percent. The high level of FPPS is not compelling in and of itself as the utility functions were developed on this data set to maximize FPPS. This did, however, demonstrate that we had produced a viable, repeatable process for assigning personnel in a sequential fashion. We were also not surprised by the large number of unassigned personnel since we were only using the SPSU function; a high success rate, with poor utilization of personnel, is commensurate with a poor overinvestment strategy of personnel. With such an underutilization of personnel assigned, no test of our Yerkes-Dodson hypothesis was evident.

We continued our efforts using simulations which included both the SPSU and the AFQTU penalty functions as parts of the Composite Utility. In multiple iterations of the simulations, FPPS reached a stabilized average of 92 percent, with roughly 5 percent unused training opportunities. Without a baseline for comparison (the existing data set has, by definition, 0 unused training opportunities), the 5 percent vacancy number was considered very good. Through multiple discussions with subject matter experts (SMEs), we were convinced that in an operational setting, 5 percent unassigned is a reasonable number, since we have a number of processes in place to make accommodations for matching these people to jobs (e.g., ASVAB waivers) and a number of business rules which prioritize which training opportunities are filled first. Based on SME suggestions in one set of iterations, we were able to obtain 0 percent unused training opportunities by assigning all Nuclear Field personnel (very high ASVAB score requirements) first and all undesignated personnel (no ASVAB requirement beyond AFQT minimum) last while maintaining FPPS around 92 percent.

While these initial efforts indicated a general usefulness of the RIDE algorithms, we engaged another team of researchers to develop and test the algorithms (EDS, 2001) prior to pilot testing in an operational environment.

Independent Validation

The simulations performed in this secondary phase were very similar to the simulation protocol described above, with the exception that FPPS was aggregated across all possible assignments (EDS, 2001) rather than the previous procedure of averaging only made assignments. In this fashion, unassigned personnel are represented as failures, whereas in the previous process they simply went unassigned. Also, when the sets of curves were developed relating QS and FPPS, data were assembled into bins of five QS points and then, if necessary, expanded by five points until each bin contained at least 10 observations. The mean score of each bin was used to plot the QS to FPPS relationship. Finally, the PDR was determined by identifying all QS bins with FPPS within 1 percent of the maximum FPPS, and using the lowest QS bin average value.

As in the previous efforts, two data sets were constructed: the Job Data set and the Applicant Data set. These data sets contained the same variables as previously described. In addition to the existing 75,000 records from 1996–1999, 75,000 records were added from 2000–2001 resulting in a total data set of roughly 150,000 records.

Multiple sequential assignment simulations were run comparing a variety of heuristics to the actual Navy (baseline) assignments. It is important to note that although the current classification system uses CLASP, operational practices can produce differences between actual assignments and CLASP recommendations. Distinctions are made between these two assignment "practices" and both are considered operational benchmarks for our efforts.

In addition to the existing utilities of the RIDE algorithms, a "hardness" or difficulty factor was added (EDS, 2001). Initial simulations in this phase were resulting in a high number of unassigned applicants. In particular (and matching what our SMEs provided as guidance in our initial efforts), Nuclear Field positions are very hard to fill, and if priority is not given to these jobs, many remain unfilled. Although including this new element confounds goodness of fit with operational concerns, the utility of this constraint in a simulation process was deemed important to test and represents actual operational practice in this simulation environment.

The Hardness Index of a job was defined as the average ASVAB subtest score at the PDR. Since the classification composites are combination of multiple subtests, taking the CS at PDR and dividing by the number of subtests in that composite was used to indicate relative difficulty or "hardness" of that rating. The Hardness Index was scaled to a range of 0–1 using the transformation:

$$\text{Hardness Factor} = (\text{Hardness} - \text{MinHard}) / (\text{MaxHard} - \text{MinHard})$$

When used in the simulations, the Hardness Factor was implemented by multiplying (correcting) SPSU by this factor.

Although a wide variety of simulations using various combinations of the available data were analyzed in this effort, the final report (EDS, 2001) focuses on results using the data sets composed of recruiting data from 1999–2000 matched to job parameters from 1996–1998 training data. In this

Table 3.1. Comparison of Algorithms Tested (EDS, 2001)

Algorithm	MOEs	
(1) W-F with IDF	80.4%	
	1,582	4,748
(2) W-F no IDF	81.1%	
	1,572	4,349
(3) W-F efficient frontier	78.2%	
	276	2,471
(4) Shadow pricing	81.9%	
	1,035	4,324
(1a) W-F with IDF HARD	81.9%	
	1,035	4,324
(2a) W-F no IDF HARD	85.8%	
	98	799
(3a) W-F efficient frontier HARD	85.4%	
	151	1,312
(4a) Shadow pricing HARD	82.2%	
	193	1,672
Baseline Navy Allocation	81.7%	
	1,719	923
CLASP algorithm	79.0%	
	2,876	3,830

Measures of effectiveness (MOEs) represent FPPS at the top center, number of waivers granted at lower left, and unfilled vacancies on the lower right.

fashion, data records for the individual applicant to be assigned are distinct from the training "demand" signal records. This distinction results in a closer approximation of an operational environment than the previously described efforts where applicants are essentially reassigned to training requirements derived from their own data.

In this round of simulations, variants of the RIDE algorithms (referred to in the EDS report as the W-F, or Watson-Folchi algorithms) were compared to other heuristics and Navy baselines. Results of the simulations from 60,000 records assigned to 75 different ratings are presented in Table 3.1. In addition to FPPS (top center) and Unfilled Vacancies (lower right), these simulations also present Waivers Granted (lower left). At the end of these simulation processes, a second iteration allowed unassigned applicants five-point waivers and ran them through an additional round of potential assignment.

These assignments count toward waivers granted and more closely approximate operational considerations. The W-F with IDF (Identity Function) cell represents the model as depicted both in Watson and Folchi (1999) and in the Technical Specifications section above. This baseline form has a procedural transformation which results in SPSU being drawn from 1 at CS to 100 at PDR. Although this variant did somewhat better than the CLASP baseline, it is surprising that it did not exceed the Navy Baseline Allocation. This may be an indication that our operational practices contribute classification productivity in addition to existing algorithms (in this case CLASP). If this is the case, it may be an uneven contrast to compare the results of the algorithm to those of the algorithm plus, what appear to be, very good operational practices. The fact that the Navy Baseline Allocation did better than CLASP in these simulations supports this interpretation.

The next variant, W-F no IDF, represents the SPSU without this transformation. Rather than transforming to 1 and 100, the SPSU values reflect the actual FPPS at CS and PDR, and the utility curve is a straight line between these two points. Results show some performance enhancement with this variant.

Neither an efficient frontier nor a shadow pricing heuristic did appreciably better than existing W-F algorithms. The most dramatic improvement was the variant which contained the Hardness Function modifying the SPSU, but without an IDF transformation of SPSU.

In summary, while RIDE did show an improvement over CLASP in the multiple sequential assignment problem, it was unexpected that there was not an improvement over Baseline Navy Allocation. However, variants of the initial specifications readily showed substantial improvements. Using non-transformed FPPS values and including a Hardness Factor were the most effective variants in these simulations.

BENEFITS TO THE NAVY

The RIDE algorithms have reliably demonstrated the capability to classify sailors to ratings while optimizing FPPS. Figure 3.6 illustrates the effectiveness of the RIDE algorithms by presenting data from over 30,000 sailors (Watson, 2004; Watson & Blanco, 2004). In these efforts, all sailor records were run through the RIDE algorithms, and the RIDE rank for the actual rating assigned was determined and compared to actual FPPS. These data depict a clear relationship between FPPS and RIDE rank: top-10 ranked classifications have a greater than 91 percent FPPS rate, while those not in the top-25 ranked classifications have a less than 87 percent FPPS rate.

Velgach and Watson (2009) present many other compelling MOEs using this same type of analysis. Using over 100,000 sailor records, RIDE again not only predicts FPPS but also predicts advancement and retention. Sailors with top-10 ranked classifications are almost twice as likely to make

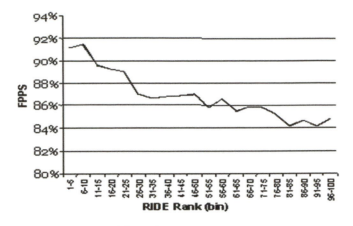

Figure 3.6.   FPPS versus RIDE rank.

E-6 pay grade during their first enlistment (average of 7%) than those not in the top-25 (3.5%). Sailors who have been classified into top-10 ranked classifications are retained in their original rating at an average of 85 percent, whereas those beneath the top-25 average 81 percent.

The RIDE models have been implemented for in-service counseling in the Fleet RIDE system. These in-service classifications occur when an unrated sailor desires to become rated (classified into a rating) or a sailor with a rating is changing to a different rating. In-service rating changes are referred to as reclassifications or rating conversions.

Velgach and Watson describe outcomes specifically related to Fleet RIDE use in these in-service classifications and reclassifications. In one comparison, the RIDE composite scores are calculated for the sailor's desired rating and compared to success on the exam used to grant admission to that rating. Exam success rates are highly correlated to RIDE score: RIDE scores above 80 utility points result in an average of 95 percent success rate; RIDE scores beneath 60 result in a 50 percent or lower success rate. For reclassifications, one comparison looked at 1,400 rating conversion requests. RIDE score was highly correlated with conversion approval: RIDE scores above 80 utility points result in 96 percent conversion approval; RIDE scores beneath 60 utility points resulted in 90 percent or lower approval rate.

RIDE and Fleet RIDE have also undergone formal pilot testing for both initial classification and in-service reclassification. Roughly 1,400 applicants were classified using RIDE between July 2001 and March 2003 and compared to the same size cohort group enlisted at the same processing center in San Diego, California. Tracking both groups through training indicated that sailors classified using RIDE demonstrated 91 percent FPPS as compared to 89 percent FPPS for those that were not. Additionally, sailors classified with RIDE tended to honor their enlistment agreement at a higher rate than those that were not.

That is, there are typically weeks or months of delay between initial classification and shipping to basic training. RIDE classified applicants showed up to ship at a rate of 91 percent as compared to local average of 89 percent. We believe that the higher ship rate was due to applicants being more satisfied with the match made by RIDE and were, therefore, more committed to fulfilling their obligation to enter active duty.

Early Fleet-RIDE pilot testing started in August 2003 and was limited to two ships homeported in San Diego, a large amphibious platform, *USS Belleau Wood* (LHA-3), and a small cruiser, *USS Valley Forge* (CG-50). The MOEs for these efforts have a different emphasis than others described. Since we already have substantial support for the RIDE methodology, these analyses focused on the value of RIDE from a system perspective. While we assume at this point that the RIDE algorithms will perform optimal sailor-rating job matching, concerns about excessive workload to counselors, as well as potential hindrance to the classification and reclassification efforts, were assessed.

All results support the utility of using the Fleet RIDE system, including reduction of non-value-added work (reading manuals, generating forms, and extracting personnel data from databases). Job screening time was reduced from 3 hours to 15 minutes. Conversion packages developed from these sessions improved in quality from an overall 70 percent error rate to an effective 0 percent error rate. Additionally, since Fleet RIDE enables the counselor and sailor to see a list of all qualified jobs, rank ordered by the RIDE composite utility, counseling session can intelligently compare as many as 90 ratings. Comparative estimates indicate that roughly three ratings are compared during non-Fleet RIDE sessions.

In summary, a broad array of criterion measures converged to validate the RIDE heuristic algorithms and the implementation of these algorithms in job counseling systems. While the heuristics were developed to maximize training success as related by FPPS, the robust nature of the algorithms is verified through their effectiveness in predicting a variety of other outcomes, including promotion rates, retention rates, and testing success. The robust nature of the RIDE model supports the belief that basing personnel decision models on valid models of human performance can dramatically add to their effectiveness and general application.

APPLICATIONS TO OTHER DOMAINS

Work-related stress is one of the greatest challenges to the health of working people and therefore to the healthiness of the work organizations (Cox, Randall, & Griffiths, 2002). In the United States, workers who suffer from a stress-related illness are off work for a median of 25 days (National Institute for Occupational Safety and Health, 2004). A survey of European Union member states found that 28 percent of employees reported stress-related illness or health problems (this equates to 41 million workers, European Foundation for the Improvement of Living and Working Conditions, 2000). On the opposite end of the Yerkes-Dodson curve, having a workforce that is not challenged can also lead to complacency and human errors (Flin, O'Connor, & Crichton, 2008). Therefore, the need for a workforce that is suitably challenged in their work is not just a concern for the USN but crucial for all high-reliability organizations. By selecting personnel with the correct attributes, in the right "quantities," we are setting up the individual to have a stimulating and productive career and providing the organization with someone who will do a good job. It is suggested that applying the selection process described in this chapter provides an empirically based method that allows the flexibility to identify a range of people that could succeed in the job.

REFERENCES

Cox, T., Randall, R., & Griffiths, A. (2002). *Interventions to control stress at work in hospital staff*. Sudbury: HSE Books.

Eitelberg, M. J. (1984). *Manpower for military occupations*. Washington, D.C.: Office of the Assistant Secretary of Defense (Force Management and Personnel).

———. (1988). *Manpower for military occupations*. Washington, D.C.: Department of Defense.

Electronic Data Systems, U.S. Government Solutions. (2001). *RIDE: Alternative algorithms for job selection*. Report prepared for the Department of the Navy. EDS, Dallas, TX.

European Foundation for the Improvement of Living and Working Conditions. (2000). *Third European survey of workers conditions*. Dublin, Ireland: European Foundation for the Improvement of Working Conditions.

Flin, R., O'Connor, P., & Crichton, M. (2008). *Safety at the sharp end: Training non-technical skills*. Aldershot, England: Ashgate Publishing Ltd.

Hunter, J. E. (1986). Cognitive ability, cognitive aptitudes, job knowledge, and job performance. *Journal of Vocational Behavior*, 29, 340–362.

Ippel, M. J. (2006). Investigation into the measurement invariance of the ASVAB scores using a multi-group confirmatory factor analysis. *CogniMetrics Research Report*, No. 06-01.

Ippel, M. J., & Watson, S. E. (2008). *ASVAB: E Pluribus Unum?* In 50th annual conference of the International Military Testing Association, Amsterdam, September 29–October 3, 2008.

Johnson, C. W. (2007). *The systemic effects of fatigue on military operations*. Second Institution of Engineering and Technology international conference on system safety (pp. 1–6).

Kass, R. A., Mitchell, K. J., Grafton, F. C., & Wing, H. (1983). Factorial validity of the Armed Services Vocational Aptitude Battery (ASVAB), Forms 8, 9, and 10; 1981 Army applicant sample. *Educational and Psychological Measurement*, 43, 1077–1087.

Kroeker, L., & Rafacz, B. A. (1983). *Classification and assignment within Pride (CLASP): A recruit assignment model* (NPRDC TR 84-9). San Diego, CA: Navy Personnel Research and Development Center.

Lacey, J. L. (1967). Somatic response patterning and stress: Some revisions of activation theory. In M. H. Appley & R. Trumbell (Eds.), *Psychological stress: Issues in research.* New York: Appleton-Century-Croft.

National Institute for Occupational Safety and Health (2004). *Worker health chartbook 2004.* Cincinnati, OH: National Institute for Occupational Safety and Health.

Sellman, W. S. (2004). *Predicting readiness for military service: How enlistment standards are set.* Report prepared for National Assessment Governing Board, Washington, D.C.

Shrivastava, P. (1986). *Bhopal: Anatomy of a disaster.* New York: Basic Books.

Velgach, S., & Watson, S. E. (2009). *Effectiveness of the rating identification engine.* Prepared for the 51st Annual Conference of the International Military Testing Association, Tartu, Estonia.

Ward, J. H. (1977). *Creating mathematical models of judgment processes: From policy capturing to policy specifying* (AFHRL-TR-77-47). Brooks Air Force Base, TX: Air Force Human Resources Laboratory.

Ward, J. H., Haney, D. L., Hendrix, W. H., & Pina, M. (1978). *Assignment procedures in Air Force procurement management information system* (AFHRL-TR-78-30). Brooks Air Force Base, TX: Air Force Human Resources Laboratory.

Watson, S. E. (2004). *The Navy's rating identification engine: Optimizing human resource allocation.* In 46th Annual Conference of the International Military Testing Association, Brussels.

Watson, S. E., & Blanco, T. A. (2004). *Fleet-RIDE: Enabling technology for sailor continuous career counseling.* Paper presented at the Interservice/Industry Training, Simulation & Education Conference (I/ITSEC), Orlando, Florida.

Watson, S. E., & Folchi, J. S. (1999). *Specifications for RIDE utility functions.* Unpublished technical report. Navy Personnel Research Studies and Technology, Millington, Tennessee.

Watson, S. E., Mills, L. J., & Arendt, C. A. (2004). *Using classification technology to support force shaping.* Paper presented at the fourth annual Navy workforce analysis conference, Alexandria, Virginia.

Welsh, J. R., Kucinkas, S. K., & Curran, L. T. (1990). *Armed Services Vocational Aptitude Battery (ASVAB): Integrative review of validity studies* (AFHRL-TR-90-22). Brooks Air Force Base, TX: Air Force Human Resources Laboratory.

Welsh, J. R., Watson, T. W., & Ree, M. J. (1990). *Armed Services Vocational Aptitude Battery (ASVAB): Predicting military criteria from general and specific abilities* (AFHRL-TR-90-63). Brooks Air Force Base, TX: Air Force Human Resources Laboratory.

Winton, W. M. (1987). Do introductory textbooks present the Yerkes-Dodson law correctly? *American Psychologist,* 42 (2), 202–203.

Yerkes, R. M., & Dodson, J. D. (1908). The relation of strength of stimulus to rapidity of habit-formation. *Journal of Comparative Neurology and Psychology,* 18, 459–482.

Chapter 4

ASSESSMENT AND SELECTION OF AVIATORS IN THE U.S. MILITARY

Tatana M. Olson, Peter B. Walker, and Henry L. Phillips IV

Many high-risk environments are characterized by complexity in both the missions being performed and the equipment and systems being used. Particularly in military aviation, advances in automation have increased the availability of real-time data, improved efficiency, and allowed for greater flexibility in aviation operations (Parasuraman & Byrne, 2003). However, the aviator remains at the center of this complex system, selectively attending to and encoding relevant information, filtering out irrelevant information, and making critical judgments and decisions. It is the effective accomplishment of these tasks that directly contribute to the primary goals of military aviation—achieving and maintaining a high level of mission readiness and, ultimately, accomplishing mission requirements (Carretta & Ree, 2003). Achieving these goals requires selecting qualified aviators with the knowledge, skills, and abilities to perform successfully in the aviation environment.

This chapter opens with a general discussion of the importance of personnel selection followed by a brief history of selection in military aviation and an overview of current theoretical and empirical work on the use of cognitive ability, psychomotor, and personality trait-related constructs as predictors of aviator performance. The remainder of the chapter focuses on current military aviation selection procedures used by the U.S. Air Force (USAF) and U.S. Navy (USN; see Chapter 5 of this book for a discussion of selection in the USN submarine force). The chapter concludes with a brief discussion of the implications of changing technology for the selection of aviation personnel.

THE IMPORTANCE OF SELECTION

Personnel selection involves a standardized procedure for identifying candidates that are likely to be good performers on the job. Depending on the occupational environment, selection can involve two sets of processes—selecting "in" and selecting "out." Selecting "in" is the most common practice for the majority of occupations and involves identifying the best suited candidates for the nature of the work. Underlying this process are five key assumptions (Guion, 1998):

1. People have abilities (e.g., mental abilities, psychomotor abilities, learned skills, habits, and personality characteristics) that are reasonably stable.
2. People differ in any given ability and it is these differences that serve as the basis for making personnel decisions.
3. Relative differences in ability remain even after training or experience. Abilities may be enhanced by training, but the individual who started out with a high level of ability will still perform better after training than the individual who started out with a lower level of ability.
4. Different jobs require different abilities and effective selection involves matching the abilities required by the job with the abilities of the individual.
5. The abilities required by the job can be measured in some way.

Selecting "out" involves screening an individual for undesirable characteristics (e.g., psychopathology) rather than identifying the extent to which they possess desirable characteristics, such as a certain level of job-relevant knowledge, skills, and abilities. Often, highly specialized and inherently dangerous occupations (e.g., military sniper and astronaut) will rely entirely on a selecting "out" process to ensure the best possible match between individual characteristics and the demands of the job (Picano, Williams, & Roland, 2006).

Identifying and selecting the "right" individual for the job can have a significant impact on organizational outcomes such as cost, safety, and productivity. This is especially true for high-risk contexts such as aviation where the job requires well-honed skills, the work environment is inherently dangerous, and the consequences of a poor selection decision can be severe. For example, the costs associated with implementing a selection program that effectively identifies candidates that possess both a higher aptitude for learning and the motivation and personality attributes necessary to succeed may be mitigated by reduced time to train, reduced attrition, and increased competency levels. In the USN, it costs up to $880,000 just to give a student aviator the training he requires in order to set foot in the type of aircraft he will end up flying (such as the F/A-18F Hornet), followed by additional costs to provide training specific to that platform (Chief of Naval Air Training, 2008).[1] Thus, even a small reduction in training attrition could result in large cost avoidance savings.

Regardless of the focus of the selection process (i.e., selecting "in" versus selecting "out"), all selection programs rely on three critical elements (Sanchez & Levine, 2001): (1) identification of the knowledge, skills, abilities, and other characteristics (KSAOs), such as personality attributes and attitudes, required to perform the job. These KSAOs can be obtained through a number of different methods, the most common of which are job analysis (Brannick, Levine, & Morgeson, 2007) and cognitive task analysis (Chipman, Schraagen, & Shalin, 2000); (2) reliable and valid measures of these KSAOs; and (3) a thorough validation process providing evidence of a statistically significant relationship between identified KSAOs (i.e., hypothesized predictors of job performance) and job performance criteria such as supervisor ratings, hands-on job ratings, and accident reports. This relationship is represented by the correlation coefficient (r) or the multiple correlation (R) if there is more than one predictor. Validity is the most critical testing and selection issue because it establishes a relationship between the characteristic(s) upon which selection decisions are based and some aspect of job performance. If that relationship does not exist, the selection process is worthless and may in fact be illegal[2] (Uniform Guidelines on Employee Selection Procedures, 1978; also see Arvey & Faley, 1992 for a discussion of legal issues in selection). In addition, the use of selection methods with good predictive validity can translate into substantial increases in both the quantity and the quality of job performance (Schmidt & Hunter, 1998).

In the arena of general personnel selection, uncorrected validity coefficients for the prediction of performance and job-related outcomes routinely fall between .20 and .25 (Levine, Spector, Menon, Narayanan, & Cannon-Bowers, 1996), although uncorrected meta-analytic validities for some types of performance criteria have been observed as high as .44 (Schmitt, Gooding, Noe, & Kirsch, 1984). This holds true within the more specific domain of aviator selection as well. For example, in a meta-analysis of 68 studies involving more than 400,000 civilian and military subjects, average validities were between .20 and .35, with very few validities in excess of .50 (Hunter & Burke, 1994).

MILITARY AVIATION SELECTION

Historical Background

Since the early 1900s, researchers and practitioners have spent considerable time and effort trying to identify the characteristics important to being a good aviator and developing methods to effectively measure those characteristics. In the USN the roots of aviation selection began in the aeromedical community with the flight physical, which assessed the physical qualifications associated with flying such as visual acuity, muscle balance, and reaction times to visual, auditory, and tactile stimuli. However, by World War I (WWI), it was clear that the flight physical did not capture a significant portion of the variance associated with flying proficiency as evidenced by the high levels of attrition from flight training (Petho, 1992). For example, Gilchrist (1918) reported that 67 out of 100 physically qualified pilots and balloonists were disqualified because of psychological problems.

Acknowledging the inherent limitations of the flight physical for predicting flying performance, researchers began to explore potential psychological attributes related to flying proficiency (what would later be known as "aeronautical adaptability"). During the period between WWI and World War II (WWII), a number of different measures, including intelligence, psychomotor skills, mechanical comprehension, spatial measures, and personality, were identified and used for pilot selection (Koonce, 1984). The period following WWII saw little progress in pilot selection methods. Emphasis was placed on the refinement of established paper and pencil tests rather than on the creation of measures in different modalities targeting previously neglected job-relevant constructs. The one exception to this lull was in the field of personality measurement, which experienced significant growth in research and development (see Hilton & Dolgin, 1991 for a review). Starting in the 1970s, as aircraft increased in performance capability and instrumentation complexity, pilot selection expanded beyond static paper and pencil tests of intelligence to dynamic computerized assessments of psychomotor performance that more closely mirrored the demands placed upon pilots by these new operating environments. Although measures of cognitive ability remain an integral component of pilot selection programs, advances in computer technology and personality theory and measurement, as well as a greater understanding of how the human mind processes sensory information, have led to a resurgence in research examining the complex relationships between personality and psychomotor skills and pilot performance.

Aviator Selection Methods

Aviator selection methods vary in content, focus, and method of administration across countries and even across services within the United States (Carretta & Ree, 2003). However, one component common to virtually every selection system is the assessment of skills, abilities, and job-related attributes. Tests assessing cognitive ability and psychomotor skills are the most common, while simulation-based tests and personality assessments are less common. The following sections provide a brief review of current pilot selection methods and examine them within the contexts of two well-established aviation selection programs—the USAF and the USN. In addition, the applicability of these selection methods within the expanding domain of Unmanned Aerial Systems (UASs) is addressed.

Cognitive Ability Tests

Cognitive ability tests assess aptitude in a number of different areas, including verbal and mathematical skills, mechanical comprehension, reasoning, and spatial ability, and have demonstrated very good validity for predicting training and job performance across a wide range of occupations

(Salgado, Viswesvaran, & Ones, 2001; Schmidt & Hunter, 1998). The selection of aviators has long included measures of cognitive ability, and they remain a mainstay of current pilot selection programs. For example, in the Norwegian Air Force, candidates are evaluated on 20 different cognitive and psychomotor tests. In a study examining the predictive validity of these tests, Martinussen and Torjussen (1998) found that the best predictors of training performance were instrument comprehension ($r = .29$), mechanical comprehension ($r = .23$), and aviation information ($r = .22$). The Royal Air Force (RAF) of the United Kingdom also relies on the assessment of five cognitive ability domains for aviator selection—attentional capacity, mental speed, psychomotor, reasoning, and spatial (Bailey & Woodhead, 1996). Finally, both the USN and the USAF incorporate cognitive ability tests in their aviator selection programs.

Several recent meta-analyses[3] have provided further support for the utility of cognitive ability tests in predicting aviator performance. Hunter and Burke (1994) conducted a meta-analysis of 68 pilot selection studies published between 1940 and 1990 in which mean validities were estimated for 16 predictor categories, including verbal, quantitative, spatial, perceptual speed, and reaction time. The predictors with the highest observed mean validities (i.e., uncorrected for statistical artifacts) were job sample ($\rho = .34$), gross dexterity ($\rho = .32$), mechanical comprehension ($\rho = .29$), reaction time ($\rho = .28$), and aviation information ($\rho = .22$). Martinussen (1996) analyzed 50 studies examining the relationship between various psychological measures and aviator performance. Similar to Hunter and Burke, she found that the best predictors of aviator performance were a combined index of cognitive and psychomotor tests ($\rho = .37$), previous flight training experience ($\rho = .30$), and general aviation information ($\rho = .24$).

Psychomotor Tests

One of the limitations of cognitive testing in aviation selection concerns the nature of job requirements in the aviation environment. The dynamic nature of the aviation environment often requires aviators to divide their attention among a number of different tasks concurrently while continuing to fly the aircraft (i.e., aviate, navigate, and communicate). To perform these tasks, aviators must effectively coordinate the varying and competing demands for information processing and attentional resources across the various tasks (Gopher, 1982; Gopher & Kahneman, 1971; North & Gopher, 1976).

One method that has been developed to measure a candidate's ability to effectively coordinate mental resources in the cockpit has been the use of psychomotor testing. Psychomotor tests typically measure the speed and accuracy with which a person can carry out tasks ranging from simple motor and reflex responses to complex coordination tasks (for reviews see, North & Griffin, 1977; Passey & McLaurin, 1966). The U.S. military has had a strong interest in the development and use of psychomotor testing (also called apparatus testing) since WWI. Early psychomotor testing involved tasks such as compensatory tracking, where an individual would track a moving object using a mechanical or electronic device (i.e., simulated joystick). According to Weybrew (1979), early validity data for these types of apparatus testing were very robust with validity coefficients ranging from $r = .20$ to $r = .40$. However, the cost to maintain the equipment was very high, and by 1955, the USAF discontinued the use of psychomotor testing and shifted almost exclusively toward paper-based tests of general cognitive ability (Carretta, 1987).

In the next few decades, as attrition rates in the services continued to rise, there was a resurgence in research examining the utility of psychomotor testing for aviation selection. Damos (1987; see also, Blower & Dolgin, 1991) combined eye–hand–foot coordination tasks with tasks involving reaction times and problem solving. Using similar testing procedures, Griffin (1987) concluded that approximately 16 percent more variance could be accounted for using psychomotor tests in conjunction with standard paper and pencil testing. Gibb and Dolgin (1989) examined the predictive validity of the compensatory tracking task based on 187 student aviators. Compensatory tracking was shown to be directly related to flight training performance. Specifically, those with poorer tracking performance exhibited weak to failing flight performance. By the early 1990s, the evidence was clear—combining psychomotor test data with standard paper and pencil testing significantly enhanced predictability in selection (Delaney, 1992).

In response to the mounting evidence for the validity of psychomotor testing in aviation selection, the USAF initiated a program to develop a computer administered test battery for pilot selection. The result of this project was the Basic Attributes Test (BAT; Carretta, 1987, 1989), a battery of subtests assessing individual differences in psychomotor skills, cognitive abilities, personality, and attitudes toward risk. The BAT included assessments of multi-limb coordination, where subjects were required to control the horizontal and vertical movement of a targeting reticule, as well as measures of information processing ability (e.g., encoding speed, mental rotation, and item recognition). Consistent with a number of previous studies that have illustrated the utility of psychomotor testing, the BAT demonstrated a reliable increase in the prediction of flight training success over traditional cognitive ability testing alone (Carretta, 1992). Carretta and Ree (1994) reported a statistically significant increase in predictive validity when BAT scores were combined with the Air Force Officer Qualifying Test (AFOQT) and previous flying experience (from $r = .31$ to $r = .38$).

More recently, the USAF revised the battery of tests included in the BAT to specifically assess aviation-related skill sets. The new test battery, called the Test of Basic Aviation Skills (TBAS; Carretta, 2005), consists of a series of cognitive, perceptual, and psychomotor tasks performed separately, and then in progressively more challenging combinations. These tasks include three- and five-digit listening tasks, one- and two-axis airplane tracking tasks, an emergency scenario test, and a test of ability to orient oneself in three-dimensional space. One such combination requires the examinee to monitor a series of numbers presented aurally and to respond when any one of a group of target numbers (e.g., 1, 2, 4, 6, or 8) is presented, as well as track two airplanes using a joystick and foot pedals. In addition to demonstrating good "face validity" among individuals being evaluated for admission into aviation training due to its incorporation of tasks directly related to activities that would be performed in the cockpit, TBAS has demonstrated good predictive validity for training performance across a number of studies (e.g., Carretta, 2005; Ree, 2003).

Personality Tests

The most important development in the literature regarding personality and aviator performance was the emerging consensus on the five-factor model (Tupes & Christal, 1961) as a robust conceptual framework for personality. These factors, known as the "Big Five," represent five broad dimensions of personality traits and were derived from numerous studies, which showed that people's descriptions of themselves or others tended to include common traits. The Big Five traits include

- *Agreeableness*: good-natured, compassionate, cooperative;
- *Conscientiousness*: dependable, organized, pays attention to detail;
- *Extroversion*: energetic, outgoing, talkative;
- *Neuroticism*: tendency to experience unpleasant emotions easily such as anger, anxiety, or depression; and
- *Openness*: open-minded, curious, imaginative, adventurous.

The predictive validity of the Big Five for job performance, especially conscientiousness and neuroticism, has been demonstrated across a wide range of contexts and occupations (Barrick & Mount, 1991; Hough & Oswald, 2000; Schmidt & Hunter, 1998) and has significantly contributed to increased research examining the role of personality in aviator performance, both within the training environment and, to a lesser extent, within operational settings.

The study of personality in aviation generally focuses on two areas (Carretta & Ree, 2003). In the first area, personality profiles of aviation candidates, students, or winged aviators are compared to the general population. A number of studies have demonstrated support for differences in personality between aviators and the general population, especially with regards to emotional stability and ability to cope with and adapt to stressful situations (see Chapter 11 of this book; Ganesh & Joseph, 2005; Voge, 1989). For example, Picano (1990) found that military aviators had more active problem-solving strategies and less reliance on emotional support, avoidance, and disengagement when coping with stress than the general population. Callister, King, Retzlaff, and Marsh (1999) used the Revised NEO-PI, a measure of the Big Five, to examine personality profiles for student aviators in the USAF. Compared to the general population, student aviators scored higher on extroversion and conscientiousness and lower on neuroticism and agreeableness. Grice and Katz (2006, 2007) found that career U.S. Army rotary wing aviators scored significantly higher on extroversion and lower on neuroticism and openness compared to a normative sample. It is important to note that although the personality profile of military aviators appears to be different than that of the general population, the population of successful aviators is not homogeneous. Based on an analysis of 10-year follow-up data from 350 USAF flight students, Retzlaff and Gibertini (1987) described three aviator prototypes: (1) the "Right Stuff," an individual characterized by low humility, argumentative behavior, self-centeredness, and impulsivity (21%); (2) the "Company Man," the typical aviator characterized as achievement-oriented, dominant, and emotionally stable (58%); and (3) the "Wrong Stuff," an individual characterized as obsessive, socially introverted, self-conscious, and serious (21%). However, across these three prototypes, they were no differences in training outcomes. These findings were further supported by Picano (1991) who identified three similar personality types among experienced and successful military aviators using a different personality measure, the Occupational Personality Questionnaire (OPQ). Thus, although there is a fairly well-defined set of personality characteristics associated with the failing aviator (e.g., low stress tolerance and high anxiety), it is likely that there is more than one personality profile for the successful aviator (Berg, Moore, Retzlaff, & King, 2002).

In the second area of personality research, scores on a personality measure are validated against some measure of training performance. Although this area has received less research attention given the difficulties in identifying reliable performance criteria, a growing number of studies have demonstrated a small to moderate relationship between personality and aviator performance. For example, Street, Helton, and Dolgin (1992) found that student naval aviators who were higher in competitiveness were less likely to attrite from training than those were not as competitive. In an examination of 274 civilian airline pilots using the Temperament Structure Scales, a measure based upon the Big Five, Hormann and Maschke (1996) found that individuals with lower scores on a global job success measure were more emotionally unstable, introverted, and aggressive than those with higher scores, and that personality added significant incremental validity above and beyond age and flying experience in predicting job performance. Among 687 USAF student pilots, Carretta and Ree (2003) found that although the personality portion of the BAT (assessment of risk-taking) exhibited only a modest relationship with pilot training performance on its own, adding the personality score to the other elements of the USAF pilot selection composite improved the overall predictive validity of the BAT. Thus, the real value in the use of personality in pilot selection may come from its ability to significantly increment the predictive validity of cognitive ability and psychomotor measures. Given the costs associated with training student pilots, even a small increase in predictive validity can translate into large cost savings.

Although numerous studies have examined the relationship between personality and aviator performance (e.g., Berg et al., 2002; Dolgin & Gibb, 1989; Retzlaff & Gibertini, 1987), empirical support for the predictive validity of personality in aviation, as discussed above, has been mixed, especially when examined in the absence of more powerful predictors such as cognitive ability. In a review of aviator selection research from 1917 to 1977, North and Griffin (1977) concluded that not one of the more than 40 different personality inventories examined had "any appreciable impact on the selection of aviator candidates." However, research efforts over the last 20 years have provided significant insight into methodological issues that may obfuscate the true relationship between personality and performance, and demonstrated the potential utility of personality variables in selection systems.

One such methodological issue involves the underlying construct that the personality test is being used to measure. Early examinations of personality and pilot performance used traditional personality inventories (e.g., Minnesota Multiphasic Personality Inventory), which were designed to detect psychopathology rather than predict variability in job performance within a "normal" population of individuals. A second methodological issue involves the criterion used to examine predictive validity. The vast majority of aviator selection studies use some measure of training performance (versus operational performance) to examine predictive validity. However, given that the training period is much more structured than the actual job environment, and individuals tend to exert maximum effort in order to "look good" (termed the Honeymoon Effect; Helmreich, Swain, & Carsrud, 1986), it may be only after this period ends that underlying personality dispositions become significant determinants of individual behavior.

The methodological issue exerting the greatest effect on personality test validity, however, may be intentional response distortion, or "faking." In instances where one response option is obviously more socially desirable than the others, applicants motivated to present themselves in the most positive light may be more likely to endorse the socially desirable option. The degree to which the phenomenon of applicant faking occurs in applicant populations and its impact on validity have been the subject of much debate (Hough, Eaton, Dunnette, Kamp, & McCloy, 1990; Griffith, Chmielowski, & Yoshita, 2007; Ones, Viswesvaran, & Reiss, 1996), but recent evidence suggests that in high-stakes military testing environments, examinee faking does result in significant scale inflation and reduced test validity (White, Young, Hunter, & Rumsey, 2008). Numerous techniques, including response time evaluation, embedded validity scales, and forced-choice response formats, have been employed to attempt to mitigate the impact of response distortion on personality test validity (Burns & Christiansen, 2006; Schmitt & Oswald, 2006) with varying degrees of success.

Summary

Research findings have clearly demonstrated the validity of cognitive ability measures for predicting aviator performance in the aviation environment. Although less conclusive, there is also considerable evidence suggesting that psychomotor skills, especially as they relate to multitasking, play an important role in determining technical performance in the cockpit when assessed in conjunction with cognitive ability. Finally, there is a growing body of research evidence supporting the predictive validity of personality, specifically those attributes related to stress coping and emotional stability, for aviation performance not only in the cockpit but within the aviation environment as a whole.

Current Applications of Aviation Selection Testing in the U.S. Military

USAF—Pilot Candidate Selection Method

The USAF's pilot selection program is composed of three components: the AFOQT, the BAT (described in the previous section), and self-reported flying experience. The AFOQT is primarily a cognitive ability and aviation interest test battery composed of 16 different tests, including verbal analogies, arithmetic reasoning, reading comprehension, data interpretation, word knowledge, scale reading, instrument comprehension, and aviation information. These tests are combined into an officer composite and two aviation composites (Pilot and Navigator-Technical; Carretta & Ree, 1996). Scores on the AFOQT, TBAS, and measure of flying experience are combined to create a measure of aptitude called the Pilot Candidate Selection Method or PCSM (Carretta, 1992). Although the AFOQT pilot composite has demonstrated the best individual predictive validity for training performance, ranging from $r = .26$ to $r = .42$, the inclusion of TBAS and previous flying experience has provided significant incremental validity (Carretta, 2005). High PCSM scores have been shown to be related to greater probability of completing jet training, fewer hours needed to complete training, higher class rank, and lower probability of attrition (Carretta, 2000).

USN—Aviation Selection Test Battery

The Aviation Selection Test Battery (ASTB) is the primary tool used by the Navy, Marine Corps, and Coast Guard to select aviation candidates. In its current form, the ASTB assesses individual aptitude in four areas:

Reading Comprehension, Mathematical Skills, Mechanical Comprehension, and Spatial Apperception. In addition, the ASTB includes a measure of job knowledge (i.e., the Aviation and Nautical Information subtest). Scores on each of the five subtests of the ASTB are regression weighted to produce three composites: the Academic Qualifications Rating (AQR), the Pilot Flight Aptitude Rating (PFAR), and the Flight Officer Flight Aptitude Rating (FOFAR).

Several studies have demonstrated the validity of the ASTB for a number of important aviation training criteria, including academic performance in Aviation Preflight Indoctrination (API)[4] and ground school, flight performance in the primary stage of flight training, and probability of completing the training pipeline (Olson, 2006a). For example, Olson (2006b) found that as much as 25 percent of the variability in performance in API and primary flight training is accounted for by an individual's scores on the ASTB. Similarly, Phillips (2004) found that student pilots achieving minimum acceptable PFAR scores were 1.64 times more likely to fail in training and that those with minimum AQR values were 5.21 times more likely to fail to complete aviation training. Additionally, it is estimated that use of the ASTB saves the Navy and Marine Corps more than $30 million annually in training attrition costs (Arnold, 2002).

One of the unique attributes of the ASTB is that it is the only military aviation selection test that is available via the Internet. The Automated Pilot Examination, or APEX, is an integrated client-server platform that creates a completely secure testing environment. Once a test is initiated on APEX, all functionality external to the platform is restricted (i.e., no cutting and pasting, screen captures, etc.), and all data that pass back and forth between the server and the client is encrypted (Olson, Phillips, & Olde, 2007). The APEX application can be downloaded from a publicly accessible Web site but cannot be installed or activated without an authentication code, which allows test administrators to monitor and limit the computer terminals from which test content is accessed. Test content is never stored on the local hard drive. Rather, each test item is downloaded as it is reached by the examinee and erased as soon as a response is provided for enhanced security. Additionally, the computer terminals used to run APEX can be used for other purposes when the application is not in use.

Since each of the ASTB subtests is timed, APEX utilizes a combination of client-side JavaScript and server-side validation to account for any time taken for the server to download and display a test item. The time that elapses between an item response and complete download of the next item is not counted against the examinee's remaining time allotted. Thus, examinees are never penalized for delays in item presentation that can result from slow Internet connections. In addition to providing the examinee with immediate scores upon completion of the test battery, APEX provides a number of useful administrative functions. All APEX users at over 150 testing locations across the United States are monitored by a single test administrator who can manage accounts, track testing activities, and troubleshoot technical problems via the APEX interface. Finally, APEX allows for quick and inexpensive revisions to test content, including the addition of alternative computer-based testing approaches, computer-adaptive testing (CAT) and psychomotor testing. Although the large item libraries required by computer-adaptive tests can be time-consuming and costly to maintain and it can be more difficult to test large numbers of individuals at once, CAT offers numerous advantages over static tests, including reduced measurement error, enhanced test security, and reduced item length requirements (Embretson & Reise, 2000), all critical considerations for high-stakes testing.

Unmanned Aerial Systems Operator Selection

The mission requirements for military aviation continue to evolve. As this process continues, the manning requirements to fulfill these missions are also changing. To meet these challenges, the U.S. military has adopted the use of Unmanned Aerial Systems (UASs; also known as Unmanned Aerial Vehicles [UAVs]). UASs are remotely piloted vehicles that fulfill a number of mission requirements for the military, including airborne reconnaissance, surveillance, target acquisition, and damage assessment (Biggerstaff, Blower, Portman, & Chapman, 1998).

Military planners have suggested that the role of the UAS is likely to expand in the coming years. This has led to a proliferation of research on UAS design, capability, and operator interface (e.g., Barnes & Matz, 1998; Tvaryanas, 2006). However, very little research has examined how UAS operators should be selected (Dolgin, Kay, Wasel, Langlier, & Hoffman, 2002).

Biggerstaff et al. (1998) attempted to develop physical and selection performance standards for the screening of candidates entering the UAV Pioneer Pilot training program. Based upon data from an extensive job task analysis and interviews, a multitasking and tracking test battery was implemented as a potential screening instrument for UAV applicants. UAV applicants were given a two-hour test battery that measured eye–hand–foot coordination, spatial/mental ability, divided auditory attention, and cognitive skills. This battery had shown good predictive validity for aviation candidates (Delaney, 1992; Street, Chapman, & Helton, 1993) as well as for Landing Craft Air Cushion operators (Dolgin & Nontasak, 1990; Nontasak, Dolgin, & Blower, 1991). Although Biggerstaff and colleagues were only able to collect data on eight individuals, their results were promising, demonstrating an adjusted R^2 of .86 for the eight psychomotor variables included in the battery. More recently, Phillips, Arnold, and Fatolitis (2003) attempted to revalidate the selection performance standards for the screening of candidates for entrance into the UAV Pioneer Pilot training program. Based upon data from 39 student UAV operators on the same test battery used by Biggerstaff and colleagues,

Phillips and colleagues created a unit-weighted, composite scoring algorithm. Their results indicated that the composite score was a significant predictor of final grade in primary UAV training ($r = .58$). In addition, mean composite scores significantly differed between students who ultimately qualified as operators in their operational fleet units and those who failed to qualify.

The USAF has taken a similar interest in the area of UAS selection. For example, Tvaryanas (2006) provided a number of recommendations for the development of aeromedical certification standards for pilots operating UASs. Following a task analysis on the MQ-1 Predator and MQ-9 Reaper training pipelines, Tvaryanas identified a number of key differences between manned and unmanned aircraft. While most of these differences focused on medical conditions that may preclude an applicant from flight training, there were a number of differences that test developers might consider for selection purposes. For example, Tvaryanas found that UAS pilots were relatively sensory deprived, lacking peripheral visual, auditory, and haptic cueing, and depending almost entirely on focal vision to obtain information on aircraft state through automation and displays. He concluded that a selection test designed to predict training in UAS performance should be structured around these sensory differences.

FUTURE RESEARCH

The aviation environment is only one of many complex, high-risk environments that individuals will continue to operate in, all of which require a high level of human performance. Given the demanding, and often dangerous, nature of this work, identification of individuals that are likely to be successful is critical in terms of mission accomplishment. We propose that the future of assessment and selection for high-risk occupations is not in the discovery of new constructs related to successful performance, but in the refinement of the measures and methods used to measure identified constructs. For example, advances in graphics design and computer technology enable researchers to explore the use of simulations and virtual environments to assess performance on many flight-related tasks. The main advantage of these types of tests over traditional forms of predictive assessment is that they provide a unique opportunity for researchers to assess an applicant's ability to perform a set of task-relevant skills in a dynamic, high-fidelity environment without the risk or costs associated with performing in a live environment. For example, researchers at Iowa State University's Virtual Reality Applications Center are currently working on a virtual reality control room for Army UAS operators. The virtual reality control room depicts the UAS within the surrounding airspace and terrain along with all the information collected by instruments and cameras, providing a more interactive and intuitive interface with significant implications for training.

Another potential avenue for future research is the use of CAT to assess both cognitive ability and personality. In a traditional testing approach, all individuals are presented with the same test items, regardless of their individual ability levels. Thus, examinees may be presented with items that are too easy or too difficult for them. If an examinee is given a traditional test composed of a set of items that are too easy for him, relatively little information about his actual ability level is yielded. All the test developer can say for sure is that the examinee's ability level is higher than the static test in question could measure. Similarly, if the same examinee is presented a set of items far too difficult for him, the test developer has the same problem. The most diagnostically valuable test items are those an examinee has roughly a 50 percent chance of answering correctly (or endorsing, in the case of personality items). This is what CAT provides: Test items presented are tailored to the examinee's ability level. The difficulty of the next item presented in the test depends upon whether the preceding item was answered correctly. Item difficulty continues to change over the course of the test until it reaches a level at which the examinee has approximately a 50 percent chance of answering correctly. Because items are tailored to the individual, fewer items are required to achieve a precise estimate of one's score, thus reducing testing time. CAT also provides greater test security because there are no discrete test forms and every examinee receives a potentially different set of items.

Similar to the assessment of cognitive ability, CAT also provides several distinct advantages over traditional testing methods in the assessment of personality. Because items are tailored to the specific individual, far fewer items are needed to reliably measure each personality attribute. Additionally, new types of computer-adaptive personality tests are less susceptible to response distortion because traits can be intermixed and/or presented in groups (e.g., pairs and triads), making it more difficult for examinees to determine the more socially desirable response (White, Young, Hunter, & Rumsey, 2008).

One promising new technique for mitigation of intentional response distortion utilizing CAT has been developed by the U.S. Army based upon the Multi-Dimensional Pairwise Preference (MDPP) model developed by Stark, Chernyshenko, and Drasgow (2005). In this approach, personality items are presented in a forced-choice format, whereby the respondent is repeatedly presented with a pair of statements and allowed to endorse only one of the two. Responses on MDPP-driven tests are much less susceptible to intentional response distortion because the two statements the applicant sees together tap different traits but are matched on their social desirability. For example, both statements in a pair could be highly desirable (e.g., "I am a hard worker" paired with "I am extremely organized") or highly undesirable (e.g., "I am often late for work" paired with "I tend not to get along with others"). Across the whole test, this essentially forces an individual to reveal his or her standing on a given trait through the series of choices he or she makes about which statements to endorse. Because the items for one trait are paired with items tapping many different traits over the course of the test, it becomes very difficult for an exami-nee to distort his or her responses on any single trait, let alone all the traits assessed (Morgeson, Campion, Dipboye, Hollenbeck, Murphy, & Schmitt, 2007). Using this approach, Stark and Chernyshenko (2003) found that, given reasonable test length, so long as 10 percent of the item pairings are unidimen-sional, consisting of two statements measuring the same trait, every applicant can be guaranteed to achieve an acceptably reliable score on every trait. The USN is currently exploring the use of CAT for both cognitive ability and per-sonality within their aviation selection program (Phillips, 2003).

Finally, we must move beyond our reliance on training outcomes as our primary criteria of interest. Longitudinal research techniques may help to (1) further clarify the relationship between predictors and performance in the operational environment, (2) better identify gaps that could inform train-ing development and future refinement of assessment and selection approaches, and (3) determine a more accurate estimate of the return on investment of selection programs.

CONCLUSION

Since WWI, the military has invested considerable time and money in the assessment and selection of pilots and other aviation personnel. Some might argue that with the increasing use of highly automated systems to control the aircraft, the role of the pilot is diminished. However, it is our position that the role of the aviator is inherently different and, in many ways, more chal-lenging. In addition to accomplishing the basic functions of "aviating, navi-gating, and communicating," the aviator now serves as the critical node in a network of interdependent systems that provide incredible amounts of infor-mation that he or she must process, prioritize, integrate, and act upon. These cognitive requirements, coupled with the high-risk and dynamic nature of the aviation environment itself, present a unique set of challenges for researchers attempting to develop reliable tests to predict flight performance. Cumulative results of these research efforts indicate that measures of cogni-tive ability demonstrate good predictive validity and, thus, will likely remain a mainstay of aviation selection programs. In addition, psychomotor tests have shown good incremental validity when used in conjunction with cogni-tive ability tests. Finally, there is a growing body of research evidence, largely due to a developing consensus regarding an underlying conceptual framework (e.g., the Big Five) and new techniques for controlling intentional response distortion, supporting personality as an important predictor of per-formance across a number of domains, including attributes tapping into emo-tional stability and stress tolerance.

The current operational environment is different than anything we have experienced in the past. Today's military faces new challenges across a range of operations. As requirements evolve, and the leading edge of technology is pushed to meet these requirements, we will be demanding more of both our platforms and our people. Future research efforts should focus not only on expanding our basic knowledge of human abilities and how they relate to performance in the aviation environment but on exploring innovative ways to measure these abilities through a multidisciplinary approach, drawing upon contributions across a range of fields, from human factors, human system integration, and individual and group psychology, to neuroscience and bioengineering. It is only through these collaborative efforts that selection programs will be able to meet the emerging challenges of the future.

NOTES

1. This figure reflects only the recoverable costs that may be avoided by preventing an aviation student from entering training.

2. It is worth mentioning that the Department of Defense (DoD) is not strictly bound by the UGESP and may permissibly employ personnel selection methods in violation of these sections of U.S. Code X. Nonetheless, all military aviation selection procedures of which the authors are aware were constructed and maintained according to the requirements outlined in this document. While the DoD is not bound by the UGESP, we act as though we were.

3. For all meta-analyses referenced in the chapter, values reported are rho correlation coefficients, which represent the average population correlations based upon a group of studies.

4. API is the first step in training for student naval aviators and flight officers. API is a six-week course composed of both classroom-based instruction on aerodynamics, aircraft system and engines, aviation weather, air navigation, and flight rules and regulations, and hands-on aviation survival training.

REFERENCES

Arnold, R. D. (2002, March 10). *The utility of the Aviation Selection Test Battery (ASTB) in the reduction of naval aviation training attrition.* Memorandum from the Naval Aerospace Medical Institute (NAMI).

Arvey, R. D., & Faley, R. H. (1992). *Fairness in selecting employees.* New York: Addison-Wesley.

Bailey, M., & Woodhead, R. (1996). Current status and future developments of RAF aircrew selection. *Selection and training advances in aviation: AGARD conference proceedings 588* (pp. 8-1–8-9). Prague, Czech Republic: Advisory Group for Aerospace Research and Development.

Barnes, M. J., & Matz, M. F. (1998). Crew simulations for unmanned aerial vehicle (UAV) applications: Sustained effects, shift factors, interface issues, and crew size. *Proceedings of the Human Factors and Ergonomics Society 42nd Annual Meeting* (pp. 143–147).

Barrick, M. R., & Mount, M. K. (1991). The Big Five personality dimensions and job performance. *Personnel Psychology, 44,* 1–26.

Berg, J. S., Moore, J. L., Retzlaff, P. D., & King, R. E. (2002). Assessment of personality and crew interaction skills in successful naval aviators. *Aviation, Space, and Environmental Medicine*, 73 (6), 575–579.

Biggerstaff, S., Blower, D. J., Portman, C. A., & Chapman, A. (1998). *Landing craft air cushion (LCAC) navigator selection system: Initial model development* (NAMRL Research Report No. 1399). Pensacola, FL: Naval Aerospace Medical Research Laboratory.

Blower, D. J., & Dolgin, D. L. (1991). *An evaluation of performance-based tests designed to improve naval aviation selection* (NAMRL Research Report No. 1363). Pensacola, FL: Naval Aerospace Medical Research Laboratory.

Brannick, M. T., Levine, E. L., & Morgeson, F. P. (2007). *Job and work analysis: Methods, research, and applications for human resource management*. Thousand Oaks, CA: Sage Publications.

Burns, G. N., & Christiansen, N. D. (2006). Sensitive or senseless: On the use of social desirability measures in selection and assessment. In R. L. Griffith & M. H. Peterson (Eds.), *A closer examination of applicant faking behavior* (pp. 113–148). Greenwich, CT: Information Age Publishing.

Callister, J. D., King, R. E., Retzlaff, P. D., & Marsh, R. W. (1999). Revised NEO personality inventory profiles of male and female U.S. Air Force pilots. *Military Medicine*, 164, 885–890.

Carretta, T. R. (1987) *Basic Attributes Test (BAT) system: A preliminary evaluation* (AFHRL-TP-87-20). San Antonio, TX: Air Force Human Resources Laboratory.

————. (1989). USAF pilot selection and classification systems. *Aviation, Space, and Environmental Medicine*, 60 (1), 44–49.

————. (1992). Recent developments in U.S. Air Force pilot candidate selection and classification. *Aviation, Space, and Environmental Medicine*, 63, 1112–1114.

————. (2000). U.S. Air Force pilot selection and training methods. *Aviation, Space, and Environmental Medicine*, 71, 950–956.

————. (2005). *Development and evaluation of the Test of Basic Aviation Skills (TBAS)*. Aviation Research Laboratory Research Report (AFRL/HTR-2005-0172). Wright-Patterson, AFB: Human Effectiveness Directorate.

Carretta, T. R., & Ree, M. J. (1994). Pilot candidate selection method (PCSM): Sources of validity. *International Journal of Aviation Psychology*, 4, 103–117.

————. (1996). Factor structure of the Air Force Officer Qualifying Test: Analysis and comparison. *Military Psychology*, 8, 29–42.

————. (2003). Pilot selection methods. In P. S. Tsang & M. A. Vidulich (Eds.), *Principles and practice of aviation psychology* (pp. 357–396). Mahwah, NJ: Lawrence Erlbaum Associates.

Chief of Naval Air Training. (2008). CNATRA actual costs per student for fiscal year 2007. Memorandum from the Chief of Naval Air Training.

Chipman, S. F., Schraagen, J. M., & Shalin, V. L. (2000). Introduction to cognitive task analysis. In J. M. Schraagen, S. F. Chipman, & V. J. Shute (Eds.), *Cognitive task analysis* (pp. 3–23). Mahwah, NJ: Lawrence Erlbaum Associates.

Damos, D. (1987). *Some considerations in the design of a computerized human information processing battery* (NAMRL Monograph 35). Pensacola, FL: Naval Aerospace Medical Research Laboratory.

Delaney, H. D. (1992). Dichotic listening and psychomotor task performance as predictors of naval primary flight-training. *International Journal of Aviation Psychology*, 2, 107–120.

Dolgin, D. L., & Gibb, G. D. (1989). Personality assessment in aviator selection. In R. S. Jensen (Ed.), *Aviation psychology* (pp. 288–320). London: Gower.

Dolgin, D. L., Kay, G., Wasel, B., Langlier, M., & Hoffman, C. (2002). Identification of the cognitive, psychomotor, and psychosocial skill demands of uninhabited combat aerial vehicles (UCAV) operators. *Survival and Flight Equipment Journal*, 30, 219–222.

Dolgin, D. L., & Nontasak, T. (1990). *Initial validation of a personnel selection system for landing craft air cushion (LCAC) vehicle operations*. Proceedings of the Psychology in the Department of Defense 12th Symposium (USAFA-TR-90-1, pp. 245–249).

Embretson, S. E., & Reise, S. P. (2000). *Item response theory for psychologists*. Mahwah, NJ: Lawrence Erlbaum.

Ganesh, A., & Joseph, C. (2005). Personality studies in aircrew: An overview. *Indian Journal of Aerospace Medicine*, 49 (1), 54–62.

Gibb, G. D., & Dolgin, D. L. (1989). Predicting military flight training success by a compensatory tracking task. *Military Psychology*, 1, 235–240.

Gilchrist, N. S. (1918). An analysis of causes of breakdown in flying. *British Journal of Medicine*, 2, 401–403.

Gopher, D. (1982). A selective attention test as a predictor of success in flight training. *Human Factors*, 24, 173–183.

Gopher, D., & Kahneman, D. (1971). Individual differences in attention and the prediction of flight criteria. *Perceptual and Motor Skills*, 33, 1335–1342.

Grice, R. L., & Katz, L. C. (2006). *Personality profiles of experienced U.S. Army aviators across mission platforms* (USARI Technical Report No. 1185). Arlington, VA: U.S. Army Research Institute for the Behavioral and Social Sciences.

———. (2007). *Personality profiles of U.S. Army initial entry rotary wing students versus career aviators* (USARI Technical Report No. 1208). Arlington, VA: U.S. Army Research Institute for the Behavioral and Social Sciences.

Griffin, G. R. (1987). *Development and evaluation of an automated series of single- and multiple-dichotic listening and psychomotor tasks* (NAMRL Technical Report 1336). Pensacola, FL: Naval Aerospace Medical Research Laboratory.

Griffith, R. L., Chmielowski, T., & Yoshita, Y. (2007). Do applicants fake? An examination of the frequency of applicant faking behavior. *Personnel Review*, 36, 341–355.

Guion, R. M. (1998). *Assessment, measurement, and prediction for personnel decisions*. Mahwah, NJ: Lawrence Erlbaum Associates.

Helmreich, R. L., Swain, L. L., & Carsrud, A. L. (1986). The honeymoon effect in job performance: Temporal increases in the predictive power of achievement motivation. *Journal of Applied Psychology*, 71 (2), 185–188.

Hilton, T. F., & Dolgin, D. L. (1991). Pilot selection in the military of the free world. In G. Gal & A. D. Mangelsdorff (Eds.), *Handbook of military psychology* (pp. 81–101). New York: Wiley.

Hormann, H. J., & Maschke, P. (1996). On the relation between personality and job performance of airline pilots. *International Journal of Aviation Psychology*, 6 (2), 171–178.

Hough, L. M., Eaton, N. K., Dunnette, M. D., Kamp, J. D., & McCloy, R. A. (1990). Criterion-related validities of personality constructs and the effect of response distortion on those validities. *Journal of Applied Psychology*, 75, 581–595.

Hough, L. M., & Oswald, F. L. (2000). Personnel selection: Looking towards the future, remembering the past. *Annual Review of Psychology*, 51, 631–664.

Hunter, D. R., & Burke, E. F. (1994). Predicting aircraft pilot training success: A meta-analysis of published research. *International Journal of Aviation Psychology*, 4 (4), 297–313.

Koonce, J. M. (1984). A brief history of aviation psychology. *Human Factors*, 26 (5), 499–508.

Levine, E. L., Spector, P. E., Menon, P. E., Narayanan, L., & Cannon-Bowers, J. (1996). Validity generalization for cognitive, psychomotor, and perceptual tests for craft jobs in the utility industry. *Human Performance*, 9, 1–22.

Martinussen, M. (1996). Psychological measures as predictors of pilot performance: A meta-analysis. *International Journal of Aviation Psychology*, 6 (1), 1–20.

Martinussen, M., & Torjussen, T. (1998). Pilot selection in the Norwegian Air Force: A validation and meta-analysis of the test battery. *International Journal of Aviation Psychology*, 8 (1), 33–45.

Morgeson, F. P., Campion, M. A., Dipboye, R. L., Hollenbeck, J. R., Murphy, K., & Schmitt, N. (2007). Reconsidering the use of personality tests in personnel selection contexts. *Personnel Psychology*, 60 (3), 683–729.

Nontasak, T., Dolgin, D. L., & Blower, D. J. (1991). Performance differences in psychomotor and dichotic listening tests among landing craft air cushion (LCAC) vehicle operator trainees. *Proceedings of the Human Factors Society 35th Annual Meeting*, San Francisco, CA (pp. 987–990).

North, R. A., & Gopher, D. (1976). Measures of attention as predictors of flight performance. *Human Factors*, 18, 1–14.

North, R. A., & Griffin, G. R. (1977). *Aviator selection 1919–1977* (NAMRL SR 77-2). Pensacola, FL: Naval Aerospace Medical Research Laboratory.

Olson, T. M. (2006a, May 16). *Navy Aviation Selection Test Battery (ASTB) program update*. Paper presented at the Department of Defense Human Factors Engineering Technical Advisory Group Meeting, Washington, D.C.

———. (2006b). *Psychometric properties of the Navy Aviation Selection Test Battery (ASTB)*. Paper presented at the ASTB Workshop, Pensacola, FL.

Olson, T. M., Phillips, H. L., & Olde, B. A. (2007). *Online delivery of the Aviation Selection Test Battery (ASTB): Development of the Automated Pilot Examination System (APEX)*. Paper presented at the American Society for Naval Engineers Human Systems Integration Symposium 2007, Annapolis, MD.

Ones, D. S., Viswesvaran, C., & Reiss, A. D. (1996). Role of social desirability in personality testing for personnel selection: The red herring. *Journal of Applied Psychology*, 81, 660–679.

Parasuraman, R., & Byrne, E. A. (2003). Automation and human performance in aviation. In P. S. Tsang & M. A. Vidulich (Eds.), *Principles and practice of aviation psychology* (pp. 311–356). Mahwah, NJ: Lawrence Erlbaum Associates.

Passey, G. E., & McLaurin, W. A. (1966). *Perceptual psychomotor tests in aircrew selection: Historical review and advanced concepts* (PRL-TR-66-4, AD-636 606). Lackland AFB, TX: Personnel Research Laboratory, Aerospace Medical Division.

Petho, F. C. (1992). *An annotated chronology on aviation psychology in the United States Navy up to 1946*. Unpublished report.

Phillips, H. L. (2003). *Plan of work for the revision and revalidation of the Aviation Selection Test Battery*. Unpublished manuscript.

———. (2004, December 9). *Considerations relevant to determination of minimum Aviation Selection Test Battery (ASTB) scores for naval aviators*. Memorandum to the Chief of Naval Personnel.

Phillips, H. L., Arnold, R. D., & Fatolitis, P. (2003). *Validation of an unmanned aerial vehicle operator selection system*. Paper presented at the Short Course on Design, Performance, and Analysis of Unmanned Aerial Vehicle Systems, Monterey, CA.

Picano, J. J. (1990). An empirical assessment of stress-coping styles in military pilots. *Aviation, Space, and Environmental Medicine*, 61, 356–360.

———. (1991). Personality types among experienced military pilots. *Aviation, Space, and Environmental Medicine*, 62 (6), 517–520.

Picano, J. J., Williams, T. J., & Roland, R. R. (2006). Assessment and selection of high-risk operational personnel. In C. H. Kennedy & E. Zillmer (Eds.), *Military psychology: Clinical and operational applications* (pp. 353–370). New York, NY: The Guilford Press.

Ree, M. J. (2003). *Test of Basic Aviation Skills (TBAS) incremental validity beyond Air Force Qualifying Test (AFOQT) pilot composite for predicting pilot criteria*. Technical Report prepared for HQ AFPC/DPPPWE. Texas: Randolph Air Force Base.

Retzlaff, R. D., & Gibertini, M. (1987). Air Force pilot personality: Hard data on the right stuff. *Multivariate Behavioral Research*, 22, 383–389.

Salgado, J. F., Viswesvaran, C., & Ones, D. S. (2001). Predictors used for personnel selection: An overview of constructs, methods, and techniques. In N. Anderson, D. S. Ones, H. K. Sinangil, & C. Viswesvaran (Eds.), *Handbook of industrial, work, and organizational psychology* (pp. 166–199). Thousand Oaks, CA: Sage Publications.

Sanchez, J. I., & Levine, E. L. (2001). The analysis of work in the 20th and 21st centuries. In N. Anderson, D. S. Ones, H. K. Sinangil, & C. Viswesvaran (Eds.), *Handbook of industrial, work, and organizational psychology* (pp. 71–89). Thousand Oaks, CA: Sage Publications.

Schmidt, F. L., & Hunter, J. E. (1998). The validity and utility of selection methods in personnel psychology: Practical and theoretical implications of 85 years of research findings. *Psychological Bulletin*, 124, 262–274.

Schmitt, N., Gooding, R. Z., Noe, R. A., & Kirsch, M. (1984). Meta-analyses of validity studies between 1964 and 1982 and the investigation of study characteristics. *Personnel Psychology*, 37, 407–422.

Schmitt, N., & Oswald, F. W. (2006). The impact of corrections for faking on the validity of noncognitive measures in selection settings. *Journal of Applied Psychology*, 91, 613–621.

Stark, S., & Chernyshenko, O. S. (2003). *Using IRT methods to construct and score personality measures that are fake-resistant*. In F. Drasgow (Chair), Innovations in Personality Assessment. Symposium conducted at the 18th Annual Meeting of the Society for Industrial and Organizational Psychology, Orlando, Florida.

Stark, S., Chernyshenko, O. S., & Drasgow, F. (2005). An IRT approach to constructing and scoring pairwise preference items involving stimuli on different dimensions: The multi-dimensional pairwise preference model. *Applied Psychological Measurement*, 29, 184–201.

Street, D. K., Helton, K. T., & Dolgin, D. L. (1992). *The unique contribution of selected personality tests to the prediction of success in naval pilot training* (NAMRL Technical Report No. 1374). Pensacola, FL: Naval Aerospace Medical Research Laboratory.

Street, D. R., Chapman, A. E., and Helton, K. T. (1993). *The future of naval aviation selection: Broad-spectrum computer-based testing*. In Proceedings of the 35th Annual Military Testing Association. Williamsburg, VA: Military Testing Association.

Tupes, E. C., & Christal, R. C. (1961). *Recurrent personality factors based on trait ratings* (Technical Report No. ASD-TR-61-97). Lackland Air Force Base, TX: US Air Force.

Tvaryanas, A. P. (2006). Human systems integration in remotely piloted aircraft operations. *Aviation, Space, and Environmental Medicine*, 77 (12), 1278–1282.

Uniform Guidelines on Employee Selection Procedures. (1978). *Federal Register*, 43, 38290–38315.

Voge, V. M. (1989). Failing aviator syndrome: A case history. *Aviation, Space, and Environmental Medicine*, 60 (7), 89–91.

Weybrew, B. (1979). *History of military psychology at the U. S. Naval Submarine Medical Research Laboratory*. Bethesda, MD: Naval Submarine Research Laboratory.

White, L. A., Young, M. C., Hunter, A. E., & Rumsey, M. G. (2008). Lessons learned in transitioning personality measures from research to operational settings. *Industrial and Organizational Psychology: Perspectives on Science and Practice*, 1, 291–295.

Chapter 5

PSYCHOMETRIC ASSESSMENT IN THE U.S. SUBMARINE FORCE

James C. Whanger, Mark N. Bing,
Alison America, and Jerry C. Lamb

Psychometrics refers to a body of theory and collection of techniques developed with the goal of refining and improving the quantitative measurement of psychological constructs (Kline, 1998; Nunnally & Bernstein, 1994). Psychometric assessment is a ubiquitous part of modern life. Knowledge tests are administered at all levels of education; achievement tests prior to entrance into institutes of higher learning; competency assessments prior to being hired by a business organization; and assessments of psychopathology when being selected into and classified within high-risk occupations such as the police, nuclear energy, or the military. These assessments are often considered *high-stakes* because the results are used to make decisions that have important consequences for an individual's life and career as well as for the success of the organization within which that individual will perform.

When designing *high-stakes* psychometric assessments such as these, it is important to develop a nuanced conceptual understanding of the environmental demands. This means a thorough rather than a cursory analysis of the knowledge, skills, abilities, and personal characteristics that will increase the probability of successful performance within the position and organization. These outcomes might include performance ratings, attrition data, job satisfaction, or perceptions of leadership climate. A nuanced conceptual understanding should be able to answer the following questions and many more about the environmental demands:

- What knowledge, skills, abilities, and personal characteristics are required to succeed at the tasks, the job, and within the organization over time?
- Which of the above are incompatible with successful performance over time?
- Which can be learned in a reasonably brief period of time?
- Which should be the focus of selection? Which should be the focus of screening?
- What is considered a reasonably brief period of time by the organization?

- Is it more effective to select for each of these competencies or train to develop them?
- Do we want to purchase off the shelf assessments or do we want to develop our own?

The focus of this chapter will be on the psychological demands created by the environment of the military submarine and the *high-stakes* psychometric assessments developed to identify those possessing the competencies necessary to perform therein. Also, a brief discussion of some of the training interventions designed to develop sailors, fresh from boot camp into capable submariners.

Environmental demands of military submarines are unlike any other. While the closed habitat has similarities to those developed for spacecraft, the number of crew members (45–150) deployed on a submarine creates a substantially different social dynamic. And, although the large group isolation experienced during submarine deployment is similar to that seen in arctic-based scientific laboratories, the sustained submergence and military missions again set the submarine apart. These two broad aspects of the submarine, a closed habitat and extended large group isolation, create environmental constraints that currently necessitate living and working in a relatively low oxygen environment, performing at a high level of technical proficiency, and coping with an interpersonally intense social climate. Additionally, the type of submarine to which one is assigned influences the operational tempo for deployments. Specifically, nuclear ballistic (SSBN) and guided missile (SSGN) submarines have two crews that trade off regularly every three months, while fast attack (SSN) submarines have variable and unpredictable deployment schedules. This latter unpredictable schedule can create additional stress for spouses and in turn for deployed submariners.

These demands have resulted in the development of technological, training, and psychometric interventions to allow the submarine force to effectively and efficiently staff submarines with capable sailors. Technological interventions have included a sophisticated air filtration system, carbon dioxide capturing, and consistent monitoring of air quality. Training interventions have included highly demanding academic training pipelines consisting of both general submarine and rating specific knowledge. The strenuous academic training creates a substantial demand on cognitive abilities such as comprehension and problem-solving skills. Thus, sailors must have higher than average academic abilities, as assessed by the Armed Services Vocational Aptitude Battery (ASVAB), in order to succeed during training for submarines. This is particularly true for those ascending through Nuclear Power School but is also the case for those ascending through Basic Enlisted Submarine School (BESS). During this training, detailed aspects of the submarine and rating-specific tasks are learned in both classroom and simulation settings before sailors are deployed where this knowledge must be demonstrated to the satisfaction of those already trained and qualified. Once the submariner has demonstrated mastery of the relevant subject matter, he too is qualified to stand watch and contribute to effective crew performance.

Along with the cognitive demands, an intense social climate, work schedule, and lack of sunlight and fresh air stretch the limit of an individual's ability to easily cope. A certain type of resilience is required, or at the very least, an absence of current or recent psychopathology. Recognition of these environmental demands resulted in the initial evaluation of commercially available psychological assessments, such as the Minnesota Multiphasic Personality Inventory (MMPI) and the California Psychological Inventory (CPI), and ultimately in the development of in-house psychological assessments at the originally named Naval Medical Research Laboratory, now the Naval Submarine Medical Research Laboratory. At the time, the decision to develop an in-house assessment was driven by the unacceptably high referral rates based on existing norms by the commercial assessments (Schlichting, 1993; Weybrew, 1967). Thus, since norms would need to be developed for the submarine force, it was decided to create a test in-house to save money.

The first of the in-house assessments developed and validated was titled the Personal Inventory Barometer (PIB) and was constructed by Benjamin Weybrew and colleagues (Weybrew & Youniss, 1957); the second evolved from a revision and expansion of the PIB and was named SUBSCREEN (Bryant & Noddin, 1986). Before diving into this, we first provide a brief outline of psychometric theory, the utility of psychometrics, and some of the challenges with psychometric assessments. Following the practical examples pulled from the sub forces, we conclude with a discussion of future directions to take with expanding psychometrics across the sub forces and to other high-risk and high-performance organizations.

BRIEF REVIEW OF PSYCHOMETRIC THEORY

This brief review of psychometric theory is put forth to highlight the importance of updating the SUBSCREEN assessment in the same way that the MMPI-2 clinical scales were updated by Tellegen, Ben-Porath, NcNulty, Arbisi, Graham, & Kaemmer (2003) and the ASVAB was in 2002, to reduce administration time and improve the validity of inferences drawn from the data. Additionally, in the case of SUBSCREEN, it could provide additional utility to the clinician conducting the referral interview.

First, we will briefly address the theoretical side of psychometrics, to provide a context within which to understand the advancements that have developed in these techniques. Consider a few important differences between classical test theory and modern test theory as applied to psychometrics.

Classical test theory assumes each individual possesses a true score (T) plus random error (E). If X represents a test score, then

$$X = T + E$$

where T is an individual's average test score over an infinite number of administrations on an infinite number of parallel tests (Nunnally & Bernstein, 1994). This results in a single test score being a behavioral sample of the construct measured by the test. Norms are then developed for given populations by conducting predictive or correlational studies with variables external to the test, such as job performance, attrition, or diagnosis. The primary problem with classical test theory is that it is unusual to administer more than one version of a test to any single individual and thus there is no way to accurately assess measurement error within this model.

In response to this, an extension of classical test theory was devised called *Generalizability theory* in which the structure of error is modeled in an attempt to better measure constructs and improve psychological research (Cronbach, Gleser, Nanda, & Rajaratnam, 1972). This approach views items as behavioral samples from a universe of normally distributed items for a particular construct. This is a substantial improvement that recognizes the problems of classical test theory; however, it is not as compelling as modern test theory.

In *Modern test theory*, the probability of a correct response or item endorsement is a function of the item, the individual, and is empirically derived from previous research on an appropriate sized sample from the population of interest. The response itself provides one piece of empirical evidence for an individual's relative position on the latent trait distribution. Each response provides an additional piece of evidence with which an individual's position on the trait curve is estimated.

Modern test theory, in contrast to a true score, assumes a latent trait. The latent trait is a conceptual representation of the target trait after item level error has been statistically accounted for (Borsboom, 2005). This perspective conceptualizes a latent trait as an emergent property of the items rather than as a summative estimation of a true score. Thus, a scale or test cannot purport to measure a construct that conceptually extends beyond what the shared covariation of the items included. Borsboom (2005) quite cogently points out, construct validity should logically be focused on a testable theory underlying item response. This means that this connection between construct and response needs to be very carefully considered during scale development in order to be justified in arguing that the scale measures what it purports to measure. Given this theoretical framework for item responses, it is important to test a set of items designed to measure a construct via measurement (Confirmatory Factor Analysis—CFA; Latent Class Analysis—LCA) and structural (Structural Equation Modeling—SEM) models. Over time, this should result in a pruning away of carelessly labeled measures.

Modern test theory further assumes a probabilistic relationship between item response and position on the trait distribution. This is accomplished by quantifying item characteristics such as item difficulty when referring to ability tests, or trait saturation when referring to personality assessments. In addition to consideration of item characteristics, response characteristics such as response time can be modeled with the goal to improve the precision with which an individual is placed on the trait distribution.

Given the same set of items from which to begin, a scale/test developer that pays careful attention to item level analysis during scale development would likely end up choosing very similar items regardless of whether a classical test theory approach was used or a modern test theory approach was used; the primary reason these theoretical distinctions are important is that the decision to embrace either classical or modern test theory will determine how we move forward with improving the measurement of psychological constructs and increasing our knowledge of complex phenomenon (Wilson, 2005). This is because a well-designed test constructed using classical test theory and traditional psychometrics will often perform quite well, but a predictive ceiling might be reached without the pursuit of innovative measurement methods. Advancement will require improvements in both psychological theory and method (Sackett & Lievens, 2008). The importance of this is discussed in the final section on the future of psychometric assessment in the submarine force.

THE UTILITY OF PSYCHOMETRIC TESTING

Psychometric tests provide utility (or value) to an organization in which individual differences in performance can have a substantial effect on organizational performance. This is especially the case when a bad selection decision or a poorly prepared employee could result in a substantial negative outcome for the organization. In this case it can be considered a risk management tool.

If a position requires executive or autonomous decision making that can potentially result in substantial losses in either the short term or long term, the greater the need for an objective methodology. This is particularly true for positions that require substantial industry knowledge, ethical behavior, personal initiative, and reliability. In contrast, companies hiring large numbers of employees into positions where 90 percent of the applicants will be selected, the process is more appropriately called screening (Weybrew, 1967).

Psychometric assessment is important because it allows for improved selection, classification, and training of personnel, which in turn can increase efficiency and improve organizational performance. This is because within any accession or training pipeline exists a sequence of assessment and prediction followed by assessment and decision. What differs between pipelines is the degree of measurement precision produced by assessment methods. Some accession pipelines make no discriminations between individuals because the training demands are modest and impact of the job may be less than mission critical. In contrast, some jobs are highly discriminating in who is selected because the job is not only highly demanding but critical to mission success.

For example, consider a large business organization that relies entirely on informal assessment via a brief unstructured phone interview followed by a series of unstructured face-to-face interviews with individuals who provide input to the ultimate decision maker. A mountain of research supports the claim that this method can be drastically improved upon by simply creating a structured interview format and that this improvement will result in improved on-the-job performance (Hough & Oswald, 2000).

When analyzing the importance of an organizational process, there are many criteria that may be used. One way to evaluate an organizational intervention like a personnel screening or selection program is financially. A business organization wants a return on an investment in terms of either cost savings or increased revenue. A military organization similarly wants a return on investment in terms of either cost savings or an improved ability to accomplish their mission. Improving the level of precision (reliability) with which predictors or assessments are measured may result in substantial improvements in personnel performance (predictive validity) at critical times. It is sometimes difficult to quantify the benefits of a selection/screening process, particularly when it is better considered within a risk management framework. If the primary focus is reduction of potentially dangerous and expensive accidents, then reducing the risk by even a small amount is likely worth the modest investment in psychometric testing.

It is important to remember, as Weybrew (1967) pointed out, that utility is contextual and is directly related to the selection ratio. A selection ratio refers to the percentage of applicants who begin an assessment process and who are subsequently hired into an organization at the end of the process period. If the selection ratio is low (10%), a top-down selection strategy, where the highest 10 percent are offered positions, will optimize the impact of the psychometric selection system. The kinds of savings that could result from a selection system like this include reduced training costs due to retention, increased productivity, increased revenue, fewer mistakes, and more satisfied personnel.

Utilizing psychometric assessments validated to be predictive of important organizational outcomes increases the likelihood of placing individuals in positions ready and able to competently and conscientiously perform their jobs. By increasing the probability of on-the-job success, both individual and organizational performance are enhanced. Furthermore, reliable and valid assessment of the full performance domain can result in a clearer understanding of both training and selection needs of the organization. If these assessments result in better matches between applicant characteristics and performance demands, then organizational performance will be optimized relative to not using such methods.

CRITICISMS OF PSYCHOMETRIC ASSESSMENT

Arguments against psychometric testing tend to take three forms. The first argument posits that psychometric tests result in discriminatory admission practices due to cultural bias. The second argument posits that psychometric tests are not predictive of actual performance. The third argument posits that psychometric tests do not measure what they purport to measure. These are reasonable issues to be raised about any standardized test and should be answered by the producers of the tests via large-scale research studies. However, though these are reasonable concerns to be raised about any given test, they in no way call into question the utility and fairness inherent in the use of objective assessment methods for admission, selection, or classification decisions. Arguments such as these three fall prey to the *fallacy of composition*: *if* there is a deficiency with a single or even a number of test(s), *then* all testing is deficient.

One can reasonably question the appropriateness of the content of the SAT, its predictive validity, or the possibility of disparate impact against minority applicants, but it is difficult to understand how this translates into criticism of psychometric testing altogether. This is because it is difficult to imagine an alternative to objective testing that is *more* predictive of performance or *fairer* to the applicants.

Psychometric testing presents a useful and fair means by which to aid those responsible to decide who to hire, where to place, and how to train people in organizations. A well-designed, reliable, and valid psychometric test can provide an objective means by which to remove bias and unfairness from admissions, selection, and training decisions. Psychometric screening tests can also help individuals avoid being placed into situations possessing psychological demands beyond their capacity to cope. In situations such as this, one might argue there is a moral obligation to endeavor to do so.

In addition to assessing individual differences, psychometric methods can help leaders identify and diagnose organizational level problems via assessments of climate and culture. Although these tools are administered to individuals, the responses are aggregated to the organizational level. These methods can also be used to identify the leadership qualities most successful within a given context, which can inform future selection and training decisions.

Finally, one caveat to our argument in support of psychometric testing is that the test must be kept up to date via ongoing quality control and evaluative research that results in appropriate revisions. Without this kind of upkeep, the reliability and validity of a test can deteriorate.

THE PATHS TO SUBMARINES

When a recruiting officer for the U.S. Navy identifies an individual they believe will be a good sailor, there are a number of assessments that are conducted in addition to the initial informal assessment of the recruiter. First, the recruit must complete the ASVAB, which assesses individual differences on the following constructs: General Science, Arithmetic Reasoning, Word Knowledge, Paragraph Comprehension, Mathematics Knowledge, Numerical Operations, Coding Speed, Auto and Shop Information, Mechanical Comprehension, and Electronics Information. Various combinations of these scales are then used to create cutoff scores that provide sailors with options consistent with assessed aptitudes, when choosing a career path. This method increases the likelihood that sailors will be placed in jobs for which they possess the abilities to learn and then apply the requisite skills. For example, as one might imagine, high scores in both verbal and math aptitude are required for entrance into the training pipeline for the Navy nuclear field. The academic demands of the training pipeline are such that selecting a substantial number of individuals below this score would result in wasted resources, increased attrition, and a likely reduction in job performance. Next, the recruit must go through a medical evaluation at the MEPS (Military Entry Processing Station) during which a number of screening questions are asked with the goal of identifying potentially disqualifying conditions. From here recruits continue to Recruit Training Command (RTC) where they are confronted with a *moment of truth* and given the opportunity to confess to anything they may have lied about to get into the Navy. After graduation from RTC, new sailors come to Groton, CT to become submariners. It is here that SUBSCREEN is administered on their first day of training at Basic Enlisted Training School.

If a sailor is flagged by the SUBSCREEN assessment, they are referred for a clinical interview. Approximately 15 percent of sailors are referred, and approximately 20 percent of those referred are transferred out of the submarine training pipeline. These sailors are either transferred to the surface fleet or separated from the Navy due to a disqualifying condition, most often coded in the training database as *personality disorder*. Thus, the ASVAB, the SUBSCREEN assessment, and clinical referral interview provide a multiple hurdle process for entry into the submarine force. Each step increases the likelihood of putting a sailor possessing the necessary competencies in the right place to perform effectively.

In a world with unlimited time, resources, and recruits we might want to allow anyone with the desire to pursue any career path to do so. However, all of these are limited and thus the means by which we make decisions should as fairly and objectively as possible increase the likelihood of a successful accession. Thus, the ultimate goal of the submarine training and accession pipeline is to develop qualified and competent sailors capable of performing at high levels of proficiency. Identifying individuals possessing or capable of learning requisite competencies is fundamental to the achievement of this goal.

As mentioned above, the environmental demands guide the identification of the relevant competencies, which guides the analysis of the type of psychometric assessment program needed. In the case of the military submarine environment, the requirement of an absence of psychopathology suggests the need for a screening procedure.

Although not ubiquitous, there is a substantial amount of confusion about psychological screening programs in military settings. This is evidenced by Wright et al.'s (2005) response to Rona, Hyams, & Wessely (2005) in the *Journal of the American Medical Association* (*JAMA*). Some have a tendency to view a psychological screening program as they might a typical medical screening program and thus attempt to evaluate it using similar criteria. Rona, Hyams, & Wessely (2005) describe a set of criteria they *believe* important for use of a mass administered psychological screening test but provide weak rationale for these. For example, they argue that a psychological screening test should provide a high yield. The logic underlying this claim is unclear as there is substantial evidence provided by Wright and colleagues, as well as work cited below from the Naval Submarine Medical Research Laboratory, that clearly demonstrates that even low yield psychological screening programs provide substantial financial, personal, and mission accomplishment utility. We would further argue that there is a moral responsibility to engage in such screening due to the fact that it is often those most in need of help who are least likely to seek it. This is why a program for educating people about access to mental health opportunities, although important and laudable, is inadequate to the realities of psychopathology in the military.

A mass psychological screening program is appropriate for three reasons: First, mass administration of psychometric assessments makes the cost of assessment small relative to typical medical tests which are often done singly and thus must include both the physician's and the laboratory technician's time in the cost analysis. Second, the cost savings of removing even a small number of individuals from an accession pipeline prior to psychological decompensation (loss of ability to cope with psychological demands) provides substantial financial and mission accomplishment utility. Finally, we believe there is a moral obligation to attempt to identify individuals likely to psychologically decompensate, for their own as well as their shipmates' safety. A similar argument can be made for the need to identify individuals with antisocial personality disorder, who are often responsible for bullying and harassing psychologically vulnerable individuals until they break (Johnson, 2009).

SCREENING ENLISTED SUBMARINERS

Beginning in 1942, research conducted by the then named Naval Medical Research Laboratory (NMRL) at Submarine Base New London focused on personnel selection for the challenging environment of a submarine. Among the challenges presented by a submarine deployment are a paucity of personal space, long periods with no sunlight, an unusual day/night schedule, and extended periods of separation from friends and loved ones with minimal communication. When we combine these with a very cognitively demanding workload, a requirement for extremely high levels of job/task proficiency, a rigid military hierarchy, and no psychiatric support underway, it becomes evident that the psychological resilience of the crew needs to be greater than that required for most jobs.

Early research at the NMRL identified three tests (intelligence test, personal inventory, and two-hand coordination test) that combined to predict psychological fitness as judged during a psychiatric interview. Of particular interest, from this report, were the two implementation strategies proposed, one of which continues to be used currently with the SUBSCREEN program. The first was the implementation of a cut score and separation from the submarine force based on that score, which resulted in a selection cost of 33 percent in return for a 70 percent reduction in the number of "bads," as they were referred to in the report. This method was rejected as being too "costly." The second method involved using the test as a referral method for a psychiatric examination and was determined more cost-effective because it effectively reduced the selection cost to include only those currently diagnosable with a disqualifying psychological disorder.

Benjamin Weybrew initiated a program of research intended to determine the effects of isolation on submariners submerged for extended periods of time and subsequently to identify psychometric tests capable of identifying prospective submariners possessing the necessary resilience, and more importantly, to identify those lacking it (Weybrew, 1954). Projects were initiated both independently and with leading academic psychologists of the day. For example, Henry Murray of Harvard, the developer of the TAT (Thematic Apperception Test), helped create and validate a Navy version using stimulus pictures involving sailors rather than the standard pictures used. Although the predictive validity of this test was good, the cumbersome and time-consuming nature of the scoring procedure made it unappealing for mass administration.

Personal Inventory Barometer

Based on findings gleaned from these early psychological studies within the submarine force, an assessment battery was developed (Weybrew & Alves, 1959) intended to identify individuals with pathologically high levels of anxiety. Based, in part, on the Taylor Manifest Anxiety Scale (Taylor, 1953), the PIB became the single psychological screening tool used at the U.S. Naval Submarine School (NSS) for submarine candidates (Weybrew & Noddin, 1974), given virtually unchanged to all BESS students for approximately 25 years. However, this test gave way to a revised and expanded version that emerged as part of a project originally intended to update the language of the PIB.

SUBSCREEN

In the early 1980s, it was recognized that some of the language used in PIB items might be out of date (e.g., "I sometimes have queer unpleasant feelings in my body"), which could attenuate the construct validity of the scales in use and thus its utility. As a result of this conclusion, work began to develop a new psychometric screening test in recognition of the facts that the demographic, ethical, and social characteristics of society inevitably change, and that definitions of psychological health also change. At approximately the same time, an analysis of causes for premature loss of nonnuclear trained enlisted individuals from submarine service was also undertaken (Bryant, 1986). Bryant's study showed that early losses were related to problems in BESS, middle losses were related to behavioral and psychological problems during deployment, and later losses (greater than three years' service) were related to misconduct offenses.

Based on the findings of this study, Bryant began a substantial revision of the PIB and named the new test SUBSCREEN. The new psychometric screening test incorporated 60 percent of the questions in the original PIB and included additional questions, some from the literature on stress and adjustment, some from the literature on organizational commitment, and some developed after consultation with BESS instructors and psychologists with experience in evaluating BESS students. SUBSCREEN and the PIB were at first administered simultaneously for several BESS classes. Once testing demonstrated that SUBSCREEN identified the same people as the PIB, and additionally identified a subset of individuals at risk for psychological disorder not identified by the PIB, use of the PIB was discontinued.

SUBSCREEN has now been in continuous use at NSS for 21 years, screening all students in BESS and all officers attending the Submarine Officer Basic Course (SOBC). The SUBSCREEN database now includes data on over 30,000 enlisted and over 4,000 officers.

Submarine Attrition Risk Test

A recent innovation in the SUBSCREEN program came in the form of a new actionable metric within the SUBSCREEN test, created in the fall of 2001. This actionable metric, or empirical predictor, was based on SUBSCREEN scale scores and was created for the purpose of predicting fleet attrition among BESS students. The Submarine Attrition Risk Test (SMART) is an optimal linear composite of scales within the SUBSCREEN test that predict adverse (e.g., misconduct and substance abuse) and early (i.e., prior to end of first enlistment) fleet attrition among BESS students. It does not provide a psychological diagnosis, only the probability with which one can expect a BESS student to separate for negative reasons once he reaches the fleet.

The SMART was created using, in essence, an actuarial procedure. Specifically, a known-group approach was utilized to determine if scales within the SUBSCREEN test could predict adverse fleet attrition. A database of fleet submariners ($n = 1172$) who had taken SUBSCREEN during training and subsequently attrited for adverse reasons prior to the end of their first enlistment (e.g., for psychological dysfunction, substance abuse, and misconduct) was merged with a database of successful fleet submariners (i.e., reenlisted persons of higher rank, $n = 1099$) who had also taken SUBSCREEN during training. A discriminant analysis was conducted, and SUBSCREEN scales that jointly contributed to maximal separation of the groups (i.e., maximal prediction of group membership) in the discriminant function were selected for inclusion into a new composite scale.

SMART has been validated against early attrition indicators, such as nonjudicial punishment (NJP) events and legal hold status, for alleged criminal activities (Bing & Eisenberg, 2003). The higher an enlisted student scores on the SMART, the more likely he or she is to commit an act that will eventually result in disciplinary action (e.g., NJP) and separation from the Navy. A recent study (Bing & Eisenberg, 2003) indicated that the SMART had a sensitivity rate of 20 percent for early separation. This means that of all adverse fleet separations (i.e., attritions) among BESS-trained submariners, one in five was identified by SMART as being "at risk" for attrition.

Additional investigations on the SMART (Bing & Eisenberg, 2003) indicated that it had a sensitivity rate that ranged from 21 percent to 28 percent for psychologically based waivers and disqualifications, and a sensitivity rate of 24 percent for psychologically based medical evacuations (MEDEVACS) from submarines. Thus, it is reasonable to assume that the SMART, if applied proactively during training for interventions, could aid in preventing many of the negative outcomes.

SCREENING OFFICER SUBMARINERS

Knowing who among SOBC officers are most likely to remain and advance within SUBFOR could be useful for accession planning. However, such planning would benefit by having an actionable metric that would allow for identification of officers most likely to continue submarine duty. The SORT study was undertaken to determine if the SUBSCREEN test could provide such an actionable metric—one which predicts which of the SOBC students are the most likely to advance in their careers to the Submarine Officer Advanced Course (SOAC), and thus progress to Department Head billets.

Preliminary analysis showed that those submarine officers with high to very high levels of job performance are much more likely to advance from SOBC to SOAC. In fact, for every four SOBC students, approximately one will ultimately attend SOAC. Because fluctuations in motivation tend to impact job performance (Barrick, Stewart, & Piotrowski, 2002), the hypothesis adopted was that, within the SUBSCREEN test, the motivational scales would be the best predictors of career progression. However, other SUBSCREEN scales were also examined, especially those that were included in the SMART for predicting attrition among enlisted submariners.

Existing SUBSCREEN data were analyzed on more than 1,000 submarine officers who had taken SUBSCREEN while attending SOBC. Records of officers from year groups 1993–1999 were used to capture data on officers whose potential time in service was long enough for the officer to reach a career point at which selection for attending SOAC was possible.

Using correlation and regression techniques, six motivational scales and one response set scale within the SUBSCREEN test were found to form an optimal linear composite that predicted which SOBC students were likely to advance to SOAC, with $R = .25$ ($p < .001$). Reweighing SUBSCREEN scales created the *Submarine Officer Retention Test* (SORT). In essence, SORT is composed of temporally stable attitudes measured by SUBSCREEN. Several advantageous initial cut-points were identified for this prediction equation.

Currently the SORT metric is not used by the submarine force to aid in selection to SOAC. And, although it would not be appropriate to select officers for advancement entirely based on this metric, it could provide a useful adjunct to current data, which would increase the predictive validity of the selection process.

FUTURE OF PSYCHOMETRIC TESTING IN THE U.S. SUBMARINE FORCE

A number of areas provide substantial opportunities for psychometric testing to contribute to the effectiveness of the submarine force. One area of opportunity is to update the SUBSCREEN assessment using modern test theory and latent variable methodology. This could be done using Wilson's (2005) construct mapping and item response modeling approach, which could result in a more sensitive assessment using fewer items. This could be properly accomplished within two years.

A second area is the potential for integration of implicit personality, particularly in the area of psychopathy and antisocial personality. This could be accomplished using a number of methods, including conditional reasoning methodology (Bing, LeBreton, Davison, Migetz, & James, 2007; James et al., 2005), implicit association methodology (Nosek, Greenwald, & Banaji, 2005), attribution styles (Seligman, Abramson, Semmel, & Von Baeyer, 1979), or implicit goals (Bargh, 2006). These methods would allow us to indirectly assess individuals possessing antisocial personality traits that create an increased likelihood of criminal misconduct, behavioral tendencies incompatible with creating a positive leadership climate, and likelihood of engaging in bullying and harassing behavior.

A third area is the potential for a subset of SUBSCREEN scales integrated with implicit personality assessments to identify those likely to engage in suicide-related behaviors. Identification of those with substantially higher odds could be funneled into psychological intervention programs designed to increase resilience (Seligman and colleagues, 1979).

Finally, an area that could be quite fruitful is the assessment of the personality and interpersonal skills necessary to be an effective leader within the submarine force. Rickover's legacy persists and although the primacy of reliability and safety related to operation of the submarine and its power plant, there is opportunity for improvement of interpersonal leadership skills. This could be accomplished using assessment center techniques, which involve behavioral simulation of managerial scenarios specific to the submarine context and evaluation of interpersonal skills followed by executive coaching to identify and initiate strategies for improving.

In summary, SUBSCREEN has provided utility to the submarine force for over 20 years. With it, NSMRL has helped to identify individuals possessing the requisite psychological resilience necessary to successfully perform in the challenging environment of a military submarine. This has contributed to both efficient use of training resources and to improved probability to accomplishing missions. Although SUBSCREEN provides substantial utility, a modest investment could bring it up to date psychometrically and improve the utility of the test for the next 20 years.

REFERENCES

Bargh, J. A. (2006). What have we been priming all these years? On the development of mechanisms, and ecology of nonconscious social behavior. *European Journal of Social Psychology*, 36, 147–168.

Barrick, M. R., Stewart, G. L., & Piotrowski, M. (2002). Personality and job performance: Test of the mediated effects of motivation among sales representative. *Journal of Applied Psychology*, 87, 1–8.

Bing, M. N., & Eisenberg, K. L. (2003). The development and validation of the Submarine Attrition Risk Scale (SARS). International Personnel Management Association Assessment Council, 27th Annual Conference, Baltimore, MD.

Bing, M. N., LeBreton, J. M., Davison, H. K., Migetz, D. Z., & James, L. R. (2007). Integrating implicit and explicit social cognitions for enhanced personality assessment: A general framework for choosing measurement and statistical methods. *Organizational Research Methods*, 10, 346–389.

Borsboom, D. (2005). *Measuring the mind: Conceptual issues in contemporary psychometrics*. New York, NY: Cambridge University Press.

Bryant, K. J. (1986). *Longitudinal analyses of involuntary turnover characteristics within the submarine service: Non-nuclear trained enlisted personnel* (NSMRL Technical Report 1077). Groton, RI: Navy Submarine Laboratory.

Bryant, K. J., & Noddin, E. (1986). *SUBSCREEN assessment* (NSMRL v.2). Groton, RI: Navy Submarine Laboratory.

Cronbach, L. J., Gleser, G. C., Nanda, H., & Rajaratnam, N. (1972). *The dependability of behavioral measurements: Theory of generalizability for scores and profiles.* New York: Wiley.

Hough, L. M., & Oswald, F. L. (2000). Personnel selection: Looking toward the future —Remembering the past. *Annual Review of Psychology*, 51, 631–664.

James, L. R., McIntyre, M. D., Glisson, P. D., Patton, T. W., LeBreton, J. M., Frost, B. C., Russell, S. M., Sablynski, C. J., Mitchell, T. R., & Williams, L. J. (2005). A conditional reasoning measure for aggression. *Organizational Research Methods*, 8, 69–99.

Johnson, S. L. (2009). International perspectives on workplace bullying among nurses: A review. *International Nursing Review*, 56, 34–40.

Kline, P. (1998). *The new psychometrics: Science, psychology and measurement.* New York, NY: Routledge.

Nosek, B. A., Greenwald, A. G., & Banaji, M. R. (2005). Understanding and using the implicit association test: Method variables and construct validity. *Personality and Social Psychology Bulletin*, 31, 166–180.

Nunnally, J. C., & Bernstein, I. H. (1994). *Psychometric theory.* New York, NY: McGraw-Hill.

Rona, R. J., Hyams, K. C., & Wessely, S. (2005). Screening for psychological illness in military personnel. *Journal of the American Medical Association*, 293, 1257–1260.

Sackett, P. R., & Lievens, F. (2008). Personnel selection. *Annual Review of Psychology*, 59, 419–450.

Schlichting, C. L. (1993). *Psychiatric screening for the submarine service: Enlisted personnel* (NSMRL Report 1193). Groton, RI: Navy Submarine Laboratory.

Seligman, M. E., Abramson, L. Y., Semmel, A., & Von Baeyer, C. (1979). Depressive attributional style. *Journal of Abnormal Psychology*, 88, 242–247.

Taylor, J. A. (1953). A personality scale of manifest anxiety. *Journal of Abnormal Psychology*, 48, 285–290.

Tellegen, A., Ben-Porath, Y. S., NcNulty, J. L., Arbisi, P. A., Graham, J. R., & Kaemmer, B. (2003). *The MMPI-2 restructured clinical scales: Development, validation, and interpretation.* Minneapolis, MN: University of Minnesota Press.

Weybrew, B. B. (1954). *Predicting success in submarine school.* Groton, CA: Navy Submarine Research Laboratory.

———. (1967). *History of military psychology at the U.S. Naval Submarine Medical Research Laboratory* (NSMRL Report 917). Groton, RI: Navy Submarine Laboratory.

Weybrew, B. B., & Alves, D. J. (1959). *Exploratory study of autonomic resiliency to manifest anxiety and selected personality traits.* Groton, CA: Navy Submarine Research Laboratory.

Weybrew, B. B., & Noddin, E. M. (1974). *A simplified procedure for identification of optimal test score cut-off points for non-rated submariner candidates* (NSMRL Report 764). Groton, RI: Navy Submarine Laboratory.

Weybrew, B. B., & Youniss, R. P. (1957). *The personal inventory barometer: Development of the questionnaire* (NSMRL Report 290). Groton, RI: Navy Submarine Laboratory.

Wilson, M. (2005). *Constructing measures: An item response modeling approach.* Mahwah, NJ: Lawrence Erlbaum Associates.

Wright, K. M., Bliese, P. D., Adler, A. B., Hoge, C. W., Castro, C. A., & Thomas, J. L. (2005). Screening for psychological illness in the military. *Journal of the American Medical Association*, 294, 42–43.

Part III: Training

Chapter 6

TRAINING INCREDIBLY COMPLEX TASKS

Wallace H. Wulfeck II and Sandra K. Wetzel-Smith

High-risk environments are those in which bad decisions or unsuccessful performance may lead to dire consequences. The point of performance enhancement in these environments is to help people better accomplish tasks and control risk.

Some tasks, such as manufacturing fireworks, using noxious chemicals in industrial processes, or operating cutting tools or heavy machinery, are inherently risky not because they are especially difficult, but because of the possibility of equipment failure, a freak of nature, or mishap due to human inattention or fatigue. In these tasks, the risk surrounding otherwise routine human performance is controlled through automation, fail-safe design, rigid procedure, redundant inspection, and stringent precaution.

More interesting though, at least from a human performance point of view, are the tasks that are "left over" after the routine or simple operations are proceduralized or automated. It has been estimated that perhaps 85 percent of training involves routine factual or procedural tasks, with the remaining 15 percent involving higher-level rule and principle-based performance (Wetzel, Van Kekerix, & Wulfeck, 1987). Some of these higher-level tasks involve extremely complicated judgment, planning, and decision making, and require extensive expert-level knowledge and skill. These sorts of tasks occur in many situations in business, law, economics, large-scale construction, and manufacturing, and they are especially prevalent in medicine, homeland security, and defense, where lives depend on competent performance. For example, the U.S. Joint Chiefs of Staff publish the Universal Joint Task List (Chairman, Joint Chiefs of Staff, 2006), which contains tasks like the following:

- plan, integrate, and coordinate global ballistic missile defense;
- develop theater courses of action;
- conduct deception in support of theater strategy and campaigns;
- coordinate battlespace maneuver and integrate with firepower; and
- conduct foreign humanitarian assistance.

In earlier work, we have described these Incredibly Complex Tasks as tasks that are almost unbelievably complicated, in that they require years of highly contextualized study and experience (Wulfeck & Wetzel-Smith, 2008). They are tasks that require deep expertise and highly focused practice for successful performance. These are the kinds of tasks that lay people speak of as "rocket science" or "brain surgery."

The same features that make tasks difficult are those that contribute to risk in performance or decision environments. Feltovich, Spiro, and colleagues (e.g., Feltovich, Spiro, & Coulson, 1991; Feltovich, Hoffman, Woods, & Roesler, 2004) have described several features of tasks and/or problems that make them difficult, and we have added additional criteria in earlier work (Wulfeck & Wetzel-Smith, 2008). This chapter will discuss some of these sources of difficulty, such as abstraction, variability, uncertainty, and ambiguity. For each source, we provide a short summary of the current training approaches. Following this, we provide a basic set of generalizable principles regarding how to train complex tasks in general to help people cope with complexity in cases not considered in this chapter.

ABSTRACTION

Although philosophers differ on the nature of abstraction (Rosen, 2008), it clearly contributes to task difficulty. Tasks performed in the "real world" on tangible objects are so-called "concrete tasks," while in abstract tasks, the task environment is (re)created conceptually by the performer(s). Performance is said to require a "mental model" (Gentner & Stevens, 1983; Johnson-Laird, 1983) or, in the case of team tasks, "shared mental models" (Cannon-Bowers, Salas, & Converse, 1990). Attention to, and processing of, the conceptual environment is often termed "situation awareness" (Endsley, 1995), and loss of situation awareness is occasionally a contributor to catastrophic error (Anderson & Hauland, 2004).

In abstract tasks, underlying physical phenomena are invisible and the underlying cause-effect relationships cannot be directly observed. These relationships therefore must either be kept in mind, which contributes to the memory and processing load imposed on the task performer by the task environment, or maintained in some sort of display system that helps the user cope with the task environment.

Several strategies help students learn to deal with abstraction. One strategy, useful for both performance-aiding display and for training, is to provide visualizations that help make the relationships observable. In prior work we have shown how the use of interactive visual display environments can help students both learn about complicated physics relationships and perform operationally in tasks that require decision making based on underlying physics principles (Wulfeck & Wetzel-Smith, 2008). A related strategy is to use visualization to demonstrate the otherwise mental manipulation of abstractions (Khan, 2008; Lewak, 2005). Visualization works not only because it helps make invisible relationships more comprehensible but also because it reduces the memory and processing load imposed by the abstraction (Wouters, Paas, & van Merrienboer, 2008).

However, extensive visualization does not necessarily reduce the need for training, expertise, or experience; in fact it may increase the requirement for training. This is because visualizations can only display four or five dimensions of variation at a time, and what is not shown may be just as important as what is presented in a display for its correct interpretation. Another way of saying this is that interpreting any visualization requires knowledge of underlying assumptions, omissions (what is left out to avoid clutter or complexity, or what is averaged or collapsed), presentation conventions (such as scaling and color or symbol mapping onto display parameters), and sufficient practice with the visualization for fluent task performance (Wulfeck & Wetzel-Smith, 2008). A corollary of this principle is, of course, that the search for a simple display that renders a task environment "intuitively obvious to the casual observer" is doomed to failure, at least for complex multivariate tasks. People must know what they are doing.

It is important during training to make the principles underlying abstractions explicit and to exemplify them completely before requiring unaided student performance. A large number of studies in the 1960s and 1970s showed the superiority of direct instructional methods, such as the Rule-Example-Practice strategy—teaching the principles, then showing how the principles apply, and finally requiring student performance to build skill (cf. Merrill, 1983; Merrill & Tennyson, 1977). In particular, worked examples help organize the problem space and reduce the cognitive load during learning. They can also help sequence and structure task performance, by showing how principles and procedures are applied (Sweller & Cooper, 1985).

Note, however, that the purpose of visualizations and examples is not only to make the problem space concrete but more importantly to increase the fluency of abstraction. Recently, Kaminski, Sloutsky, and Heckler (2008) showed the advantage of using abstract rather than concrete examples—they found increased transfer to new situations when instruction concentrated on underlying principles.

One of the largest applications of visualization technologies to deal with abstraction and complexity in both training and performance aiding is the Interactive Multisensor Analysis Training project (IMAT; Wetzel-Smith & Wulfeck, 2009; Wulfeck, Wetzel-Smith, & Dickieson, 2003). The IMAT project developed visualizations in the use of Sonar for antisubmarine warfare aboard Navy ships, including:

- training systems which integrate computer models of physical systems with scientific visualization technologies;

- performance support systems which use modeling and visualization to aid real-world planning; and

- simulation systems which emulate real-world sensor systems for training and mission rehearsal.

The most important design strategy in IMAT was to use computer models of underlying physical phenomena, together with databases of geophysical and environmental input parameters, to drive scientific visualization systems. This had several effects: First, the computer models explicitly identify, and allow manipulation and visualization of, the physical parameters underlying successful sensor employment. Second, the visualizations can be used in both training and performance support systems to represent the tasks to be learned and performed. And third, they provide interactive "laboratories" in which to explore the effects of input variation or changes in decision strategy. These effects aid both training and operational planning.

MULTIPLE SOURCES OF VARIATION

In multivariate problems, several different underlying causes can affect an outcome. Multivariable problems are more difficult than univariate tasks because they increase the cognitive load involved in dealing with the problem (Pollock, Chandler, & Sweller, 2002). Until performance is highly practiced, these tasks often require attention switching among different sources of variation.

There is relatively broad consensus that humans have a limited-capacity working memory. According to Baddeley and Logie (1999):

> working memory refers to aspects of on-line cognition—the moment-to-moment monitoring, processing, and maintenance of information both in laboratory tasks and in everyday cognition. Our own definition of working memory is that it comprises those functional components of cognition that allow humans to comprehend and mentally represent their immediate environment, to retain information about their immediate past experience, to support the acquisition of new knowledge, to solve problems, and to formulate, relate, and act on current goals (pp. 28–29).

Working memory is limited in that it can only maintain a relatively small number of "chunks" of information (Miller, 1956). When new information must be kept in mind, it either displaces some older information or requires time for re-coding and updating new and old information together.

The popular press often extols the virtues of "multitasking" and claims that young people, raised on television, video games, or ipods, are somehow better at it (e.g., Aratani, 2007). In fact, except for highly practiced tasks that require little attention, people do not process multiple tasks "at once," but rather "context-switch" their (limited) attention among tasks (Hamilton, 2008).

Unfortunately, context-switching takes time and involves error, and the more difficult the tasks, the more difficult it is to maintain or reconstruct the context. Almost no studies have looked at context-switching among seriously complicated tasks. Pashler (1992) notes that while tasks such as driving and carrying on a conversation can be performed more or less "at the same time," in fact both activities are highly practiced and usually may involve relatively few actual response selection decisions requiring explicit attention. As complexity increases, for example, when a traffic anomaly occurs, conversation ceases. When both tasks require serious attentional resources, they can only be done by switching among them, not simultaneously. Further, in highly complex tasks, people are likely to load shed, for example, through recognition-primed decision making (Klein, 1998) rather than deep analysis.

Trafton and his colleagues have looked at the effects of interruptions on performance of tasks. On simple tasks, interruptions sometimes result in faster performance, but on complex tasks, interruptions lead to cognitive capacity shortfalls, resulting in increased error rates and longer time to complete primary tasks (Ratwani, Trafton, & Myers, 2007). The effects of interruption on task resumption performance can be mitigated by suitably designed displays which include an event timeline or Interruption Recovery Assistance tools (Scott, Wan, Sasangohar, & Cummings, 2008).

The main training strategy, of course, is to control memory load and minimize interruption during task performance, including during the presentation of worked examples and practice. The process begins with selection of the most salient dimensions of variation. Then, variation is held constant on all but one dimension at a time, and the effects of variation along that dimension are fully explored. Note that it is important to use a single coherent representation (Wilson & Cole, 2001) rather than varying the presentation based on different dimensions of variation.

INTERACTIVITY

Unfortunately, the strategy of isolating variability to one dimension at a time fails when interaction effects are involved. Here the effects of one source of variation are different depending on the action of another source of variation. Again, this increases difficulty because of memory-load requirements to maintain both dimensions in mind to reason about outcomes. Halford, Baker, McCredden, and Bain (2005) showed that performance on five-way interactions is essentially at chance level, and that a four-way interaction is difficult even for experienced adults to process without external aids. Happily, however, such high-way interactions are rare, and often do not constitute large effects. But when they occur, perhaps the only mitigation for training this kind of complexity is to (a) find more basic underlying principles from which reasoning is less intensive, (b) find ways to re-code several interacting dimensions into a more superordinate dimension, or (c) develop performance support systems with displays or processing which can collapse across sources of variation.

DYNAMISM, CONTINUITY, AND SIMULTANEITY

In dynamic problems, the process of variation itself is the subject of analysis rather than end or intermediate states. These types of problems are difficult because people seem to think of change as a succession of states rather than as a process of continuous interaction. Discrete sequences of states are generally easier to learn, because they can be memorized, or represented as static displays, and task-oriented performance aids can be built which help keep track of state and remind users of inputs to transition to other states.

In contrast, simultaneous variation and continuity often occur together in dynamic systems. Among the simplest of such systems are those that employ some sort of output feedback to help the system adjust itself.

Figure 6.1 gives a simplified schematic view of a spring-loaded pressure-reducing valve.[1] The purpose of such a valve is to keep fluid pressure on the outlet side of the valve from exceeding a set limit. When pressure on the

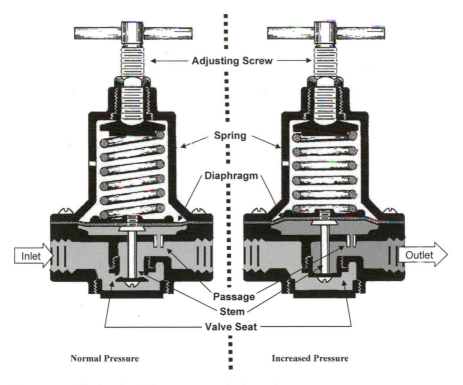

Figure 6.1.   Spring-loaded pressure-reducing valve.

outlet side of the valve is "normal," the valve is open at the valve seat (Figure 6.1, Left Panel). On the outlet side of the valve, fluid is led through a passage to the underside of the diaphragm. The diaphragm is attached to a valve stem which moves with the diaphragm. When pressure rises, fluid tends to press upward on the diaphragm, overcoming spring pressure, which tends to raise the valve stem and close the valve (Figure 6.1, Right Panel). The pressure necessary to raise the diaphragm can be adjusted using the adjusting screw to compress the spring. Note that when this valve is correctly adjusted and is operating properly, it is rarely in any fixed state—the static pictures in Figure 6.1 are quite misleading. Rather the diaphragm "floats" continuously while modulating pressure.

One of the difficulties with such systems is that while the valve operates "continuously," the language used to describe it is sequential, as in "fluid is led through . . . press upwards . . . close the valve." This means that verbal descriptions are poor instruction, because of the difficulty of describing simultaneity. In these cases, animated visual representations are clearly a medium of choice.

Visual animation may work to help explain such relatively simple mechanical devices, but these sorts of feedback systems are common in many other areas such as electronics or economics, where the inputs, outputs, and control signals are invisible abstractions. This means that instructional and performance support systems must properly represent the underlying relationships, and, as described above, properly employ visualization of abstraction.

In many control or piloting tasks, the rate of change of some measure is of central importance, sometimes more so than the actual measurement itself. For example, a standard task in ship navigation is to determine the relative motion of another ship versus our own ship, when both are moving. An important parameter is the bearing (azimuth or direction) to the other ship relative to own ship. However, the bearing at any particular point in time may be of less interest than the rate of change in bearing with time (often called the bearing rate). The reader is invited to consider the implications of a zero bearing rate.

When the dimensions of variation are continuous, instruction should focus on the functional relationships involved rather than on discrete state changes. Outcomes vary continuously with changes in underlying variables rather than as a succession of states. Instruction and practice should focus on the nature of the cause-effect relationships rather than on linear explanations of inputs and outputs.

NONLINEARITY

In nonlinear problems, the relationship of outcome to an underlying dimension is not a simple straight-line function; rather relationships may be exponential, logarithmic, or even more complex. Again, training and instruction can focus on the nature of the underlying functional relationships.

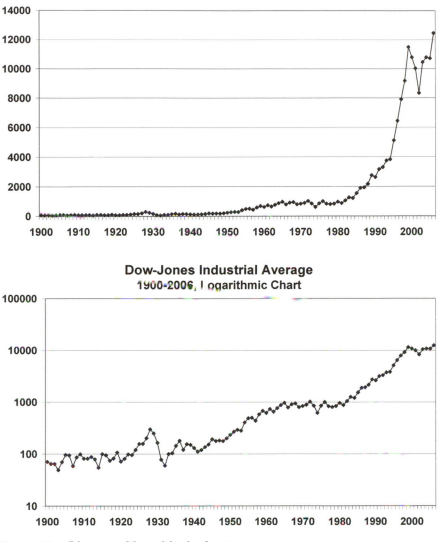

Figure 6.2. Linear and logarithmic charts.

Performance support displays can "linearize" observations, for example, by transforming measurement scales. A simple example is the use of logarithmic scales for compound interest (which is by definition an exponential function) or stock market displays (which investors hope will show exponential growth).

Figure 6.2 shows linear and logarithmic charts for the Dow-Jones Industrial Average from 1900 to 2006. The difference is that the linear chart shows equal dollar gains (or losses) on the vertical axis, while the logarithmic chart shows equal percentage gains (or losses). Here, it is much easier to see periods of growth or no growth. The more general point is that different choices for the representation of data lead to different perceptions or conclusions from the data, and different ways to reason about the data and underlying principles.

Another training strategy is well known to math and science teachers: explore the "interesting" parts of the graphs of functional relationships, such as zero-crossings, maxima and minima, inflections, and discontinuities. In general, the goal is to provide for systematic exploration of the performance environment rather than conventional repeated practice (Pierce, Duncan, Gholson, Ray, & Kamhi, 1993).

CONDITION

Relationships among variables and outcomes may depend on particular boundary conditions or other contextual events. There may be conditional exceptions to general rules or principles may apply only in certain circumstances and not in others. Instruction should adopt an approach to problem-solving or prediction that involves conditional analysis as an early phase of problem solution.

As an example, in sonar operations, an important parameter is the speed at which sound travels. The speed of sound in seawater depends on several factors, including salinity, temperature, and pressure. Salinity is normally fairly constant, but temperature and pressure generally vary with depth. The resulting sound-speed gradient leads to refraction of sound energy as it travels through the water, which in turn may lead to differential enhancement or attenuation of the original sound energy at a given distance. However, on occasion, salinity may decrease at shallow depths (because the density of fresh water is less than salt water) near the outflows of rivers, particularly after major storms, or near melting ice in the Polar regions in the summer, at least until sufficient mixing has occurred. Sonar operators are taught to consider these sorts of boundary conditions during day-to-day operations.

AMBIGUITY

Under ambiguity, the same combination of circumstances may result in multiple outcomes, or the same outcome may be the result of different combinations of circumstances. Sometimes ambiguity can result from simple physics. For example, linear sensor arrays are more sensitive at 90 degrees to their linear axes (more generally in conical regions at other angles depending on element phasing) so that there is always ambiguity for the position of a received signal, or alternatively for the position of the array to optimize signal reception from a given direction. (Try rotating an AM radio at night to receive a distant weak station—the maximum or minimum signal strength is reached with each 180 degrees of rotation, so there are two choices for radio orientation to maximize reception.) For a radio operator using a dipole antenna or a sonar operator using a line array, there is ambiguity as to the direction of a received signal. In other more complicated situations, such as in medicine, several different diseases may result in similar symptoms, such as fever. Training and performance support systems should therefore involve specific procedures for resolving ambiguity. For sonar operations these involve deliberate maneuvering techniques, and in medicine, ambiguity reduction is called "differential diagnosis" and is explicitly taught.

UNCERTAINTY

In most risky situations and complex real-world problems, there is significant uncertainty. Exact values on underlying variables may not be known precisely. They may be subject to measurement imprecision, and some values may be interpolations, estimates, or approximations. Estimates of trends may depend on other underlying uncertainty. There is a large body of psychological research suggesting that people have difficulty dealing with estimation and uncertainty (e.g., Tversky & Kahneman, 1981).

There is significant research underway concerning how to construct visualizations of uncertainty (see, for example, work on visualizing uncertainty in weather prediction at the University of Washington, 2008), in part because visualization can increase the apparent precision of otherwise uncertain data (Deitrick & Edsall, 2006). Although graphical devices such as error bars or high-low lines have been used for years on two-dimensional charts, there are many more possibilities in, for example, three-dimensional volume visualizations. These include variations in hue, saturation, density, texture, blur, and motion in animations. To date, there is little consensus concerning the "best" ways to visualize uncertainty, and the efficacy of various techniques is likely to be domain-specific. Further, as Deitrick and Edsall (2006) suggest, it is not at all clear that uncertainty visualizations, even if they increase comprehensibility of data, will improve decision quality.

Training can focus on the nature of uncertainty and involve "best-case/worst-case" trade-off analysis in the design of worked examples and practice. Note that while we advocate teaching about probabilistic outcomes, we do not advocate introducing stochastic modeling into simulated task environments rather than employing deterministic modeled predictions. Doing so cloaks variation and uncertainty in statistical error rather than making them objects of study where, for training complex tasks, they belong (Wetzel-Smith and Wulfeck, 2009).

TRAINING INCREDIBLY COMPLEX TASKS:
SOME GENERAL PRINCIPLES

So far, our main prescriptions for training complex tasks are to provide extensive training on the principles underlying successful performance in the task area of interest, then to give examples and provide practice so as to reduce the cognitive load associated with performance. We also advocate developing task environments which support memory and decision making. However, we do not advocate conventional training wherein tasks are broken down into disconnected but manageable chunks. As Feltovich, Spiro, and Coulson (1991) point out,

> common strategies of simplification ... such as teaching topics in isolation from related ones (compartmentalizing knowledge), presenting only clear instances (and not the many pertinent exceptions), and requiring only reproductive memory in assessment are often in conflict with the realities of advanced learning—where components of knowledge are fundamentally interrelated, where context-dependent exceptions pervade, and where the ability to respond flexibly to "messy" application situations is required.

We therefore advocate providing principles, examples, and practice in fully complex task environments, but carefully designing the progression of experience so as to control cognitive load. This includes three prescriptions:

Train the whole task. Provide a fully elaborated task environment which properly models all of the variables and cause-effect relationships.

Always make the terminal goal explicit.[2] A corollary of the first prescription is to make the end goals of complex tasks as explicit as possible. As Feltovich, Spiro, and Coulson (1991) point out, tasks should not be fractionated or taught as "part tasks" without first being included in whole-task context.

Do not oversimplify. The reductive bias described by Feltovich, Spiro, and Coulson (1991) (also see Feltovich, Hoffman, Woods, & Roesler, 2004) leads to poor learning. Also, it is tempting to leave out complicating sources of variation or difficulty in constructing task environments for deliberate authentic practice. Doing so may omit key parameters, may lead to a lack of fidelity, and may make eventual fielding of the training system more expensive and difficult because of the need to re-implement it for physical accuracy (Wetzel-Smith & Wulfeck, 2009).

In addition to all the factors that contribute to task difficulty, the fact is that without training and experience, many people are not very good problem solvers, nor are they rational decision makers. Instead people are subject to capture by prior experience or expectation (e.g., functional fixedness or *einstellung*), biased in high or low likelihood situations, and inattentive to base rates. For example:

> I invested $100 in the stock market on Monday. The market went down 40 percent on Tuesday, but its OK, it went up 50 percent on Wednesday, so I'm ahead!

This means that in addition to domain-specific principles, examples, and practice, training for complex tasks also must include special purpose domain-related instruction in more general techniques for problem solving, judgment, and decision making.

In problem solving, there are many techniques for understanding task environments through careful analysis, choice of representation, and selection of appropriate solution methods (cf. Polya, 1957). Note, however, that these must be taught in the domain-specific context, not as general purpose problem-solving tools.

Judgment and decision making must also be taught explicitly. Hastie and Dawes (2001) specifically address the question of what makes a decision difficult:

> there are many intellectual aspects of a decision that make it difficult: the number of alternatives under consideration; the potential for loss if a bad choice is made; the degree of uncertainty about the outcomes that will occur if different choices are made; and, especially, the number and difficulty of the trade-offs that must be made on the way to selecting just one from many courses of action. And there are more emotional aspects as well: the degree to which cherished values are involved and even threatened by the choice alternatives, the intensity of the emotions associated with the choice process or evoked when evaluating the possible consequences of the alternatives, and the presence of time pressure and other threats to a smooth decision process (p. 45).

Finally, the perception of both high-risk and high-task difficulty will contribute to increased stress. This has two effects: first, it increases the intensity of emotion as described above, and second, it reduces cognitive fluency and flexibility. Stress is known to lead to reduced memory performance and to overfocusing on supposed problem solutions. In an extensive review of stress and cognition, Bourne and Yaroush (2003) conclude:

> At high enough levels, stress has adverse effects of performance and cognition. There is an extensive literature, spanning basic and applied research, to document these effects. In contrast, unfortunately, there is little empirical data on effective countermeasures to stress. There is considerable speculation, but little that we can be sure about. The best established countervailing condition is practice or training, or better over-training. The more thoroughly versed in the requirements of a task the performer is, the less the adverse effect of stress. Beyond normal training, training that incorporates exposure to potential stressful events is also useful (p. 103).

Training therefore should be designed to prepare job performers for complexity and risk, and should include sufficient examples and practice opportunities involving sufficient task context and consequence so that stress can habituate.

CONCLUSION

In this chapter, we described factors that contribute to task complexity. We recommend training environments for complex tasks that:

- teach principles underlying abstraction;
- help learners cope with multiple sources of variability in the task environment;
- provide aids or displays that reduce memory load so learning and effective performance can occur;
- provide strategies for dealing with uncertainty and ambiguity;
- provide training in problem solving, judgment, and decision making; and
- provide sufficient practice so that people learn to cope with the stress of complexity and risk.

These training strategies are especially important in preparing people for high-risk environments, where the consequences of performance failure can be catastrophic. There is growing appreciation for the necessity of training incredibly complex tasks. Fletcher (2009) notes the central importance in the military of simulation-based systems for training incredibly complex tasks to "compress years of experience into intense instructional interactions with a comprehensive range of realistic situations" (p. 73).

A vivid demonstration of the importance of training for complexity occurred in the successful ditching of U.S. Air Flight 1549 on January 15, 2009 in New York's Hudson River. In a later interview, Captain Chesley Sullenberger described his thought process in conducting an unpowered water landing for his Airbus 320:

> I needed the wings exactly level at touchdown. I needed to make the rate of descent survivable. I needed to touch down at nose-up attitude. And I needed to touch down just above our minimum flying speed. And all those needed to occur simultaneously (Couric & Sullenberger, 2009).

This is a classic description of complexity. It succinctly describes the mental abstraction of the multivariate nonlinear simultaneous relationships among attitude, airspeed, and rate of descent; Captain Sullenberger ascribed his and his crew's performance to training and experience. Happily, this saved all 155 people aboard his aircraft.

NOTES

1. For a more detailed explanation of the conceptual difficulties and qualitative reasoning required to make sense of this sort of system, see Forbus (1993).

2. This principle was independently discussed by both Ed Hutchins and John Anderson at the *Annual ONR Contractors Meeting for Instructional Theory and Advanced Training Systems*, Stanford University, Stanford, CA, January 1980. Although included in Anderson's subsequent tutoring systems, it has been little discussed in the professional literature since. Violation of this principle is one of the reasons why pure discovery learning often fails (Mayer, 2004) and constructivist approaches to instruction are less effective than direct instruction (Kirschner, Sweller, & Clark, 2006).

REFERENCES

Anderson, H. H. K., & Hauland, G. (2004). Studying operator behaviour during a simple but safety critical task. In C. W. Johnson & P. Palanque (Eds.) *Human error, safety and systems development* (pp. 209–222). Norwell, MA: Kluwer.

Aratani, L. (2007). Teens can multitask, but what are costs? *Washington Post*, February 26, 2007. http://www.washingtonpost.com/wp-dyn/content/article/2007/02/25/AR2007022501600.html (accessed March 12, 2009).

Baddeley, A. D., & Logie, R. H. (1999). Working memory: The multiple-component model. In A. Miyake & P. Shah (Eds.). *Models of working memory. Mechanisms of active maintenance and executive control* (pp. 28–61). Cambridge: Cambridge University Press.

Bourne, L. E., Jr., & Yaroush, R. A. (2003). Stress and cognition; a cognitive psychological perspective. NASA Technical Report. NAG2-1561. NASA Ames Research Center. Downloaded January 29, 2009 from http://psych-www.colorado.edu/~lbourne/StressCognition.pdf.

Cannon-Bowers, J. A., Salas, E., & Converse, S. A. (1990). Cognitive psychology and team training: Training shared mental models and complex systems. *Human Factors Society Bulletin*, 33, 1–4.

Chairman, Joint Chiefs of Staff. (2006). *Universal joint task list, CJCSM 3500.04D*. Washington, D.C.: Joint Staff.

Couric, K., & Sullenberger, C. (2009). Interview concerning US Air 1549. *CBS News 60 Minutes*, February 8, 2009.

Deitrick, S., & Edsall, R. (2006). The influence of uncertainty visualization on decision making: An empirical evaluation. In A. Riedl, W. Kainz, & G. A. Elmes (Eds.) *Progress in spatial data handling* (pp. 719–738). Berlin: Springer.

Endsley, M. R. (1995). Towards a theory of situation awareness. *Human Factors*, 37 (1), 32–64.

Feltovich, P. J., Hoffman, R. R., Woods, D. R., & Roesler, A. (2004). Keeping it too simple: How the reductive tendency affects cognitive engineering. *IEEE Intelligent Systems*, 90–94. Available online: http://www.ihmc.us/research/projects/EssaysOnHCC/ReductiveExplanation.pdf.

Feltovich, P. J., Spiro, R. J., & Coulson, R. L. (1991). Learning, teaching, and testing for complex conceptual understanding. In N. Frederiksen, R. J. Mislevey, & I. I. Bejar (Eds.), *Test theory for a new generation of tests* (pp. 181–217). Hillsdale, NJ: Lawrence Erlbaum Associates.

Fletcher, J. D. (2009). Education and training technology in the military. *Science*, 323, 72–75.

Forbus, K. D. (1993). Qualitative process theory: Twelve years after. *Artificial Intelligence*, 59, 115–123.

Gentner, D., & Stevens, A. L. (Eds.) (1983). *Mental models*. Hillsdale, NJ: Lawrence Erlbaum.

Halford, G. S., Baker, R., McCredden, J. E., & Bain, J. D. (2005). How many variables can humans process? *Psychological Science*, 16 (1), 70–76.

Hamilton, J. (2008). Think you're multitasking? Think again. *National Public Radio Morning Edition*, October 2, 2008. Retrieved October 18, 2008 from http://www.npr.org/templates/story/story.php?storyId=95256794.

Hastie, R., & Dawes, R. M. (2001). *Rational choice in an uncertain world: The psychology of judgment and decision making.* Thousand Oaks, CA: Sage.

Johnson-Laird, P. (1983). *Mental models.* Cambridge, MA: Harvard University Press.

Kaminski, J. A., Sloutsky, V. M., & Heckler, A. F. (2008). The advantage of abstract examples in learning math. *Science,* 320, 454–455.

Khan, S. (2008). Model-based teaching as a source of insight for the design of a viable science simulation. *Technology, Instruction, Cognition and Learning,* 6 (2), 63–78.

Kirschner, P. A., Sweller, J., & Clark, R. E. (2006). Why minimal guidance during instruction does not work: An analysis of the failure of constructivist, discovery, problem-based, experiential, and inquiry-based teaching. *Educational Psychologist,* 41 (2), 75–86.

Klein, G. A. (1998). *Sources of power: How people make decisions.* Cambridge, Mass: MIT Press.

Lewak, J. (2005). *Method of presenting and teaching abstract concepts by animating abstract symbols.* United States Patent 6856318. Retrieved October 14, 2008 from http://www.freepatentsonline.com/6856318.html.

Mayer, R. (2004). Should there be a three-strikes rule against pure discovery learning? The case for guided methods of instruction. *American Psychologist,* 59 (1), 14–19.

Merrill, M. D. (1983). Component display theory. In C. M. Reigeluth (Ed.). *Instructional-design theories and models: An overview of their current status.* Hillsdale, NJ: Erlbaum.

Merrill, M. D., & Tennyson, R. (1977). *Teaching concepts: An instructional design guide.* Englewood Cliffs, NJ: Educational Technology Publications.

Miller, G. A. (1956). The magical number seven, plus or minus two: Some limits on our capacity for processing information. *Psychological Review,* 63, 81–97.

Pashler, H. (1992). Attentional limitations in doing two tasks at the same time. *Current Directions in Psychological Science,* 1 (2), 44–48.

Pierce, K. A., Duncan, M. K., Gholson, B., Ray, G. E., & Kamhi, A. G. (1993). Cognitive load, schema acquisition, and procedural adaptation in nonisomorphic analogical transfer. *Journal of Educational Psychology,* 85 (1), 66–74.

Pollock, E., Chandler, P., & Sweller, J. (2002). Assimilating complex information. *Learning and Instruction,* 12, 61–86.

Polya, G. (1957). *How to solve it.* Boston, MA: Princeton University Press.

Ratwani, R. M, Trafton, J. G., & Myers, C. (2007). Helpful or harmful? Examining the effects of interruptions on task performance. *Human factors and ergonomics society annual meeting proceedings, cognitive engineering and decision making,* pp. 372–375(4).

Rosen, G. (2008). "Abstract objects," *The Stanford Encyclopedia of Philosophy (Fall 2008 Edition).* Retrieved October 15, 2008 from http:/plato.stanford.edu/archives/fall2008/entries/abstract-objects/.

Scott, S. D., Wan, J., Sasangohar, F., & Cummings, M. L. (2008). Mitigating supervisory-level interruptions in mission control operations. In *Proceedings of 2nd Int'l Conference on Applied Human Factors and Ergonomics,* July 14–17, 2008, Las Vegas, NV.

Sweller, J., & Cooper, G. A. (1985). The use of worked examples as a substitute for problem solving in learning algebra. *Cognition and Instruction,* 2 (1), 59–89.

Tversky, A., & Kahneman, D. (1981). The framing of decisions and the psychology of choice. *Science*, 211 (4481), 453–458.

University of Washington. (2008). UW Probcast: Integration and visualization of multi-source information for mesoscale meteorology, statistical and cognitive approaches to visualizing uncertainty. Retrieved October 22, 2008 from http://www.stat.washington.edu/MURI/.

Wetzel, C. D., Van Kekerix, D. L., & Wulfeck, W. H. (1987). *Analysis of navy technical school training objectives for microcomputer based training systems*. San Diego, CA: Navy Personnel Research and Development Center.

Wetzel-Smith, S. K., & Wulfeck, W. H. (2009). Virtual technologies for training, interactive multisensor analysis training. In J. Cohn, D. Nicholson, & D. Schmorrow (Eds.). *The PSI handbook of virtual environments for training and education: Developments for the military and beyond. Volume 3: Integrated systems, training evaluations, and future directions*. Westport, CT: Praeger.

Wilson, B. G., & Cole, P. (2001). Cognitive teaching models. In D. H. Jonassen (Ed.), *Handbook of research for educational communications and technology* (pp. 601–621). Bloomington, IN: Association for Educational Communications and Technology.

Wouters, P., Paas, F., & van Merrienboer, J. J. G. (2008). How to optimize learning from animated models: A review of guidelines based on cognitive load. *Review of Educational Research*, 78 (3), 645–675.

Wulfeck, W. H., & Wetzel-Smith, S. K. (2008). Use of visualization to improve high-stakes problem solving. In E. L. Baker, J. Dickieson, W. H. Wulfeck, & H. F. O'Neal (Eds.), *Assessment of problem solving using simulations* (pp. 223–238). New York: Lawrence Erlbaum Associates.

Wulfeck, W. H., Wetzel-Smith, S. K., & Dickieson, J. L. (2003). *Interactive multisensor analysis training*. San Diego, CA: Space and Naval Warfare Systems Center.

Chapter 7

THE U.S. NAVY'S CREW RESOURCE MANAGEMENT PROGRAM: THE PAST, PRESENT, AND RECOMMENDATIONS FOR THE FUTURE

Paul E. O'Connor, Robert G. Hahn, and Eduardo Salas

Crew resource management (CRM) training is the most widely applied technique for providing human factors and team training to operations personnel in high-reliability organizations (HROs; see Flin, O'Connor, & Mearns, 2002 for a review). CRM training can be defined as "a set of instructional strategies designed to improve teamwork in the cockpit by applying well-tested tools (e.g., performance measures, exercises, feedback mechanisms) and appropriate training methods (e.g., simulators, lectures, videos) targeted at specific content (i.e., teamwork knowledge, skills, and attitudes)" (Salas, Prince, Bowers, Stout, Oser, & Cannon-Bowers, 1999, p. 163). Since its inception over 20 years ago in commercial aviation, CRM training is now recommended by the major civil aviation regulators (e.g., Federal Aviation Authority, FAA; and Joint Aviation Authorities, JAA) and used by virtually all the large national and international airlines and U.S. military aviation. The goal of U.S. Navy (USN) CRM[1] training is to "improve mission effectiveness by minimizing crew preventable errors, maximizing crew coordination, and optimizing risk management" (Chief of Naval Operations, 2001). Every naval aviator must receive ground training and a CRM evaluation during an actual, or simulated, flight by a CRM instructor, or facilitator, once a year.

Unlike commercial aviation, the USN considers CRM training to be an *operational* training program, as opposed to a safety training course. However, with more than 80 percent of naval aviation mishaps attributed to human error (Naval Safety Center, 2006), if CRM's goal of reducing preventable crew errors is achieved, improvements in safety would also be an inevitable outcome of CRM training.

The purpose of this chapter is to discuss the development of CRM training in U.S. Naval aviation, and how that training is managed in a large organization with many different airframes and squadrons (a squadron consists total of 12–24 aircraft, depending on aircraft type commanded by a single senior officer). This chapter also discusses early evaluations of the effectiveness of Navy CRM training and suggests considerations for improving the program. Although this chapter is written with reference to the USN's CRM program, this chapter is of interest to any organization attempting to implement, or improve, the effectiveness of CRM training.

THE DEVELOPMENT OF CRM TRAINING IN THE USN

The impetus for CRM training in the USN came directly from commercial aviation. Throughout the 1970s and 1980s, commercial aviation sponsored increasing amounts of research to identify how failures of human performance had contributed to mishaps. As a result of this research, commercial carriers developed training to reduce error and increase flight crew effectiveness (the first comprehensive CRM program was initiated by United Airlines in 1981; Helmreich & Foushee, 1993).

The first attempt to start a CRM training program in naval aviation was initiated by the Naval Safety Center in 1989 (Alkov, 1989). The program was based heavily upon the training that was being provided in civil aviation at that time. However, the training was not universally accepted by naval aviators across all communities due to the "one-size-fits-all" nature of the training (Prince & Salas, 1993). Oser, Salas, Merket, and Bowers (2001) point out that "for the naval CRM program to be successful and accepted, it had to be developed for aviators, by aviators" (p. 334). Therefore, CRM training research was started by the Navy with the purpose of designing a program specifically for the needs of naval aviators to coordinate their resources. A brief description of the nine steps that were used to design and deliver the Navy's CRM training program is provided below (for a more detailed discussion of the development of the program, see Oser et al., 2001; Oser, Salas, Merket, Walwanis, & Bergondy, 2000; and Prince & Salas, 1993).

Steps 1 and 2: Identify operational requirements and assess training needs and coordination demands. Existing training curricula, standard operating procedures, mishap data, and interviews with naval aviators were carried out to identify the skills and behaviors required for effective and ineffective performance (Oser et al., 2001).

Step 3. Identify teamwork competencies and knowledge, skills, and attitudes. The particular emphasis at this stage was on skills. The research goal was to "develop and demonstrate a methodology that could be used by the various aviation communities to build validated, mission-oriented, skill-based training for aircrew coordination which could be integrated with other aircrew training" (Prince & Salas, 1993, p. 355). Seven critical skill areas were identified: decision making, assertiveness, mission analysis, communication, leadership, adaptability/flexibility, and situational awareness (Prince & Salas, 1993).

Step 4. Determine team training objectives. For each teamwork knowledge, skill, and attitude competency, training objectives were written. The training objectives then guided the development of the content of the course. Training objectives are crucial as these can be empirically evaluated to assess whether or not they were achieved through the training (Goldstein & Ford, 2002).

Step 5. Determine instructional delivery method. Different instructional strategies were examined to establish the most effective method for training the skills identified from the research. Based upon prior research on training effectiveness, it was decided to use a combination of information (lectures), demonstration (video clips of good and poor examples of CRM), practice (practice the behaviors in the simulator), and feedback to the training participants (Oser et al., 2001).

Step 6. Design scenario exercises and create opportunity for practice. Scenario-based (or event-based) training was used to provide the participants the opportunity to practice the skills they had learned in a simulated environment. "Event based training is an instructional approach that systematically structures training in an efficient manner by tightly linking learning objectives, exercise design, performance measurement and feedback" (Dwyer, Oser, Salas, & Fowlkes, 1999, p. 191). For each training objective, specific learning objectives are identified for inclusion in the training exercises. The next stage is to identify "trigger events" for each learning objective. These events are the stimulus conditions and cues which are embedded in the exercises and require a response by the participants.

Step 7. Develop performance assessment/measurement tools. In association with the design of the scenarios, tools were developed to assess the performance of the participants. These tools included behavioral-based checklists, subjective evaluation forms, and outcome metrics and criteria (Salas, Fowlkes, Stout, Milanovich, & Prince, 1999; see the next section for more details on these measures).

Step 8. Design and tailor tools for feedback. Guidance was provided to instructors as to how to provide feedback to participants on their performance. The purpose of the guidance was to provide instructors with help diagnosing the causes of poor performance, as well as aiding in providing feedback on improving performance in the future.

Step 9. Evaluate the extent of improved teamwork in the cockpit. The FAA (2004) states that for CRM training "it is vital that each training program be assessed to determine if CRM training is achieving its goals" (p. 12). Using the tools developed in step seven, a number of studies were carried out on the effectiveness of the training. The next section provides a detailed description of this research.

Evaluation of the USN's CRM Program

As has been the case with CRM in commercial aviation (see O'Connor, Flin, & Fletcher, 2002; Salas, Burke, Bowers, & Wilson, 2001; Salas, Wilson, Burke, Wightman, & Howse, 2006 for reviews), evaluations of the effectiveness of the USN's CRM training have been reported in the scientific literature. Kirkpatrick's (1976) evaluation hierarchy provides a useful framework to assess the effects of a training intervention on an organization by considering training evaluations at different levels. The hierarchy consists of four different levels of evaluation: reactions, learning, behavior, and organization.

- Reactions (level one) are concerned with how the participants react to the training. Evaluating reactions is the equivalent of measuring customer satisfaction. For example, did the participants like the training?

- Learning is the second level in the hierarchy and refers to "the principles, facts, and skills which were understood and absorbed by the participants" (Kirkpatrick, 1976, p. 11). This level is concerned with whether the participants have acquired knowledge, or have modified their attitudes (a tendency to respond in a certain manner when confronted with a certain stimuli or situation; Oppenheim, 1992) or beliefs as a result of attending the training course.

- An evaluation at the behavior level (level three) is the assessment of whether knowledge learned in training actually transfers to behaviors on the job, or a similar simulated environment.

- The organizational level is the highest in Kirkpatrick's (1976) hierarchy. The ultimate aim of any training program is to produce tangible evidence at an organizational level, such as an improvement in safety and productivity. The problems with the evaluation of training at this level are that it can be difficult both to establish discernible indicators and to be able to attribute these to the effects of a single training course.

Table 7.1 summarizes the eight scientific studies of the effectiveness of the USN's CRM program that have been reported in the literature.

Level 1: Reactions. In the five studies that reported an evaluation of reactions, naval aviators were found to be enthusiastic in their reactions to the training (see Table 7.1). To illustrate, the first study reported by Salas, Fowlkes, et al. (1999) reported a strong endorsement of the usefulness of the training (a mean of 4.3 out of 5).

Level 2: Learning. Six studies examined the effect of CRM training on the attitudes of course participants (see Table 7.1). These studies used adaptations of the cockpit management attitudes questionnaire (CMAQ; Helmreich, 1984) to assess attitude change. It can be seen that the studies generally reported a positive shift in the attitudes of CRM participants.

Four studies examined the effects of CRM training on the knowledge of course participants using multiple choice tests, with three of the studies reporting a significant increase in knowledge (see Table 7.1). For example,

Table 7.1. Evaluations of the Effectiveness of the USN's CRM Program

Author(s)	Participants	Reactions	Learning	Behavior	Organization
Alkov (1989); Alkov & Gaynor (1991)	90 aircrew		Positive shift in attitudes.		Aircrew error mishap rate declined.
Baker, Bauman, & Zalesny (1991)	41 helicopter pilots	Positive reaction			
Brannick, Prince, Prince, & Salas (1995)	51 aircrew			Better than average in performing CRM behaviors.	
O'Connor & Jones (under review)	364 aviators		Senior aviators were significantly more supportive of an open cockpit climate than junior aviators.		
Salas, Fowlkes, et al. (1999)	35 pilots & 34 enlisted helicopter aircrew	Positive reaction	No significant difference in attitudes pre- and post-training. Significant increase in CRM knowledge.	Trained crews performed better than untrained crews.	

Author	Participants	Reaction	Learning	Behavior	Results
	27 helicopter pilots (12 serving as controls)	Positive reaction	No significant difference in attitudes between trained and controls. Trained aviators scored significantly better on knowledge test than controls.	Trained better during preflight brief, and greater number of teamwork behaviors during high workload.	
Stout, Salas, & Fowlkes (1997)	42 student aviators (20 experimental, 22 control)	Positive reaction	Positive shift in attitudes. Significant increase in knowledge of CRM principles.	Trained crews performed better than untrained crews.	
Stout, Salas, & Kraiger (1996)	12 helicopter pilots (10 serving as a control group)	Positive reaction	Positive change in attitudes, but not significant. No significant difference in scores on knowledge test than controls.	Trained participants performed on average 8% more desired behaviors than control as measured by TARGETs.	
Wiegmann & Shappell (1999)	290 naval aviation mishap (1990–1996) causal factors				56% of the mishaps had at least one CRM causal factors. Comparable to the 58% aircrew error rate found by Yacavone (1993) in an examination of 308 naval aviation mishaps (1986–1990).

Salas, Fowlkes, et al. (1999) found that, although CRM training did not show an effect on the pilots' attitudes, it did appear to increase their CRM-related knowledge. Those who had participated in the CRM training scored significantly better than the baseline group that had not received any training (a mean of 12.6 out of 17, compared to 9.8, respectively).

Level 3: Behavior. Four out of the five studies that assessed behaviors used a behavioral marker system called Targeted Acceptable Responses to Generated Events or Tasks (TARGETs) to assess team performance, with Brannick et al. (1995) using a precursor to TARGETs (see Table 7.1). Behavioral markers are "a prescribed set of behaviors indicative of some aspect of performance" (Flin & Martin, 2001, p. 96). The TARGETs system was based upon the seven critical aircrew behaviors that are taught in the Navy's CRM training (Fowlkes, Lane, Salas, Franz, & Osler, 1994). For each stimulus event in a scenario, there is a predefined set of acceptable behaviors; each is rated as present or absent. It is a measure of crew performance rather than individual performance. All five of the studies reported an increase in CRM behaviors. For example, Salas, Fowlkes, et al. (1999) found that CRM-trained helicopter crews performed 15 percent better than the untrained crew during the preflight brief and 9 percent better during high workload segments.

Level 4: Organizational impact. The ultimate aim of any training program is to produce tangible evidence at an organizational level, such as an improvement in safety and productivity. Only two studies reported an evaluation at the organizational level. Alkov (1989) and Alkov and Gaynor (1991; both studies used the same data) reported a decrease in the mishap rate for three naval aircraft communities (helicopters, attack bombers, and multi-placed fighters) as a result of CRM training. However, Wiegmann and Shappell (1999) argued that the initial success of the Navy's CRM program may have been short-lived.

An analysis of the causes of naval aviation mishaps from 1990 to 1996 found that 56 percent involved at least one CRM failure (Wiegmann & Shappell, 1999). This can be compared to an aircrew error rate of 58 percent in naval aviation mishaps from 1986 to 1990—prior to the introduction of CRM (Yacavone, 1993). Wiegmann and Shappell (1999) attributed the lack of change in the aircrew error rate to the absence of specific tailoring of the CRM program to the particular needs of the different aviation communities. There certainly could be some truth to this argument, particularly considering that the CRM training was only beginning to be applied in naval aviation during this time period. However, there are other factors that may have contributed to a perceived lack of change in the aircrew error rate. To illustrate, CRM training may have led to an increase in the awareness and understanding of aircrew error. Therefore, there may have been a greater willingness of the mishap investigation board to identify human factors as causal to the mishap than prior to widespread participation in CRM training.

To summarize the findings from the evaluation studies, apart from the conclusions of Wiegmann and Shappell (1999), there would generally appear to be a positive effect of the Navy's CRM training at each of the levels of Kirkpatrick's evaluation hierarchy. In the next section the methodology for implementing the training to every naval aviator is described.

The Implementation of CRM Training in the USN

As described above, after the initial limited success in implementing the civil aviation-modeled CRM training to naval aviators in 1989, the scientifically grounded course was introduced in 1993. This section is concerned with how the training was, and continues to be, implemented in an organization as large as the U.S. Navy, operating a highly diverse range of aircraft types.

Implementation of the "new" CRM programs into naval aviation began in 1993 and was initiated by the Naval Air Warfare Center Training Systems Division (NAWCTSD). To execute this new far-reaching program required an architecture, or command and control system, suited to the organization it would serve. However, only a portion of the funding required for full-scale implementation was made available. Therefore, when the program was first launched, the extent to which it was put into practice varied considerably from platform to platform (Osei et al., 2001). To this day, there is some variability between both communities and squadrons in the quality of CRM training provided to naval aviators. The effectiveness of the program is greatly influenced by the support of the squadron Commanding Officer and the enthusiasm of the CRM facilitator.

The Navy's CRM program is governed by a Chief of Naval Operations (CNO) Instruction—OPNAVINST 1542.7C. This instruction sets the basic administrative organization of the CRM program and outlines a basic framework for CRM in the USN and Marine Corps. The CNO instruction outlines a rudimentary foundation of CRM program academics and the behaviors the program aims to achieve. The instruction sets out the roles and responsibilities of the key personnel in the CRM program (see Table 7.2).

The naval CRM program can be viewed as 42 separate CRM programs (run by the Curriculum Program Managers and their Curriculum Model Managers) united by a common CRM language and basic tenants as outlined in the CNO instruction. At the same time, the Curriculum Program Managers have the license to make the basic CRM program specific to their aircraft, crew composition, and mission. The CRM IMM trains the Curriculum Model Managers. This gives rise to a "train the trainer" system. IMM instructors train the Curriculum Model Managers who train CRM Facilitators who in turn train aviators in the squadrons. It should be pointed out that the only position that is a full-time "job" is that of the IMM. For all of the other positions, the CRM duty is performed in addition to all of their other duties (e.g., flying,

Table 7.2.   Roles and Responsibilities of Key Personnel in the CRM Program

Roles	Responsibilities
Chief of Naval Operations	The resource sponsor for the CRM program.
Controlling Custodians	Ensure compliance with the program; forward resource needs to higher authority for various CRM program initiatives; allocate quotas for training of personnel at the Instructional Model Manager's CRM course.
Curriculum Program Managers	Implement the CRM programs that are specific to their type-model aircraft.
Curriculum Model Managers	Responsible for training squadron CRM facilitators within their aircraft community.
CRM Facilitators	Monitor CRM programs in their squadron, and conduct squadron-level CRM training.
CRM Instructional Model Manager (IMM)	Providing CRM training to the Curriculum Model Managers. In this capacity, the IMM sets the overall academic theme of naval CRM training.

instructing, and safety officer). Due to the size and complexity of naval aviation, this system is functionally expedient.

The IMM has an additional responsibility not often delegated to "schoolhouses"—that of conducting periodic site visits to the Curriculum Program Manager sites. In this capacity the IMM provides oversight to the naval CRM program. This oversight is limited and advisory in nature, rather than punitive. The IMM looks for basic compliance with the CNO instruction in the Program Managers' programs and ensures that academic literature in the Curriculum Program Managers' CRM training covers the basic academic tenants addressed in the CRM curriculum. In this manner, naval CRM achieves both broad standardization in language, basic academics, and implementation, and relevance in specific CRM programs which have been adapted to address the particular issues in a given aircraft model. This unique IMM duty helps serve to provide a form of standardization in the naval CRM program.

The organization of the USN CRM program has remained intact since its inception. Although there have been minor updates to the IMM's curriculum, the basic CRM instruction in naval aviation has not changed greatly in the last decade. The last systematic update of the training curriculum was in 1999 by NAWCTSD (Oser et al., 2001). There are cases, however, of some Curriculum Program Managers making exhaustive efforts to improve CRM in their communities. Some training commands have drawn extensively on airline models for multi-place CRM training, while the MV-22 Osprey program has developed robust CRM courseware and models for their CRM program.

The CRM curriculum in these communities exceeds the basic requirement in the CNO instruction and augments the curriculum promulgated by the IMM. These are generally the exception; most Curriculum Program Managers' CRM programs reflect the basic academics taught by the IMM. Promulgating the latest academic themes in a "train the trainer" system is sometimes a challenge in a large organization.

RECOMMENDATIONS FOR THE USN'S CRM PROGRAM

It is possible to make a number of suggestions for improving the USN's CRM program. However, these recommendations do not only apply to the USN but have implications for any large HRO that has, or is developing, a CRM training program.

Use and Apply What We Know from the Science of Team Training

The design and delivery of training is a science (Salas & Cannon-Bowers, 2000), grounded in a systematic process of creating a robust learning environment. Training should be based on theoretically driven and empirically validated instructional principles to drive the design of the instructional process (Salas, Wilson, Burke, Wightman, & Howse, 2006). The design and delivery of *team* training is no different. And over the last two decades a wealth of knowledge has emerged about how to design and deliver team training (Salas et al., 2006). There are now solid principles, guidelines, tips, and specifications that can be applied to update and modernize CRM programs.

Conduct Evaluations of the Effectiveness of the CRM Program

It is important to track the effects of CRM training to allow for the identification of topics for recurrent programs and to ensure that it continues to improve performance despite changes in aircraft design, operational conditions, emerging risks, and pilot demographics. However, the majority of the studies evaluating the Navy's CRM program were carried out in the 1990s. Very little has been done to evaluate the effectiveness of CRM training in the last decade. Therefore, there is a need to regularly collect data at as many levels of Kirkpatrick's evaluation hierarchy as is feasible. This evaluation data could be used for internal performance auditing, as well as for benchmarking across different aircraft types to ensure an optimal return on CRM training investment.

Update and Improve the Content of the Existing Training Course

Much has changed in the 20 years since CRM training was first introduced in the Navy. A wealth of more recent research that is relevant to CRM training has been published. Examples of this research include situation awareness (e.g., Endsley & Robertson, 2000), naturalistic decision making (e.g., Klein, 1999), metacognition (e.g., Cohen, Freeman, & Wolf, 1996), shared mental models (Campbell & Kuncel, 2001), and teamwork (e.g., Salas, Burke, & Stagl, 2004). Further, naval aircraft have become increasingly automated, so for many aviation platforms there is also a need to increase the training provided on the effects of automation on crew coordination (e.g., Woods & Sarter, 2000).

As discussed in the previous section, thanks to the dedication of the individuals that have run the Navy CRM program over the years, the training has not remained stagnant—one of the largest recent changes has been the introduction of the concept of threat and error management (see Helmreich, Wilhelm, Klinect, & Merritt, 2001 for a discussion). However, these changes have been made on a piecemeal basis and vary between aviation communities. Therefore, there is a need to systematically evaluate if the training is meeting its objectives and whether updates should be implemented to the content based upon recent research and changes in aircraft design.

Exploit the Use of Simulation to Practice and Provide Feedback on Team Performance

Follow the science of simulation-based training. There is a wealth of research on designing effective simulator scenarios (e.g., Shrestha, Prince, Baker, & Salas, 1995), training simulator instructors (e.g., MacLeod, 2005), and tools for providing feedback to participants on performance (Flin, O'Connor, & Crichton, 2008). The design of scenario exercises was part of the original nine steps for designing and delivering CRM training. However, the effective utilization of simulators to provide aviators with the opportunity to practice and receive objective feedback on their CRM behaviors is largely missing from a number of the Navy's CRM programs. This fact is detrimental to the impact of the training. In a recent meta-analysis of CRM evaluation studies, those studies that were found to be most effective were those in which the training participants were given the opportunity to practice the behaviors they had learned in CRM training course, in a simulator (O'Connor, Campbell, Newon, Melton, Salas, & Wilson, 2008). A combination of lectures, the opportunity to practice desirable behaviors, and feedback regarding performance is a well-established mechanism for delivering effective training (Baldwin & Ford, 1988, Bandura, 1977).

Establish CRM in Other Navy Communities

Despite the fact that CRM training has been used in the USN for almost two decades, there has been no systematic effort to expand the training to communities beyond naval aviators. Bridge Resource Management (BRM) was introduced into the curriculum of the Surface Warfare Officers School (the command that trains officers who will work on ships) three years ago. However, it is still in the process of becoming established. The only other isolated examples of the use of CRM training by non-aviation personnel are naval medicine and navy diving (O'Connor & Muller, 2006). However, outside the military, CRM training is being applied in a wide range of high-reliability industries. Those industries that adopted it first were, unsurprisingly, involved in the aviation business. However, CRM training has also begun to be used in a number of other high-reliability industries unrelated to aviation (see Flin, O'Connor, & Mearns, 2002 for a review). Civilian applications of CRM training that directly related to the roles of USN personnel include aviation maintenance, air traffic control, nuclear power generation, commercial shipping, and medicine. However, if naval aviation CRM is to be adapted for other military domains, the training materials must be customized. As in the example of naval aviation, this effort must be fully supported at all levels from the deck plates to the CNO. The framework of nine steps for designing and delivering training will service as a guide for developing CRM training in other domains (see Salas, Wilson, Burke, & Wightman, 2006 for a further refinement of this approach).

For the training to be effective, it is imperative that the skills which are required be identified through a training needs analysis. The language and psychological concepts of the research effort must be translated for ease of use and understanding of by participants. Relevant practical examples and case studies should be used to illustrate the concepts. The training is not likely to be effective unless examples poignant to the particular domain are used. One of the main criticisms of participants of the early aviation CRM courses was that there was too much psychological theory and not enough relevance to aviation (Helmreich, Merritt, & Wilhelm, 1999). "I am not suggesting the mindless import of existing programs; rather, aviation experience should be used as a template for developing data driven actions reflecting the unique situation of each organization" (p. 784).

CONCLUSION

An organization's CRM training program must not remain stagnant. Much has occurred in the two decades since CRM training was first introduced in the USN. It is reasonable to suggest that a program that two decades ago delivered on its goal to improve mission effectiveness needs review to ensure its vitality. As new glass cockpit aircraft (e.g., V-22 Osprey) are brought into the Marine Corps, new behavioral-based safety training and monitoring are needed to match these machines (e.g., operational risk management and military flight operational quality assurance; see O'Connor & O'Dea, 2007 for details). These new programs must be assessed to ensure they are meeting naval aviation's operational needs.

Given that more than 50 percent of naval aviation mishaps have been attributed to CRM failures (Wiegmann & Shappell, 1999), a robust, scientifically driven CRM training program is an important mechanism for addressing the human component of aviation mishaps in the USN.

NOTE

1. For the purposes of this chapter, reference to the USN CRM program includes U.S. Marine Corps aviation. Similarly, use of the word *naval* includes both the sea services as both comprise the Department of the Navy.

REFERENCES

Alkov, R. A. (1989). The US Naval aircrew coordination program. In R. Jensen (Ed.), *Proceedings of the Fifth International Symposium on Aviation Psychology* (pp. 368–371). Dayton, OH: Ohio State University.

Alkov, R. A., & Gaynor, J. A. (1991). Attitude changes in Navy/Marine flight instructors following aircrew coordination training course. *International Journal of Aviation Psychology*, 1 (3), 245–253.

Baker, D., Bauman, M., & Zalesny, M. D. (1991). Development of aircrew coordination exercises to facilitate training transfer. In R. Jensen (Ed.), *Proceedings of the 6th International Symposium on Aviation Psychology* (pp. 314–319), Columbus, Ohio.

Baldwin, T. T., & Ford, J. K. (1988). Transfer of training: A review and direction for future research. *Personnel Psychology*, 42, 331–342.

Bandura, A. (1977). *Social learning theory*. Englewood Cliffs, NJ: Prentice Hall.

Brannick, M. T., Prince, A., Prince, C., & Salas, E. (1995). The measurement of team process. *Human Factors*, 37, 641–651.

Campbell, J. P., & Kuncel, N. R. (2001). Individual and team training. In N. Anderson, D. S. Ones, H. K. Sinangil, & C. Viswesvaran (Eds.), *Handbook of industrial work and organizational psychology*. London: Sage.

Chief of Naval Operations. (2001). *Crew resource management program, OPNA-VINST 1542.7C*. Washington, D.C.: Chief of Naval Operations.

Cohen, M. S., Freeman, J. T., & Wolf, S. (1996). Metacognition in time-stressed decision making: Recognizing, critiquing, and correcting. *Human Factors*, 38, 206–219.

Dwyer, D. J., Oser, R. L., Salas, E., & Fowlkes, J. (1999). Performance measurement in distributed environments: Initial results and implications for training. *Military Psychology*, 11 (2), 189–215.

Endsley, M. R., & Robertson, M. M. (2000). Training for situation awareness in individuals and teams. In M. R. Endsley & D. J. Garland (Eds.), *Situation awareness analysis and measurement* (pp. 349–365). Mahwah, NJ: Lawrence Erlbaum.

Federal Aviation Authority. (2004). *Advisory circular no. 120-51E: Crew resource management training*. Washington, D.C.: Federal Aviation Authority.

Flin, R., & Martin, L. (2001). Behavioral markers for crew resource management: A review of current practice. *International Journal of Aviation Psychology*, 11, 95–118.

Flin, R., O'Connor, P., & Crichton, M. (2008). *Safety at the sharp end: Training non-technical skills*. Aldershot, England: Ashgate Publishing Ltd.

Flin, R., O'Connor, P., & Mearns, K. (2002). Crew resource management: Improving safety in high reliability industries. *Team Performance Management*, 8, 68–78.

Fowlkes, J., Lane, N., Salas, E., Franz, T., & Osler, R. (1994). Improving the measurement of team performance: The TARGETs methodology. *Military Psychology*, 6 (1), 47–61.

Goldstein, I. L., & Ford, K. J. (2002) *Training in organizations: Needs assessment, development, and evaluation*. Belmont, CA: Wadsworth.

Helmreich, R. (1984). Cockpit management attitudes. *Human Factors*, 26, 583–589.

Helmreich, R. L., & Foushee, H. C. (1993). Why crew resource management? Empirical and theoretical bases of human factors training in aviation. In E. L. Wiener, B. G. Kanki, & R. L. Helmreich (Eds.), *Cockpit resource management* (pp. 3–41). New York: Academic Press.

Helmreich, R. L., Merritt, A. C., & Wilhelm, J. A. (1999). The evolution of crew resource management training in commercial aviation. *International Journal of Aviation Psychology*, 9, 19–32.

Helmreich, R. L., Wilhelm, J. A., Klinect, J. R., & Merritt, A. C. (2001). Culture, error, and crew resource management. In E. Salas, C. A. Bowers, & E. Edens (Eds.), *Improving teamwork in organizations: Applications of resource management training* (pp. 305–331). Mahwah, NJ: Lawrence Erlbaum Associates.

Kirkpatrick, D. L. (1976). Evaluation of training. In R. L. Craig & L. R. Bittel (Eds.), *Training and development handbook* (pp. 18.1–18.27). New York: McGraw Hill.

Klein, G. (1999). *Sources of power: How people make decisions*. Boston, MA: MIT Press.

Macleod, N. (2005). *Building safe systems in aviation. A CRM developer's handbook*. Aldershot: Ashgate.

Naval Safety Center. (2006). *Aviation 3750*. Norfolk, VA: Naval Safety Center.

O'Connor, P., Campbell, J., Newon, J., Melton, J., Salas, E., & Wilson, K. (2008). Crew resource management training effectiveness: A meta-analysis and some critical needs. *International Journal of Aviation Psychology*, 18 (4), 353–368.

O'Connor, P., Flin, R., & Fletcher, G. (2002). Methods used to evaluate the effectiveness of CRM training: A literature review. *Journal of Human Factors and Aerospace Safety*, 2, 217–234.

O'Connor, O., & Jones, D. (October 2009). *Attitudes of U.S. Naval aviators towards the human factors skills required for effective flight operations*. Paper presented at the Human Factors and Ergonomics Society meeting, San Antonio, Texas.

O'Connor, P., & Muller, M. (June 2006). *A novel human factors training curriculum for U.S. Navy diving*. Paper presented at the Undersea and Hyperbaric Medical Society meeting, Orlando, Florida.

O'Connor, P., & O'Dea, A. (2007). The U.S. Navy's aviation safety program: A critical review. *International Journal of Applied Aviation Studies*, 7 (2), 312–328.

Oppenheim, A. N. (1992). *Questionnaire design, interviewing, and attitude measurement.* London: Pinter.

Oser, R. L., Salas, E., Merket, D. C., & Bowers, C. A. (2001). Applying resource management training in naval aviation: A methodology and lessons learned. In E. Salas, C. A. Bowers & E. Edens (Eds.), *Improving teamwork in organizations: Applications of resource management training* (pp. 283–301). Mahwah, NJ: Lawrence Erlbaum Associates.

Oser, R. L., Salas, E., Merket, D. C., Walwanis, M. M., & Bergondy, M. L. (2000). Can applied research help naval aviation?: Lessons learned implementing crew resource management training in the Navy. *Transportation Human Factors,* 2 (4), 331–345.

Prince, C., & Salas, E. (1993). Training and research for teamwork in the military aircrew. In E. Wiener, B. Kanki, & R. Helmreich (Eds.), *Cockpit resource management* (pp. 337–366). San Diego: Academic Press.

Salas, E., Burke, C. S., Bowers, C. A., & Wilson, K. A. (2001). Team training in the skies: Does crew resource management (CRM) training work? *Human Factors,* 41, 161–172.

Salas, E., Burke, C. S., & Stagl, K. C. (2004). Developing teams and team leaders: Strategies and principles. In D. Day, S. J. Zaccaro, & S. M. Halpin (Eds.), *Leader development for transforming organizations* (pp. 325–357). Mahwah, NJ: Lawrence Erlbaum Associates.

Salas, E., & Cannon-Bowers, J. A. (2000). The anatomy of team training. In L. Tobias & D. Fletcher (Eds.), *Training and retraining: A Handbook for business, industry, government, and the military* (pp. 312–335). New York: Macmillan.

Salas, E., Fowlkes, J. E., Stout, R. J., Milanovich, D. M., & Prince, C. (1999). Does CRM training improve teamwork skills in the cockpit?: Two evaluation studies. *Human Factors,* 41, 326–343.

Salas, E., Prince, C., Bowers, C., Stout, R., Oser, R. L., & Cannon-Bowers, J. A. (1999). A methodology for enhancing crew resource management training. *Human Factors,* 41, 161–172.

Salas, E., Wilson, K. A., Burke, C. S., & Wightman, D. C. (2006). Does CRM training work? An update, extension and some critical needs. *Human Factors,* 14, 392–412.

Salas, E., Wilson, K. A., Burke, C. S., Wightman, D. C., & Howse, W. R. (2006). A checklist for crew resource management training. *Ergonomics in Design,* 14, 6–15.

Shrestha, L. B., Prince, C., Baker, D., & Salas, E. (1995). Understanding situation awareness: Concepts, methods, and training. In W. B. Rouse (Ed.), *Human/technology interactions in complex systems* (vol. 7, pp. 45–85). Greenwich, CT: JAI Press.

Stout, R. J., Salas, E., & Fowlkes, J. E. (1997). Enhancing teamwork in complex environments through team training. *Group Dynamics: Theory, research, and practice,* 1, 169–182.

Stout, R. J., Salas, E., & Kraiger, K. (1996). The role of trainee knowledge structures in aviation psychology. *International Journal of Aviation Psychology,* 7, 235–250.

Wiegmann, D. A., & Shappell, S. A. (1999). Human error and crew resource management failures in naval aviation mishap: A review of U.S. Naval Safety Center data, 1990–96. *Aviation, Space, Environmental Medicine,* 70 (12), 1147–1151.

Woods, D. D., & Sarter, N. B. (2000). Learning from automation surprises and "going sour" accidents. In N. Sarter and R. Amalberti (Eds.), *Cognitive engineering in the aviation domain* (pp. 327–356). Hillsdale, NJ: Erlbaum.

Yacavone, D. W. (1993). Mishap trends and cause factors in naval aviation: A review of Naval Safety Center data, 1996–90. *Aviation, Space, Environmental Medicine*, 64 (5), 392–395.

Chapter 8

MEASURING RETURN ON INVESTMENTS IN TRAINING AND HUMAN PERFORMANCE

J. D. Fletcher and Ralph E. Chatham

Admiral Isaac Kidd, retired head of Naval Materiel Command and chair of several Defense Science Board review panels, often challenged the human performance community by asking, "What is a pound of training worth?" The question highlights issues that high-level Defense policy decision makers face. Should they, for example, buy a pound of training, a pound of jet propulsion fuel, or a pound of munitions? They could, with some precision, estimate how much more flying time fuel would provide and the expected number and type of targets destroyed by different munitions. But how might they relate training to system and operational effectiveness with sufficient and equivalent precision to inform their decisions? Many decision makers are willing to take the value of training and human performance on faith, but faith only goes so far when budgets are under scrutiny.

Although this chapter focuses on human performance obtained through military training, the same issue arises in civilian training (Phillips, 2003) and civilian education (Levin & McEwan, 2001). More broadly, it occurs as a perennial problem in managing human resources for business. For instance, Becker, Huselid, and Ulrich (2001) emphasize that the necessary data are rarely, if ever, found in a commercial firm's financial and/or managerial accounting systems. They then discuss ways to collect the necessary data using a human resources scorecard to balance a firm's human resources costs, including those for training, with the resources needed to ensure implementation of its strategic business plan.

Those who recognize the difficulty of answering Admiral Kidd's question directly may choose to avoid the issue, but interest in such assessment began in the manufacturing sector almost a century ago and has now worked its way through the service, health care, and public sectors (Bassi & Van Buren, 1998; Phillips, 2003). It has finally arrived at training. The time may have come to address this issue directly.

Today, we can determine fairly well the costs of training investments, along with other means for developing and/or enhancing human performance. But how should we evaluate the return? How, in quantitative terms that are comparable to the returns we can calculate for investments in materiel, ordnance, supplies, and the like, should we assess the increases in system and operational effectiveness that are affected by investments in training? Techniques for assessing cost-effectiveness, cost-benefits, and, particularly, return on investment (ROI) come to mind.

Most practical decision-making does not focus on anticipated benefits alone, but must additionally consider what must be given up to get them. Costs in particular help inform decisions by taking into account both investment, what must be given up, and what we get in return.

Cost-effectiveness, for instance, is especially useful when the metrics of investment and return must be expressed in different terms (e.g., dollars in investment, operational effectiveness in return). Such analyses can be found for both military and nonmilitary training and education (e.g., Orlansky & String, 1977; Ross, Barkaoui, & Scott, 2007, respectively). However, cost-effectiveness is a relative term, and relevant decision alternatives must be identified and defined in assessing it. Despite common usage, we cannot properly say an investment, all by itself, is or is not cost-effective.

Instead, we can calculate and present a benefits-costs ratio (BCR) or a ROI for a single course of action by identifying the investment and return using whatever metrics we choose. But in these cases the terms for input and output must be commensurable—both must be assessed using the same units of measure. Usually, the resources required for investment are most easily expressed in monetary units. On the other hand, returns may be more amenable to terms better suited to the productivity and effectiveness being sought. Nonetheless, monetary units tend to be those most readily translated from whatever returns are produced to meet BCR and/or ROI requirements for commensurability. The examples considered in this chapter all key on costs.

This chapter mostly concerns investments in training because that is where human performance data are mostly readily found—scarce though they may be. Overall, the point we want to make is that more could, and should, be done by behavioral scientists to assess ROI. It is unlikely that anyone else will do it for them.

We present a brief, introductory discussion of ROI analysis and then some specific examples where sufficient data were available to assess ROI. These examples attempt to relate training investments directly to operational effectiveness. After discussing these examples, we finish by mentioning, yet again, the need for ROI analyses in the area of human performance and end with a brief exhortation to decision makers to seek such analyses more frequently, if not more insistently, and to behavioral scientists to perform them more often, if not routinely.

ANALYZING RETURN ON INVESTMENT

BCR and ROI ratios have been with us for some time. In 1667, public health officials in London found that expenditures to combat the plague would yield a BCR of 84:1 (Thompson, 1980). In the United States, the River and Harbor Act (1902) and Flood Control Act (1936) mandated that projects to support them be justified by examining and then reporting their benefits as cost ratios. This mandate later evolved into the 1973 "Principles and Standards for Planning Water and Related Land Resources," which required BCR and ROI analyses of trade-offs between national economic development, regional economic development, environmental quality, and social well-being (Sassone & Schaffer, 1978).

Accountability for Lyndon Johnson's Great Society programs in the 1960s was intended to be informed by systematic ROI analyses that were required by the Planning, Programming, and Budgeting System, which was specifically implemented for these programs and now remains a core issue in preparing today's Future (or Five) Year Defense Plans. This continuing emphasis on accountability and identifying quantitative relationships between investments and their returns suggests that it may be time to begin seriously applying these techniques to investments in enhanced human performance, including, of course, investments in training.

However, training and education are more often viewed as expenses than investments—as the infrastructure costs of doing business. In military accounting practice, training is often bundled with travel, transit, hospitalization, and incarceration. Of course, the core business of military organizations is not education and training, but the successful execution of military operations. However, the direct and substantial contributions of human performance to system and operational effectiveness suggest that education and training are better characterized as investments than expenses. BCR and ROI analyses seem applicable if not essential.

As discussed by Phillips (2003), among others, BCR is calculated as:

$$\frac{\text{Value of the result}}{\text{Cost of the investment}}$$

It tells us, in nicely quantified terms, how many units of value we get for every unit of cost. The basic formula for calculating ROI is as straightforward as its name suggests. Again, as discussed by Phillips (2003) and others, it is:

$$\frac{\text{Value of the result} - \text{Cost of the investment}}{\text{Cost of the investment}}$$

This ratio is sometimes multiplied by 100 so it can be expressed as a percent rather than a proportion. We left it as a proportion in this chapter, so that any ROI greater than 1.0 indicates a positive net return. ROI is almost always calculated for some period of time, such as a year. The length of time is, of course, up to the analyst. ROI may be calculated for a particular kind of activity, such as a sales event or a military operation covering a variable period of time. In these cases, costs may be averaged over several of the activities.

A related means of calculating ROI may be used for investments undertaken as projects lasting several years. In early years of the project, the return from the investment may be zero or something very close to it. In later years, when the project begins to pay off, the required investment may be considerably reduced and the return considerably increased. ROI in these multiyear projects must take account of the net flow of resources (inflow minus outflow) over several years. In deciding whether to make this investment today, we would like to know what is the value, in terms of today's resources, of the investment after it has been carried out over an agreed upon number of years.

Resource values for these projects are inevitably measured in today's monetary units, i.e., cash, and calculated using a standard technique called, among other things, net present value (NPV). Resources other than cash might be used, but examples of NPV calculated without it are rare. The value of the cash must be adjusted over the anticipated years of return using adjustments for inflation and the discount rate, which, roughly, is the return that might be realized from investing the cash in financial markets with levels of risk similar to those of the proposed project. Calculation of NPV is more complicated than those discussed above, but only mildly so thanks to tables routinely produced in the United States by the Office of Management and Budget and widely accepted for discounting cash. NPV commonly used to estimate ROI anticipated from multiyear research and/or development projects. It is not discussed further in this introductory chapter, but the reader is referred to Mishan and Quah (2007) for more detail.

All these analyses require "Value" and "Cost" to be commensurable—expressed in the same units of measure, which is usually monetary. Of BCR and ROI we prefer the latter because it indicates how many units of *net* benefits are obtained, after investment costs have been subtracted out, for each unit invested. Readers will note that these processes may require a certain amount of curve smoothing. There are, of course, spikes, dips, and diminishing returns to be considered with differently timed units of investment, but we have kept this chapter at an introductory level, hoping to inspire enthusiasm for follow-on study and development by interested readers. In addition to the Mishan and Quah (2007) economics text just mentioned, an easier next step is Phillips (2003) book, which is directly focused on training and performance improvement.

In calculating ROI, the devil, as usual, infests the details. There are no one-size-fits-all cost analyses—they rarely, if ever, satisfy the needs of all decision makers who turn to them for assistance—but they can, and should, be made as explicit as possible. Decision makers should receive enough information to determine for themselves the degree to which any analysis is relevant, credible, and sufficient to inform whatever decision they must make.

The issues that arise with the investment side of ROI usually concern what cost elements should be included, how specifically to define them, and what values should be assigned to parameters such as discount, interest, depreciation, inflation, and amortization rates. These are not simple issues, but they are easier to resolve than finding data to quantify returns arising from units of enhanced human performance.

How can we best measure the value of human performance? What units of performance should we use? In particular, how can we assess success in military operations with metrics that are commensurable with investment costs? Secondary and tertiary effects abound in human performance areas, and some of them may have as much effect on ROI as primary effects. Again, it is impossible to be perfect in performing these analyses, but at least we can be explicit. We have done what we could in presenting the following examples.

SOME EXAMPLES: ESTIMATES OF ROI IN TRAINING

We can borrow from Kirkpatrick (e.g., 1987) and identify four levels of assessment for interventions, such as training, that are intended to increase human performance. Level 1 uses surveys to collect the opinions of those affected by the intervention. Level 2 uses objective measures to determine if the intervention achieved its objectives. Level 3 assesses the impact of the intervention on performance in the field. Level 4 assesses the impact of the intervention on the effectiveness of the organization that was intended to benefit from it. Chapter 7 of this book provides more detailed discussion of these levels, along with examples drawn from their review of crew resource management studies.

In Peter Drucker's terms (e.g., 1993), Kirkpatrick's Levels 1 and 2 are primarily concerned with doing things right. In this regard, Nesselrode (2007) provides good ROI examples and data relating returns from investments in modeling and simulation to the achievement of training objectives. Levels 3 and 4 are concerned with doing the right things. These levels address the ultimate impact, value, and purpose of an investment. They are emphasized in the examples presented here. They focus on returns from training in the form of enhanced productivity and operational effectiveness.

Kirkpatrick's Levels 3 and 4 are particularly relevant to human performance in high-stress environments but are rarely measured. Both the 2001 and 2003 Defense Science Boards on training lamented the infrequency with which we link training investments to operational effectiveness (Braddock & Chatham, 2003; Chatham & Braddock, 2001). We measure process (e.g., number of sorties flown and number of field exercises completed) and achievement of training objectives, but we usually skip Levels 3 and 4, which tell us if the investment in training was worth making at all. To understand the value of efforts intended to enhance human performance, we need to measure their return in performance on the job and their impact on the performance of military operations in general.

It is difficult to measure value at Level 3 and extraordinarily hard to do so at Level 4. What is the return for deterring a major war by investing in a standing army? If a war does occur, how should we measure the value of alternate weapon systems or competent operators in terms of warfare outcomes? If we develop a language and cultural training tool, how can we determine the value of avoiding tactical and strategic blunders? Trainers and others who invest in improving human performance face the same dilemma as epidemiologists—if they prevent a disaster, nobody knows it. If they fail to prevent one, everyone knows it.

The problem is compounded by the difficulty of sorting the lucky from the good within the small sample sizes history allows us. Assigning causes for good or bad performance in war is almost always confounded by its chaos; success depends on far too many variables, influenced by many actors and many events that are unmeasured or simply not measurable. Each phase occurs in a different place with different players and different initial conditions.

Unfortunately for analysts, and fortunately for the rest of us, there are too few wars to apply statistical procedures that filter out these factors (March, Sproull, & Tomuz, 1991). This measurement problem applies to both the identification and the quantification of possible causative factors and to the assessment of performance in operations. The problem is further confounded by the uniqueness of every military engagement, which is clearly indicated by simulations developed to recreate specific battles in precise and extensive detail, as was done for 73 Easting in Desert Storm (Christianson & Zirkle, 1992; Orlansky & Thorpe, 1992) and more recently for Mazar-e-Sharif (Knarr & Richbourg, 2008) in the Afghanistan campaign. As March, Sproull, and Tomuz (1991) point out, "the expected error in estimation can be decreased by aggregating over several events, but history limits the number of comparable events . . . Measurement error, model misspecification, and system complexity introduce substantial noise into observations and interpretations" (pp. 7–8).

Further, eyewitness reports are not reliable sources of information. Researchers who have studied these reports have noted their frequent inaccuracy (Loftus, 1996). Some inaccuracy may be unavoidable. William James (1890/1950) first observed this in defining his General Law of Perception, "whilst part of what we perceive comes through our senses from the object before us, another part (and it may be the larger part) always comes out of our mind" (p. 747). His observation has been verified by much subsequent research as reviewed by Neisser (1967), Baddeley and Hitch (1974), Von Glaserfeld (1989), and others who have studied the constructive nature of perception and memory. We might well conclude that history is overwhelmingly an interpretation of interpretations. All these difficulties notwithstanding, there are examples from the military that can provide measures of output value for input investment. The Top Gun experience is a case in point.

Top Gun "Experiment": Air-to-Air Warfare

Background

In the late 1960s, the U.S. Navy was understandably concerned by its deteriorating air-to-air engagement performance over Vietnam. During a six-month period in 1968, the exchange ratio had actually dropped to less than one-to-one—9 enemy aircraft shot down with the loss of 10 Navy aircraft (Armed Forces Journal, 1974). Fortunately and for a variety of reasons, there was a hiatus in the air war from 1968 to 1970. Concerned about its losses, the Navy used this time to create a new kind of training, colloquially called Top Gun. Over the years 1968–1973, 300 aircrews received this training.

Top Gun was intended to mimic as closely as possible the Vietnam air-to-air combat environment. The best Navy pilots were assigned to an existing air base, put in MIG-like aircraft, and trained to act as an opposing Red Force using enemy doctrine, procedures, and tactics. The next best pilots were then sent to this "graduate school of dog-fighting," where, over a period of five weeks, they fought the Red Force in their F-4E Phantom II aircraft during 32 hours of mock combat as a Blue Force. Although the Blue Force pilots routinely lost to Red Force pilots, they improved quickly and substantially.

The basic elements of the process became known as engagement simulation. As described by Gorman (1990), Fletcher and Chatelier (2000), and Chatham (2009a), actions in the mock battles were measured in extensive detail by instruments installed in the aircraft and on the combat range, producing a precise, objective record of what happened. Outcomes were not determined by force of personality or by who got to the chalkboard first. After each engagement there was a free-flowing after action review (AAR) where lessons learned were not presented didactically by observers but facilitated and drawn out of the trainees themselves (Morrison & Meliza, 1999). The facilitators asked questions such as: When you were here, what did you see? What did you do? What were you thinking then? What could you have done better? What worked? What failed? Then the process was repeated.

The results were dramatic. When the air war resumed in 1970, the Navy's exchange ratio increased from 2.4:1, drawn from the four years prior to Top Gun, up to 12.5:1 (Armed Forces Journal, 1974; Chatham, 2009a; Fletcher & Chatelier, 2000; Gorman, 1990). This level of performance continued through the next four years.

The Air Force provided a natural control group. With nearly the same equipment and weaponry as the Navy, the Air Force exchange ratio, of 2.2:1 before the 1968–1970 hiatus, dropped to 2.0:1 for the four years following the Navy's introduction of Top Gun. Soon thereafter, the Air Force adopted the same engagement simulation process for training its own pilots. The general process has now been adopted in combat training centers by the land warfare services. In the Army, the AAR has revolutionized not only training but Army culture as well (Bolger, 1986; Braddock & Chatham, 2003; Chatham, 2009a, 2009b; Chatham & Braddock, 2001; Fletcher & Chatelier, 2000; Morrison & Meliza, 1999).

Payoffs and Costs for Top Gun

In calculating ROI for Top Gun, we started with the return—the warfare value of post–Top Gun proficiency improvements. Had the Navy pilots (aviators) sustained the exchange level (2.4:1) of the four years before Top Gun graduates arrived in the fleet, they would have lost 10 aircraft while shooting down 25 MiGs. If the Navy had matched the ratio (2.0.1) that the Air Force experienced after the air war resumed, their 25 MiG kills would have been accompanied by 12–13 Navy aircraft lost. In the actual event only two Navy F-4E aircraft were lost.

To simplify the arithmetic, we assumed the absence of Top Gun would have led to 10 extra losses. Adopting Knaack's (1978) figures, the cost of an F-4E, in 2008 dollars, would be about $16.4 million. Thus the cost of losing 10 fighter-bombers, not counting logistics and tactical costs, would have been about $164 million. If we add in the $2 million actuarial cost of an American life today (Ashenfelter & Greenstone, 2004) and $100,000 for pilot training, the cost of 10 lost F-4E aircraft and their pilots would be about $185 million.

Now for the investment costs: Given the establishment of the Navy Fighter Weapons School at Naval Air Station Miramar, which was already in place, little extra money was likely to have been applied to upgrade the facilities already there to accommodate Top Gun training. To be conservative, we estimated an additional $10 million in facilities and instrumentation. We then looked for investment costs in the extra flying hours that Top Gun training required. We assumed that all the hours the trainees flew in Top Gun would have been expended at home station had they not been in the school. Thus we assumed that the increases in flying hours for Top Gun were those used by the Red Force.

Taking Red Force flying hours as equal to Blue Force hours, we calculated Red Force flying hours through 1974 at 300 trainees times 32 hours of mock battle for a total of 9,600 hours. However, we found from the Top Gun safety record that by 1974 the number of these hours was only a little over 7,000. At $6,119 per hour in 2008 money, the cost of those hours was about $43 million. Adding in the $10 million for facilities and instrumentation, we get a total investment cost in Top Gun of about $53 million.

Return on Investment

Comparing the cost of Top Gun Red Force flying hours ($53 million) to the cost of 10 aircraft not shot down ($185 million) yields an ROI in Top Gun of about $(185 - 53)/53 = 2.49$. The ROI calculated for the Top Gun example is summarized in Table 8.1.

Discussion

These ROI results would have increased had we been able to include the *tactical* cost of losing the extra aircraft or if Red Force aircraft were cheaper to fly than the Blue Force F-4Es. The ROI results would have decreased if Top Gun increased the number of Blue Force flying hours over and above what would have occurred at home station absent Top Gun.

If we use the Navy's 1968 exchange ratio of 9:10 in the months just prior to Top Gun (Armed Forces Journal, 1974) and take 26 as the number of lost aircraft avoided (28 at the 1968 9:10 exchange ratio minus the two F-4Es actually lost), the ROI would be about $(481 - 53)/53 = 8.1$.

Given that the total of Navy kills before Top Gun was 29 (including the 18 kills by F-8s) and total Navy losses were 12, one can infer that the Navy F-4E exchange ratio was very close to 1:1 for the four years before 1969. This adds credibility to the high end (i.e., 8:1) of the ROI range for Top Gun.

The principal Navy air-to-air aircraft throughout the war was the F-4E Phantom II (as it was, in different versions, for the Air Force). The Navy also had a second-line fighter, the F-8 Crusader, but all 18 Navy MiG kills by the F-8 were pre–Top Gun (Armed Forces Journal, 1974). They are not included in the ROI analysis.

Conclusion

Estimating the cost of aircraft and pilots that would have been lost had the Navy not established Top Gun and relating that to the cost of extra flight

Table 8.1. Example ROI: Top Gun

Investment		Return	
7,000 more Red Force flying hours	$7000 \times 6120 =$ $43M	10 F-4E saved	$10 \times 16.4M =$ $164M
Added instrumentation	$10M	10 pilots saved	$10 \times 2.1M = 21M$
Total Investment	**$53M**	**Total Return**	**$185M**
ROI over four years: $(185 - 53)/53 = 2.49$			
Assumes: No increase in Blue Force flying hours. Four-year Navy loss/exchange ratio = 2.4:1			

hours that the opposing Red Force expended along with some costs for instrumentation, we estimated ROI for the Top Gun school intervention to be somewhere in the range of 2.5–8.1.

In-Transit Sustainment Training: Air Support Warfare

Background

The Defense Science Board Task Force on Training Superiority and Training Surprise was told that a substantial loss of proficiency had been observed in air squadrons serving on aircraft carriers deployed to the Persian Gulf (Chatham & Braddock, 2001). A generalized form of Top Gun training was then delivered to each deploying squadron as a unit for a period of three weeks. At the start of the training, their average bombing hit rate was 30 percent of targets attacked. By the end of the third week, their accuracy had improved to 70 percent.

After their Top Gun training, it took the squadrons two to four months to arrive on station, ready to launch aircraft strikes from the Gulf. Skill decay of the type needed for air-to-ground attacks has a time constant of the order of three months (Chatham, 2009a). Operational statistics suggested that bombing accuracy on the first day of action for a squadron deployed on station was roughly 40 percent. By the third day of bombing, accuracy improved to the 70 percent that the squadrons had achieved after three weeks of Top Gun training.

The pilots in the deployed squadron had no way, en route to the Gulf, to refresh or refine their skills in coordinated, multiple aircraft air-to-ground missions. The result was that they required about two days of refresher training in their first combat missions. The only recourse available in 1999 was to shorten the time between the squadrons' Top Gun training and initiation of their combat operations.

But suppose squadron members could create, or "author," realistic, low-cost PC-based training environments that provide coordinated, multiple aircraft training for air-to-ground operations and that could be used to provide sustainment training while traveling to their duty stations. The last decade has seen that possibility become reality (Chatham, 2009b). A user-authoring revolution started with a land combat trainer, DARWARS Ambush! developed by DARPA in 2004. The DARPA RealWorld project has since expanded these authoring capabilities significantly. Effective refresher training can now take place using these user-authored, PC-based environments (Kaufman, 2008; Lunceford & Kaufman, 2009).

Payoffs and Costs for Air-to-Ground Collective, In-Transit Training

Starting again with the return side of ROI, we assumed that user-authored, PC-based training simulation could enable pilots in the deploying squadron to retain their Top Gun-created skills and achieve 70 percent bombing accuracy on their first day of combat. Since no planes were shot down, we assumed that the cost avoided would come from the additional flying hours and the extra munitions needed to hit targets when performance was below 70 percent.

Using a cost per flight hour for F/A-18s in 2008 dollars of $7,000 (Murdock, 2008), three flight hours per sortie, and the cost of a Mark 84 (dumb) bomb of $3,100, a single plane sortie dropping one bomb (excluding support costs of the aircraft) would then cost about $24,100. At 70 percent accuracy, each target would require 1.4 sorties at a cost per target of $34,000. At a first-day-in-combat accuracy of 40 percent (see Table 8.2 for a summary of these calculations), it would take a newly arrived squadron lacking any in-transit training 2.5 sorties per target at a cost of about $60,000 per target hit, an increase of $26,000. Assuming that accuracy for the squadron on the second day would have improved (linearly) to 55 percent, the cost of bombing inaccuracy relative to 70 percent would be about $9,000. By the third day, and given a return to 70 percent accuracy, the cost would have dropped to the standard $34,000 per target hit.

Assuming that the squadron had 10 targets per day, the cost of skill decay on the first day would be about $260,000 and $90,000 on the second. Therefore, we assumed a cost of $350,000 per squadron for its two days of refresher training in combat. On the investment side, we estimated how much in-transit, PC-based training might cost today using DARPA's RealWorld authoring capabilities to create a realistic, multi-ship, mission rehearsal environment.

RealWorld allows terrain to be created from whatever sources are available. It also includes physics and connectivity simulation capabilities that

Table 8.2.   Example ROI: In-Transit Sustainment Training

Investment		Return	
		1st day cost saved/ target	$(2.5 \times 24.1K) - 34$ = $26K
Cost for four trainers with user-authoring software	$4 \times 20K = \$80K$	2nd day cost saved/target	$(1.8 \times 24.1K) - 34$ = $9K
		Total saved, 10 targets/day for two days	$(35K \times 10) =$ $350K
ROI per squadron deployment: (350 − 80)/80 = 3.37			
Assumes: Accuracy without trainers, 1st day = 40%, 2nd day = 55%, 3rd day = 70%. Three-hour sorties at $7K per flight hour and $3.1K per bomb = $24.1K per target. Cost per target at 70% accuracy (1.4 × $24.1K) = $34K. No cost for authoring by squadron.			

are available to government users at no cost but their labor (Kaufman, 2008). In 2007, a RealWorld-developed A-10 trainer was certified by the Air Force Air Combat Command to qualify A-10 pilots to shoot a new air-to-ground missile. Conventional training system developers had estimated the cost per A-10 trainer to be over $350,000. RealWorld delivered the trainer in 2006 for under $30,000 apiece, including the development cost. The large-screen display ($15,000) contributed half of the cost. Today RealWorld authoring software has advanced further and the cost of displays of the same size has dropped by a factor of 10.

All this suggests that compact collaborative, multi-aircraft simulation trainers could be procured and delivered to the fleet for under $20,000 each, including development costs. We would need at least four PC trainers if we were to provide multi-ship, coordinated training for the squadron, so the total investment for the PC trainers would be about $80,000.

Given RealWorld authoring capabilities, a detailed, three-dimensional representation of the targets to be attacked could be created by squadron members within a day or less. Pilots could then practice in that environment repeatedly before going on the mission.

Return on Investment

Taking only the cost for a single aircraft's flight hours and munitions expended, and assuming $20,000 investment costs, the savings from the first target on the first day for that single aircraft would be $(2.5 \times 24.1K) - \$34K = \$26K$. Assuming 10 targets on Day One, that would amount to a savings on Day One of $260,000. Assuming (linearly) an improvement to 55 percent accuracy on Day Two would yield a savings of $(1.8 \times 24.1) - \$34K = \$9K$ per target or $90,000 for 10 targets. For both days, the ROI amounts to $(350 - 80)/80 = 3.375$.

Discussion

The above calculations may underestimate ROI, because it only takes into account the aircraft hours and munitions costs. Planes do not go out alone. For each target attacked by a bombing plane, there are more aircraft (e.g., wingmen, electronic warfare support aircraft, air-controlling aircraft, and tankers) that support the sortie. We also excluded the extra fuel used by the battle group to support the early sorties. The cost of the weapon could have a large impact on ROI as well. We assumed the cheapest large bomb in the inventory. ROI increases if this skill-decay-induced accuracy decrement is applied to the more expensive weapons such as smart bombs, which cost around $20,000 apiece. ROI would also increase if the practice provided by PC-based air-to-ground combat trainers raises the level of accuracy above the 70 percent level achieved after three weeks of Top Gun training. Finally, we have probably overestimated the cost of the trainers.

Factors decreasing ROI would include the use of professional developers rather than squadron members to produce the training environment. Additionally, all the team member roles may have to be played by humans. An earlier Synthetic Teammates for Anywhere Real-Time Training (STRATA) program at DARPA created cognitive models of all the roles in air-to-ground attacks complete with human errors and human time constants (Bell, Ryder, & Pratt, 2008). It allowed trainees to practice alone or with as many human collaborators as they wanted. The system was never deployed, but developing synthetic teammates would have increased the cost to develop the system, although they would have reduced the time, costs, and scheduling required to assemble a team of humans for training.

We assumed that such a PC-based system would, in fact, sustain the pilots' bombing abilities. It is not an unreasonable assumption given reviews of the issue by Bell, Ryder, and Pratt (2008) and by Pohlman and Fletcher (1999), but direct empirical assessment of this application would be needed. The answer, of course, may lie somewhere between full recovery of accuracy to 70 percent and Day One accuracy of 40 percent.

Finally, we provide a caution about how to use effectiveness data. If we had looked for gains from lightweight flight simulators beyond the third day of bombing, we would have found little value, even though there was a great deal of value for the first few days. Training often delivers its highest value early in the learning process and looking for large returns at the shallow-sloped, far end of the learning curve may be less fruitful.

Conclusion

A networked PC-based air-to-ground attack simulator could prevent decay of skill as well-trained Navy pilots are transported to duty stations. Although the pilots only took two days to return to the skill level they had attained three to four months earlier, it is neither efficient nor safe for anyone to do refresher training in combat.

Sonar Antisubmarine Warfare Proficiency

Background

A key element of performance in the submarine force is its ability to conduct effective acoustic search, and, once a contact is found, to identify it and maintain track on it. During the 1980s, the submarines of the world became substantially quieter, but oceans did not. This situation dramatically reduced the acoustic search area for submarines (Chatham, 1984). Expensive attempts to enlarge the search area through improved sensor hardware and technology met with only modest success.

Wulfeck and Wetzel-Smith (2010) and Wulfeck and Wetzel-Smith (2008) are psychologists who taught themselves to be sonar experts. They tried another tack by creating a training system that improved the abilities of sonar operators to visualize the complex behavior of sound in the ocean. It enabled them to effectively understand and use the tools that technology gave them. Without this capability many sonar operators were being overwhelmed by the complexity of the ocean environment.

Wetzel-Smith and Wulfeck have described the work of sonar operators as an example of an incredibly complex task. These tasks are abstract involving invisible phenomena and the relationships between them, multivariate with multiple causes affecting multiple interacting effects, dynamic and continuously changing involving nonlinear interactions among their components, and uncertain, ambiguous, and probabilistic rather than certain and deterministic. Demand for performing these tasks has been increasing for a number of years in both military and civilian sectors (*Technology for the United States Navy and Marine Corps*, 1997). They are especially at a premium in high-risk environments, where decisions must be made quickly and correctly.

The training system Wetzel-Smith and Wulfeck produced for sonar operators, the Interactive Multisensor Analysis Trainer (IMAT), gave junior sonar operators the ability to do something that physics Ph.D. submarine Operations Officers[1] could not. It enabled them to create an acoustic search plan that was practicable and effective.

Payoff and Costs for IMAT

A five-day exercise was conducted in 1999 with eight submarines. One of them had PC-IMAT aboard. After two days of training, its effective search area increased by a factor of 10.5 and, once gained, no contact was ever lost. In effect, the submarine with IMAT-trained sonar operators was able to do the work of 10 submarines without them (Chatham & Braddock, 2001).

The cost of the IMAT program up to that point amounted less than $10 million (Wulfeck & Wetzel-Smith, 2008). Submarines cost well over $2 billion each when people, parts, power plant, provisions, and shore support are included. It is not safe to pack 10 submarines into the space that IMAT-trained operators can control, so a direct, experimental comparison has not been performed. However, one could argue that the return on this $10 million investment could be one submarine for 10, suggesting a savings of 9 submarines and an ROI of $(18B - 0.01B)/0.01B$ yields a net return that might, with some reason, be measured in billions of dollars. Moreover, the cost of physical acoustic technology to deliver an improvement equivalent to that delivered by IMAT through improved human performance is vastly greater than the $10 million spent on IMAT. With the shrinking number of U.S. submarines, there is significant military value in making the most of those that we have.

IMAT Conclusion

A PC-based tool, IMAT, developed by psychologists to train people to visualize the complex behavior of sound in the ocean, delivered an order of magnitude increase in sonar search area coverage—along with a number of other harder-to-measure benefits. IMAT made a $2 billion platform 10 times more effective after spending less than $10 million over a five-year period. The implied ROI is sizable.

Technology-Based Instruction: Training Time Reduction

Background

One of the most stable results to emerge from reviews of several hundred studies comparing standard classroom instruction (e.g., lectures, text- and workbooks, and some hands-on laboratory experience) with the use of technology-based instruction is a reduction in time to learn of about 30 percent (Fletcher, 1997, 2004, 2009a, 2009b). Research suggests that this finding results from the capability of computers (i.e., those who program computers) to tailor the pace, content, and sequence of instruction to the needs of each learner. Absent computer technology, such a capability has long been viewed as desirable, but unaffordable.[2] As argued by Fletcher (1992, 1997) and later by Corbett (2001), computer technology permits substitution of technology for human tutors, making this instructional imperative affordable. It can replace many of the tutoring opportunities lost to the economic necessity of grouped, classroom instruction.

Knowing that we can reliably reduce the time to achieve many training objectives, particularly those involving journeyman skills such as remembering, understanding, and applying facts, simple concepts, and straightforward procedures, what might the return be from investing in it?

Based on an earlier analysis (Angier & Fletcher, 1991), the Naval Studies Board (NSB) reviewed the return side of this ROI issue (*Technology for the United States Navy and Marine Corps*, 1997). Although the use of computer-assisted training could be applied more widely, the NSB focused on Specialized Skill Training, which, roughly, is the post-induction training intended to turn novices into certified journeymen for work in specific military occupations, about 86 percent of which have civilian equivalents (Fletcher & Chatelier, 2000).

Payoff and Costs for Technology-Based Instruction

Assuming a 30 percent reduction in training time, what ROI might we expect if 40 percent of specialized skill training students were to use technology-based instruction? The average Specialized Training course length across all four services is about 57 days or about 400 hours[3]

(*Military Manpower Training Report*, 2002). About 357,700 officers and enlisted personnel completed Specialized Training in FY02. Forty percent of that number amounts to 143,080 learners who then amass about 57.2 million hours spent in specialized training per year. If we were to reduce that training time by 30 percent, that would save about 17.2 million hours in specialized training per year.[4]

Assuming an average composite hourly rate of $42 for enlisted personnel early in their careers (E1 – E2), we can then estimate a total return from this level of investment in technology-based training of about $722.4 million (Office of the Under Secretary of Defense, 2009).

How much, then on the investment side, would it cost to produce the necessary computer-assisted specialized skill training? Estimates to produce an hour of computer-assisted training range widely depending on the content, instructional strategy used, and pay and allowances for the course subject matter experts, "authors," and computer programmers. One source of estimates come from the Joint Knowledge Development and Distribution Capability (JKDDC), which is producing Web-based individual training programs for joint assignments and operations.

As of April 2009, JKDDC had produced over 300 courses with more than 185,000 course completions (Camacho, 2009). In the first quarter of FY08, the costs for JKDDC to develop an hour of instruction were about $14,000 and about $10 to deliver it. How many hours of instructional material would be needed for a 57-day course? Setting study time aside, we might conservatively assume that personnel in specialized skill training receive about 44 hours of instruction per week, so about 352 hours of technology-based instruction would be developed and delivered for a 57-day course. On the basis of the JKDDC figures, we assumed that it would cost about $4.9 million to produce that amount of technology-based specialized skill training and an additional $201.5 million to deliver it to 143,080 students. The investment, then, for the first year of this training would cost about $206.4 million.

Return on Investment

Plugging these considerations and assumptions into an ROI calculation yields a value of (722.4 – 206.4)/206.4 = 2.50 (see Table 8.3 for a summary of these calculations).

Discussion

After the first year, of course, the costs to develop the instruction could be removed from the ROI calculation, but the ROI is not particularly sensitive to development costs. It seems to be far more sensitive to delivery costs, which are considered for the delivery of the technology-based instruction but not for the classroom instruction it replaces. For this reason technology-based instruction is placed at a disadvantage in this calculation, especially with

Table 8.3.   Example ROI: Distributed Learning for Specialized Skill Training

Investment		Return	
Produce 352 hours of instruction	352 × $14,000 = $4.9M	Total average hours spent by 40% of learners in training	143,080 × 352 = 57.2M
Deliver 352 hours of instruction to 40% of learners	143,080 × 352 × $4 = $201.5M	Total hours saved	57.2M × 0.3 = 17.2M
		Composite personnel P&A cost per hour × hours saved	$42 × 17.2M = $722.4M
Total investment	**$206.4M**	**Total return**	**$722.4M**
ROI per year: (722.4 – 206.4)/206.4 = 2.50			
Assumes: 30% time reduction to train 40% of 357,700 (i.e., 143,080) learners. Average course length of 352 hours. $14,000/hour to produce and $4/hour to deliver technology-based training. $42 average hourly cost (pay and allowances) per person.			

regard to its scalability. If the savings in training delivery costs were fully considered in this calculation, the ROI would probably increase. Also, 30 percent time savings is likely to be an underestimate of the student time in training that can be saved. Fifty percent and more time savings appear in the data. Finally, specialized skill training is a very promising area for application of technology-based instruction. It is likely that 60–80 percent of specialized skill training could be delivered this way, thereby increasing ROI further.

Less time in school means more time on the job. Savings in time needed to reach training objectives not only reduce training costs but also increase the supply of people for operational forces without increasing the number of people in uniform—they amount to a force multiplier. Ways to account for accompanying increases in readiness and effectiveness due to force multiplication remain to be determined, but they, rather than savings in training costs, may be the most significant impact of reducing time to reach performance levels required by operational forces.

Conclusion

There appears to be a significant ROI from converting some proportion of training to technology-based delivery. This value arises primarily from the reduction of student time spent in the training infrastructure. Even with technology-based instruction, some training, mentoring, and monitoring must be provided by seasoned military personnel to people early in their careers, and certainly the camaraderie and esprit de corps gained by students undergoing the rigors of training together must be balanced against the economic value of technology-based learning. Still the administrative efficiencies, improved tracking of student progress, assurance of student success, and other benefits provided by technology-based training that were not considered in this analysis have their place and would continue to argue for its use.

THE UTILITY OF ROI IN HUMAN PERFORMANCE ASSESSMENTS

Admiral Kidd's question seems as relevant today as it was 20 years ago. If the behavioral science community is to respond to the needs of Defense (and industry) decision makers, it needs to address cost. Few behavioral scientists have been trained in the fine points of costing, but as we hoped to show with the above examples, credible analyses are possible even with crude, approximate measures.

Phillips (2003) points out that ROI analyses allow behavioral scientists to join a transformation beginning in the manufacturing sector, then progressing through the service, health, nonprofit, and public sectors until finally arriving in education and training sectors. The ROI approaches we discuss in this chapter may all be used to assess enhancements of human performance in high-risk environments and in some cases are already there, doing that (Phillips, 2003). Completing this progression with its cost accounting requirements will transform education and training program evaluation from reactive efforts starting only after a program is fielded to something more proactive, beginning much earlier in the development cycle.

Such a transformation toward more proactive assessment in education and training will more closely link program effects to specific requirements and objectives, more strongly emphasize performance effectiveness at Kirkpatrick's Levels 3 and 4, more effectively communicate results to decision makers, help set priorities, and, overall, focus program reporting on output. Notably, it will better inform budget decisions when adjustments are called for.

Some caution is inevitably advisable. Kirkpatrick's Levels 1 and 2 may reveal significant improvements in human performance after a training intervention that is the subject of an ROI analysis. However, when we seek further validation at Kirkpatrick's Level 3 and go to the field or some other operational venue where the training was intended to improve performance, we should acknowledge the multifaceted, stochastic properties of the real world. To some extent what we observe is a result of the training provided, and to some unavoidable extent it is not. The influence of factors other than training must be kept in mind.

Taylor, in a 2000 paper presentation discussed by Flin, O'Connor, and Crichton (2008), suggested application of a causal operator to adjust ROI for such factors as changes in morale, organizational climate, performance conditions, improvements in equipment, and the like that may have contributed to improvements that are observed in Kirkpatrick's Level 3 assessments but are independent of the training intervention and not otherwise accounted for in the ROI calculation. If a reliable correlation between one or more of these factors is available, it may, as Taylor suggested, be used to attenuate the improvements observed and thereby provide a more valid assessment of ROI. The recommended ROI calculation is then:

$$\frac{(\text{Value of the result} - \text{Cost of the investment}) \times \text{Causal Operator}}{\text{Cost of the investment}}$$

The Causal Operator is the amount of variance accounted for by the factor or combination of factors not otherwise attributable to the training intervention under consideration. It is simply the square of the correlation between the operational improvements observed and the factor or factors not otherwise included in the calculation. It may be applied under the assumption that the correlation between these factor(s) and the training intervention provided is near zero—that they are effectively independent.

The ROI calculations in the examples presented in this chapter are not difficult, but the data (including correlations needed for Taylor's Causal Operator) that they require are often absent, with the result that ROI calculations may require assumptions that can vary widely. Exactitude and precision are not needed, "ballpark" estimates may be enough to inform many of these decisions, but the estimated data itself may require extrapolations from what is known. Methodology and managerial commitments remain needed to make ROI assessments involving human performance more accurate, useful, and routinely available in decision making.

Final Word

In 1959 Fred Muckler pointed out a pressing need for specific and detailed metrics to be used in evaluating human performance as a necessary and inevitable component of all system performance. He called for a mobilization of the human research community to launch a concentrated, serious effort to develop them. Human performance measures are typically more variable and less precise than those of equipment performance, but they can lend themselves to the cost and effectiveness trade-offs that are an inevitable and proper component of managerial and administrative decision-making. Such trade-offs and the decisions based on them can be substantially informed by analyses of cost-effectiveness, benefit-cost, and ROI. It may be time for the human performance community to begin including them routinely in their assessments.

NOTES

1. For instance, R. E. Chatham.
2. Exceptions are made for high-stress, high-value environments such as surgery and piloting aircraft. In these cases, the investment is costly, but the expected return (e.g., avoidance of loss) is equally or more valuable.
3. Skill Progression Training after Specialized Skill Training is not included in this calculation.
4. The 2002 Military Manpower Training Report is the last such report issued by the Office of the Under Secretary of Defense for Personnel and Readiness. There would have been some changes in Specialized Skill Training since 2002, but these changes are assumed to have been small.

REFERENCES

Angier, B., & Fletcher, J. D. (1991). *Interactive Courseware (ICW) and the cost of individual training* (IDA Paper P-2567). Alexandria, VA: Institute for Defense Analyses.

Armed Forces Journal. (1974). "You fight like you train" and TOP GUN crews train hard. *Armed Forces Journal International*, May, 25–27.

Ashenfelter, O., & Greenstone, M. (2004). Using mandated speed limits to measure the value of a statistical life. *Journal of Political Economy*, 112 (2, Part 2), S226–S267.

Baddeley, A. D., & Hitch, G. J. (1974). Working memory. In G. A. Bower (Ed.), *The psychology of learning and motivation: Advances in research and theory* (vol. 8, pp. 47–89). New York: Academic Press.

Bassi, L., & Van Buren, M. (1998). State of the industry report. *Training and Development*, 58 (1), 22–42.

Becker, B. E., Huselid, M. A., & Ulrich, D. (2001). *The HR scorecard: Linking people, strategy, and performance*. Boston, MA: Harvard Business School Press.

Bell, B., Ryder, J., & Pratt, S. N. (2008). Communications and coordination training with speech-interactive synthetic teammates: A design and evaluation case study. In D. A. Vincenzi, J. A. Wise, M. Mouloua, & P. A. Hancock (Eds.), *Human factors in simulation and training* (pp. 385–413). New York: Academic Press.

Bolger, D. P. (1986). *Dragons at war*. Novato, CA: Presidio Press.

Braddock, J. V., & Chatham, R. E. (2003). *Training for future conflicts*. Washington, D.C.: Defense Science Board, Department of Defense.

Camacho, J. (2009). *Joint Knowledge Online brief to the Norwegian Armed Forces Norwegian Defence University College*. Paper presented at the ADL conference 2009 Training, Simulation and Education, Bergen, Norway.

Chatham, R. E. (September 1984). The quiet revolution. *Naval Institute Proceedings*, 110, 42–46.

————. (2009a). The 20th century training revolution. In K. A. Ericsson (Ed.), *Development of professional expertise: Toward measurement of expert performance and design of optimal learning environments* (pp. 27–60). Cambridge, UK: Cambridge University Press.

————. (2009b). Toward a second training revolution: Promise and pitfalls of digital experiential training. In K. A. Ericsson (Ed.), *Development of professional expertise: Toward measurement of expert performance and design of optimal learning environments* (pp. 215–246). Cambridge, UK: Cambridge University Press.

Chatham, R. E., & Braddock, J. V. (2001). *Training superiority and training surprise.* Washington, D.C.: Defense Science Board, Department of Defense.

Christianson, W. M., & Zirkle, R. A. (1992). *73 Easting battle replication—a Janus combat simulation* (IDA Paper P-2770). Alexandria, VA: Institute for Defense Analyses.

Corbett, A. (2001). Cognitive computer tutors: Solving the two-sigma problem. In M. Bauer, P. J. Gmytrasiewicz, & Y. Vassileva (Eds.), *User modeling* (pp. 137–147). Berlin: Springer-Verlag.

Drucker, P. F. (1993). *Managing for results.* New York, NY: Harper Collins.

Fletcher, J. D. (1992). Individualized systems of instruction. In M. C. Alkin (Ed.), *Encyclopedia of educational research* (pp. 613–620). New York, NY: Macmillan.

————. (1997). What have we learned about computer based instruction in military training? In R. J. Seidel & P. R. Chatelier (Eds.), *Virtual reality, training's future?* (pp. 169–177). New York, NY: Plenum Publishing.

————. (2004). Technology, the Columbus effect, and the third revolution in learning. In M. Rabinowitz, F. C. Blumberg, & H. Everson (Eds.), *The design of instruction and evaluation: Affordances of using media and technology* (pp. 139–157). Mahwah, NJ: Lawrence Erlbaum Associates.

————. (2009a). From behaviorism to constructivism: A philosophical journey from drill and practice to situated learning. In S. Tobias & T. D. Duffy (Eds.), *Constructivist theory applied to education: Success or failure?* (pp. 242–263). New York: Taylor and Francis.

————. (2009b). Education and training technology in the military. *Science, 323,* 72–75.

Fletcher, J. D., & Chatelier, P. R. (2000). Military training. In S. Tobias & J. D. Fletcher (Eds.), *Training and retraining: A handbook for business, industry, government, and the military* (pp. 267–288). New York, NY: Macmillan.

Flin, R., O'Connor, P., & Crichton, M. (2008). *Safety at the sharp end.* Aldershot, UK: Ashgate.

Gorman, P. F. (1990). *The military value of training* (IDA Paper P-2515). Alexandria, VA: Institute for Defense Analyses (DTIC/NTIS No. ADA 232 460).

James, W. (1890/1950). *Principles of psychology: Volume I.* New York: Dover Press.

Kaufman, D. (2008). Private communication from Kaufman, the RealWorld program manager at DARPA, with Ralph Chatham December 12, 2008.

Kirkpatrick, D. L. (1987). Evaluation. In R. L. Craig (Ed.), *Training and development handbook* (pp. 301–319). New York, NY. McGraw-Hill.

Knaack, M. S. (1978). *Encyclopedia of US Air Force aircraft and missile systems: Volume 1 Post-World War II fighters 1945–1973*. Washington, D.C.: Office of Air Force History.

Knarr, W., & Richbourg, R. (2008). *Learning from the first victory of the 21st century: Mazar-e Sharif* (IDA Document D-3380). Alexandria, VA: Institute for Defense Analyses.

Levin, H. M., & McEwan, P. J. (2001). *Cost-effectiveness analysis*. Thousand Oaks, CA: Sage.

Loftus, E. F. (1996). *Eyewitness testimony*. Cambridge, MA: Harvard University Press.

Lunceford, D., & Kaufman, D. (2009). RealWorld paper.

March, J. G., Sproull, L. S., & Tomuz, M. (1991). Learning from samples of one or fewer. *Organization Science*, 2, 1–13.

Military Manpower Training Report. (2002). Washington, D.C.: Defense Manpower Data Center, U.S. Department of Defense.

Mishan, E. J., & Quah, E. (2007). *Cost-benefit analysis*. London: Routledge.

Morrison, J. E., & Meliza, L. L. (1999). *Foundations of the after action review process* (IDA Document D-2332). Alexandria, VA: Institute for Defense Analyses.

Muckler, F. A. (1959). Human factors research on weapon systems project teams. *Human Factors*, 1 (4), 28–31.

Murdock, H. C., Commander, United States Navy. (2008). F-18 fighter is IAF's best bet: US Navy, quoted in Express India May 09, 2008. Web reference: http://www.expressindia.com/latest-news/F18-fighter-is-IAFs-best-bet-US-Navy/307414/.

Neisser, U. (1967). *Cognitive psychology*. New York, NY: Appleton, Century, Crofts.

Nesselrode, M. C. (2007). *Determining the return on investment (ROI) for joint training*. Norfolk, VA: Virginia Modeling Analysis and Simulation Center, Old Dominion University (DTIC/NTIS No. ADA 488 217).

Office of the Under Secretary of Defense. (2009). *Department of Defense (DoD) military personnel composite standard pay and reimbursement rates*. Washington, D.C.: Office of the Under Secretary of Defense (Comptroller). Available from http://www.dod.mil/comptroller/rates.

Orlansky, J., & String, J. (1977). *Cost effectiveness of computer based instruction in military training* (IDA Paper P-1375). Arlington, VA: Institute for Defense Analyses.

Orlansky, J., & Thorpe, J. (Eds.). (1992). *73 Easting: Lessons learned from desert storm via advanced distributed simulation technology* (IDA Document D-1110). Alexandria, VA: Institute for Defense Analyses.

Phillips, J. J. (2003). *Return on investment in training and performance improvement programs*. Oxford, UK: Butterworth-Heinemann.

Pohlman, D. L., & Fletcher, J. D. (1999). Aviation personnel selection and training. In D. J. Garland, J. A. Wise, & V. D. Hopkin (Eds.), *Handbook of aviation human factors* (pp. 277–308). Boca Raton, FL: CRC Press.

Ross, J. A., Barkaoui, K., & Scott, G. (2007). Evaluations that consider the cost of educational programs. *American Journal of Evaluation*, 28, 477–492.

Sassone, P. G., & Schaffer, W. A. (1978). *Cost-benefit analysis: A handbook*. New York: Academic Press.

Taylor, J. C. (2000). *A new model for measuring return on investment (ROI) for safety programs in aviation: An example from airline maintenance resource management (MRM)*. Paper number 2001-01-90 presented at the Advances in Aviation Safety Conference, Daytona Beach, FL.

Technology for the United States Navy and Marine Corps, 2000–2035: (Vol. 4) Human Resources. (1997). Washington, D.C.: National Academy Press.

Thompson, M. S. (1980). *Benefit-cost analysis for program evaluation*. Beverly Hills, CA: Sage Publications.

Von Glaserfeld, E. (1989). Cognition, construction of knowledge, and teaching. *Synthese*, 801, 121–140.

Wulfeck, W. H., & Wetzel-Smith, S. K. (2008). Use of visualization techniques to improve high-stakes problem solving. In E. Baker, J. Dickieson, W. Wulfeck, & H. F. O'Neil (Eds.), *Assessment of problem solving using simulations* (pp. 223–238). Florence, KY: Taylor and Francis–Lawrence Erlbaum Associates.

———. (2010). Training incredibly complex tasks. In P. E. O'Connor & J. Cohn (Eds.), *Performance enhancement in high risk environments* (pp. 74–89). Westport, CT: Praeger.

Chapter 9

PHYSIOLOGICAL MEASURES OF VIRTUAL ENVIRONMENT TRAINING

Anna Skinner, Marc Sebrechts, Cali Fidopiastis, Chris Berka, Jack Vice, and Corinna Lathan

Virtual environments (VEs) and simulations are being employed for training applications in a wide variety of disciplines, both military and civilian. Technological advances are enhancing the ability of developers to create VEs with visual, auditory, haptic, and even olfactory realism. Such VEs enable training of skills that are too costly, too dangerous, or are otherwise impossible to practice. While significant research has been conducted examining the transfer of training from VEs to operational tasks, traditional methods of training evaluation are limited and objective metrics of transfer are needed. This chapter will provide an overview of the limitations related to training within high-risk environments, the benefits of VE-based training for such domains, and the current methods for assessing transfer of training from virtual to operational environments. Additionally, the use of physiological measures as assessment metrics, within the VE design cycle, and specifically for the determination of VE fidelity requirements will be examined.

TRAINING IN HIGH-RISK ENVIRONMENTS

By definition, training for high-risk environments is precarious and involves uncertainty. While many basic tasks typically performed in high-risk environments can initially be trained with very little risk involved (i.e., training a firefighter to carry a hose or training an infantry warfighter to dig a fighting position), such training is not comprehensive and does not prepare the trainee for the operational task. As training progresses to higher order tasks, even these basic skills must be executed in a high-risk setting (i.e., a burning building or battlefield with bullets flying overhead) in order to provide the trainee with operationally relevant experience. This presents significant safety, and thus logistics, challenges.

Military ground combat operations provide an example of extremely volatile, violent, and hazardous task conditions. Thus, realistic training for ground combat operations is inherently high risk. During live fire training for such tasks, many of the risks involve the violent nature of the tools being used. Ricocheting supersonic bullets, fragments from explosives, and blast cones of rockets and missiles are all extremely dangerous, even within a controlled environment. Additional examples of specific dangers associated with ground combat operations include operating large vehicles in close proximity to infantry personnel, negotiating hazardous obstacles, mountaineering, helicopter entry and exit, and exposure.

Within the military domain, the goal is for personnel to train as they fight; however, for ground combat operations, safety and training effectiveness are often in opposition. If the training is so safe that trainees are never injured, the training is likely ineffective and may result in increased injuries or casualties during actual operations. Alternatively, if the training environment is excessively hazardous, unacceptable injuries or fatalities may occur during training, and performance and learning may be negatively impacted. Finally, given the dangers of realistic training, significant logistical overhead exists for such training events. Even a small-scale live fire exercise requires extensive planning, preparation, and execution support due to the inherent safety concerns. Large-scale training exercises, such as the Marine Corps Mojave Viper pre-deployment training program, involve massive logistics and safety considerations.

BENEFITS OF VE TRAINING

Simulation refers to the substitution of real objects or tasks with a model or system representation. Historically, simulation-based training is substituted for real-world operational environments when the cost of training (e.g., large-scale war games) is exceedingly high or when the learning task may pose dangers to the trainee or others such as with surgical training (Stedmon & Stone, 2001). A three-dimensional (3D), interactive computer-generated VE permits errors and other behaviors such as exploration that occur naturally during the learning processes without risk of harm. The representation of 3D space is generally considered a hallmark of VEs (Wann, Rushton, & Mon-Williams, 1996), as are real-time interactivity (Stone, 2001) and the sense of presence (Riva, 2003; Slater & Wilbur, 1997).

The benefits of VEs have already been shown in several areas, most prominently in aviation, where the cost of mistakes can be enormous in terms of life and material. Flight simulations have proven sufficiently compelling to allow the use of simulator hours toward pilot certification. Training in virtual medical procedures provides another example of significant research; specific techniques can be learned without patient risk prior to medical personnel implementing those procedures under high-risk and time constraint conditions. At the same time, it may be precisely the stressful conditions that influence performance; thus, the ability to simulate those factors is another potential advantage of VEs.

Virtual or simulation-based training has many advantages in addition to increased safety and decreased costs. VEs can provide training in places with limited physical space and can be widely distributed, minimizing the need for significant travel. While infantry training has traditionally required soldiers or Marines go to a training site, portable VE systems, such as laptop-based systems, enable the training system to deploy with the unit and be used wherever the unit is stationed. One example is the Deployable Virtual Training Environment (DVTE), developed by the Office of Naval Research Virtual Training Environments (VIRTE) program. The DVTE is a laptop-based system designed to provide combined arms or joint forces Marine Corps training and sustainment, including Call For Fire (CFF) planning and execution.

Another primary advantage of VE-based training is the ability to vary the training parameters. For example, within the domain of ground combat training, environmental components such as weather conditions, terrain (i.e., mountainous, jungle, urban, and densely wooded), and lighting conditions can easily be adjusted. Additionally, altering any number of mission-specific details within the simulated environment can be used to generate a multitude of scenario variations, emphasizing a wide variety of skill sets and addressing multiple training objectives. VE training systems also provide the ability to train in environments not easily accessible. This includes training within various foreign cultures, as well as various types of cityscapes having distinct construction and architecture features, making up the battleground in an urban warfare scenario. Furthermore, VEs provide the ability to train in reproductions of actual places such as the "Green Zone" in Iraq, a specific U.S. embassy, or a specific objective building. Finally, simulation training enables a diversity of training within hazardous and inaccessible environments with minimal expense and logistical overhead. Thus, trainees can afford to rehearse scenarios that they may rarely experience, but that require sufficient training when encountered.

TRANSFER OF TRAINING FROM VES TO REAL-WORLD TASKS

Most explicit training occurs in a context other than the one in which performance is required. As a consequence, the utility of training depends on the extent to which there is *transfer* of what is learned in the training context to the performance context. VEs provide a promising context for such transfer of training, with potential benefits of increased safety, reduced cost, simpler distribution, and ease of modification of training materials.

Early transfer studies such as Williams and Flexman (1949) and Flexman, Roscoe, Williams, and Williges (1972) assessed measurement of pilot training transfer from simulators to aircraft. In recent years, transfer of training has been applied to both virtual and traditional training methodologies across a wide range of domains. The evaluation of training alternatives and their impact on transfer, however, remains complicated. There is no direct measure of transfer; it is measured indirectly by the relationship between training and performance. Kirkpatrick (1959) proposed a framework for evaluation consisting of four levels: reaction, learning, behavior, and results; measuring changes in behavior that occur as a result of training programs, the final results occurring as a result of training programs, comment sheets completed by participants at the end of training programs, and the learning that takes place in the classroom as measured by increased knowledge, improved skills, and changes in attitude. In the most common model, a variety of training situations are compared with a variety of performance outcomes (see NATO Advisory Group for Aerospace Research and Development, 1980). It is assumed that better performance reflects better training. However, this general comparative evaluation strategy is problematic due to the immense variety of possible training scenarios and the difficulty of testing them all.

To constrain the possible training scenarios, there are two prevalent approaches to improving and evaluating transfer. The training environment can be designed by matching the target performance task and environment, or it can be designed by decomposing the overall task into core components and logical structure. In either case, the most common evaluation metrics to date are: (1) measures of technical match of environments; and (2) behavioral measures. Each of these serves specific evaluation goals.

Match to Performance Environment

Given the assumption that training in the real-world performance environment is optimal, the goal of achieving the best transfer is satisfied by making the training context match the performance task as much as possible; the more the training environment matches the target environment, the better the transfer will be. This is commonly referred to as maximizing *fidelity*. Fidelity is defined as the degree to which features (e.g., visual and auditory) in the VE match features in the real environment. This approach is supported by a view that transfer occurs when two contexts share "identical elements." That view, proposed by Thorndike (1906), has had some support from psychological studies. Individuals who were presented with a multipronged attack strategy for a military operation, for example, were unable to recognize its applicability to a similar medical context that required a multipronged use of radiation (Gick & Holyoak, 1980). The extent of this specificity of encoding (Tulving, 1983) was highlighted by a study in which an individual was trained for 200 hours and expanded his short-term recall from 7 or 8 digits to 81 digits, but showed no memory span increase for letters (Chase & Ericsson, 1982). Consider how the technical, psycho-behavioral, and physiological measures function in this model of transfer.

Visual fidelity, which is critical for the majority of VE training systems, consists of a number of components, including frame rate, resolution, polygon count, texture mapping, contrast, lighting effects, color depth, and physics. Chalmers, Cater, and Maffioli (2003) found that viewers completing a visual task did not notice a quality difference in images, some of which cost much less than others. Another approach is to degrade fidelity components that do not directly relate to performance of the targeted task. A study conducted by O'Sullivan, Howlett, McDonnell, Morvan, and O'Conor (2004) suggested that people do not notice a difference in high- and low-resolution images when not performing a task related to the images. In this study, only 20 percent noticed a difference in resolution in this condition, compared to 80 percent that noticed a difference while performing a task relating to the images; low-resolution objects were characterized as looking the same as high-resolution objects in the former condition. Thus, minimum fidelity requirements exist for tasks involving visual discrimination of images. In such instances, Wickens and Hollands (1999) assert that the degree of training stimuli variability should be equivalent to the degree of actual instance variability within the real-world task.

Technical developments of a VE provide a straightforward way to evaluate simulated environments. As the rate of rendering fidelity components such as polygon count increases, the visual appearance of the VE is more like that of real environments. As the frame rate increases concurrently, the change of scenes more closely resembles that of real environments. Some aspects of VE fidelity such as movement within the environment are more difficult to increase than others. While the ability to walk as though in a larger environment is increased by VE locomotion devices such as omnidirectional treadmills or VirtuSpheres, movements remain limited and may result in negative transfer. Users must adapt to walking in a moving platform, having limited visual feedback, and integrating motion cues with physical responses (Medina, Fruland, & Weghorst, 2008). Additionally, maneuvers commonly used in the targeted operational environments, such as walking fast and turning, have been shown to be difficult within such locomotion systems (Darken, Cockayne, & Carmein, 1997). Less obtrusive head-mounted displays, the presence of a Cave Automatic Virtual Environment (CAVE), or greater degrees of freedom in visual updates may increase the similarity to unencumbered movement; however, such improvements are often costly. Similarly, interfaces for virtual tools such as weapons and optics may result in negative transfer if they behave differently (better or worse) than in the real-world environment. For example, if virtual thermal imaging devices do not display changes in effectiveness for scenarios with varied ambient temperature conditions, negative transfer is likely to occur.

Despite significant advances, the technical specifications of VEs continue to fall short of the reality and promise to do so for some time to come. Stoffregen, Bardy, Smart, and Pagulayan (2003) even make a reasonable case for the argument that simulations can never achieve identity with reality. Thus, it is often argued that the adequacy of specific technical developments is relevant only insofar as they are reflected in psychological and behavioral measure of sensory-perceptual, cognitive-emotional, and motor response. In psychological terms, this is a matter of "affordances" (Gibson, 1979), the range of possible human interaction that is made possible by the environment. This approach asks about the environment properties in terms of behavioral consequences, determined in a variety of self-reports and specific behavioral assessments. To what extent does the environment foster a sense of presence? How similar are VE-based movement patterns to those found in a physical space? Are judgments of object distance the same in a virtual and real environment? Is it easier or more difficult to distinguish hostile from friendly combatants?

Core Components and Logical Structure

A second approach to transfer evaluation is to identify the core components that facilitate transfer. This approach finds support in the argument that not everything is essential to transfer. One does not need identical elements, but common logical structure (Singley & Anderson, 1989). Dennis and Harris (1998) and Koonce and Bramble (1998) have reported positive transfer between low-fidelity PC-based training devices and aircraft. Among others, Salas, Bowers, and Rhodenizer (1998) have investigated problems relating to determining how much simulator complexity is required for training and identified a number of assumptions relating to overreliance on high-fidelity simulation. Specifically, cognitive fidelity, a measure of the similarity between the mental processes required to complete the virtual and real-world tasks, has been identified as critical for effective skill transfer.

The utility of matching as a model of transfer depends on the training objective. If one were training for only one specific real-world event, then virtual replication of that specific context would be optimal. However, the ability to exactly capture a real environment is limited at best. Furthermore, it is rare to train for just one circumstance. Few sailors will work on only one specific ship; few soldiers will drive an armored vehicle through only one specific type of terrain; and even when a specific performance context is anticipated, it is important to be prepared for changes in conditions between training and performance. In all of these cases, exact replication of one specific environment would introduce a number of variables that may be task irrelevant. Given these constraints, a focus on fidelity to a particular real-world context can be problematic. In a fixed training environment, there is a risk of learning a specific solution that depends on the particular contingencies in that environment. Such "mechanization" of a solution (the Einstellung effect; Luchins, 1942) can lead to misuse of one strategy even when another simpler option is presented.

Within this transfer framework, VEs offer an especially apt context for training transfer by allowing isolation of key components, thereby avoiding potential attention allocation to irrelevant details, which may distract from the core task during the learning phase. Emphasis on minimal core tasks during training has been shown to minimize error and lead to better long-term performance (Carroll & Rosson, 1984). Similar benefits can be achieved by training on part of a task, while complementing that training with virtual fill-in of the rest of the task (Wightman & Lintern, 1985).

Thus, transfer of training must be evaluated in a way that allows appropriate decomposition of the tasks while capturing core components. In this case, however, the application of fidelity to transfer has somewhat different constraints. Technical matching is still important, but primarily for components that are otherwise identified as relevant for the logical structure of the task. Behavioral comparisons can help to isolate the relevant features, although that approach tends to have a rather long time lag, and can depend to varying degrees on subjectivity or bias in recollection. Thus, additional, objective metrics of transfer are needed.

PHYSIOLOGICAL MEASURES AS ASSESSMENT METRICS

Accelerated development and application of complex simulation-based training environments is escalating the need for evaluation methodologies that are more sensitive than behavioral comparisons, expert observations, or subjective reports obtained from users. As a result, significant advances are being made in the capability to objectively assess operator cognitive state changes in real time through the use of a variety of physiological sensors and computational metrics.

Advances in computational processing and miniaturization of electronics now support real-time acquisition in operational environments of the electrocardiogram or ECG (heart rate and heart rate variability [HRV]), galvanic skin response (GSR), electromyogram or EMG (muscle activity), electrooculogram or EOG (eye movements and eye blinks), eye tracking (eye gaze and pupillometry), respiration, oximetry (oxygen levels in the blood), and brain activity with the electroencephalogram (EEG) or functional near infrared (fNIR) imaging. These biological signals have been employed alone or in combination to detect cognitive state changes (Berka et al., 2004, 2005a; Gevins, Smith, McEvoy, & Yu, 1997; Gevins et al., 1998; Kramer & Parasuraman, 2005; Kramer, Trejo, & Humphrey, 1996; Russell & Wilson, 2006; Scerbo, Freeman, & Mikulka, 2001). Functional magnetic resonance imaging (fMRI), which measures the hemodynamic response related to neural activity, and positron emission tomography (PET), a nuclear imaging technique which produces a 3D image of functional processes in the body, provide valuable metrics, particularly for spatial localization of brain activity; however, fMRI and PET apparatus tend to be large, expensive, and restrictive in terms of tasks that can be performed during imaging due to movement and electromagnetic restrictions. Table 9.1, which expands upon a summary provided by Andreassi (2006), presents a breakdown of some of the more common physiological indices and methods of assessment.

A number of studies have revealed a direct link between user state (Rowe, Sibert, & Irwin, 1998), specifically mental effort, and HRV (Aasman, Mulder, & Mulder, 1987) as well as arousal. Nonspecific and specific event-related GSR peaks and spikes may also provide a reliable measure of peripheral arousal (Boucsein, 1992). Additionally, due to the fact that GSR measurements are easy to perform, it is one of the few parameters that have been measured in physically demanding settings (Matthews, McDonald, & Trejo, 2005). EMG can provide evidence of specific muscle activation during a movement task or can provide nonspecific indication of increasing stress or frustration (Tassinary & Cacioppo, 2000). Skin conductance is related to sweat gland activity and has long been used to indicate stress levels (Dawson et al., 2000; Iacono, 2007). It is relatively slow to change, highly nonspecific, and does not relate to any specific emotional response.

Eye tracking devices monitor cognitive state by assessing pupil reflexes that occur when an individual experiences effortful cognitive processing. The pupils dilate when an individual engages in different types of cognitive acts such as reading text, listening to instructions, searching a display, or interpreting a graph. Thus, changes in pupil diameter can be used to assess

Table 9.1. Common Physiological Measures by Nervous System Branch

Autonomic nervous system	Central nervous system	Somatic nervous system
Heart rate (ECG, HRV, BVP)	EEG (electroencephalogram)	EMG (electromyogram)
Blood pressure	ERP (event-related potential)	EOG (electrooculogram)
Pulse oximetry	fNIR (functional near infrared)	
Respiration	fMRI (functional magnetic resonance imaging)	
Electrodermal activity (GSR)	PET (positron emission tomography)	
Pupil response (eye tracking)		

cognitive workload and decision making (Einhäuser, Stout, Koch, & Carter, 2008). Eye tracking can also be used to determine the pattern of search within a visual search task rather than simply determining if a target object is found, providing a measure, not only of outcome, but also of efficiency in performing the task.

ERPs can assist in the identification of attention allocation by measuring changes in specific brain potentials rather than having to use a verbal protocol in which individuals report what they notice. Identifying attention allocation during training is especially important in light of our understanding of encoding specificity (Tulving, 1983), the finding that the learning depends on what is noticed at the time that learning takes place. In addition, physiological measures provide information in real time and capture characteristics that may influence performance even without subjective awareness.

In addition to ongoing fluctuation in the EEG signals, when the EEG analysis is synchronized to the introduction of specific stimuli or responses, ERPs can be derived. ERPs offer excellent temporal resolution and tracking of neural activity representing the flow of information from sensory processing and analysis to initiation of a response. Event-related EEG signals have been linked to the processing of visual, auditory, olfactory, and tactile inputs as well as to the preparation for or anticipation of a motor activity (Fabiani, Gratton, & Federmeier, 2007). In addition, a variety of cognitive events have been linked to specific neural signatures in the EEG, including the identification of a target, the recognition of events previously encoded, and surprise at the introduction of a highly novel stimulus (Polich & Comerchero, 2003) or at a semantically incongruent word at the completion of a sentence (Hald, Bastiaansen, & Hagoort, 2006). Past research also indicates the feasibility of using EEG/ERP to differentiate between correct responses (i.e., hits and correct rejections) and highly biased responses (e.g., false alarms and misses), thus supporting the potential for using neurotechnology for characterizing accuracy of decision making within the simulation environment.

As an alternative to examining the ERPs within the raw EEG signal, it is often useful to obtain the event-specific signatures using mean power spectra time-locked to the stimulus, response, or other event of interest (termed "PERPs," power event-related potentials). To calculate the PERPs, the EEG is segmented into windows. The EEG analysis window is then positioned over either a specific stimulus presentation event or a response event to calculate the EEG power associated with processing of a stimulus or with generation of a response. The EEG signal can also be decomposed using a wavelets transformation and the wavelets coefficients can also be used to characterize event-related EEG features (Murata, 2005).

Event-related theta as detected in the PERP can be useful in monitoring the encoding of new items in learning and memory tests and in characterizing the processing of sentences (Bastiaansen, van der Linden, ter Keurs, Dijkstra, & Hagoort, 2005) and chemistry sequences. Increased event-related theta has been suggested as evidence of accurate encoding as well as showing the build up of a mental model during sentence processing and comprehension (Bastiaansen et al., 2005). These data suggest the viability of using the neural signatures to establish whether specific material has been correctly encoded or whether repetition of specified items is required to ensure learning is complete within a training environment.

The advent of wireless, easily applied EEG systems holds great promise for evaluations in the simulation environment. The EEG has been shown to accurately reflect subtle shifts in alertness, attention and workload that can be identified and quantified on a second-by-second time frame. Significant correlations between EEG indices of cognitive state changes and performance have been reported based on studies conducted in laboratory and simulation and operational environments (Berka et al., 2004, 2005b; Gevins et al., 1997; Gevins et al., 1998; Kramer & Parasuraman, 2005; Kramer, Trejo, & Humphrey, 1996; Russell & Wilson, 2006; Scerbo, Freeman, & Mikulka, 2001). Real-time classifiers have proven useful in quantifying drowsiness-alertness, mental workload, and spatial and verbal processing in simple and complex tasks, as well as characterizing alertness and memory in patients with sleep and neurological disorders and identifying individual differences in susceptibility to the effects of sleep deprivation (Berka et al., 2004, 2005c, 2005d, 2005e, 2006, 2007; Mitler et al., 2002; Westbrook et al., 2004).

Scientists and researchers have been collecting physiological measures in a variety of virtual and operational (real-world) environments at an increasing rate. Healey and Picard (2004) conducted a study in which drivers' stress levels were recorded using ECG, EMG, skin conductance, and respiration measures as drivers followed a set route. Backs, Lenneman, and Sicard (1999) have also conducted work examining heart period changes between low- and high-workload flight tasks to determine which physiological measures of cardiovascular activity are most related to changes in pilot performance. In the air traffic environment, Ahlstrom and Friedman-Berg (2006) recorded eye movement activity for air traffic controllers during simulation to predict cognitive workload levels. These studies speak not only to the ability to reliably collect such data in real-world environments but also to the feasibility within simulated environments.

Physiological sensors have also proven useful in gauging situational awareness (SA) in both individuals and teams (Berka et al., 2006; Pancerella et al., 2003; also see Chapter 15 of this book for a discussion), which is imperative within high-risk environments such as ground combat operations. Pancerella reported on an adaptive awareness and decision making using an agent-based infrastructure that monitored heat flux, skin temperature, GSR, and heart rate and the environment to direct personal and small group awareness and decision making. Doser (2003) reported that real-time physiological SA evaluation in a team environment, using ECG, electromyograph (EMG), GSR, respirometer, and pulse oximeter, provided information that characterized emergent and desirable group behavior and improved task performance. Specifically, events of interest (e.g., cooperation, conflict, and leadership), when time synchronized and compared to heart rate data, showed evidence of group cooperation (Doser et al., 2003). Real-world studies such as this can help simulation designers determine which physiological measures are best correlated between simulated and real-world environments to maximize the likelihood of transfer of training and aid in determining simulation acquisition decisions.

USE OF PHYSIOLOGICAL MEASURES WITHIN THE VE DESIGN CYCLE

While traditional measures of virtual training environment effectiveness and transfer are useful and provide a measure of face validity, there is a concern that the measures can be subjective and that self-reports often depend on recollection and reconstruction. Additionally, there is no guarantee that these subjective measures are directly related to behavior or transfer of training. In fact, there is a history of empirical evidence supporting the disassociation between subjective and behavioral measures. Vidulich and Wickens (1983), as well as Vidulich and Bortolussi (1988), demonstrated this disassociation with respect to workload measures. These findings do not discount the use of subjective measures, but rather highlight the importance of using multiple measures for obtaining convergent validity.

A newer and more compelling approach is to examine the extent to which physiological measures for an individual are similar across real and simulated environments. Puinetti, Meehan, and Mendozzi (2001) published a review of physiological correlates of virtual reality indicating that physiological signals could be used, among other applications, "to develop more effective virtual environments" and "to study the effect of varying system parameters on physiological reaction evoked." Rather than asking trainees to rate their presence or stress, researchers can use psychophysiological metrics to identify whether specific scenarios are provoking a similar physiological response to that evoked under real-world conditions. While significant research has been conducted examining the transfer of training from VEs (e.g., Lathan, Tracey, Sebrechts, Clawson, & Higgins, 2002; Sebrechts, Lathan, Clawson, Miller, & Trepagnier, 2003), only a limited number of efforts have used physiologically based measures to do so. For example, Meehan, Insko, Whitton, & Brooks (2001) and Dussault, Jouanin, Philippe, and Guezennec (2005) demonstrated HRV and EEG-derived metrics to be more sensitive than most of the self-reported measures for characterizing operator workload and task engagement, and as such are excellent candidates for assessing presence in VEs.

The advent of wireless, unobtrusive psychophysiological sensors and their respective software analysis tools offers developers and evaluators of simulated environments the opportunity to monitor users while they perform operational tasks and thus provide objective measures of the effectiveness of the interface and the impact of the design on the user's attention, workload, and task engagement. Moreover, physiological sensors have utility for assessing some of the more challenging experiential aspects of the VE, including the importance of fidelity, the amount of "presence" evoked in users, and the positive transfer between a training system and real-world operations. Issues such as fidelity are typically challenged during the initial stages of the VE design cycle, yet it took the sensor technology advances of the last decade to formally consider psychophysiological measures as a part of this process. In preliminary investigations, physiological responses have been suggested as reliable, valid, sensitive, and objective measures across simulation platforms.

VE design must consider a number of critical issues. Users' opinions of the design as well as their input on the usability of the VE setup become essential to ensuring effective learning outcomes. As such, the International Standard ISO 13407, the Human-Centered Design Processes for Interactive Systems, was issued in 1999 to provide guidelines for including the user in the iterative loop of the design and implementation cycle (Earthy, Sherwood-Jones, & Bevan, 2001). Of primary importance in this design scheme is delineating the functional relationship between the user and the technology whereby assessing the understandability, learnability, and operability of the system from the users' perspective naturally contributes to effectiveness, safety, and satisfaction of the interactive training environment (Stedmon & Stone, 2001).

The importance of creating international standards speaks to the diverse fields employing virtual technologies and thus assures that commercial as well as academic institutions are abiding by specific rules and including similar design features. For example, VE-based trainers for medical and military applications involving healthy persons have been successfully designed using the ISO 13407 framework (Stedmon & Stone, 2001; Riva, 2003). However, usability is not the only criteria important for determining fundamental components of the VE system such as the level of presence, generally defined here as the subjective experience of being in the VE training scenario rather than the physical setup of equipment required by such trainers (Slater, 1999; Witmer & Singer, 1998). Further, the standard is not specific as to the measures necessary to fulfill the recommendations, thus leading to a level of subjectivity that may hinder cross-validation of similar VE design efforts.

Recognizing the limitation of the ISO guidelines and the growing human factors concerns identified by expanded VE technology use, the European Information Society Technologies (IST) initiative tackled these issues in a project entitled Virtual and Interactive Environments for Workplaces of the Future, VIEW of the Future (Wilson & D'Cruz, 2006). One result of this European collaborative effort was an extended usability test battery (UTB) manual that included traditional usability testing (e.g., cognitive walkthrough; Bowman, Gabbard, & Hix, 2002) and newer methods derived from psychophysiological measures (e.g., heart rate; Mager et al., 2003).

VIEW researchers identified several physiological measures that could potentially determine user internal factors such as mental and physical work-load, cybersickness, emotion, arousal, and attention. These measures included eye tracking (point of gaze and eye blinks), electrodermal activity (skin conductance responses), HRV (inter-beat heart rate interval), and EEG wave patterns (e.g., alpha and beta waves). However, as discussed by Karaseitanidis et al. (2006), confounding variables such as mood are difficult to distinguish from the construct being measured; psychophysiological sensors generate an enormous amount of data and necessitate the development of better acquisition systems; and environmental issues such as a change in temperature affect internal states being measured. These drawbacks hamper the capability to dissociate among problematic system issues, individual differences, and data collection methods. More importantly, these concerns need solutions if psychophysiological measures are to extend to real-world operational environments.

In some cases, physiological assessment has been used to drive closed-loop systems. Assessment needs of such VE systems parallel those of biocybernetic or adaptive systems where changes in automation or learning material are triggered through the use of psychophysiological measures (Vartak, Fidopiastis, Nicholson, Mikhael, & Schmorrow, 2008). For example, the National Aeronautics and Space Administration (NASA) has conducted research using physiological measures for the application of adaptive automation for pilots. This research also has been extended to include the measurement of ERPs (Prinzel, Pope, Freeman, Scerbo, & Mikulka, 2001). Adaptive systems foundationally require the added constraint of real-time analysis of psychophysiological data (Fairclough & Venables, 2006). This constraint necessitates a system architecture designed to synchronize, log, feature detect, error correct, and "fuse" multiple data streams of psychophysiological data (Kemper, Davis, Fidopiastis, & Nicholson, 2008).

While data aspects are not the only obstacles facing psychophysiology-based usability, data strategies elucidated for adaptive system design may provide the framework to overcome some of the major difficulties facing VE system design. The resulting capabilities may assist in fulfilling the promise of these objective measures and fully exploit their capability of providing reliable, valid, sensitive, and objective measures across simulation platforms.

USE OF PHYSIOLOGICAL MEASURES TO DETERMINE FIDELITY REQUIREMENTS FOR VIRTUAL TRAINING ENVIRONMENTS

Based on the "Match to Performance Environment" approach to improving and evaluating transfer, one can argue that a VE with maximum fidelity would result in transfer of training equivalent to real-world training given that the two environments would be impossible to differentiate (Waller, Hunt, & Knapp, 1998). However, developers are limited by practical restrictions such as cost, time, and development resources. Furthermore, as previously noted, some researchers hold that exact replication of the real world is unattainable through a VE (Stoffregen et al., 2003). Thus, trade-offs are necessary. There is currently a limited understanding of the specific trade-offs between increases in simulation fidelity and operator behavior, and essentially no guarantee to developers that a particular level/area of simulation fidelity is sufficient to provide effective transfer of training. There is also evidence to suggest that very specific changes in VE fidelity components may be required to elicit changes in operator behavior. For example, Bürki-Cohen et al. (2003) reported that while an initial study of the potential benefits of adding motion to flight simulators had no effect with respect to pilot training and evaluation, a subsequent study reported that if the motion was of a particular type (i.e., enhanced hexapod motion), motion benefits were found.

Meehan, Razzaque, Insko, Whitton, and Brooks (2005) hypothesized that a VE experience that is perceived as similar to the real world (i.e., high fidelity) will evoke similar physiological responses in both contexts. Given that VE fidelity is a primary contributor to transfer of training within operational tasks, Vice, Lathan, Lockerd, and Hitt (2007) proposed a novel approach to determining fidelity requirements for simulation design using physiologically based measures. The premise of this hypothesis is that a physiologically based system capable of dynamically detecting changes in operator behavior and physiology throughout a VE experience and comparing those changes to operator behavior and physiology in real-world tasks could potentially determine which aspects of VE fidelity will have the highest impact on transfer of training. While many transfer of training approaches focus on maximizing effectiveness based on the ability to elicit desired behaviors from operators during simulations, this approach hypothesizes that transfer of training will be maximized and VE fidelity requirements will be best determined by matching an operator's physiological responses in the simulated environment with those collected in the real-world environment.

Physiological measurement provides several significant advantages over other measurement methods (e.g., subjective or behavioral) in determining VE fidelity requirements for effective skill transfer. Physiological data can be collected continuously with large sample sizes and can be monitored continuously and examined for dynamic changes against a baseline or other criterion data. Additionally, it is more difficult to "fake" physiological data; participants can deceive subjective measures and can alter behavior for performance measures or alter responses to self-report metrics; however, physiological responses are extremely difficult to control. In addition to assessing technical similarities between VE and real-world tasks, physiological measures have especially high potential in the logical structure approach to VE transfer of training. They provide an objective means to compare aspects of virtual training and real-world performance environments. As variations are imposed on the VE, physiological measures can provide direct comparisons of an individual's response. In addition, it is possible to "read" responses in real time concurrently with variation in task characteristics, thereby avoiding potential contamination by interpretation or delayed recollection. Of course, these evaluations need to be combined with relevant changes in the technical specifications for the environment and with behavioral measures of performance. Finally, it is worth noting that in the limit case, a number of VE tasks become the performance domain, as more and more operations and vehicles become computer-controlled. In those cases, physiological measures of the VE interaction provide direct performance information.

Research and development is currently being conducted by the Office of Naval Research (ONR) Human Performance, Training, and Education (HPTE) research division to validate this approach and apply it to military virtual training systems. Key to this research is identifying which training effects can be accomplished using low-fidelity simulation and which high-fidelity components provide the greatest impact on transfer to real-world tasks, specifically visual perceptual skills tasks. Thus, the development costs associated with a uniformly high-fidelity simulator can be avoided.

SUMMARY

Virtual training environments provide a means for developing and practicing skills required for operational tasks in high-risk environments such as medical, aviation, and military operations. Traditional methods for assessing positive transfer of skills from virtual to real-world environments are limited and often involve subjective measures. Meanwhile, the use of physiological measures in understanding human behavior has made significant progressions during the last few decades. The ability to collect multiple sources of physiological data, advances in computing power, decreases in apparatus physical size, and the ability to couple human physiology with behavior and cognitive functioning all contribute to these advances. Given the limitations of traditional training evaluation metrics, physiologically based approaches have been proposed. Preliminary research utilizing physiological measures as objective metrics for transfer of training evaluation and VE design guidance has demonstrated promise and warrants further investigation.

REFERENCES

Aasman, J., Mulder, G., & Mulder, L. J. M. (1987). Operator effort and the measurement of heart-rate variability. *Human Factors*, 29 (2), 161–170.

Ahlstrom, U., & Friedman-Berg, F. J. (2006). Using eye movement activity as a correlate of cognitive workload. *International Journal of Industrial Ergonomics*, 36 (7), 623–636.

Andreassi, J. L. (2006). *Psychophysiology: Human behavior & physiological response*. Hillsdale, NJ: Lawrence Erlbaum Associates.

Backs, R. W., Lenneman, J. K., & Sicard, J. L. (1999). The use of autonomic components to improve cardiovascular assessment of mental workload in flight simulation. *International Journal of Aviation Psychology*, 9, 33–47.

Bastiaansen, M., van der Linden, M., ter Keurs, M., Dijkstra, T., & Hagoort, P. (2005). Theta Responses are involved in lexical-semantic retrieval during language processing. *Journal of Cognitive Neuroscience*, 17 (3), 530–541.

Berka, C., et al. (2004). Real-time analysis of EEG indices of alertness, cognition, and memory acquired with a wireless EEG headset. *International Journal of Human-Computer Interaction*, 17 (2), 151–170.

Berka, C., Levendowski, D., Davis, G., Lumicao, M., Ramsey, C., Stanney, K., et al. (2005a). *EEG indices distinguish spatial and verbal working memory processing: Implications for real-time monitoring in a closed-loop tactical tomahawk weapons simulation*. Paper presented at the First International Conference on Augmented Cognition, Las Vegas, NV.

Berka, C., Levendowski, D., Ramsey, C. K., Davis, G., Lumicao, M., Stanney, K., et al. (2005b). Evaluation of an EEG-workload model in an aegis simulation environment. In J. A. Caldwell & N. J. Wesensten (Eds.), *Proceedings of SPIE Defense and Security Symposium, Biomonitoring for Physiological and Cognitive Performance during Military Operations* (vol. 5797, pp. 90–99). Orlando, FL: SPIE, The International Society for Optical Engineering.

Berka, C., Levendowski, D., Westbrook, P., Davis, G., Lumicao, M., Olmstead, R., et al. (2005c). EEG quantification of alertness: Methods for early identification of individuals most susceptible to sleep deprivation. In J. A. Caldwell & N. J. Wesensten (Eds.), *Proceedings of SPIE Defense and Security Symposium, Biomonitoring for Physiological and Cognitive Performance during Military Operations* (vol. 5797, pp. 78–89). Orlando, FL: SPIE, The International Society for Optical Engineering.

Berka, C., Levendowski, D., Westbrook, P., Davis, G., Lumicao, M., Ramsey, C., et al. (2005d). *Implementation of a closed-loop real-time EEG-based drowsiness detection system: Effects of feedback alarms on performance in a driving simulator*. Paper presented at the First International Conference on Augmented Cognition, Las Vegas, NV.

Berka, C., Westbrook, P., Levendowski, D., Lumicao, M., Ramsey, C. K., Zavora, T., et al. (2005e). *Implementation model for identifying and treating obstructive sleep apnea in commercial drivers*. Paper presented at the International Conference on Fatigue Management in Transportation Operations, Seattle, WA.

Berka, C., Levendowski, D., Davis, G., Whitmoyer, M., Hale, K., & Fuchs, S. (2006). Objective measures of situational awareness using neurophysiology technology. In D. Schmorrow, K. Stanney, & L. Reeves (Eds.), *Augmented cognition: Past, present and future* (pp. 145–154). Arlington, VA: Strategic Analysis, Inc.

Berka, C., Davis, G., Johnson, R., Levendowski, D., Whitmoyer, M., Fatch, R., et al. (2007). Psychophysiological profiles of sleep deprivation and stress during marine corps training. *Sleep*, 30, A132.

Boucsein, W. (1992). *Electrodermal activity*. Plenum Press: New York.

Bowman, D. A., Gabbard, J. L., & Hix, D. (2002). A survey of usability evaluation in virtual environments: Classification and comparison of methods. *Presence*, 11 (4), 404–424.

Bürki-Cohen, J., Go, T. H., Chung, W. W., Schroeder, J., Jacobs, S., & Longridge, T. (2003). Simulator fidelity requirements for airline pilot training and evaluation continued: An update on motion requirements research. *Proceedings of the 12th International Symposium on Aviation Psychology.*

Carroll, J. M., & Rosson, M. B. (1984). Minimalist training. *Datamation*, 30, 125–126.

Chalmers, A., Cater, C., & Maffioli, D. (2003). Visual attention models for producing high fidelity efficiently. *Spring conference on computer graphics* (pp. 39–45). New York: ACM.

Chase, W. G., & Ericsson, K. A. (1982). Skill and working memory. In G. H. Bower (Ed.), *The psychology of learning and motivation* (pp. 1–58). New York: Academic Press.

Darken, R. P., Cockayne, W. R., & Carmein, D. (1997). The omni-directional tread-mill: A locomotion device for virtual worlds. In *Proceedings of UIST 1997*, pp. 213–221.

Dawson, M. E., Schell, A. M., & Filion, D. L. (2000). The electrodermal system. In J. T. Cacioppo, L. G. Tassinary, & G. G. Nernston (Eds.), *Handbook of psychophysiology* (pp. 200–223). New York, NY: Cambridge University Press.

Dennis, K. A., & Harris, D. (1998). Computer-based simulation as adjunct to an intro to flight training. *International Journal of Aviation Psychology*, 8 (3), 261–276.

Doser, A. B., Merkle, P. B., Johnson, C., Jones, W., Warner, D., & Murphy, T. (2003). *Enabling technology for human collaboration* (No. SAND 2003-4225). Sandia National Laboratories.

Dussault, C., Jouanin, J., Philippe, M., & Guezennec, C. (2005). EEG and ECG changes during simulator operation reflect mental workload and vigilance. *Aviation Space and Environmental Medicine*, 76 (4), 344–351.

Earthy, J., Sherwood-Jones, B., & Bevan, N. (2001). The improvement of human-centred processes—facing the challenge and reaping the benefits of ISO 13407. *International Journal of Human Computer Studies*, 55, 553–585.

Einhäuser, W., Stout, J., Koch, C., & Carter, O. (2008). Pupil dilation reflects perceptual selection and predicts subsequent stability in perceptual rivalry. *Proceedings of the National Academy of Sciences of the United States of America*, 105, 1704–1709.

Fabiani, M., Gratton, G., & Federmeier, K. D. (2007). Event-related brain potentials: Methods, theory, and applications. In J. T. Cacioppo, L. G. Tassinary, & G. G. Berntson (Eds.), *Handbook of psychophysiology* (pp. 85–119). New York: Cambridge University Press.

Fairclough, S. H., & Venables, L. (2006). Prediction of subjective states from psycho-physiology: A multivariate approach. *Biological psychology*, 71, 100–110.

Flexman, R. E., Roscoe, S. N., Williams, A. C., Jr., & Williges, B. H. (1972). *Studies in pilot training* (Aviation Res. Monographs, vol. 2, #1). Savoy, IL: University of Illinois, Institute of Aviation.

Gevins, A., Smith, M. E., Leong, H., McEvoy, L., Whitfield, S., Du, R., et al. (1998). Monitoring working memory load during computer-based tasks with EEG pattern recognition methods. *Human Factors*, 40 (1), 79–91.

Gevins, A., Smith, M. E., McEvoy, L., & Yu, D. (1997). High-resolution EEG mapping of cortical activation related to working memory: Effects of task difficulty, type of processing, and practice. *Cerebral Cortex*, 7 (4), 374–385.

Gibson, J. J. (1979). *The ecological approach to visual perception*. Boston: Houghton Mifflin.

Gick, M. L., & Holyoak, K. J. (1980). Analogical problem solving. *Cognitive Psychology*, 12, 306–355.

Hald, L. A., Bastiaansen, M. C. M., & Hagoort, P. (2006). EEG theta and gamma responses to semantic violations in online sentence processing. *Brain and Language*, 96, 90–105.

Healey, J. A., & Picard, R. W. (2004). *Detecting stress during real-world driving tasks using physiological sensors*. Cambridge Research Laboratory, HPL-2004-229. HP Laboratories, Cambridge, MA.

Iacono, W. G. (2007). Detection of deception. In J. T. Cacioppo, L. G. Tassinary, & G. G. Berntson (Eds.), *Handbook of psychophysiology* (pp. 688–703). New York: Cambridge University Press.

Karaseitanidis, I., Amditis, A., Patel, H., Sharples, S., Bekiaris, E., Bullinger, A., & Tromp, J. (2006). Evaluation of virtual reality products and applications from individual, organizational and societal perspectives. *Human-Computer Studies*, 64, 251–266.

Kemper, D., Davis, L., Fidopiastis, C. M., & Nicholson, D. M. (2008). A first step towards a generalized psychophysiological measurement framework. In the *Proceedings of Human Factors and Ergonomics Society 52nd Annual Meeting*, 615–618.

Kirkpatrick, D. L. (1959). Techniques for evaluating training programs. *Journal of the American Society of Training and Development*, 13, 3–9.

Koonce, J. M., & Bramble, W. J., Jr. (1998). Personal computer-based flight training devices. *International Journal of Aviation Psychology*, 8 (3), 277–292.

Kramer, A., & Parasuraman, R. (2005). Neuroergonomics: Application of neuroscience to human factors. In J. T. Cacioppo, L. G. Tassinary, & G. G. Berntson (Eds.), *Handbook of psychophysiology*. New York: Cambridge University Press.

Kramer, H. C., Trejo, L. J., & Humphrey, D. G. (1996). *Psychophysiological measures of workload: Potential applications to adaptively automated systems*. New Jersey: Lawrence Erlbaum Associates.

Lathan, C. E., Tracey, M. R., Sebrechts, M. M., Clawson, D. M., & Higgins, G. (2002). Using virtual environments as training simulators: Measuring transfer. In K. Stanney (Ed.) *Handbook of virtual environments: Design, implementation, and applications* (pp. 403–414). Mahwah, NJ: Lawrence Erlbaum Associates.

Luchins, A. (1942). Mechanization in problem solving: The effect of einstellung. *Psychological Monographs*, 248, 54–56.

Mager, R., Stoermer, R., Schaerli, H., Estoppey, K. H., Bullinger, A. H., Patel, H., Stedmon, A., Nichols, S. C., & D'Cruz, M. (2003). *Usability test-battery manual. Deliverable for the European Commission, IST Project VIEW of the Future, IST-2000-26089*. Retrieved May 15, 2006 from http://www.view.iao.fraunhofer.de/pdf/D3_2.pdf.

Matthews, R., McDonald, N. J., & Trejo, L. J. (2005). Sensor techniques: An overview. *Proceedings of the 2005 HCI International Conference*, Las Vegas.

Medina, E., Fruland, R., & Weghorst, S. (2008). VIRTUSPHERE: Walking in a human size VR "hamster ball." In *Proceedings of the Human Factors and Ergonomics Society 52nd Annual Meeting* (pp. 2102–2106). New York, NY: HFES.

Meehan, M., Insko, B., Whitton, M., & Brooks, F. P. (2001). Physiological measures of presence in virtual environments. *Proceedings of 4th International Workshop on Presence* (pp. 21–23). Philadelphia, PA.

Meehan, M., Razzaque, S., Insko, B., Whitton, M., & Brooks, F. P., Jr. (2005). Review of four studies on the use of physiological reaction as a measure of presence in stressful virtual environments. *Applied Psychophysiology and Biofeedback*, 30.

Mitler, M. M., et al. (2002). Validation of automated EEG quantification of alertness: Methods for early identification of individuals most susceptible to sleep deprivation. *Sleep*, 25, A147–A148.

Murata, A. (2005). An attempt to evaluate mental workload using wavelet transform of EEG. *Human Factors*, 47 (3), 498–508.

NATO Advisory Group for Aerospace Research and Development. (1980). *Fidelity of simulation for pilot training*. Brussels, Belgium: NATO.

O'Sullivan, C., Howlett, S., McDonnell, R., Morvan, Y., & O'Conor, K. (2004). Perceptually adaptive graphics. *Eurographics*, 141–164.

Pancerella, C. M., Tucker, S., Doser, A. B., Kyker, R., Perano, K. J., & Berry, N. M. (2003). *Adaptive awareness for personal and small group decision making*. Albuquerque. NM: Sandia National Laboratories.

Polich, J., & Comerchero, M. D. (2003). P3a from visual stimuli: Typicality, task and topography. *Brain Topography*, 15, 141–152.

Prinzel, L. J., Pope, A. T., Freeman, F. G., Scerbo, M. W., & Mikulka, P. J. (2001). *Empirical analysis of EEG and ERPs for psychophysical adaptive task allocation* (Technical Report No. TM-2001-211016). Langley, VA: NASA.

Puinetti, L., Meehan, M., & Mendozzi, L. (2001). Psychophysiological correlates of virtual reality: A review. *Presence*, 10, 384–400.

Riva, G. (2003). Applications of virtual environments in medicine. *Methods of Information in Medicine*, 42, 524–534.

Rowe, D. W., Sibert, J., & Irwin, D. (1998). Heart rate variability: Indicator of user state as an aid to human-computer interaction. In *Proceedings of CHI-98: Human Factors in Computing Systems* (pp. 480–487). New York: ACM Press.

Russell, C., & Wilson, G. F. (2006). Operator functional state classification in uncertainty. In D. D. Schmorrow, K. M. Stanney, L. M. Reeves (Eds.), *Foundations of augmented cognition* (pp. 19–26). Arlington, VA: Strategic Analysis, Inc.

Salas, E., Bowers, C. A., & Rhodenizer, L. (1998). It is not how much you have but how you use it: Toward a rational use of simulation to support aviation training. *International Journal of Aviation Psychology*, 8 (3), 197–208.

Scerbo, M. W., Freeman, F. G., & Mikulka, P. J. (2001). *The efficacy of psychophysiological measures for implementing adaptive technology* (TP-2001-211018). Hampton, VA: NASA.

Sebrechts, M. M., Lathan, C. E., Clawson, D. M., Miller, M. S., & Trepagnier, C. (2003). Transfer of training in virtual environments: Issues for human performance. In L. J. Hettinger & M. W. Haas (Eds.), *Virtual and adaptive environments: Applications, implications, and human performance issues* (pp. 67–90).

Mahwah, NJ: Lawrence Erlbaum Associates.

Singley, M. K., & Anderson, J. R. (1989). *Transfer of cognitive skill.* Cambridge, MA: Harvard University Press.

Slater, M. (1999). Measuring presence: A response to Witmer and Singer presence questionnaire. *Presence: Teleoperators and Virtual Environments,* 8 (5), 560–565.

Slater, M., & Wilbur, S. (1997). A framework for immersive virtual environments (FIVE): Speculations on the role of presence in virtual environments. *Presence: Teleoperators and Virtual Environments,* 6, 603–616.

Stedmon, A. W., & Stone, R. J. (2001). Re-viewing reality: Human factors of synthetic training environments. *International Journal of Human-Computer Studies,* 55, 675–698.

Stoffregen, T. A., Bardy, B. G., Smart, L. J., & Pagulayan, R. J. (2003). On the nature and evaluation of fidelity in virtual environments. In L. J. Hettinger & M. W. Haas (Eds.), *Virtual and adaptive environments: Applications, implications, and human performance issues* (pp. 111–128). Mahwah, NJ: Erlbaum.

Stone, R. J. (2001). Virtual reality for interactive training: An industrial practitioner's viewpoint. *International Journal of Human-Computer Studies,* 55, 611–699.

Tassinary, L. G., & Cacioppo, J. T. (2000). The skeletomuscular system: Surface electromyography. In J. T. Cacioppo, L. G. Tassinary, & G. G. Berntson (Eds.), *Handbook of psychophysiology* (pp. 163–199). New York: Cambridge University Press.

Thorndike, E. L. (1906). *Principles of teaching.* New York: A. G. Seller.

Tulving, E. (1983). *Elements of episodic memory.* New York: Oxford University Press.

Vartak, A. A., Fidopiastis, C. M., Nicholson, D. M., Mikhael, W. B., & Schmorrow, D. (2008). Cognitive state estimation for adaptive learning systems using wearable physiological sensors. *Biosignals,* 2, 147–152.

Vice, J. M., Lathan, C., Lockerd, A. D., & Hitt II, J. M. (2007). Simulation fidelity design informed by physiologically-based measurement tools. *Proceedings the Human Computer Interaction International Conference.*

Vidulich, M. A., & Bortolussi, M. R. (1988). A dissociation of objective and subjective workload measures in assessing the impact of speech controls in advanced helicopters. In *Proceedings of the Human Factors Society 32nd Annual Meeting* (pp. 1471–1475).

Vidulich, M., & Wickens, C. (1983). *Processing phenomena and the dissociation between subjective and objective workload measures* (Tech Report EPL-83-2/0NH-83-2). University of Illinois Engineering Psychology Laboratory.

Waller, D., Hunt, E., & Knapp, D. (1998). The transfer of spatial knowledge in virtual environment training. *Presence: Teleoperators and Virtual Environments,* 7, 129–143.

Wann, J. P., Rushton, S., & Mon-Williams, M. (1996). What does virtual reality NEED?: Human factors issues in the design of three-dimensional computer environments. *International Journal of Human-Computer Studies,* 44, 829–847.

Westbrook, P., Berka, C., Levendowski, D., Lumicao, M., Davis, G., Olmstead, R., et al. (2004). Quantification of alertness, memory and neurophysiological changes in sleep apnea patients following treatment with nCPAP. *Sleep,* 27, A223.

Wickens, C. D., & Hollands, J. G. (1999). *Engineering psychology and human performance*. Upper Saddle River, NJ: Prentice Hall.

Wightman, D. C., & Lintern, G. (1985). Part-task training for tracking and manual control. *Human Factors*, 27, 267–283.

Williams, A. C., & Flexman, R. E. (1949). *An evaluation of the Link SNJ operational training as an aid in contact flight training*. Port Washington, NY: Office of Naval Research, Special Devices Center.

Wilson, J., & D'Cruz, M. (2006). Virtual and interactive environments for work of the future. *International Journal of Human-Computer Studies*, 64, 158–169.

Witmer, B. G., & Singer, M. J. (1998). Measuring presence in virtual environments: A presence questionnaire. *Presence: Teleoperators and Virtual Environments*, 7 (3), 225–240.

Part IV: Safety

Chapter 10

MILITARY AVIATION SAFETY POLICY AND MANAGING THE CULTURE OF RISK

Andrew Bellenkes

> After the ship has sunk, everyone knows how she might have been saved.
> —Italian proverb

> The fault, dear Brutus, is not in our stars, but in ourselves.
> —W. Shakespeare, *Julius Caesar* (I, ii, 140–141)

Safety policy is "written in blood." This is an "old saw" among some safety professionals asserting that safety doctrine and policies often come about as post hoc responses to an event (or series of events) in which injuries or loss of life may have been a tragic result. Whatever their origins, flight safety policies have been designed ostensibly to minimize the hazards and risks associated with flight operations. As human performance plays a central role in these operations, it comes as no surprise that a number of safety policies focus on aircraft system operators and maintainers. The foundations upon which these policies have evolved are not all new; indeed, the origins of a great deal of this work stems from the earliest days of human flight. Many of the tenets upon which these policies have been based are couched in terms of risk analysis and management—a process called Operational Risk Management (ORM). ORM is a means of providing individuals with an approach to identifying, assessing, and controlling risk, thereby facilitating the decision-making process in high-risk environments (Bellenkes, 2000a). In this way, the effective use of ORM can minimize risks to acceptable levels by systematically applying controls to each unacceptable risk. While certain aspects of military operations differ little from that of commercial and general aviation counterparts, the unique nature of many of its varied operational requirements dictates the need for specialized doctrine, especially one grounded in risk analysis associated with human performance capabilities and limitations. Thus, while employing ORM may prove efficacious in any high-risk environment, the use of this process of risk assessment and management is particularly important to military aviation.

When one considers the tragedy associated with the loss of life, it is of little solace to note that, despite the nature and scope of missions flown, military aviation mishaps occur with remarkable infrequency. Still, with every mishap investigation, a host of lessons learned are added to the cumulative portfolio of preemptive measures to be taken in order to prevent such a mishap from ever happening again. Sadly, despite the best efforts of safety professionals and their commanders, the lessons learned tome continues to grow, lives and aircraft are lost, and unit operational readiness may be placed in jeopardy. This notion suggests a propensity to "respond" rather than "prevent"; to react quickly and decisively to analyze and understand what has already transpired to prevent it from happening again. It is in this desire to be proactive that we create standards and programs that, if enforced, are meant to ensure that operations can indeed be carried out as safely and effectively as possible.

The ORM process enables mission planners to assess risk based on identified hazards associated with a mission, personnel, material, and operational factors with a probability assessment of the impacts of these hazards (Bellenkes, 2000b). As such employing ORM processes not only facilitates the making of informed decisions but also provides mission planners with the ability to implement controls designed to bring risk levels down to acceptable levels (VanVactor, 2007). It provides a means for mission planners and commanders to assess how mission-related decisions can be carried out in such a manner so as to maximize readiness while minimizing *unnecessary* risk to aircrews and support personnel (Bellenkes, 2000b, 2002).

First developed for use by industry, ORM has also found its way into military standard operating procedures and its principles have become an important part of warfighting doctrine. There are a large number of organizational risks inherent to training for and conducting military operations; many are specific to the nature and mission of the particular unit in question. These hazards could range from those that could physically endanger individuals and/or small groups of personnel to those safety and non-safety variables that could impact the success of a mission or even the outcome of an entire campaign.

As per OPNAVINST 3500.39 (U.S. Dept. of the Navy, 2004a), "Operational Risk Management is an effective tool for maintaining readiness in peacetime and success in combat without infringing upon the prerogatives of the Commander . . . It provides a means to help define risk and control it where possible, thereby assisting the Commander in choosing the best course of action and seize opportunities which lead to victory."

Based on the understanding that risk exists and as such must be managed, the basic tenets of ORM can be couched in four primary principles (U.S. Dept. of the Navy, 2004a, 2004b):

a. *Accept no unnecessary risk.* It is not always prudent to carry out an activity or mission when doing so entails unnecessary risk. ORM provides a means to identify and facilitate the avoidance of such "unnecessary" risks associated with a particular task, activity, or operation.

b. *Make risk decisions at the appropriate level.* The decision to carry out a task or mission where risk may be involved should be made by those directly accountable and responsible for the activity. It should also be the activity/mission leadership's responsibility to inform subordinates as to the level of risk acceptable in their efforts, and, if necessary, to raise the decision-making authority to a higher level in their chain of command.

c. *Accept the risk when the benefits outweigh the costs.* It may be decided that although there is some (even high) level of risk, an operation should nevertheless be conducted, the results outweighing the possible costs due to risk. ORM provides a means to identify and manage these risk(s).

d. *Anticipate and manage risk by planning.* Risk can be better anticipated and, if not precluded, controlled by instituting ORM processes at the onset of mission planning. Doing so may reduce costs and enhance ORM's overall effectiveness.

To best understand how ORM can be applied to the unique missions associated with military air operations, it is first necessary to briefly review the means to identify and control for organic (internal) and extrinsic (external) hazards. The following section therefore briefly describes the five primary steps involved in the ORM process.

THE FIVE STEPS IN THE ORM PROCESS

Figure 10.1 illustrates the five-step ORM process. It begins with the identification of hazards, after which these hazards are assessed for the probability and extent to which they may impact operations. If the risk of such impacts is great, then mission planners must create and then implement defenses (controls) that, whether through doctrine, design, or changes to operations throughout the hierarchy of a command, will minimize if not negate the impacts of these hazards. Finally, all parts of this process are monitored (supervised). This is especially critical with regard to the supervision of controls; if they do not provide the required defense against a given hazard, then it may become necessary to modify existing controls or institute new controls. It should be noted that this process is cyclic; that is, a continuous, ongoing set of activities designed to be carried out prior to the start of a mission, operation, or activity. This proactive approach to employing the five-step process is most critical for minimizing potential risk.

Identifying Hazards

The first step in the ORM process is to identify the often numerous hazards facing an aircrew, organization, or system. They manifest themselves as actual, perceived, or potential conditions (VanVactor, 2007) and can appear in a plethora of forms at all levels of the command hierarchy (Reason, 1990, 1997). In the aviation environment, hazards normally can be generically

Figure 10.1.   The Risk Management paradigm. Mission planners must supervise each of the steps in the ORM process. Adapted from Bellenkes (2004a).

defined as any weapon, system, procedure, or policy that, by either use, inappropriate use, or lack of use, could lead to (a) injury or harm, (b) property damage, and/or (c) mission/performance degradation.

There exist a number of tools designed to facilitate the identification of hazards derived both from sources outside (external) and from within (internal) a system or organization. These tools include the use of unrestrictive association and hypothesis generation ("Brainstorming" and "What If" analyses) and the generation of visual guides (flow charts, "Cause-Effect" and "Affinity" diagrams; Bellenkes, 2004a). However, there are other existing processes that can be adapted as tools to facilitate hazard identification. Two of these are the Critical Mission Task Analysis (CMTA) and the use of human system integration (HSI) domains as frameworks within the context of which hazards might be classified.

Critical Mission Task Analysis (CMTA)

One especially effective tool that can be used to identify hazards is what we can call a CMTA; a modified form of Critical Task Analysis (CTA) methodology. CTA has been successfully employed in system design and evaluation (Kirwan & Ainsworth, 1992) to identify human factors-related issues that have the potential to negatively impact human-system performance. This is done by breaking down into sometimes minute detail all of the actions being carried out by the components (including human) and subcomponents of a system in order to perform a specific action or task. The CMTA would similarly employ a "parsing" approach; breaking down a mission into its components and assessing risk in each separately. By parsing apart the various elements or phases of a given mission and then assessing each separately for hazards, it may be possible to more effectively identify hazards. Doing so may, in turn, provide data for the creation of means to minimize or negate the impacts these hazards could have on operational readiness and mission success.

Application of Human-System Integration Domains to the CMTA

As noted, the CMTA explores hazards originating from both within and without an organization. One way to facilitate this process is by defining the relationships between those personnel carrying out a task or mission and the systems in which they operate. An excellent foundation for this pursuit can be found in the domains that define HSI. For the purposes of the current discussion, one need only refer to the HSI domains as a means of categorizing possible hazards (Bellenkes, 2004b; Booher, 2003). These domains include:

Human Factors Engineering

As per U.S. Department of Defense instruction (U.S. Dept. of Defense, 2003), the requirements of system users and maintainers to perceive, interpret, and respond to vast amounts of data have led designers to incorporate technologies designed to ensure enhanced system performance while decreasing user workloads. Too often, however, designers have created these systems despite rather than as a function of user performance limits and capabilities. The result has been an unfortunate paradox; the higher the state of technology employed, the greater the user workload. Flight station design sometimes ignores sound ergonomic principles in order to integrate newer automated systems. An excellent example can be seen in the use of multifunction displays that require substantial "heads down" time in order for pilots to navigate through cumbersome software tableaus when they should be scanning instruments. Switches are still designed and located so as to permit inadvertent or incorrect activation. Workload is increased, performance is degraded, and sometimes deadly mishaps occur. Such design hazards could put a mission at risk and as such must be identified and controlled for prior to the start of a mission.

Today, much of the data concerning the effectiveness of ORM in a human factors engineering context has been manifested into defense-wide system safety-based doctrine. The latter is most clearly defined in MIL-STD 882 (U.S. Dept. of Defense, 2000), Standard Practice for System Safety; a document outlining the process of establishing and monitoring a hazard identification program covering every activity of the design and acquisition processes during the entire life cycle of a system (Kritzinger, 2006).

Manpower

Unit manpower requirements are based on the nature of the current types of missions to be performed and the numbers of aircrews, ground crews, maintainers, and support personnel it will take to carry out these missions. A manpower-related hazard would be identified if there were not sufficient personnel on hand to carry out a mission. For example, towing an aircraft with fewer than required "wing walkers" (ground support personnel who ensure sufficient clearance between the aircraft they are monitoring and nearby aircraft, objects, and structures) out of a hangar may possibly result in one of the wings striking maintenance support gear, resulting in damage severe enough to prevent the aircraft from being able to carry out its mission.

Manpower and Personnel

Manpower defines the "scope" of forces available to fly and maintain an aircraft and its ancillary systems. *Personnel*, on the other hand, is a variable that examines the "nature" of those individuals available and/or required. This is accomplished by defining the human performance characteristics of the user population. Most important in determining personnel is a description of the aviation system in question, the projected characteristics of target occupational specialties (those whose special skills may be required), and the recruitment and retention trends. These latter factors are critical, for the success of a system may depend on the selective recruitment and retention of certain warfare specialties.

All aviation-based weapon systems (including robotic and other unmanned devices) require humans to operate, maintain, and otherwise support them. Thus, Manpower and Personnel are very critical elements in the hazard identification process. Without the effective number and types of personnel, the chance for hazards existing and not being identified increase, and with that the risk of a mission not carried out successfully. The use of ORM, however, provides mission planners with the means to identify and assess the severity of these hazards. They are then better able to weigh the costs and benefits of carrying out the mission even when the numbers and types of personnel on hand may not be optimal.

Training

Without an effective training program, the risk for aircrew and ground crew and maintainer-related hazards increases manifold. The nature and scope of training is based both on system complexity and the form of training provided. In this regard, training-based hazards can originate in any of the other HSI domains. Most important of all considerations is whether the information provided by a training program can successfully transfer to actual performance of the task(s) at hand. There are a host of factors that can affect transfer of training. These include the:

- skill and personality of the instructor,
- setting in which training occurs,
- validity of the training process for a specific system,
- type of skills required for a given task or set of tasks, and
- fidelity of the simulator or other training aids (i.e., how realistic is the simulated task, scenario, or environment when compared with the actual task and performance environment).

Personnel Survivability

One of the primary goals of risk management is to optimize operational capability and readiness by managing natural and man-made hazards in such a way as to accomplish the mission with minimal loss. In this regard the domain of personnel survivability can be defined as "system design features that reduce the risk of fratricide, detection, and the probability of being attacked; and that enable the crew to withstand man-made hostile environments without aborting the mission or suffering acute chronic illness, disability, or death" (Defense Acquisition University, DAU Guidebook, 2009, p. 6.2.6.1).

In terms of aviation risk management, personnel survivability entails the use of administrative, doctrinal, and material means to control and reduce hazards encountered by those who fly, maintain, and support unit activities. Examples of this include (a) the employment of systems that assist crews in the avoidance of detection; (b) the use of communications or material schemes to preclude the possibility of fratricide (such as friend or foe technologies), and the provision of aviation crews and ground personnel with training and material means for use as protection against weapons and other man-made (chemical, biological, radiological, nuclear, and explosive) hazards having the potential to debilitate, cause injury, or result in death; and (c) ensuring that maintenance activities are accomplished in environments located in environments and/or designed in such a manner so as to make personnel less vulnerable to enemy fire. Clearly, hazards associated in this domain, if unchecked, would certainly have the potential to increase the risk of injury or death.

Safety and Occupational Health

There may exist hazards in the natural or man-made environment that could impact the safety and health of those carrying out a mission. Working in extreme or unhealthy environmental conditions or with unsafe equipment, for example, could result in injuries or loss of life. The resulting loss of personnel could impair unit operational readiness. It is critical, therefore, that conditions resulting in safety and health hazards be proactively detected and mitigated (U.S. Dept. of the Navy, 1997). ORM provides the means to "identify and minimize (the) impact of health hazards associated with the operation/maintenance of a system" (U.S. Dept. of Defense, 2003).

Assess Hazard Risk(s)

After the hazards have been identified, the unit mission-planners must then determine the level of risk associated with each hazard, particularly with regard to both the severity of consequences resulting from exposure to the hazard and the probability that a loss will occur should an event take place.

Severity

There are four subjective classes of hazard severity (Bellenkes, 2004a):

- *Catastrophic*—may result in loss of personnel (death) and/or loss or grave damage to facilities and resources;
- *Critical*—may result in severe injury or severe illness or major damage and/or severe degradation in the effective use of facilities, resources, and related assets;
- *Marginal*—may cause minor injury, minor illness, or minor damage and/or minor degradation in the effective use of facilities, resources, and assets; and
- *Negligible*—a disruptive hazard, but one that would not cause illness or physical damage, and minimal degradation to the effective use of assets. This data is then used to determine the relative "priority" that a given hazard should have during planning.

Probability

The probability of a hazard having impact can vary as a function of a host of environmental and human factors variables and is described in terms of its likelihood of occurring over a given period of time (Bellenkes, 2004a).

- *Imminent*—will occur frequently and within a very short period of time,
- *Likely*—expected to occur a few times and very soon,
- *Probable*—may occur once and soon, and
- *Unlikely*—low probability that hazard will occur.

A matrix such as that described by Bellenkes (2004a) is then created to illustrate the relationships between hazard severity and probability (Table 10.1). These relationships are defined by the assignment of Risk Assessment Codes (RAC; Decker, 2001a, 2001b) to each severity–probability pairing. The RAC provides a means for mission planners to then identify which hazards may pose higher risk than others.

In assessing risks, the ORM process not only describes the hazard(s) but also provides a foundation for the steps that follow whereby "controls" designed to mitigate the effects of hazards can be identified and employed.

Table 10.1. ORM Hazard Matrix

Threat severity	Event probability			
I	1	1	2	3
II	1	2	3	4
III	2	3	4	5
IV	3	4	5	5

Adapted from Bellenkes (2004a).

Make Hazard (Risk) Control Decisions

In addition to identifying risks unique to a particular mission, unit mission-planners must also be able to develop control options designed to best mitigate risk. A control is any type of defense that eliminates hazards or reduces the risk of hazards impacting performance (Reason, 1997).

Controls come in three primary forms: (a) Engineering controls—Controls that reduce risks by the engineering of system design, (b) Administrative controls—Controls that reduce risks through specific administrative actions, and (when appropriate) (c) Protective controls—The use of protective equipment and systems that would create barriers between personnel and the hazard(s) at hand. Engineering and Administrative controls are preventive controls, designed to reduce the probability of exposure to a hazard. Protective controls would be implemented should exposure to a hazard actually occur, and would be designed to reduce hazard severity (Bellenkes, 2004a).

Mission planners employ controls aimed at the root causes (rather than the symptoms) of the hazards identified and are guided in control implementation by the priorities illustrated in the matrix described above.

What follows is a list of general measures that can be used as a basis for the identification and assessment of specific controls designed to reduce/eliminate risk. They have been adapted from a list by Reason (1997) who looked at the types of measures associated with "error management." These measures include:

- minimizing liability (individual or group) associated with hazard identification;
- reducing "risk vulnerability" of tasks or their elements;
- discovering, assessing, and then eliminating hazards;
- diagnosing organizational factors (institutional hazards) that can lead to increased risk;
- enhancing hazard detection;
- increasing tolerance of certain amounts of risk;
- making latent conditions (those hazards that may or may not directly contribute to risk) visible to mission planners; and
- improving an organization's intrinsic resistance to human fallibility.

In order to make effective control decisions, mission planners must first start with the most serious risk and select controls that will reduce the probability of event-related losses occurrence or the severity of loss should the event nevertheless occur. Once these controls have been selected, the planner is then able to balance the costs and benefits of using a particular control. Should the costs associated with a certain control outweigh its benefits, then the control is eliminated and another decided upon to be set in place.

Implement Hazard (Risk) Controls

Once the control or set of controls have been chosen, they must then be implemented and monitored for their effect(s) against the hazard(s). Effective and enduring application of controls to a given hazard may require that mission planners (a) make the case for implementation clear, (b) establish a chain of accountability in the use of said control, and (c) ensure that as long as the control is "in place," it will receive full support from all levels of authority.

Supervise-Monitor the Effect(s) of Control Implementation

Mission planners must then ensure that controls are effective and in place and be aware of any changes to hazard priorities and probabilities (as described earlier) that may necessitate performing the entire five-step process again. This could result in the reevaluation of the original control decisions that, in turn, could lead to the addition, withdrawal, or alteration of controls already in place. Indeed, if the result of this reevaluation is that controls are not effective, or if changes to the nature and scope of hazards become apparent, it will be necessary to repeat the entire five-step ORM process, looking for new hazards.

Although it is the final step in the ORM process, supervision is not relegated just to the monitoring of controls. Rather, each of the steps in ORM must be supervised by a credible, knowledgeable authority of the ORM process. As can be seen in Figure 10.1, supervisory oversight is recommended at all steps, from hazard (risk) identification through the implementation of controls. The authority who oversees the process may or may not be the same authority that monitors the controls.

In summary, ORM is a five-step process whereby hazards are identified, assessed for level of risk, and then controls are chosen, implemented, and their effects monitored for a reduction of risk to acceptable operational levels. It must be noted at this juncture that the ability to process through these five steps can be impacted by how much time is available to complete the process. These "temporal constraints" can, in certain circumstances, place considerable pressure on mission planners, the results of which can impact mission success. Indeed, under certain conditions, it may become necessary for mission planners to perform ORM within a very limited period of time (time-critical ORM). They would have to make immediate decisions (short-fuse planning) based on a cursory version of the process during the execution phase of operations/training and for crisis response planning. This type of ORM can also be referred to as "intuitive ORM," for it often involves exploiting experience, weighing real-time risks, and executing immediate control decisions (Bellenkes, 2004a).

Still, under other circumstances where time is not so constrained, planners may have fewer temporal constraints within which to carry out all the five steps (deliberate ORM). As with time-critical ORM, deliberate ORM requires a good understanding of the issues based on experience.

Finally, if time is not a constraint, and missions are being planned far ahead of their start dates, then planners may have the luxury of performing slow, methodical risk analyses, a process known as in-depth ORM. There has been a change of plans; your squadron is not due to deploy for 15 months. Now you and your mission planners have even more time to perform an ORM analysis. In this case, you will probably elect to carry out an "in-depth" ORM analysis. As with time-critical and deliberate ORM, in-depth ORM uses the five steps described earlier. However, as more time is available for planning, in-depth ORM stresses the first two steps of the process; that is, mission planners spend a greater amount of time researching possible hazards for their severity and probability of occurring. Further, a more in-depth analysis of target vulnerabilities can be made using the results of tools such as scenario modeling, testing, research, and intelligence data (Bellenkes, 2004a).

To this point, we have discussed the nature of ORM and the process by which it is employed to reduce risk. After describing how ORM has been used by industry and other nonmilitary applications, we will briefly turn to how the tenets of ORM have been (and continue to be) employed in military aviation operations and safety.

Nonmilitary ORM Applications

First developed for use in the insurance industry (Bogardus & Moore, 2007), risk assessment and management (later, ORM) has since been employed in a plethora of government and industry safety programs, including those for finance and budgeting (U.S. Government Accounting Office, 2005), building and highway design and construction (Zurich Services Corporation, 2009), food security (U.S. Food and Drug Administration, 2001), chemical safety (Embry, Kontogiannis, & Green, 1994), and, more recently, homeland security, civilian emergency preparedness, and response to weapons of mass destruction (Bellenkes, 2004a; Moser, Whilte, Lewis-Younger, & Garrett, 2001; U.S. Government Accounting Office, 2007, 2008). ORM has also played a critical role in the process of system design (Swallom, Lindberg, & Smith-Jackson, 2003).

ORM has also found applications in civilian air and space flight (Brooker, 2007; U.S. Dept. of Transportation, Federal Aviation Administration, 2000, 2005). For example, the Federal Aviation Agency (FAA) has long recognized the importance of managing risk in commercial flight through training geared specifically toward effective and timely decision-making (Ashley, 1999). The FAA has therefore inculcated ORM into its operations policies and procedures (U.S. Dept. of Transportation, Federal Aviation Administration, 2000) whereby all Federal Aviation Administration personnel are empowered to play a role in critical decision-making. The same ORM training has been extended to general (civil) aviation aircrews as part of what the FAA calls the "3-P's": Perceive hazards, Process to evaluate the level of risk, and Perform risk management (U.S. Dept. of Transportation, Federal Aviation Administration, 2005).

Similarly, the National Aeronautics and Space Administration (NASA) has employed what they refer to as Integrated Risk Management (IRM) processes to facilitate risk-informed management decision-making for aeronautical and space operations (Stamatelatos, 2008). Using IRM principles, NASA leadership continues to conduct research designed to identify and control risks anticipated during manned and unmanned operations (NASA, 2009). The tenets of ORM have also been formally documented and disseminated throughout NASA as an agency-wide instruction (NASA, 2008).

Risk Management in U.S. Military Aviation Operations

For the U.S. military, the concept of ORM is best defined as "the competent and effective application of principles to preserve the combat power of your forces for use against the enemy, rather than the squandering of your soldiers against useless accident statistics" (Burke, 1999). Although not referred to as such, variants of risk management have been employed throughout the history of warfare (Tanner, 1997). Since the integration of ORM processes into warfighting practice, it has been observed to facilitate operational performance and safety in combat (U.S. Dept. of the Navy, 2002a, 2002b; U.S. Dept. of the Army, 2003), in joint service mission planning (LaTrash, 1999), and with issues associated with homeland security, specifically in the protection against and response to chemical and biological weapons hazards (Bellenkes, 2004a; Lunch, 2002; Rose, 1989). The Defense Science Board Task Force on Aviation Safety recommended that ORM be instituted as part of U.S. Department of Defense-wide aviation safety practice (U.S. Dept. of Defense, 1997).

U.S. Army

The U.S. Army first recognized the need to create a means to evaluate and control risk during their reviews of battlefield "accidents" (hereafter referred to as "mishaps")—those mishaps with little or no direct relation to combat. Such mishaps could impact field operations and, in doing so, hurt operational readiness. During World War II, the application of a risk management process was employed by the Army in support of its airlift operations in the South Pacific (VanVactor, 2007). It was only some years later, in the late 1980s, that the Army began to require that ORM processes become part of the operational culture of both its ground and air assets. The Army did report a drop in Class A mishaps (those involving death and/or material losses of $1 million or greater) subsequent to the implementation of their ORM program, but there has been some question as to whether or not this mishap rate fell as a function of ORM being employed (Ashley, 1999).

It has since become a deliberate means for commanders of all Army activities to mitigate risks in the various hazard-rich mission types (such as aviation), in essence, becoming a central part of the military decision-making process impacting all levels and phases of decision making, training, personnel assignments, ground, aviation, workplace, and maintenance activities (Rains, 2008; U.S. Dept. of the Army, 1998). The Army formally incorporated the tenets of ORM into its flight safety program and ORM is routinely employed as a doctrinal requirement (U.S. Dept. of the Army, 1997a, 1997b). It has successfully integrated risk management into flight mission planning, preparation, and execution ensuring that the appropriate decision makers accept no unnecessary risk (VanVactor, 2007). The Army has also incorporated ORM into the command and control of unmanned vehicles (U.S. Dept. of the Army, 1999); such practices are critical as the use of such devices has substantially increased in recent years.

U.S. Navy and Marine Corps

It was not long after the Army first employed ORM to facilitate operational readiness that the other armed services likewise found that the processes and practices associated with ORM could be applied to their operational cultures. In 1997, the Chief of Naval Operations and Commandant of the United States Marine Corps first promulgated Department of the Navy, OPNAVINST 3500.39 and Marine Corps Order 3500.27, respectively (U.S. Dept. of the Navy, 1997), in order to introduce ORM and standardize ORM-related practices throughout the fleet. The Navy and Marine Corps specifically wanted all of their officers, enlisted personnel, and civilians to be thoroughly couched in the theory and practice of ORM and, as such, be able to recognize and mitigate risk on a daily basis both on and off duty and at all levels within individual commands. It was stressed that sailors and marines would face that "uncertainty" and risk daily as a part of all their activities, and as such, must be considered when planning for operations rather than in response to mishaps. Later revisions of these instructions (U.S. Dept. of the Navy, 2004b) emphasized the necessity for both the Navy and the Marine Corps to provide comprehensive ORM throughout all facets of general and warfare specialty training syllabi.

ORM training was subsequently provided throughout the fleet, a task facilitated by the creation of a very successful "Train the Trainer" program. Unit Naval Safety Officers began to create and implement their own local ORM training programs. It soon became apparent, however, that a standardized ORM curriculum would be necessary to ensure fleet-wide common practice.

In 2000 as a response to this need, the Naval Postgraduate School's School of Aviation Safety incorporated ORM into their syllabi of their Naval Aviation Safety Officer (ASOs) and senior officer Command courses. As such, the ASOs were then able to take the fundamentals of ORM, teach them to their aircrews and ground crews, implement local ORM-based safety policies, and institute ORM practices into preflight mission planning; all of this under the cognizance and with the support of senior squadron/wing leadership (Executive and Commanding Officers).

At the same time, specialists in Naval Aerospace Medicine (serving both Navy and Marine Corps aviation units) developed a strategic goal to ensure that all of their Flight Surgeons, Aerospace Physiologists, and Aerospace Experimental Psychologists would receive standardized training in ORM (Bellenkes, 2000b). To accomplish this, a team of representatives from each of the naval aeromedical specialty areas developed a standardized one-day "ORM for Docs" course. The program included an intensive survey of ORM with emphasis placed on those issues and areas specific to aeromedicine. "Field Classes" were taught by a specialized instruction team of ORM subject matter experts. Classes were administered to aeromedical specialists already assigned to operational Navy and Marine fleet units, training facilities, clinics, and other activities to which aviation Medical and Medical Service Corps personnel had been assigned. These classes were taught to members of Student Flight Surgeon and Aerospace Residency classes.

U.S. Air Force

The U.S. Air Force began to inculcate ORM into its operational culture in 1996, and it was considered fully implemented two years later (Cho, 2002). ORM directives on how to carry out unit-level ORM processes were subsequently promulgated via "AFP 91-214, Operational Risk Management Implementation and Execution" (U.S. Dept. of the Air Force, 1997). Air Force leadership has since endeavored to ensure that ORM would be a part of the changing culture toward improved safety, to be used on a daily basis as a part of "doing business." As a result, ORM has become an operational imperative—a central part of the training and education continuum at all levels of enlisted and officer corps throughout the Air Force. In flight operations, it has since been employed as a standardized set of preflight briefing points and as a means to ensure increased safety during particularly hazardous operational evolutions (Hunt, 2002).

In 2006, the Air Force Air Mobility Command (AMC) along with the Air National Guard and Reserve endeavored to create a "single-standard end-to-end aviation ORM program" (Hale, 2007). The rationale behind the creation of such a standard ORM program for aviation was that doing so required the use of a "common language"—a common frame of operational reference among and between all air command flight personnel. This program was found to be quite successful in the Tanker Airlift Control Community (TACC) and has since begun to be promulgated throughout the Air Force's various tactical, strategic, and support squadrons.

U.S. Coast Guard

The U.S. Coast Guard likewise employs risk-based decision making methodologies with ORM in all their daily operations (U.S. Dept. of Homeland Security, U.S. Coast Guard, 1999, 2008), but in a slightly modified form incorporating seven steps. Aviation commanders routinely perform a preflight CMTA after which hazards from each mission phase are identified. They then assess risks and identify controls ("options"). They then evaluate the risk as a function of gain, implement the option(s), and monitor the results. Coast Guard aviation units and, indeed, all Coast Guard assets in essence already apply a number of the HSI domains as part of their CMTA by "ensuring sufficient personnel are available to safely and effectively perform unit missions, ensuring a training program is maintained, ensuring needed equipment is available and operational, ensuring needed logistical support is available, ensuring required infrastructure is maintained, ensuring the flow of information and ensuring that effective safety risk management principles are incorporated into the planning and execution of on- and off-duty evolutions and activities" (U.S. Dept. of Homeland Security, U.S. Coast Guard, 2008, pp. 2–9).

SUMMARY

It is a general canard in military aviation that safety doctrine and procedures are all too often "written in blood"; that is, the reactive "lessons learned" from mishaps that have already occurred. However, it is a goal of aviation leadership and safety personnel to prevent mishaps from taking place—to save invaluable lives and expensive aircraft and, in doing so, maintain the highest levels of operational readiness.

This chapter described how ORM has been employed as a means to reduce risks by identifying and controlling hazards that could potentially lead to mishaps. It was seen that the process of ORM has, via policy, doctrine, training, and practice, been inculcated into military aviation. It was also proposed that the consideration of human-system interaction domains could facilitate an ORM-based CMTA by better defining the relationships between those personnel carrying out a task or mission and the systems in which they operate.

The use of ORM, then, is one way that mission planners and safety personnel can be proactive in their approach to managing risks, save lives and material resources, and in doing so, maintain high levels of unit operational readiness.

REFERENCES

Ashley, P. D. (1999). *Operational risk management and military aviation safety* (unpublished thesis, Air Force Institute of Technology, Ohio).

Bellenkes, A. H. (2000a). *Operational risk management training for naval aeromedical personnel.* Paper presented at the Meeting of the Navy Aerospace Medicine Strategic Planning Group, Houston, Texas.

———. (2000b). *Operational risk management as an international standard in aviation safety.* Paper presented at the 48th International Congress of Aviation and Space Medicine, Rio de Janeiro, Brazil.

———. (2002). *Operational risk management as a weapon for homeland defense.* Paper presented at the 73rd Annual Congress of the Aerospace Medical Association, Montreal, Canada.

———. (2004a). Effective risk management in the human factors assessment of chemical/biological threats. In J. Kocik, M. K. Janiak, & M. Negut (Eds.), *Preparedness against bioterrorism and re-emerging infectious threats* (pp. 89–104). Amsterdam, The Netherlands: IOS Press.

———. (2004b). *An introduction to human systems integration for systems engineers.* Ft. Belvoir, MD: Defense Acquisition University.

Bogardus, J., & Moore, R. (2007). Lloyds of London: The early days. Retrieved November 1, 2008 from http://www.irmi.com/Expert/Articles/2007/Bogardus09.aspx.

Booher, H. R. (2003). Introduction: Human systems integration. In H. R. Booher (Ed.), *Handbook of human systems integration* (pp. 1–30). Hoboken, New Jersey: A. John Wiley & Sons.

Brooker, P. (2007). Air traffic safety: Continued evolution or a new paradigm? Presented at the Imperial College of London as the Lloyd's Register Educational Trust Transport Risk Management Lecture. Retrieved November 1, 2007 from https://dspace.lib.cranfield.ac.uk/bitstream/1826/1967/1/Air%20Traffic%20Safety-Transport%20Risk%20Management%20Lecture-2007.pdf.

Burke, C. M. (1999). Risk management for brigades and battalions: Task Force XXI update. *CALL Newsletter*, 99-5.

Cho, M. G. (2002). *The Air Force operational risk management program and aviation safety* (unpublished thesis, Air Force Institute of Technology, Ohio).

Decker, R. J. (2001a). *Homeland security: Key elements of a risk management approach.* U.S. Government Accounting Office-02-150T. Washington, D.C.: U.S. General Accounting Office.

———. (2001b). *Homeland security: A risk management approach can guide preparedness efforts.* U.S. Government Accounting Office-02-208T. Washington, D.C.: U.S. General Accounting Office.

Defense Acquisition University. (2009). Defense acquisition guidebook. Retrieved November 1, 2007 from https://akss.dau.mil/default.aspx.

Embry, D., Kontogiannis, T., & Green, M. (1994). *Guidelines for preventing human error in process safety.* New York: American Institute of Chemical Engineers.

Hale, M. (March 2007). Looking for signs of risk? *Flying safety.*

Hunt, P. C. (2002). Hot pit refuelling at night: Operational risk management gave us tools so we could prove we were able to safely hot pit at night. *Combat edge*, June. Retrieved November 1, 2007 from http://findarticles.com/p/articles/mi_m0JCA/is_1_11/ai_89380917.

Kirwan, B., & Ainsworth, L. K. (1992). *A guide to task analysis*. London, England: Taylor and Francis.

Kritzinger, D. (2006). *Aircraft system safety: Military and civil aeronautical applications*. Cambridge, England: Woodhead Publishing Ltd.

LaTrash, F. (1999). *Risk management: An integral part of operational planning*. Report. Newport, RI: Naval War College.

Lunch, W. (2002). Bioterrorism: Then and now. *NRA News*, January.

Moser, R., Whilte, G. L., Lewis-Younger, C., & Garrett, L. C. (2001). Preparing for expected bioterrorism attacks. *Military Medicine*, 166 (5), 369–374.

National Aeronautics and Space Administration. (2008). NASA procedural requirements: Agency risk management procedural requirements. NPR 8000.4a. Retrieved November 1, 2007 from http://nodis3.gsfc.nasa.gov/displayDir.cfm?Internal_ID=N_PR_8000_004A_&page_name=main.

National Aeronautics and Space Administration. (2009). Mission operations risk management. Retrieved November 1, 2008 from http://www.nasa.gov/centers/ames/research/technology-onepagers/mission_ops_risk_mngt.html.

Rains, W. (2008). Risk management for the aviation staff. *CALL Report*, 01-07. Retrieved November 1, 2008 from http://www.globalsecurity.org/military/library/report/call/call_01-7_ch10.htm.

Reason, J. (1990). *Human error*. New York: Cambridge University Press.

———. (1997). *Managing the risks of organizational accidents*. Aldershot, UK: Ashgate Publishing Ltd.

Rose, S. (1989). The coming explosion of silent weapons. *Naval War College Review*, Summer: 339–354.

Stamatelatos, M. (2008). NASA integrated risk management process. Paper presented at the TRISMAC Conference, ESTEC, The Netherlands, April 2008. Retrieved November 1, 2008 from http://www.congrex.nl/08a04/presentations/2-P2/01_Stamatelatos.pdf.

Swallom, D. W., Lindberg, R. M., & Smith-Jackson, T. L. (2003). System safety principles and methods. In H. R. Booher (Ed.), *Human systems integration handbook* (pp. 497–540). New York: Wiley Interscience.

Tanner, J. C. (1997). *Operational risk management at the operational level of war*. Report. Newport, RI: Naval War College.

U.S. Department of the Air Force. (1997). *USAF instruction AFP 91-214: Operational risk management and execution*. Washington, D.C.: U.S. Government Printing Office.

U.S. Department of the Army. (1997a). *AR 95-1: Flight regulations*. Washington, D.C.: U.S. Government Printing Office.

———. (1997b). *FM 101-5: Staff organization and operation: Annex J—Risk management*. Washington, D.C.: U.S. Government Printing Office.

———. (1998). *FM 100-14: Risk management*. Washington, D.C.: U.S. Government Printing Office.

————. (1999). *Range safety criteria for unmanned air vehicles. U.S. Army White Sands Missile Range Report. 323-99.* Washington, D.C.: U.S. Government Printing Office.

————. (2003). *FM 25-101: Battle-focused training.* H1-3. Washington, D.C.: U.S. Government Printing Office.

U.S. Department of Defense. (1997). *Report of the Defense Science Board Task Force on aviation safety.* Washington, D.C.: U.S. Government Printing Office.

————. (2000). *MIL-STD 882D: Standard practice for system safety.* Washington, D.C.: U.S. Government Printing Office.

————. (2003). *Operation of the defense acquisition system. Enclosure E-7: Human systems integration* (E-7, 36–37). Washington, D.C.: U.S. Government Printing Office.

U.S. Department of Homeland Security, U.S. Coast Guard. (1999). *Operational risk management. Commandant Instruction: COMDTINST 3500.3.* Washington, D.C.: HQ, U.S. Coast Guard.

————. (2008). Risk based decision making and operational risk management. In *U.S. Coast Guard sector organization manual. Commandant Instruction: COMDTINST M5401.6* (section 2-B-6, 2–7). Washington, D.C.: HQ, U.S. Coast Guard.

U.S. Department of the Navy. (1997). *OPNAV Instruction 3500.39/Marine Corps Order 3500.27: Introduction to operational risk management.* Washington, D.C.: U.S. Government Printing Office.

————. (2002a). *Medical operational risk management (ORM) in Marine Forces Reserve HM/DT Sustainment/Enhancement Training (SET) program.* Washington, D.C.: U.S. Government Printing Office.

————. (2002b). Operational risk management. *HQ US Marine Corps Document ORM 1-0.* Washington, D.C.: U.S. Government Printing Office.

————. (2004a). Operational risk management (ORM). *OPNAV Instruction 3500.39B.* Washington, D.C.: U.S. Government Printing Office.

————. (2004b). Operational risk management (ORM), *Marine Corps Order 3500.27B.* Washington, D.C.: U.S. Government Printing Office.

U.S. Department of Transportation, Federal Aviation Administration. (2000). Operational risk management (ORM) in U.S. Dept. of Transportation, Federal Aviation Administration. In *System safety handbook* (pp. 15-2–15-23). Washington, D.C.: U.S. Government Printing Office.

————. (2005). General aviation pilot's guide to online safety resources. Retrieved November 1, 2008 from http://www.avhf.com/html/Publications/FAA/ga_safety_-sourcebook_2005.pdf.

U.S. Food and Drug Administration, Center for Food Safety and Applied Nutrition. (2001). *Food safety and security: Operational risk management systems approach.* Washington, D.C.: U.S. Printing Office.

U.S. Government Accounting Office. (2005). *Strategic budgeting: Risk management principles can help DHS allocate resources to highest priorities. U.S. Government Accounting Office-05-824T.* Retrieved November 1, 2008 from http://www.gao.gov/new.items/d05824t.pdf.

————. (2007). *Risk management: Applying risk management principles to guide federal investments. U.S. Government Accounting Office-07-386T*. Retrieved November 1, 2008 from http://www.gao.gov/new.items/d07386t.pdf.

————. (2008). *Risk management: Strengthening the use of risk management principles in homeland security*. U.S. Government Accounting Office-08-904T. Retrieved November 1, 2008 from http://www.gao.gov/new.items/d08904t.pdf.

VanVactor, Jerry D. (2007). Risk mitigation through a composite risk management process: The U.S. Army risk assessment. *Organization Development Journal*, Summer.

Zurich Services Corporation. (2009). Risk management for highway construction. Zurich Services Seminar Series. Retrieved November 1, 2008 from http://www.buildsafe.org/confnews/2009/Proc/8G-highway.pdf.

Chapter 11

COPING WITH STRESS IN MILITARY AVIATION

Justin S. Campbell and Paul E. O'Connor

Military aviation exacts a costly toll in psychological stress from those who choose to pursue the occupation (Stokes & Kite, 1994). A prime example is landing on an aircraft carrier, a task which physiological indices and subjective accounts both rate as one of the most stressful in aviation (Miller, Rubin, Clark, Crawford, & Ransom, 1970). The intense psychological pressure associated with a career in military aviation makes military aviators an ideal population for understanding individual differences in robust functioning in high-stress environments. Such an understanding benefits not only those seeking to develop aviation selection and classification instruments but also those interested in identifying important protective factors relevant to alternative military and civilian occupations in which personnel are expected to operate sophisticated systems while exposed to profound stress. Unfortunately, popular mythology and stereotypes of aviator stress coping tend to outnumber empirically based profiles of military aviators (Kern, 2006). This chapter is an attempt to provide an empirically grounded starting point for those seeking a better understanding of stress coping among military aviators. The chapter will try to provide a brief review of stress-coping theories germane to the aviation literature. The objective of the literature review is not to synthesize the variety of approaches and theories encompassed in that literature. Instead, the intention is to provide the reader with a unique opportunity to formulate their own conclusions with respect to the emergence or absence of a theoretical paradigm for this nascent, multidisciplinary field of study.

STRESS COPING

The Transactional Model of Stress Coping

Pioneering stress research conducted by physiologists such as Cannon (1915) and Selye (1956) paved the way for interdisciplinary approaches to the study of stress coping by stoking an interest in the interaction between psychological and physiological aspects of stress. A prominent example of such an approach is the transactional model of stress developed by Lazarus and Folkman (1984). According to the transactional model, stress is defined as "a particular relationship between the person and the environment that is appraised by the person as taxing or exceeding his or her resources and endangering his or her well-being" (Lazarus & Folkman, 1984, p. 19).

Within the transactional model of stress, coping is defined as "cognitive and behavioral efforts to manage specific external and/or internal demands that are appraised as taxing or exceeding the resources of the person" (Lazarus & Folkman, 1984, p. 141). The transactional model further delineates coping into problem-focused and emotion-focused subtypes. Problem-focused coping starts with an effort to define the problem or source of stress, followed by generation of competing solutions that are subjected to a cognitive cost-benefit analysis that ideally results in selection and initiation of the most desirable coping strategy. Alternatively, emotion-focused strategies aim to reduce or manage one's experience of unpleasant feelings induced by stressors. Examples of emotion-focused strategies include venting, acting out, emotional denial, and acceptance.

Avoidant versus Attentive Coping

Another distinction that can be made when discussing stress coping is between avoidant and attentive coping (Krohne, 1993; Suls & Fletcher, 1985). Avoidant stress-coping strategies are ways of thinking about stressful situations such as denial, distraction, repression, and suppression that act to shift an individual's attention away from (a) the stressor and (b) their immediate emotional reaction to the stressor. On the other hand, attentive coping focuses attention on the stressor and one's response to it. These ways of thinking, or more technically cognitive schemata (Brewer, 1987), can be both conscious and unconscious processes.

The Compass of Shame Coping

The compass of shame (Nathanson, 1992) offers a third theoretical perspective grounded in emotions/affect theory (Tomkins, 1970) that describes how aviators might respond to stress. The compass of shame is composed of four poles of maladaptive shame coping that constitute stable individual tendencies for coping with the self-conscious emotion of shame. The first two poles, attack-self and withdrawal, are conceptualized as internalizing coping strategies that focus the unpleasant experience of shame upon the self. The second two poles, attack-other and avoidance, are conceptualized as externalizing coping because both responses cognitively distance the self from the source of shame. Initial studies investigating the relationship between coping styles and general trait dispositions suggest that internalizing coping styles are related to personality styles that are susceptible to anxiety and depressive disorders (Elison, Lennon, & Pulos, 2006). However, it should also be noted that sole reliance upon externalizing coping styles has been linked to a tendency to endorse antisocial personality traits—e.g., emotionally callous, narcissistic, and antiauthority (Campbell & Elison, 2005). More relevant to aviation, evidence suggests that aviators, compared to the general population, may be reluctant to utilize internalizing coping strategies. Pilots and aircrew who are reluctant to utilize a limited but healthy level of internalizing coping when the inevitable error or miscalculation occurs in the cockpit or flight deck may be at risk for disrupted crew communication. Specifically, Brown and Moren (2003) studied commercial aviation students in simulated cockpit exercises and found that aviators may be overly reluctant to engage in attack-self coping, instead focusing exclusively on externalizing coping strategies that make little allowance for the acknowledgment of mistakes.

OBJECTIVES AND METHODS OF THE REVIEW

With respect to stress coping in military aviation, it remains unclear which theoretical perspective, if any, has come to dominate the literature, much less specify any specific distinctions between emotion/problem or avoidant/attention coping and their contribution to the adaptation of stress in military flight environments. The literature review that follows is narrative and undertaken to identify some consistent themes regarding coping styles and other mediating factors that impact the manifestation of stress in aircrew confronted with both acute and chronic stress. In doing so, the focus of the review is to create a starting point for unifying the currently disparate theoretical threads that run through the study of stress coping in aviation.

A computerized search of the literature was conducted utilizing PsycINFO, Google Scholar, Medline, and Defense Technical Information Center. Keywords for the computerized search of the literature were "stress," "anxiety," "emotional stability," and "neuroticism." The review identified a total of 10 studies with substantive material concerning psychologically induced stress in military aviators. These studies are described in chronological order below and summarized in Table 11.1. The term stress-coping models will be used to refer collectively to the three stress-coping models (i.e., transactional, avoidant/attentive, and compass of shame coping) in the narrative reviews of each study.

STUDIES OF STRESS COPING IN MILITARY AVIATION

Ursano (1980)

Ursano (1980) presented three case histories to illustrate the necessity of contemplating not just biological origins of presenting symptoms in aviators

Table 11.1. Summary of Stress-Coping Studies

Study	Population	Theory of stress	Definition of stress	Measures	Findings
Ursano (1980)	Three U.S. Air Force officers (case studies)	(a) General Adaptation Syndrome (Selye, 1956) (b) Life Change (Holmes & Rahe, 1967)	(a) A threatening event (b) Any event that causes change	(a) N/A (b) N/A	Aviators are emotionally stable but tend to use emotion-focused coping techniques when their stress threshold has been surpassed.
McCarron and Haakonson (1982)	Canadian Forces: 158 aviators, 127 ground crew, and 46 non-aviation officers	Life Change (Holmes & Rahe, 1967)	Aviation stress factors: flight conditions, emergency situations, flight-related anxiety, and personal risk factors (e.g., divorce and demotion)	(a) Recent Life Change Questionnaire (b) Social Readjustment Rating Scale	The levels of stress associated with life changing events were significantly lower in aviators than ground personnel or non-aviation officers.
Alkov, Borowsky, and Gaynor (1982)	501 U.S. Naval aviators who had been involved in a mishap	General Adaptation Syndrome	The nonspecific response of the body to any demand made upon it	(a) Human Factors Aircraft Accident Investigation (b) Psychological Background Questionnaire	At-fault aviators were significantly more likely to use emotion-focused coping and have particular "life stressors" than not-at-fault aviators.

Study	Sample	Approach	Stressor	Measure	Findings
Alkov, Gaynor, and Borowsky (1985)	Data obtained, from flight surgeons, on 259 U.S. Naval aviators who had been involved in a mishap	Method implies Life Change approach	Not specifically defined, financial difficulties, recent marital engagements, career decisions examples of stressors	U.S. Navy Stress & Personality Questionnaire	Aviators who caused a mishap were more likely to have problems with interpersonal relationships and display symptoms of inadequate stress coping compared to non-mishap aviators.
Picano (1990)	U.S. Army: 465 pilots, 143 aircrew, and 50 non-aviation personnel	Dispositional approach to stress coping	Not specifically defined, implied as emotionally challenging events	Coping Orientation to Problems Experienced	The pilots were significantly more likely to use problem-focused coping strategies and less likely to use emotion-focused strategies than the non-aviators.
Takla, Koffman, and Bailey (1994)	Literature review	Combat stress	Not specifically defined. Threat of injury or death, injury or death of friends, requirement to destroy	N/A	Aviators (particularly young pilots) have better psychological well-being than non-aviators.

Study	Sample				Findings
Siem and Murray (1994)	100 U.S. Air Force pilots	BIGFIVE Personality	Emotional stability	N/A	Conscientiousness was rated as the most desirable trait for aviators.
Parsa and Kapadia (1997)	57 U.S. Air Force pilots participating in combat operations	(a) Stimulus model (b) Response-based model (c) Transactional model	A physical or psychological stimulus which, when impinging on an individual, produces strain or disequilibrium	Beck Depression Inventory	The pilots were not experiencing high levels of stress despite participating in combat operations.
Otsuka, Onozawa, and Miyamoto (2006)	Japanese Air Self-Defense Force: 30 student aviators and 33 instructor aviators	(a) Stimulus model (b) Response-based model	Levels of urinary catecholamine and salivary cortisol	Levels of urinary catecholamine and salivary cortisol	Students became better able to cope with the stress of flight training as they became more experienced.
Lurie et al. (2007)	57 Israeli Air Force Officers: 25 pilots and 22 non-pilots	(a) Dispositional approach to stress coping (b) Response-based model	The bond between the environmental demands toward the individual and his ability to cope with them	(a) Folkman coping-style questionnaire (b) Dental assessment	Bruxism was noticeable in 69% of pilots and 27% of non-pilots. Pilots suffering from bruxism are more likely to use less effective coping strategies than non-pilots suffering from bruxism.

but also the individual aviator's personality (e.g., Type A personality), socio-cultural background (e.g., marital and childhood), and symbolic representation (e.g., aviation as adult status or childhood dream). In his introduction, Ursano emphasized the need to investigate these three areas, in large part due to a perception that aviators tend to ignore their internal emotional life and focus on tangible concerns. When faced with stress, Ursano argued that, aviators are less apt to employ psychological defenses, and consequently the symptoms presented are more tangible physiological symptoms as opposed to psychological. In all three case studies, biological bases for presenting physical symptoms could not be established. The author concluded that con-current investigation of personality, sociocultural, and symbolic histories was essential for identifying the course of psychiatric treatment implemented for the three aviators described in the case histories.

In terms of stress susceptibility, the authors appeared to support the notion that military aircrew are elevated in emotional stability, while the coping strategy of choice for the aviator whose stress threshold has been surpassed is often some form of externalizing response in which direct confrontation of unpleasant emotions is avoided but manifest as physiological or somatic complaints. The implication of this study, when discussed from the perspective of the stress coping models introduced at the start of this chapter, is that aviators who rely upon avoidant/internalized stress coping may have a tendency to clinically present with physical ailments that are an unconscious manifestation of their underlying battle with stress.

McCarron and Haakonson (1982)

McCarron and Haakonson (1982) adopted Holmes and Rahe's life change conceptualization of stress (Holmes & Rahe, 1967) in their study of life change stress among Canadian aviators. The life change theory attributes stress to the frequency of life change events, which regardless of emotional valence of the event, leads to more stress as the frequency of life change events increases. The Recent Life Change Questionnaire (RLCQ as cited in McCarron & Haakonson, 1982) was used to compare life change units across health, work, family, social, and financial domains, between pilots ($n = 158$), aircraft maintenance ground crew ($n = 127$), and non-aviation officers ($n = 46$). No significant differences emerged between the various aviation communities with respect to the number of life change events (the mean number for pilots, aircraft maintenance, and non-aviation personnel were 11.8, 13.4, and 13.1 life changing events, respectively). The results indicated the aviator sample had fewer life change units overall compared to other communities, especially ground crew ($p < .05$). Significant differences in life change units (a numerical value ranging from 11 to 100 units describing the quantity of life changing events) indicated aviators experienced less life change stressors compared to ground crew for health ($p < .01$), family ($p < .05$), and social ($p < .05$) domains. Compared to the much smaller sample of non-aviation officers, only one significant difference from the aviation sample emerged for the family domain ($p < .05$). The findings from this study highlight the potential differences between aviators and other members of the aviation community with respect to the frequency and intensity of stressors encountered. Potential reasons for the differences between the groups were not discussed.

Referencing the stress-coping models introduced at the start of the chapter, the Life Change model of stress avoids discussion of specific coping strategies in favor of a model that equates the quantity of stressful events with the outcome, thus assuming that at some point too much stress simply outstrips one's ability to cope. Such an approach is contradictory to the transactional, avoidant/attentive, and compass coping models which share the assumption that stable individual differences in coping strategies account for at least some between-person variability in the degree to which stress adversely impacts an individual.

Alkov, Borowsky, and Gaynor (1982)

Alkov and colleagues (1982) attempted to test the hypothesis that inadequate stress-coping strategies contribute to mishaps (i.e., substantial destruction of property or bodily injury) in U.S. Naval aviation. The authors instructed U.S. Navy (USN) flight surgeons to complete a 22-item questionnaire about life style changes and personality characteristics they had observed among Naval aviators involved in mishaps. Completed questionnaires ($N = 501$) were returned to the authors, who later divided the questionnaires into two groups: (a) "at-fault" aviators ($n = 248$) with an attributed mishap and (b) "not-at-fault" aviators ($n = 230$) not implicated in a mishap. Twenty-three aviators were involved in a mishap for which the cause was undetermined. These 23 questionnaires were omitted from the final analysis, resulting in a final $N = 478$. A one-tailed Fisher-Irwin Exact significance test was conducted to examine differences in non-normal responses between the at-fault and not-at-fault groups. Significant differences were found between the at-fault and not-at-fault aviators for 9 of the 22 questions. Among the items with significant differences, five were significant at the $p < .01$ level, and four were significant at the $p < .05$ level. The content of the items with significant differences suggests deficits in stress coping for the at-fault aviators. The at-fault group was more likely to have (a) marital problems, (b) problems with interpersonal relationships, (c) recent trouble with supervisors, and (d) recent trouble with peers.

Relating this study to the stress-coping models, Alkov, Borowsky, and Gaynor (1982) concluded that ineffective coping strategies, namely "acting out" aggression (an emotion-focused coping strategy), contribute significantly to the probability of an aviator being involved in a mishap. Therefore, the authors urge that individuals in supervisory positions should be alert to signs of ineffective stress coping, such as acting-out behaviors, denial, defensiveness, oversensitivity to criticism, argumentativeness, arrogance, and chronic interpersonal problems, as indicators of suitability for flight duty.

In terms of trait dispositions, the sample itself was again described as relatively free of neuroticism. Yet there is a potential liability for emotional stability: when the stress-coping envelope of an aviator is finally breached, such individuals are relative novices at dealing with their emotions. Aviators in this study who may have crossed this threshold were described as being overreliant upon externalizing coping strategies (e.g., attack-other) that can have deleterious impact upon performance and, ultimately, safety.

Alkov, Gaynor, and Borowsky (1985)

In a second expanded study, Alkov, Gaynor, and Borowsky (1985) asked USN flight surgeons to rate Naval aviators involved in mishaps (1980–1982) on 26 items that assessed dimensions of externalizing stress coping (poor familial and work relationships, risk-taking, and absentmindedness on the job). Although Alkov and colleagues acknowledged that military aviators, as a group, are "recognized as high stress copers" (p. 244), they hypothesized that certain stress-coping personality traits could differentiate between mishap-involved pilots who were, and were not, identified as contributing to a mishap. From the Lazarus and Folkman perspective (Lazarus, 1983; Lazarus & Folkman, 1984), Alkov and colleagues suggested that young aggressive Naval aviators, forced into emotion-focused coping, are more likely to adopt externalizing or "acting-out" strategies likely to be manifested in interpersonal relationship problems (familial and job-related) rather than adopt internalizing coping strategies characterized by quiet anxiety and depression.

The questionnaire was completed by flight surgeons for 381 mishap-attributed and 356 non-mishap-attributed Naval aviators. A significant proportion of the sample (Fisher-Irwin Exact Test, $p < .001$, one-tailed) endorsed the following four items: (a) recent major decision, (b) not professional in flying, (c) trouble with superiors, and (d) incapable of quickly assessing trouble. Mishap-attributed aviators appeared more likely to engage in externalizing stress coping compared to the non-mishap-attributed aviators.

Unfortunately, it is difficult to make much of the findings reported in this study given the dearth of psychometric information regarding the questionnaire (e.g., neither reliability nor validity information reported). Moreover, the use of single-item comparisons may have elevated experiment-wise

(Type I) error, especially in conjunction with the use of a one-tailed *p* value. Notwithstanding, the findings provide a descriptive survey of how flight surgeons have come to conceptualize the failing aviator as being more stress-prone than their adaptive counterparts, combined with an overreliance upon externalizing/avoidant coping mechanisms when forced to engage in emotion-focused coping.

Picano (1990)

Picano (1990) conducted a survey of aviator coping styles to examine the belief that aviators emphasize problem-focused coping strategies. Using a mail-in survey procedure, the Coping Orientation to Problems Experienced (COPE; Carver, Scheier, & Weintraub, 1989) questionnaire was completed and returned by U.S. Army pilots (*n* = 465), aircrew (*n* = 143), and non-aviation military (*n* = 50) personnel. The COPE has an empirically supported factor structure that groups several subscales into the following coping styles: problem-solving, support-seeking, avoidance, acceptance, and religion. To reduce potential confounds due to gender, 35 surveys completed by females were not included in the final sample of Army personnel. First, the pilot sample (*n* = 465) was compared to a collegiate norm sample (*n* = 1030). Using Cohen's *d* (1977) as a reference, only three scales reached the "large" effect size of .5 or greater. Two of these scales were facets of the support-seeking dimension (support-seeking for emotional reasons, venting of emotions), on which pilots scored significantly lower than the college sample. Pilots also scored significantly lower than the college sample on the mental disengagement facet of the avoidance dimension.

These findings offer further support for the portrayal of pilots as individuals who are reluctant to engage in emotion-focused coping and prone to externalize if confronted with emotion. When compared with aircrew and non-aviation military samples, the pilot sample again evidenced significantly lower emotional venting, mental disengagement, and denial. Another significant difference was observed with respect to the support-seeking dimension, as pilots scored significantly higher on this facet than aircrew or non-aviation military personnel. Picano further attempted to delineate the coping styles of the pilot sample by comparing COPE scores across the various aircraft flown by the sample (utility, scout, attack, cargo, and fixed-wing utility). However, no significant differences emerged. Despite the amount of psychometric support for the COPE that distinguishes this study from that of Alkov and colleagues (Alkov, Borowsky, & Gaynor, 1982; Alkov, Gaynor, & Borowsky, 1985), the self-selecting nature of the sample raises questions about the generalizability of the findings. Taken in conjunction with the other studies reviewed thus far, the Picano effort lends additional support to the description of pilots as predominately externalizing, avoidant, and problem-focused when confronting stress.

Takla, Koffman, and Bailey (1994)

In their extensive literature review, Takla and colleagues (1994) noted a paucity of data devoted to the subject of combat-induced stress in modern military aviation. Applying a Freudian psychoanalytic perspective, the authors reviewed the dynamics of general combat stress reactions, noting that aviators' ability to aggress against an enemy can aid in stress coping by providing the opportunity to discharge anxiety. The authors argued that a loss of narcissistic (self-admiration, self-centeredness, and self-regard) defenses is a predisposition that often leads to combat fatigue. Takla et al. (1994) further declared that military aviators, especially between the ages of 21 and 28, sustain psychological well-being better than other aircrew in combat deployments, especially when compared to ground crew. The authors argued that aviators may be less susceptible to stress than ground crew because the aviators' active participation in combat duties facilitates an internal locus of control that is psychologically protective. Oppositely, ground crews are less likely to perceive an internal locus of control for the outlet of their stress while performing the more passive duties of support staff.

Takla and colleagues also noted that support staff may be more likely to adopt feelings of helplessness because of the fixed position of their bases, which renders them more susceptible to random attacks from the enemy. One limitation of this paper, as the authors were quick to note, is the dearth of empirical evidence substantiating the proposed psychodynamic perspective on combat stress coping in aviators and aircrew. Nevertheless, the authors clearly stipulated that aviators prefer externalizing coping styles as a group and tend to be emotionally stable when contrast against other members of the flight crew. In some cases, externalizing coping may take the form of engaging the enemy during combat operations. Given such a perspective, it creates the expectation that aviators, relative to other combat operators, have less of a risk for developing stress-related disorders in conjunction with combat deployments. Returning to the stress-coping models, this study again portrays aviators as problem-focused, avoidant, and externalizing, and in doing so suggests these traits are psychologically protective when aviators are exposed to the stress and danger of air combat operations.

Siem and Murray (1994)

Siem and Murray (1994) provided limited empirical evidence to paint a portrait of personality traits pilots themselves desire in successful combat pilots. In their study, 100 U.S. Air Force (USAF) pilots, 43 with combat experience in Operation Desert Storm, were asked to utilize six personality dimensions to create a composite personality profile of a highly effective combat pilot. Those six dimensions derived from interviews with pilots were (a) flying skills and knowledge, (b) compliance (with flight rules/regulations), (c) crew management and mutual support, (d) leadership, (e) situational awareness (SA), and (f) planning. Comparing the relative desirability of specific personality traits within those dimensions, a personality trait that resembles the BIGFIVE (Barrick & Mount, 1991) trait of conscientiousness (dependable, responsible, and decisive) was rated as the most important. The next most desirable personality factors were culture ("bright" or appearance of intelligence) for flight skills, leadership, SA, planning, and emotional stability. Conscientiousness also emerged as the most highly valued personality type for combat pilots across aircraft type.

When interpreting this result it is important to keep in mind that this profile is a subjective reflection of self-rated "desirable" traits in combat aviators as opposed to a performance-based profile. Therefore, it is best to interpret the profile as a type of "ideal" character type aviators hope to find in their colleagues, especially during combat situations. Given the complementary nature of conscientiousness and "culture," it is not surprising that pilots find these to be desirable characteristics in fellow pilots, regardless of whether or not the setting is a combat zone. Moreover, the results from this study do not provide any empirical evidence that links conscientiousness (or any other personality factors) to mental well-being and adjustment under combat conditions, an outcome variable that may be, in some cases, distinct from combat performance.

Linking the BIGFIVE model to the three stress-coping models discussed at the start of the chapter could prove to be a valuable integration, especially considering that individual differences in coping styles may very well be a function of larger underlying personality traits (Buss, 1996). Some obvious linkages are that elevated conscientiousness, emotional stability, and extroversion described here as desirable in fighter pilots are traits consistent with a problem-focused personality that can flexibly move between avoidant and attentive coping as situations dictate but decidedly oriented toward externalizing emotional coping.

Parsa and Kapadia (1997)

Parsa and Kapadia (1997) compared USAF pilots ($N = 57$) across five different squadrons (all of which were involved in combat operations at the time) with respect to their scores on the Beck Depression Inventory (BDI; Beck & Steer, 1994). Individuals who scored 10 or greater, according to the BDI manual, were identified as experiencing excessive stress. A significant ($p < .01$) test of proportions was observed using a positive screen for depression as the criterion. The results indicated the sample was not experiencing elevated stress levels despite their participation in combat operations. Moreover, no significant differences in BDI scores were observed between the squadrons. The small sample size utilized in this study render it descriptive, yet again, whatever evidence can be gleaned from the data continue to support the supposition that on average, military pilots are emotionally stable individuals who are not easily given to depressive and anxiety disorders.

The results from this study are consistent with the problem-focused, avoidant, emotionally externalizing portrait of an effective combat aviator also described by Takla, Koffman, and Bailey (1994), as well as Siem and Murray (1994). In particular, avoidant and externalizing emotional coping are thought to be protective with respect to internalizing disorders such as depression (Elison, Lennon, & Pulos, 2006).

Otsuka, Onozawa, and Miyamoto (2006)

Otsuka and colleagues (2006) attempted to differentiate between student and instructor pilots at different stages of flight training using physiological stress indicators that consisted of urinary adrenaline and noradrenaline levels, in addition to salivary cortisol. The sample of 30 students and 33 instructors were sampled from initial phase I training that involved instruction on a T-3 dual-seat propeller aircraft. A sample of 17 students and 15 instructors were sampled from the more advanced phase II training that involved instruction on a T-4 jet engine aircraft. Urine and saliva samples were taken pre- and postflight for all participants, with the ratio of pre- to postflight adrenaline, noradrenaline, and cortisol utilized to indicate the amount of stress incurred during the flights.

The results indicated that during the early training level (phase I), students evidenced significantly higher differences from instructors for all three hormones (from pre- to postflight). On the other hand, no such student/instructor differences were observed in students at more advanced stages of training. The disappearance of student/instructor differences in stress-related physiology at advanced stages of training supports the notion that training helps students acclimate to the stressors of flight training. Perhaps more importantly, this study was the first in the review to introduce objective indicators of individual differences in stress response by employing physiological indicators of stress, which in conjunction with the comparison of students against instructors at various levels of training, made the design possibly the most methodologically rigorous in the present literature review.

With respect to individual trait differences in stress susceptibility, the findings from this study suggest that while pilots seem to experience stress when they first encounter the demands of military aviation, successful student aviators have the capacity to physiologically adapt to the stressors of aviation training. From another perspective, the results suggest that performance might interact with stress susceptibility, such that students who are unable to improve their performance in a timely manner are also more likely to experience greater stress for a longer duration. The result of this interaction is deteriorating performance and a greater likelihood of training attrition. Further application of this methodology combined with an analysis of coping styles might shed light on the degree to which coping strategies mediate such habituation. Establishing bio-physiological markers for a personality

(Canli, 2006) oriented toward problem-focused, flexibly avoidant, and emotionally externalizing coping could provide a powerful new approach to aviation training selection as well as to those interested in studying stress resilience in other applied areas.

Lurie et al. (2007)

Lurie et al. (2007) evaluated work-related stress as a potential cause of bruxism in Israeli Air Force officers (35 pilots and 22 non-pilots). Bruxism is a common habit which causes grinding of teeth by rhythmic contractions of the masseter and other jaw muscles (Attanasio, 1997). Abnormal tooth wear is a symptom of bruxism. Following a dental examination, it was found that 69 percent of the pilots suffered from bruxism compared to 27 percent of the non-pilots (the incidence of bruxism is between 5 and 10 percent of Western populations; Lurie et al., 2007). The participants also completed a coping-style questionnaire based upon the Folkman and Lazarus model (1980). There was not a significant difference in the levels of stress reported by the pilot and non-pilot groups. However, Lurie et al. (2007) reported that pilots suffering from bruxism were relatively more likely to use emotion-focused coping styles and denial when compared with socioeconomically matched non-pilots suffering from bruxism. It was not reported whether this difference was significant. This study represents an interesting use of objective physical markers as a measure of stress. However, the sample size was extremely small and there was little detail regarding statistical analysis, particularly in the reporting of significance testing.

DISCUSSION

Considering that adaptive stress coping is a necessity for aviators who function at high levels of competency under tremendous psychological and physiological stress, we were surprised to find so few studies devoted to the topic. Nevertheless, it is possible to draw a number of conclusions regarding the role of personality and coping styles with respect to the impact of stress on military aviators. These conclusions and recommendations for further inquiry are presented next.

Integrating the Findings with Stress-Coping Theories

The transactional, avoidant/attentive, and compass of shame coping models can be described as cognitive-affective psychological theories characterized by an interaction between cognitive coping schemas and the affective states to which they are responding (Nathanson, 1992; Tomkins, 1970). The transactional and avoidant/attentive models suggest that a person and situation interaction determine the foci of cognitive information processing during exposure to psychological stress: either toward one's emotions or the specifics of the stress-evoking environment. In cases where attention is focused on one's emotional reaction to the stressor, attentive coping takes place. Attentive coping opens the door to the influence of stable individual differences in emotional coping (e.g., internalizing/externalizing shame coping). Individual differences in emotional coping tendencies describe how an individual is most likely to integrate his or her emotional coping with his or her more long-term schema of the self (Lewis & Junyk, 1997). When taken to an extreme, internalizing coping strategies magnify tendencies toward depressive and mood disorders, while excessive externalizing coping might take the form of personality disorders such as narcissism, antisocial personality, and various somatoform disorders (Nathanson, 1992).

Based on the literature review, the coping style most consistent with attaining a career in military aviation is a problem-focused and avoidant coping style. Further, for those aviators who do engage in emotion-focused or attentive coping, the tendency is to minimize the impact of emotions through externalizing coping strategies that result in somatic complaints or aggressive, acting-out behavior which minimize direct confrontation with unpleasant emotion. Therefore, one could say that the psychological stress-coping literature for military aviators portrays a subpopulation more likely to have a problem-focused, avoidant cognitive focus, and when pressed to deal with emotions, given to externalizing coping.

How is the emerging military aviator stress-coping portrait relevant to human performance? To start, it would appear aviators are ideally equipped to deal with acute, high-stress situations that benefit for maximal allocation of attention to purely cognitive and physical aspects of the stressor (Wickens, 2003). Emergency scenarios which require split-second decisions with life and death consequences are not uncommon in military or civilian aviation. Cockpit emergencies call for a problem-focused, emotionally avoidant individual to flawlessly execute rehearsed troubleshooting procedures under life-threatening pressure. Yet when it comes to dealing with chronic stress, aviators may suffer from an inability to switch to attention-based coping. Over the long-term, self-reflection and refinement are more likely to follow from attention-based coping (Suls & Fletcher, 1985). Moreover, the literature review indicated that when aviators do attend to their emotions, their particular style of coping is likely to be externalizing. Unfortunately, aviators' infrequent encounters with emotion-focused coping may mean their coping skills lack refinement; thereby predisposing aviators to engage in various forms of socially inappropriate acting-out behavior when forced to confront their emotions (Alkov, Borowsky, & Gaynor, 1982; Alkov, Gaynor, & Borowsky, 1985; Ursano, 1980). A similar finding from another applied domain was reported by Glendon and Glendon (1992), who found that ambulance staffs experiencing increased stress were likely to adopt emotion-focused coping strategies. In sum, the literature indicated aviators tend to avoid dealing with the emotional aspects of stress. In doing so, aviators are not immune to stress, but instead more prone to utilize externalizing coping. When taken to the extreme, externalizing coping may prove to be as equally debilitating and socially maladaptive as internalizing coping styles.

Personality

A consistent theme in the literature review was that military aviators are emotionally stable and therefore less prone to anxiety and depressive disorders associated with neuroticism (Alkov, Borowsky, & Gaynor, 1982; Alkov, Gaynor, & Borowsky, 1985; Parsa & Kapadia, 1997; Takla, Koffman, & Bailey, 1994; Ursano, 1980). Such a personality profile is indicative of individuals who are able to perform well under stressful conditions (Flin, O'Connor, & Crichton, 2008; Musson, Sandal, & Helmreich, 2004). This finding is fairly unsurprising. Given the stress placed upon military aviators during flight school, those individuals who are unable to cope with stress are unlikely to become military aviators as they would attrite during training. Indeed, a recent meta-analysis of personality measures as predictors of military aviation training (Campbell, 2006) found a significant, negative, mean effect for the relationship between scores on measures of neuroticism, its sub-facet anxiety, and the dependent variable of success in military aviation training. These findings are also consistent with empirical findings that military aviators as a group tend to be lower than normative samples with respect to neuroticism (Lambirth, Dolgin, Rentmeister-Bryant, & Moore, 2003; Retzlaff & Gilbertini, 1987).

Life Changing Events

McCarron and Haakonson (1982) found no significant differences in the number of life changing events when comparing military aviators with military ground personnel and non-aviation military officers. However, when military aviators experienced life changing events, the level of stress they experienced was significantly lower compared to ground personnel or non-aviation military officers. The authors of the study did not attempt to account for these findings, but from examining the study it is possible to offer some explanations. To start, military aviators are arguably less likely to suffer from medical issues as their health is carefully screened. Military aviators may also benefit from a uniquely strong social support network due to the camaraderie that accompanies squadron membership. The aviators were more homogenous in rank than the ground personnel or non-aviation officers, making sampling differences more of a plausible explanation for the differences between the two groups. Lastly, aviators may underreport health concerns because it is a major determinant as to whether they can fly or not. Therefore, care should be taken when extrapolating these findings to military aviators in general.

Turning to Alkov's finding that mishap-involved military aviators are prone to major life stressors (Alkov, Borowsky, & Gaynor, 1982; Alkov,

Gaynor, & Borowsky, 1985), this finding is consistent with the results reported by other researchers who have examined accident causation (Li, Chen, Wu, & Sung, 2001; McCarron & Haakonson, 1982). For example, Loewenthal, Eysenck, Lubitsh, Gortin, and Bicknell (2000) found a significant relationship between the levels of psychological stress of civilian pilots and whether or not they had been involved in an air traffic incident. Taken together, these studies suggest the identification of abnormally high stress in aviators should be considered an important function of mishap intervention programs that emphasize stress management techniques.

Training

The arduous selection and qualification process through which military aviators must pass necessitates the ability to perform effectively while exposed to stress. Further, the stress exposure endured during military flight training improves the ability of the flight students to cope with stress in the aircraft (Otsuka, Onozawa, & Miyamoto, 2006). The finding that stress exposure improves the ability of individuals to cope with stress in the future is supported elsewhere. For instance, in their review of 37 articles concerned with stress exposure training, Saunders, Driskell, Johnston, and Salas (1996) found the majority of studies supported the effectiveness of stress exposure training. Further, there is evidence that the skills learned during exposure to a specific stressor or stressful situation can be generalized to novel settings and stressors (Driskell, Salas, & Johnson, 2001).

CONCLUSION

The purpose of this chapter was to consolidate the disparate literature pertaining to stress coping in military aviators. Although this review of stress coping in military aviation did not uncover a dominant theoretical or methodological paradigm, one consistent theme was that military aviators on average tend to be one of the most stress resilient populations in the military and, by extension, the general public. Aviators as a whole were commonly described as being emotionally stable (low in neuroticism), a trait well suited to preventing acute stress from interfering with the performance of complex flight skills under intense time pressure. Yet with respect to chronic stress (e.g., divorce and failed relationships), the evidence suggested that aviators who do succumb to this type of stress (i.e., forced to engage in emotion-focused coping) are prone to engage in externalizing and often self-destructive behavior (e.g., acting-out/attack-other behavior and presentation of somatic complaints while avoiding direct acknowledgment of emotional problems). In conclusion, few attempts have been made to replicate or extend the aviation stress-coping literature. To address this limitation, we recommend the development and utilization of a standardized method for evaluating individual differences in the ability to withstand and cope with stress. Aviation and military psychology might look to the developmental literature on emotional regulation (Cicchetti, Ackerman, & Izard, 1995) as an example of a more theoretically and methodologically developed approach to dealing with issues of individual differences in coping. The development of a standardized method for measuring and discussing stress coping would add a new dimension to human performance in aviation with the potential to improve the selection, training, and sustainment of military aviators while providing a basis for comparing stress responses in personnel across a range of high-risk industries.

NOTE

All opinions stated in this chapter are those of the authors and do not necessarily represent the opinion or position of the USN, Navy Bureau of Medicine and Surgery, or the Naval Postgraduate School.

REFERENCES

Alkov, R. A., Borowsky, M. S., & Gaynor, J. A. (1982). Stress coping and the U.S. Navy aircrew factor mishap. *Aviation, Space, and Environmental Medicine*, 53, 1112–1115.

Alkov, R. A., Gaynor, J. A., & Borowsky, M. S. (1985). *Aviation, Space, and Environmental Medicine*, 56, 244–247.

Attanasio, R. (1997). An overview of bruxism and its management. *Dental Clinics of North America*, 41, 229–241.

Barrick, M. R., & Mount, M. K. (1991). The big five personality dimensions and job performance: A meta-analysis. *Personnel Psychology*, 44, 1–26.

Beck, A. T., & Steer, R. A. (1994). *The Beck depression inventory manual*. San Antonio, TX: Harcourt, Brace, & Co.

Brewer, W. F. (1987). Schemas versus mental models in human memory. In P. Morris (Ed.), *Modeling cognition* (pp. 187–197). Chichester, UK: Wiley.

Brown, N. M., & Moren, C. R. (2003). Background emotional dynamics of crew resource management: Shame emotions and coping responses. *International Journal of Aviation Psychology*, 13, 269–286.

Buss, D. M. (1996). Social adaptation and five major factors of personality. In J. S. Wiggins (Ed.), *The five factor model of personality*. New York: The Guilford Press.

Campbell, J. S. (2006). Personality assessment in naval aviation. In *Proceedings of the annual convention of the American Psychological Association* (p. 258), New Orleans, LA.

Campbell, J. S., & Elison, J. (2005). Shame coping styles and psychopathic personality traits. *Journal of Personality Assessment*, 84, 96–104.

Canli, T. (2006). *Biology of personality and individual differences*. New York: The Guilford Press.

Cannon, W. B. (1915). *Bodily changes in pain, hunger, fear, and rage*. New York: Appleton.

Carver, C. S., Scheier, M. F., & Weintraub, J. K. (1989). Assessing coping strategies: A theoretically based approach. *Journal of Personality and Social Psychology*, 56, 267–283.

Cicchetti, D., Ackerman, B. P., & Izard, C. E. (1995). Emotions and emotion regulation in developmental psychopathology. *Development and Psychopathology*, 7, 1–10.

Cohen, J. (1977). *Statistical power analysis for the behavioral sciences*. San Diego: Academic Press.

Driskell, J. E., Salas, E., & Johnson, J. (2001). Stress management: Individual and team training. In E. Salas, C. Bowers, & E. Edens (Eds.), *Improving teamwork in organizations: Applications of resource management training* (pp. 55–72). Mahwah, NJ: Lawrence Erlbaum Associates.

Elison, J., Lennon, R., & Pulos, S. (2006). Investigating the compass of shame: The development of the compass of shame scale. *Social Behavior and Personality*, 34, 221–238.

Flin, R., O'Connor, P., & Crichton, M. (2008). *Safety at the sharp end*. New York: Lawrence Erlbaum.

Folkman, S., & Lazarus, R. S. (1980). An analysis of coping in a middle-aged community sample. *Journal of Health & Social Behavior*, 46, 159–162.

Glendon, A. I., & Glendon, S. (1992). Stress in ambulance staff. In E. J. Lovesey (Ed.), *Contemporary ergonomics 1992: Ergonomics for industry* (pp. 174–180). London: Taylor & Francis.

Holmes, T. H., & Rahe, R. H. (1967). The social readjustment rating scale. *Journal of Psychosomatic Research*, 11, 213–218.

Kern, T. (2006). *Darker shades of blue: The rogue pilot*. Weston, FL: Convergent.

Krohne, H. W. (1993). *Attention and avoidance*. Seattle: Hogrefe & Huber Publishers.

Lambirth, T., Dolgin, D., Rentmeister-Bryant, H., & Moore, J. L. (2003). Selected personality characteristics of student naval aviators and student naval flight officers. *International Journal of Aviation Psychology*, 13, 415–427.

Lazarus, R. S. (1983). The costs and benefits of denial. In S. Breznitz (Ed.), *The denial of stress* (pp. 1–30). New York: International Universities Press.

Lazarus, R. S., & Folkman, S. (1984). *Stress, appraisal and coping*. New York: Springer Publishing Company.

Lewis, M. D., & Junyk, N. (1997). The self-organization of psychological defenses. In F. Masterpasqua & P. Perna (Eds.), *The psychological meaning of chaos* (pp. 41–74). Washington, DC: American Psychological Association.

Li, C. Y., Chen K. R., Wu, C. H., & Sung, F. C. (2001). Job stress and dissatisfaction in association with non-fatal injuries on the job in a cross-sectional sample of petrochemical workers. *Occupational Medicine*, 51, 50–55.

Loewenthal, K. M., Eysenck, M., Lubitsh, G., Gortin, T., & Bicknell, H. (2000). Stress, distress and air traffic incidents: Job dysfunction, and distress in airline pilots in relation to contextually-assessed stress. *Stress Medicine*, 16 (3), 179–183.

Lurie, O., Zadik, Y., Einy, S., Tarrasch, R., Raviv, G., & Goldstein, L. (2007). Bruxism in military pilots and non-pilots: Tooth war and psychological stress. *Aviation, Space, and Environmental Medicine*, 78, 137–139.

McCarron, P. M., & Haakonson, N. H. (1982). Recent life change measurement in Canadian forces pilots. *Aviation, Space, and Environmental Medicine*, 53, 6–13.

Miller, R. G., Rubin, R. T., Clark, B. R., Crawford, W. R., & Ransom, J. A. (1970). The stress of aircraft carrier landings. I. Corticosteroid responses in naval aviators. *Psychosomatic Medicine*, 32 (6), 581–588.

Musson, D. M., Sandal, G. M., & Helmreich, R. L. (2004). Personality characteristics and trait clusters in final stage astronaut selection. *Aviation, Space, and Environmental Medicine*, 75, 342–349.

Nathanson, D. (1992). *Shame and pride: Affect, sex, and the birth of the self*. New York: Norton.

Otsuka, Y., Onozawa, A., & Miyamoto, Y. (2006). Hormonal responses of pilots to training flights: The effects of experience on apparent stress. *Aviation, Space, and Environmental Medicine*, 77, 410–414.

Parsa, B. B., & Kapadia, A. S. (1997). Stress in Air Force aviators facing the combat environment. *Aviation, Space, and Environmental Medicine*, 68, 1088–1092.

Picano, J. (1990). An empirical assessment of stress-coping styles in military pilots. *Aviation, Space, and Environmental Medicine*, 61, 356–360.

Retzlaff, P. D., & Gilbertini, M. (1987). Air Force personality: Hard data on the right stuff. *Multivariate Behavioral Research*, 22, 383–389.

Saunders, T., Driskell, J. E., Johnston, J., & Salas, E. (1996). The effect of stress inoculation training on anxiety and performance. *Journal of Occupational Health Psychology*, 1, 170–186.

Selye, H. (1956). *The stress of life*. New York: McGraw-Hill.

Siem, F. M., & Murray, M. W. (1994). Personality factors affecting pilot combat performance: A preliminary investigation. *Aviation, Space, and Environmental Medicine*, 65 (A, Suppl.), A45–A48.

Stokes, A., & Kite, K. (1994). *Flight stress: Stress, fatigue, and performance in aviation*. Burlington, VT: Ashgate.

Suls, J., & Fletcher, B. (1985). The relative efficacy of avoidant and nonavoidant coping strategies: A meta-analysis. *Health Psychology*, 4, 249–288.

Takla, N., Koffman, R., & Bailey, D. (1994). Combat stress, combat fatigue, and psychiatric disability in aircrew. *Aviation, Space, and Environmental Medicine*, 65, 858–865.

Tomkins, S. S. (1970). Affect as the primary motivational system. In M. Arnold (Ed.), *Feelings and emotions* (pp. 101–110). New York: Academic Press.

Ursano, R. J. (1980). Stress and adaptation: The interaction of the pilot personality and disease. *Aviation, Space, and Environmental Medicine*, 51, 1245–1249.

Wickens, C. D. (2003). Pilot actions and tasks: Selections, execution, and control. In P. Tsang & M. Vildulich (Eds.), *Principles and practice of aviation psychology* (pp. 239–264). Mahwah, NJ: Lawrence Erlbaum Associates.

Chapter 12

INTEGRATING HUMAN FACTORS INTO SYSTEM SAFETY

Scott Shappell and Douglas A. Wiegmann

When you get it right mighty beasts float up into the sky. When you get it wrong people die.

—Roger Bacon, ca. 1384

Roger Bacon could not have envisioned that people would be flying around in large jet aircraft more than six centuries into the future. Nevertheless, his thoughts ring true even today. This is why organizations such as the Federal Aviation Administration (FAA), National Transportation Safety Board (NTSB), and military safety centers exist and why aviation safety professionals endeavor to make an already safe industry even more secure. Put simply, when the regulators and industry "get it right," people are able to fly safely. When they "get it wrong," the consequences can be very unforgiving.

In recent years, those entrusted with the safety of the aviation industry have focused more and more on the investigation of human factors associated with accidents and incidents. This may be due to the fact that while the number of aviation accidents attributable solely to mechanical failures has decreased sharply over the past 40 years, those attributed to human factors continue to be linked to 70–80 percent of civil and military aviation accidents (O'Hare, Wiggins, Batt, & Morrison, 1994; Wiegmann & Shappell, 2003).

The purpose of this chapter is to discuss the application of system safety as it relates to human factors associated with accidents occurring in aviation and other high-risk industries. Toward these ends, we will briefly review a fundamental model of system safety, highlighting the different stages in the system safety process and identifying aspects of the process that could be improved by the use of better human factors tools and techniques. We will then briefly describe two such tools—the Human Factors Analysis and Classification System (HFACS) and the Human Factors Intervention Matrix (HFIX). Finally, we will provide an example of how these tools can be used to improve human factors data analysis and intervention development within aviation to improve overall safety.

FUNDAMENTALS OF SYSTEM SAFETY

In attempt to close the gap and address the human component of aviation safety, many safety professionals have embraced a system safety approach similar to the one illustrated on the right side of Figure 12.1. While there are several variations to the basic approach, most models include the following components: data acquisition, hazard identification, hazard assessment, identification of intervention/mitigation strategies to address specific hazards, an assessment of those intervention/mitigation strategies, intervention implementation, and system monitoring. Ideally, this is a dynamic process involving the real-time identification of hazards, identification and implementation of interventions, and some process for monitoring changes in the health and safety of the overall system.

Historically, the system safety approach has been effective when addressing mechanical issues within aviation and other industries. Indeed, the number of accidents attributed to mechanical/engineering failures has decreased markedly since the middle of the twenty-first century. Although the reasons can be debated, many would agree that the success of system safety could be attributed, at least in part, to a number of engineering and mathematical tools capable of quantifying decisions at each step in the process.

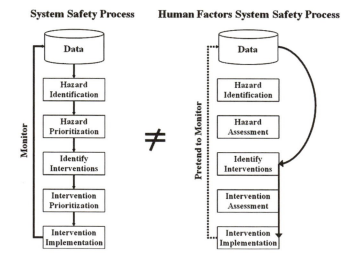

Figure 12.1.   The lack of effective human factors tools results in key steps in the human factors system safety process being skipped.

Encouraged by the success of this approach in the engineering world, many safety professionals have understandably looked to this same methodology when addressing human error in aviation. As a result, the last 10–15 years have witnessed a move toward the collection of more normative data for hazard identification and assessment—particularly within the scheduled air carrier industry. Programs such as Flight Operations Quality Assurance (FOQA), the Aviation Safety Action Program (ASAP), and Line Oriented Safety Audits (LOSA) have expanded our understanding of human factors associated with air carrier accidents and incidents. In fact, when combined with traditional data sources from accident, incident, and near-miss databases maintained by the NTSB and National Aeronautics and Space Administration (NASA), data from FOQA, ASAP, and LOSA have provided the air carrier industry a unique perspective of human error.

Nevertheless, as important as data collection is, it is still only *part* of the solution. After all, it can be argued that even without programs such as FOQA, ASAP, and LOSA, the aviation industry is still collecting valuable accident, incident, and near-miss data (Shappell & Wiegmann, 2003a). The problem is identifying hazards within a veritable cornucopia of data that already exist within these databases. Combined with the cumbersome nature of many of the larger data repositories, manipulation and analysis of the existing data is difficult, at best. As a result, even the most well-intentioned safety professionals may be forced to focus on selected cases or small subsets of the data rather than more global analyses.

Left without a systematic, albeit standardized, and generally accepted means to examine human error data, the only viable option available to safety managers may be to tacitly address or bypass altogether the next two critical steps in the system safety process (hazard identification and assessment) and jump straight to identifying interventions (Figure 12.1). However, the human factors system safety process does not get any easier when identifying interventions. After all, effective tools for systematically generating effective intervention programs that target specific forms of human error have been lacking. As illustrated in Figure 12.1, this often leaves safety professionals with no choice but to sidestep the next steps in the safety management process (identifying and assessing intervention strategies) and simply implement safety initiatives that look and feel "good," yet do not necessarily target any specific error form.

In the end, organizations may have no alternative but to rely on simple intuition, expert opinion, or "pop psychology" when addressing human factors, thereby ignoring the larger database altogether. Unfortunately, such an approach can lead to omnibus and unfocused initiatives based more on personality and anecdotes than aggregate data.

This is not to say that a system safety approach to human error within the industry is not feasible. Quite the contrary, it is conceivably a very good idea. However, to date few valid and reliable tools exist that would enable it to be systematically employed throughout the aviation industry and beyond into other industrial settings. As a result, system safety as an approach for addressing human factors associated with accidents/incidents has arguably met with limited success.

MERGING HUMAN FACTORS AND SYSTEM SAFETY

Over the past several years, we have been working on ways to improve the integration of human factors into the system safety process. As both scientists and practitioners, we have strived to develop methods for managing human error that are scientifically derived, empirically tested, and proven in the field. The results of our efforts have been the successful *development of a compendium of* tools and techniques, including the HFACS and the HFIX, for use by safety professionals. The balance of this chapter will describe these tools and how they can be combined to facilitate hazard analysis and intervention development within the context of aviation and other industries.

THE HUMAN FACTORS ANALYSIS AND CLASSIFICATION SYSTEM

It is generally accepted that aviation accidents are typically the result of a chain of events that often culminate with the unsafe acts of operators (aircrew). The aviation industry is not alone in this belief. The safety community has embraced a sequential theory of accident investigation since Heinrich first published his axioms of industrial safety in 1931 (Heinrich, Petersen, & Roos, 1980). However, it was not until Reason published his "Swiss cheese" model of human error in 1990 that the aviation community truly began to examine human error in a systematic manner.

Drawing upon Reason's (1990) concept of latent and active failures, HFACS describes human error at each of four levels: (1) the unsafe acts of operators (e.g., aircrew, maintainers, and air traffic controllers), (2) preconditions for unsafe acts, (3) unsafe supervision (i.e., middle management), and (4) organizational influences. In other words, the HFACS framework goes beyond the simple identification of *what* an operator did wrong to provide a clear understanding of the reasons *why* the error occurred in the first place. In this way, errors are viewed as consequences of system failures and/or symptoms of deeper systemic problems; *not* simply the fault of the employee working at the "pointy end of the spear." A brief description of each causal category within HFACS is provided in Table 12.1, and the structure of HFACS is presented graphically in Figure 12.2.

Although HFACS was originally developed and used as an aviation accident investigation and analysis tool for the U.S. Navy and Marine Corps, the framework has been adopted by a number of other aviation, transportation,

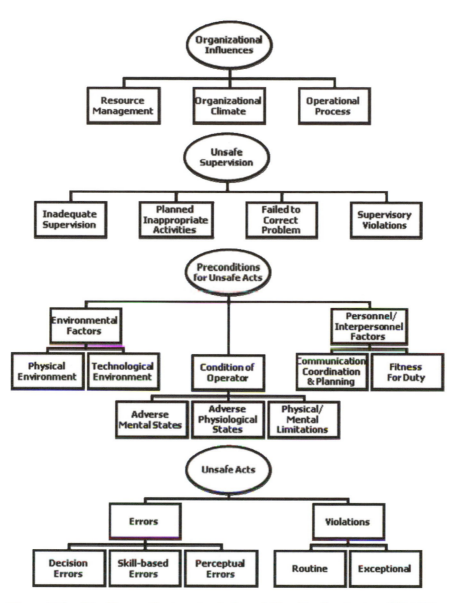

Figure 12.2.   The Human Factors Analysis and Classification System (HFACS).

Table 12.1. Description of HFACS Causal Categories

ORGANIZATIONAL INFLUENCES
Organizational climate: Prevailing atmosphere/vision within the organization, including such things as policies, command structure, and culture.
Operational process: Formal process by which the vision of an organization is carried out, including operations, procedures, and oversight among others.
Resource management: How human, monetary, and equipment resources necessary to carry out the vision are managed.
UNSAFE SUPERVISION
Inadequate supervision: Oversight and management of personnel and resources, including training, professional guidance, and operational leadership among other aspects.
Planned inappropriate operations: Management and assignment of work, including aspects of risk management, crew pairing, and operational tempo.
Failed to correct known problems: Those instances when deficiencies among individuals, equipment, training, or other related safety areas are "known" to the supervisor, yet are allowed to continue uncorrected.
Supervisory violations: The willful disregard for existing rules, regulations, instructions, or standard operating procedures by management during the course of their duties.
PRECONDITIONS FOR UNSAFE ACTS
Environmental Factors
Technological environment: This category encompasses a variety of issues, including the design of equipment and controls, display/interface characteristics, checklist layouts, task factors, and automation.
Physical environment: Included are both the operational setting (e.g., weather, altitude, and terrain) and the ambient environment, such as heat, vibration, lighting, and toxins.
Condition of the Operator
Adverse mental states: Acute psychological and/or mental conditions that negatively affect performance such as mental fatigue, pernicious attitudes, and misplaced motivation.
Adverse physiological states: Acute medical and/or physiological conditions that preclude safe operations such as illness, intoxication, and the myriad of pharmacological and medical abnormalities known to affect performance.
Physical/Mental limitations: Permanent physical/mental disabilities that may adversely impact performance such as poor vision, lack of physical strength, mental aptitude, general knowledge, and a variety of other chronic mental illnesses.

Personnel Factors
Communication, coordination, and planning: Includes a variety of communication, coordination, and teamwork issues that impact performance.
Fitness for duty: Off-duty activities required to perform optimally on the job such as adhering to crew rest requirements, alcohol restrictions, and other off-duty mandates.
<div align="center">**UNSAFE ACTS**</div>
Errors
Decision errors: These "thinking" errors represent conscious, goal-intended behavior that proceeds as designed, yet the plan proves inadequate or inappropriate for the situation. These errors typically manifest as poorly executed procedures, improper choices, or simply the misinterpretation and/or misuse of relevant information.
Skill-based errors: Highly practiced behavior that occurs with little or no conscious thought. These "doing" errors frequently appear as a breakdown in visual scan patterns, inadvertent activation/deactivation of switches, forgotten intentions, and omitted items in checklists. Even the manner or technique with which one performs a task is included.
Perceptual errors: These errors arise when sensory input is degraded as is often the case when flying at night, in poor weather, or in otherwise visually impoverished environments. Faced with acting on imperfect or incomplete information, aircrew run the risk of misjudging distances, altitude, airspeed, etc., as well as responding incorrectly to a variety of visual/vestibular illusions.
Violations
Routine violations: Often referred to as "bending the rules," this type of violation tends to be habitual by nature and is often enabled by a system of supervision and management that tolerates such departures from the rules.
Exceptional violations: Isolated departures from authority, neither typical of the individual nor condoned by the management.

and high-risk industries. All branches of the U.S. military, as well as the Canadian Defense Force, Royal Dutch Air Force, Hellenic Air Force, and Indian Air Force, have now adopted HFACS. It has also been employed in civilian aviation settings (e.g., Australian Transportation Safety Board, Air Canada, and Alaska Airlines) as a tool for analyzing the role of human error in aviation accidents. This is not to say that HFACS is only applicable to aviation. Indeed, it has also been proven to be effective in the analysis of errors within a variety of other industrial settings (e.g., health care—ElBardissi, Wiegmann, Dearani, Daly, & Sundt, 2007) as well as other modes of transportation (e.g., railroad—Baysari, McIntosh, & Wilson, 2008 and Reinach & Viale, 2006; maritime—Celik & Cebi, 2009; and driving—Iden &

Shappell, 2006). Given its theoretical foundation, HFACS can be applied in virtually any operational context.

THE HUMAN FACTORS INTERVENTION MATRIX

HFACS has proven useful with the identification and prioritization of human causal factors. The next step in the system safety process is to identify and assess current, planned, and potential interventions to address the hazards identified. Stated plainly, simply knowing that a problem exists does not necessarily translate into an effective solution.

Consider, for example, ACME Airlines, which has recently seen a large number of perceptual errors in the ramp area. In particular, there has been a marked increase in damage caused by baggage handlers inadvertently driving their baggage conveyors into the side of aircraft (presumable due to baggage handlers misjudging the distance between the conveyor and the aircraft). Surely, there are any number of interventions that might be effective in reducing these aggravating and costly collisions. However, depending on whom you talk to, you might get different types of interventions. For example, if you ask a manager, he or she might suggest administrative fixes (e.g., additional policies/procedures or some form of enforcement action). On the other hand, if you ask an engineer, he or she would likely come up with an engineering fix (e.g., bumpers on the end of the conveyor, collision avoidance systems, or automatic braking). All are good ideas, but which one is best and are there others?

To help address this need, the HFIX was developed to broaden the scope of potential interventions and force safety professionals to consider a broad spectrum of interventions rather than the same two or three that always seem to find their way into existing safety programs (Shappell & Wiegmann, 2006). Specifically, the HFIX tool contrasts the causal factors identified within HFACS (e.g., decision errors, skill-based errors, perceptual errors, and violations) against five approaches to accident intervention and mitigation identified in the literature (Figure 12.3).

While a complete description of HFIX is beyond the scope of this chapter, in general HFIX employs five broad areas around which interventions can be developed: (1) administrative, (2) human, (3) technological, (4) task, and (5) operational environment. Each is briefly summarized below.

- *Administrative*
  - *Human resource management*: Adequacy of staff in specific situations, the need for additional personnel, and the evaluation of individual skills of employees.
  - *Rules/Regulations/Policies*: Issuing, modifying, establishing, amending, and/or reviewing policies, rules, or regulations.

	Organizational/ Administrative	Human/ Crew	Technology/ Engineering	Task/ Mission	Operational/ Physical Environment
Decision Errors					
Skill-based Errors					
Perceptual Errors					
Violations					

Figure 12.3.   The *H*uman *F*actors *I*ntervention Matri*X* (HFIX). For simplicity, only the four unsafe acts are illustrated.

- ○ *Information management/Communication*: Improvements in disseminating, storing, archiving, and publishing information. Also included are recommendations regarding collection of data, issuing information, and reporting activity.
- ○ *Research/Special study*: Conducting research to determine the impact of recent technological advances or call for special studies to review processes, develop/validate methodologies, etc.
- • *Task*
- ○ *Procedures*: Amending, reviewing, modifying, revising, establishing, developing, and validating procedures.
- ○ *Manuals*: Reviewing, revising, issuing, and modifying manuals, bulletins, checklists, and other instructions or guidance.
- • *Technological*
- ○ *Design/Repair*: Specific manufacturing changes, including the design of parts. Also included is the modification, replacement, removal and/ or installation, or repair of parts and equipment.
- ○ *Inspection*: Maintenance inspections, overhauling, detecting damage, including day-to-day operations such as inspecting fuel, oil level, and recommended safety checks.

- *Operational Environment*
  - *Operational/Physical environment*: Modifications to the operational environment (e.g., weather, altitude, and terrain) or the ambient environment, such as heat, vibration, lighting, and eliminating toxins, to improve performance.
- *Human/Crew*
  - *Training*: Reviewing, developing, and implementing training programs. Also included is the training of personnel in handling emergencies.

When employing HFIX, whether with an individual accident or larger, more aggregate problems like those experienced by ACME Airlines, the goal is to identify multiple interventions within each of the five approaches. To accomplish this within larger, aggregate scenarios like the ACME Airlines example, we would typically identify about 20 individuals from multiple lines of business within the airline to generate candidate interventions. The goal is to get as wide a variety of expertise in the room as possible, from management to ramp personnel, pilots to executive secretaries, maintenance to logistics.

Once the group is convened and the problem explained, individuals are randomly assigned to one of five groups to generate candidate interventions. Note that we do not introduce individuals in the room to each other since it might stifle intervention generation if individuals were aware of each other's rank in the organization. Each group is then assigned to one of the five approaches and instructed to generate as many interventions as possible within 30 minutes to address the problem (i.e., collisions between baggage conveyors and aircraft in our example). They are instructed that no intervention is too ridiculous, just list them, and we will sort out the good from the bad ideas later. After about 15 minutes, the groups are provided with a sheet of questions to further stimulate their intervention generation. These questions are:

- How can warnings or alarms be improved to increase operators' awareness of hazards or the presence of abnormal conditions?
- How can tools or technologies be redesigned to enter into "fail-safe" mode when problems occur?
- How could safeguards or personnel protective equipment be improved to reduce the consequences of errors?
- How could tools, checklists, manuals, or displays be redesigned to reduce confusion and errors (e.g., boldface items in checklist that are most important and/or should be memorized)?
- How could automation help in reducing the dependency on human performance of certain tasks?

- Are better tools currently on the market but not purchased by the company? What are these tools and how would they reduce errors on the job?
- How could technologies be developed to reduce the task demands on the human decision-making processes, perceptual processes, or physical limitations?
- How could operator tools be more effectively designed to improve operator performance and/or reduce injuries?
- How could controls be more easily identified and/or better designed in terms of shape, size, and other relevant considerations?
- How could information sources be integrated or located in a more effective manner?
- How can the provision for adequate redundancy in the system be improved, especially of critical functions? One form of redundancy is the implementation of backup or parallel components (persons or machines).
- How could the design/operation of tools, workplaces, vehicles, etc., be standardized to prevent negative transfer or confusion?
- How could tools/technology be developed to reduce the physical demand on the operator?
- How could equipment be redesigned for convenient maintenance?
- Is there adequate clearance space for reaching parts that need to be repaired or replaced?
- Can individual parts be repaired or replaced easily?
- Are proper tools and adequate troubleshooting aids available? Are there adequate instructions for maintenance and repair?

After a short break, the groups are then assigned a new intervention approach (e.g., the administrative group is now assigned human/crew intervention development) and the process is repeated. Our experience has shown that three rounds of intervention generation are optimal although some organizations repeat the process until all five groups have had a turn identifying interventions in each of the five approaches.

While groups occasionally identify the same or similar interventions, this process usually results in between 100 and 200 unique interventions ranging from the very unique and promising to the utterly ridiculous. More important, interventions are identified across a wide spectrum of approaches. For example, some of the more useful interventions ACME Airlines identified were:

- the assignment of at least one person whose job it is to spot the baggage conveyor as it approaches the aircraft (organizational/administrative);
- the purchase and use of a baggage conveyor simulator for training of ramp personnel (organizational/administrative);
- selection of ramp personnel with 20/20 vision normally or corrected with eyeglasses (human/crew);
- proximity detectors on the end of the baggage conveyor (technological);

- elimination of baggage conveyors to remove bags from aircraft, use soft slides instead (task/mission); and

- improved lighting in the ramp area (operational environment).

In contrast to the above candidate interventions, there are always some that, while potentially effective (e.g., shock collars that transmit an electric shock to the baggage handler if the conveyor touches the aircraft), certainly would not find their way onto an airport ramp! Clearly then, some sort of prioritization must be done. While individual safety managers could scan the list and pick and choose their favorite interventions much like they would a dinner entrée at their favorite restaurant, we prefer a more systematic approach that we refer to as FACES (Figure 12.4). That is, we typically convene a second, smaller group to "rate" the candidate interventions on each of the five dimensions (i.e., feasibility, acceptability, cost, effectiveness, and sustainability) using a scale of 1 to 5 with 1 representing "poor" and/or "undesirable" and 5 representing "excellent" and/or "desirable."[1] Clearly, factors such as *feasibility* (i.e., How easy will it be to implement the intervention or does it actually exist?), *acceptability* (i.e., Will the pilot community accept the proposed intervention?), *cost* (i.e., Can the organization afford the intervention?), *effectiveness* (i.e., What is the likelihood that it will reduce general aviation (GA) accidents?), and *sustainability* (i.e., Will the intervention last or will it need to be updated or reinforced regularly) are all important to the successful employment of safety interventions.

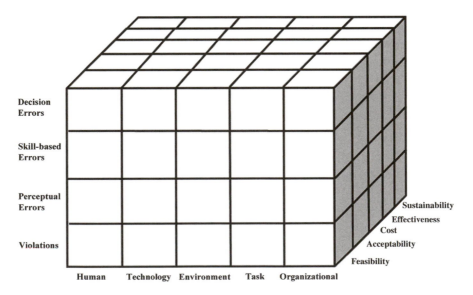

Figure 12.4.   HFIX with FACES.

By rating each candidate intervention across the FACES dimensions, an element of quantitative rigor can be introduced into the prioritization process. By averaging the ratings across the group, one can get a sense of which candidate interventions would prove most useful. Furthermore, by manipulating the weighing of the dimensions, different candidate interventions might move to the top of the list. For instance, some organizations may be more interested in cost than others, particularly in economic downturns. Others may be more interested in effectiveness or even acceptability. By weighing the dimensions, safety professionals can tailor intervention strategies to their organizations' needs.

In effect, by mapping candidate interventions onto HFIX and prioritizing them with FACES, it would be readily apparent to senior officials within the organization the breadth of a proposed safety program (i.e., is the program uni- or multidimensional) and exactly what aspects of human behavior were targeted.

PUTTING IT ALL TOGETHER: THE CASE OF GENERAL AVIATION ACCIDENTS

Most would agree that if the aviation industry is to reduce the accident rate beyond current levels, it would be reasonable to address the human factors component of accidents and incidents. Toward these ends, the FAA began using HFACS in 1999 as a tool to examine human factors associated with GA accidents—the leading cause of fatalities in the civil aviation domain.[2] Particularly germane to this discussion is a series of investigations of GA accident data conducted by the FAA's Civil Aerospace Medical Institute (CAMI) over the last several years (Detwiler et al., 2006; Shappell & Wiegmann, 2001, 2003a, 2003b, 2004; Shappell et al., 2006; Wiegmann & Shappell, 2001a, 2001b, 2003; Wiegmann et al., 2005). We will use these studies to illustrate how HFACS and HFIX can be used together to improve hazard identification and analysis, as well as intervention development and evaluation.

Identification of Hazards

Representative of the body of work referenced above was the examination of over 14,000 GA human factors-related accidents that occurred between 1990 and 2000 (see Wiegmann et al., 2005). Using HFACS, several interesting findings emerged (Figure 12.5). First, the proportion of accidents associated with at least one skill-based error, decision error, perceptual error, and violation has remained largely unchanged over the 11-year period examined. That is, all trend lines remained relatively flat.

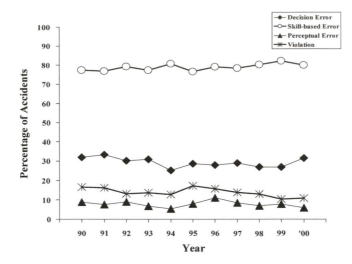

Figure 12.5. Percentage of accidents associated with at least one instance of a given unsafe act. (Note that because each accident can be associated with multiple causal factors, the percentage of accidents for a given year will not equal 100%.)

This finding suggests that although the overall GA accident rate declined from 7.85 to 6.85 accidents per 100,000 flight hours during that time frame (NTSB, 2006), safety efforts directed at GA in the late 1980s and mid-1990s had little impact on any specific type of human error. The only exceptions seemed to be a small decline in the percentage of accidents associated with decision errors in 1994, as well as a very gradual decline in violations observed from 1991 to 1994, and then again from 1995 to 2000. With decision errors, however, the trend quickly reestablished itself at levels consistent with the overall average. This was true whether one considered the data overall or separately for fatal and nonfatal accidents.

Second, skill-based errors were the most prevalent form of human error associated with GA accidents—having been implicated in roughly four out of every five accidents since 1990. This is not to say that poor decisions did not figure prominently in GA accidents. After all, nearly a third of all fatal GA accidents were associated with at least one decision error and a little less than 20 percent were associated with violations of the rules. Moreover, this pattern of human error was evident whether one looked at all human causal factors or just the first (i.e., primary) human causal factor in the chain of events leading to the accident.

Finally, while the percentage of fatal and nonfatal accidents associated with skill-based, decision, and perceptual errors was relatively equal, the proportion of accidents associated with violations was considerably higher for fatal accidents. In fact, the data suggest that pilots who violate the rules and are involved

Table 12.2. Specific Types of Errors Associated with General Aviation Accidents (perceptual errors are not shown due to the low frequency)

Aircrew unsafe act	Frequency (%)
Skill-based Errors	
Directional control on the ground	2,345 (12.9%)
Airspeed	2,008 (11.1%)
Stall/Spin	1,400 (7.7%)
Aircraft control in the air	1,359 (7.5%)
Compensation for wind conditions	1,179 (6.5%)
Total Skill-based Errors Committed	18,136 (100%)
Decision Errors	
In-flight planning/decision making	1,061 (18.2%)
Takeoff/landing from unsuitable terrain	431 (7.4%)
Preflight planning/making	393 (6.7%)
Refueling	367 (6.3%)
Go-around	354 (6.1%)
Total Decision Errors Committed	5,845 (100%)
Violations	
VFR flight into IMC	269 (10.7%)
Operating with known deficiencies	269 (10.7%)
Failure to adhere to procedures/directives	260 (10.4%)
Flight into known adverse weather	223 (8.9%)
Aircraft weight and balance	162 (6.5%)
Total Violations Committed	2,503 (100%)

in an accident are four times more likely to perish or fatally injure someone. This latter finding was particularly striking since pilots are repeatedly told that the "rules are written in blood"—a lesson apparently true even today.

Assessment of Hazards

The next logical step in the system safety methodology is to *assess the hazards* within each HFACS error category (e.g., skill-based errors, decision errors, perceptual errors, and violations) to determine which errors were most common. A summary of this assessment is presented in Table 12.2. The numbers alone would seem to imply that the largest threat to GA safety are skill-based errors such as directional control on the ground (e.g., ground loops) as well as concerns regarding control of airspeed and control surfaces leading to inadvertent stalls/spins. Equally important, however, were in-flight planning and decision errors, as were violations associated with visual flight rules (VFR) flight into instrument meteorological conditions (IMC), particularly given the emphasis within the FAA on reducing fatal GA accidents (FAA, 2006). Notably, while the loss of directional control on the ground occurs quite frequently, it typically does not result in fatalities. By comparison, stalls/spins, errors associated with in-flight planning/decision making, and VFR flight into IMC may not occur as frequently, but are often fatal when they do.

A logical extension of Table 12.2 would be to develop a so-called "Top-10 list of human error threats to GA safety." Although by no means an official list, a reasonable list of threats (in no particular order) might include:

- VFR flight into IMC and control of airspeed;
- recovery from stalls/spins;
- in-flight decision making;
- directional control on the ground;
- refueling issues;
- compensation for wind conditions;
- takeoff and landing from unsuitable terrain;
- operating with known deficiencies; and
- failure to adhere to procedures/directives.

Identification of Interventions

One area of particular interest to the FAA is VFR flight into IMC. While not all instances of VFR flight into IMC are willful and therefore a violation, many are (Detwiler et al., 2006) making this specific cause of GA accidents a reasonable place to evaluate the use of HFIX as a means to generate interventions.

To illustrate how HFIX can be used to identify interventions, we enlisted the support of 218 participants with expertise in a variety of aviation specialties (i.e., pilots, flight instructors, student pilots, aerospace engineers, air traffic controllers, mechanics, aviation administrators, government regulators, and aviation faculty) from five locations: Embry-Riddle Aeronautical University (ERAU), Canadian Helicopter Corporation (CHC), Transportation Safety Institute (TSI), FAA, and Alaska Airlines. At each location, participants were divided into five equal groups, assigned a particular approach, and instructed to generate as many interventions within that particular approach as possible. For instance, if assigned to the human approach, participants were instructed to generate programs that would reduce the likelihood that a pilot would initiate flying into IMC when VFR only by changing the behavior of the aircrew.

Ideas such as "conducting annual training to review/enhance knowledge of the adverse effects of weather on flying" and "creating a mentoring program for all new pilots" were typical of this group.

As described earlier, each group was given 15 minutes to generate as many interventions as possible. They were then provided with a list of questions intended to stimulate additional intervention development within a given approach and an additional 15 minutes to generate interventions. After a 15-minute break, the groups were assigned to another approach (e.g., the human-centered group was then tasked with developing organizational interventions). In total, three rounds of intervention development were conducted.

Not surprising, several of the interventions generated were either the same or very similar. Therefore, after interventions were collected from each location, the compiled list of interventions was edited to eliminate duplications. The final list included 136 unique interventions.

Assessment of Interventions

The next step involved assessing the candidate interventions using FACES. Unfortunately, the last assessment category, sustainability, was not added until 2008, and therefore, only the first four categories were used in this assessment (i.e., feasibility, acceptability, cost, and effectiveness). Nevertheless, for illustrative purposes we will present the "FACE" data alone.

For this phase of the process, we solicited the help of five subject matter experts (i.e., instructor pilots). Three of the instructor pilots were fixed-wing pilots and two were helicopter pilots. They had an average of 26.4 years of aviation experience, with the least amount of experience being 12 years and the greatest being 37 years.

There are many ways to rank the interventions using FACES. For instance, one could treat each dimension equally and merely sort the potential interventions based upon the overall average of the four ratings. By treating each dimension equally, a "top-10" list of interventions was identified and is presented in Table 12.3.

What is apparent from the list is that many of the candidate interventions involve some degree of training. Whether that training deals with preventing pilots from flying into instrument conditions (i.e., information regarding the hazards associated with VFR flight into IMC beyond current levels) or how to survive once one gets there (e.g., spatial disorientation training and the importance of communicating with air traffic control and flight service stations when in adverse weather), many of the higher-rated interventions seem almost intuitive. Indeed, many are already being considered at some level within the GA community. In those cases, this analysis may provide some additional support for continuing existing efforts. In contrast, where the interventions identified here were novel, they may provide those charged with GA safety a fresh approach to a historical problem.

Table 12.3. Top-10 Interventions by Average on a Scale of 1 (Worst) to 5 (Best)

Intervention	Effectiveness	Acceptability	Feasibility	Cost	Average
Standardize initial flight training that covers VFR into IMC.	4.8	4.2	4.6	4.0	4.4
Require spatial disorientation training for all pilots.	4.6	4.4	4.4	4.0	4.4
Make VFR into IMC training a special emphasis on the Biennial Flight Review.	4.4	4.0	4.6	4.2	4.3
Conduct awareness training within ground school that demonstrates flight in weather (e.g., videos of A/C exceeding structural capabilities).	4.4	4.4	4.2	3.8	4.2
Include training on the importance of communication and radio calls for items that may seem trivial or embarrassing (e.g., informing ATC that unfamiliar with the area).	4.0	3.6	4.6	4.4	4.2
Require that instructors are able to complete all the maneuvers they teach.	4.4	3.8	4.2	4.2	4.2
Add a weather update to the en route checklist.	3.8	3.6	4.0	5.0	4.1
Create an incentive program that teams with insurance programs.	4.2	4.0	3.6	4.0	4.0
Mandate minimum standards and training for all equipment used in an aircraft.	4.2	4.0	4.2	3.4	4.0
Include training on decision making versus skill in dealing with the hazards of flying in IMC.	4.0	3.6	3.8	4.2	3.9

Intervention Implementation and Monitoring

Obviously, the next step in the system safety process is the implementation of a given intervention or combination of interventions. After all, human error is by its very nature complex and multidimensional. Therefore, it seems reasonable that any strategy for addressing it would likewise be multidimensional and represent a "strategy" or "program" rather than an individual intervention.

Once the intervention strategy has been identified and implemented, the last step in the process is to monitor the data. Again, using HFACS the process starts anew. The difference is that rather than simply monitoring overall accident rates, safety professionals will be able to track improvements among specific forms of human error; in the current case, VFR flight into IMC by GA pilots.

This is a departure from the historical norm where safety professionals typically monitor the "overall" accident rate to assess whether a given human factors intervention was effective. Imagine if organizations used the same rationale for assessing intervention effectiveness when addressing mechanical failures. Would it make sense to examine the overall accident rate when determining if improvements to the production and maintenance of the rudder on the Boeing 737 were effective? Of course not. What do accidents, incidents, and near misses associated with the Beech King Air have to do with the rudder on the Boeing 737? Moreover, why would one even look at all Boeing 737 events when the rudder was the issue?

In a similar fashion, it makes no sense to examine overall accident rates to assess the impact of a given human factors intervention(s). Likewise, it may not make sense to look at HFACS categories per se—at least not as the final analysis. Rather, it may make more sense to look at the HFACS category first (e.g., violations) and the specific error form (e.g., VFR flight into IMC) to determine whether the intervention(s) were effective. Unfortunately, that data remain to be collected for the example provided.

CONCLUDING REMARKS

Socrates once said, "Prescription without diagnosis is malpractice." Perhaps he was speaking of more than just medicine. Maybe his words make sense within the realm of aviation safety as well. If indeed that is true, then clearly the use of system safety when addressing human factors associated with GA accidents makes sense and perhaps efforts like the ones outlined in this report have brought us one step closer to a methodology for practicing human factors system safety.

This report began with a brief overview of system safety and the difficulties safety professionals have faced implementing it within the complex field of human factors. Given the data presented here, perhaps some of those concerns have been resolved or are resolving.

There is no denying that system safety concepts have proven very beneficial within the aviation domain. However, its utility within human factors has yet to be fully leveraged within the aviation industry. In the end, it is hoped that tools like HFACS and HFIX will ensure that *human factors* system safety will become a reality and that ultimately accidents attributed to human error will be markedly reduced.

NOTES

1. Note that cost is reverse coded. That is high cost is considered "poor" and low cost is considered "excellent."
2. General aviation refers to the operation of civilian aircraft for purposes other than the transport of goods or passengers for hire and includes personal, business, and instructional flying.

REFERENCES

Baysari, M., McIntosh, A., & Wilson, J. (2008). Understanding the human factors contribution to railway accidents and incidents in Australia. *Accident Analysis and Prevention*, 40, 1750–1757.

Celik, M., & Cebi, S. (2009). Analytical HFACS for investigating human errors in shipping accidents. *Accident Analysis and Prevention*, 41, 66–75.

Detwiler, C., Boquet, A., Holcomb, K., Hackworth, C., Wiegmann, D., & Shappell, S. (2006). *Beyond the tip of the iceberg: A human factors analysis of general aviation accidents in Alaska and the rest of the United States*. Office of Aerospace Medicine Technical Report No. DOT/FAA/AM-06/07. Office of Aerospace Medicine, Washington, D.C.

ElBardissi, A., Wiegmann, D., Dearani, J., Daly, R., & Sundt, T. (2007). Application of the human factors analysis and classification system methodology to the cardiovascular surgery operating room. *Annals of Thoracic Surgery*, 83, 1412–1419.

Federal Aviation Administration. (2006). Federal Aviation Administration flight plan 2007–2011. Obtained from the World Wide Web at http://www.faa.gov/about/plans_reports/media/flight_plan_2007.pdf.

Heinrich, H. W., Petersen, D., & Roos, N. (1980). *Industrial accident prevention: A safety management approach* (5th ed.). New York: McGraw-Hill.

Iden, R., & Shappell, S. (2006). A human error analysis of U.S. fatal highway crashes 1990–2004. *Proceedings of the 50th Annual Meeting of the Human Factors and Ergonomics Society*, San Francisco, CA.

National Transportation Safety Board. (2006). Table 10. Accidents, fatalities, and rates, 1986 through 2005, U.S. general aviation. Obtained from the World Wide Web at http://www.ntsb.gov/aviation/Table10.htm.

O'Hare, D., Wiggins, M., Batt, R., & Morrison, D. (1994). Cognitive failure analysis for aircraft accident investigation. *Ergonomics*, 37, 1855–1869.

Reason, J. (1990). *Human error*. New York: Cambridge University Press.

Reinach, S., & Viale, A. (2006). *Human factors root cause analysis of accidents/incidents involving remote control locomotive operations* (DOT/FRA/ORD-06/05). Washington, D.C.: Federal Railroad Administration.

Shappell, S., Detwiler, C., Holcomb, K., Hackworth, C., Boquet, A., & Wiegmann, D. (2006). Human error and commercial aviation accidents: A comprehensive, fine-grained analysis using HFACS. Office of Aerospace Medicine Technical Report No. DOT/FAA/AM-06/18. Office of Aerospace Medicine, Washington, D.C.

Shappell, S., & Wiegmann, D. (2001). Unraveling the mystery of general aviation controlled flight into terrain accidents using HFACS. *Proceedings of the Eleventh International Symposium on Aviation Psychology*, Ohio State University.

————. (2003a). Reshaping the way we look at general aviation accidents using the human factors analysis and classification system. *Proceedings of the Twelfth International Symposium on Aviation Psychology*, Dayton, Ohio.

————. (2003b). A human error analysis of general aviation controlled flight into terrain (CFIT) accidents occurring between 1990–1998. Office of Aerospace Medicine Technical Report No. DOT/FAA/AM-03/4. Office of Aerospace Medicine, Washington, D.C.

————. (2004). HFACS analysis of military and civilian aviation accidents: A North American comparison. *Proceedings of the Annual Meeting of the International Society of Air Safety Investigators*, Gold Coast, Australia.

————. (2006). Developing a methodology for assessing safety programs targeting human error in aviation. Office of Aerospace Medicine Technical Report No. DOT/FAA/AM-06-24. Office of Aerospace Medicine, Washington, D.C.

Wiegmann, D., Boquet, A., Detwiler, C., Holcomb, K., Faaborg, T., & Shappell, S. (2005). Human error and general aviation accidents: A comprehensive, fine-grained analysis using HFACS. Office of Aerospace Medicine Technical Report No. DOT/FAA/AM-05-24. Office of Aerospace Medicine, Washington, D.C.

Wiegmann, D., & Shappell, S. (2001a). Human error analysis of commercial aviation accidents: Application of the human factors analysis and classification system (HFACS). *Aviation, Space and Environmental Medicine*, 72, 1006–1016.

————. (2001b). Human error analysis of commercial aviation accidents: Application of the human factors analysis and classification system (HFACS). *Proceedings of the Eleventh International Symposium on Aviation Psychology*, Ohio State University.

————. (2003). *A human error approach to aviation accident analysis: The human factors analysis and classification system*. Burlington, VT: Ashgate.

Part V: Design

Chapter 13

IT'S ALL ABOUT YOU: IMPLEMENTING HUMAN-CENTERED DESIGN

Regan H. Campbell and Geoffrey Eaton

In April of 1979, an ammunition ship was on its way to the Hawaiian Islands independently steaming across the Pacific. Unexpectedly, a U.S. Navy SH-3 Sea King helicopter appeared, hovering off the port side. The SH-3 crew began frantically gesturing to the crew of the ammunition ship. One of the ship's crew used hand signals to indicate a radio frequency on which they could communicate. The SH-3 pilot came on the circuit and stated, "We need to land, we are out of gas."

The crew of the ammunition ship immediately set emergency flight quarters. As the SH-3 approached and settled on the flight deck, it ran out of gas. There were no injuries, and there was no damage to the helicopter. How could such an event have happened?

As it turns out, the SH-3 was attached to an aircraft carrier and was conducting a standard surface surveillance mission. During watch turnover aboard the aircraft carrier, the off-going Tactical Action Officer (TAO) neglected to state there was a helicopter aloft. Shortly after assuming the watch, a Soviet surveillance plane was reported nearby. The new TAO received orders to set full electromagnetic emissions control to prevent detection of the aircraft carrier through emission detection devices by the Soviets. The carrier turned off its radios, aircraft navigation beacons, and proceeded due North at full speed—leaving the helicopter airborne without any way to locate or communicate with the carrier.

The helicopter crew happened to pick up the navigational beacon of the ammunition ship, reaching them just in time. Typically, this type of ship would not have a beacon on, since it was independent and not performing helicopter operations. However, four days earlier the ammunition ship rendezvoused with a helicopter for a passenger transfer. During the ensuing watch turnover, no one mentioned the aircraft navigation beacon was on . . . and it was still on four days later (P. M. Baumgartner, personal communication, May 16, 2008).

The story above includes two human errors, one of which fortunately compensated for the other. However, they are still errors, and errors oftentimes result in catastrophic events, particularly when synergistically compounded. Though there are many classifications for error types coupled with an equally diverse means for mitigation, the underlying solution frequently resides in proper human-centered design.

The concept of human-centered design is not new. In fact, the origins of human-centered design as a discipline began with the industrial revolution in the early 1900s (Sanders & McCormick, 1993). This early work was done by Frank and Lillian Gilbreth and other motion engineers, who were primarily focused on operator fatigue and time-motion studies that led to improved workstation layout (Chapanis, 1996; Sanders & McCormick, 1993). By World War II (WWII), the need for human-centered design became apparent after several military aviation accidents. Research found that selecting and training humans was not enough to successfully operate complex equipment, particularly with new environmental stressors. A new paradigm was required; fit the equipment to the person (Booher, 2003; Sanders & McCormick, 1993). The first formal process integrating human-centered design requirements to achieve optimized performance in military aircraft was in WWII, when joint U.S.-UK engineering psychology efforts were used to develop a design (Booher, 2003). This effort marked the beginning of a systems engineering approach which incorporated both combat ability of the aircraft and the human's ability to control the craft in order to achieve its mission requirements. This first step in the infancy of human-centered design marked a dramatic paradigm shift. Over the years since WWII, the importance of proper human-centered design has become apparent in many different arenas. Chapanis (1996) points out that we have changed from an agricultural and manufacturing society to an information society, which resulted in additional considerations to account for in human-centered design. Thus, the focus of human-centered design expanded from equipping the human and workstation layout to concern for all areas that impact the human in the system, including such things as training, selection, human–computer interaction, ergonomics, safety, survivability, habitability, quality of life, and human performance in extreme environments (e.g., space, underwater, and Polar expeditions).

The ability for the operator to optimally use a system is not the only requirement of human-centered design; the system must also be safe to use, including enhancements to increase the chances of operator survivability in the event of an incident. On a tragic day in the fall of 1966, the importance of safety considerations became all too apparent.

On October 26, 1966, two sailors aboard the USS Oriskany *were restoring aircraft flares which were off-loaded from an aircraft returning from combat operations in Vietnam. One of the sailors dropped a flare. Somehow, during the off-load procedures, the flare had not been set to safe and the safety lanyard was pulled. Another sailor picked up the flare and put it into a locker which also contained 2.75-inch rocket warheads. A short time later, the flare ignited in the locker, causing secondary explosions from the rocket warheads.*

The fire spread and eventually ignited a liquid oxygen tank—killing 44 sailors and injuring 156 (The Ordnance Shop, 2008).

Analysts questioned how such a simple careless act could have occurred and how it could have such devastating consequences. Why did the design of the flare not prevent such an incident, and why did the storage locker not contain the fire and prevent it from spreading? These and other safety questions were making their way into becoming acquisition requirements, but it would take time, and another lesson would have to be learned.

Just a short eight months after *USS Oriskany* fire, the U.S. Navy (USN) faced another tragic incident.

On July 29, 1967, a ZUNI rocket aboard the USS Forestall *was accidently fired from an aircraft being readied for a mission. The rocket streamed across the deck and struck another aircraft, igniting a fuel fire. The fire, in all likelihood, could have been contained had the fire not ignited a bomb, killing or wounding all of the on-scene fire fighters. The fire spread and continued to ignite bombs, warheads, and rockets, eventually killing 134 and injuring 161 crew members* (The Ordnance Shop, 2008).

To prevent such tragic accidents like those aboard the *USS Oriskany* and *USS Forestall* from occurring again, the USN initiated a safety review board. Now called the Weapons System and Explosive Safety Review Board (WSESRB), its charter is to provide independent oversight of weapons program safety. The mission of WSESRB is to prevent mishaps by reviewing all systems that involve weapons or ordnance. The analysis and ensuing recommendations provided by WSESRB, if followed, ensure a safe operating environment involving the use and handling of weapons or ordnance systems (Naval Sea Systems Command, 1997).

In the early 1980s, the USN extended its human-centered vantage point beyond safety and began the initial steps to incorporate human-centered design as a specification requirement for new acquisition programs. The USN awarded the Lockheed Shipbuilding Company of Seattle, Washington a contract to build the LSD-41 Whidbey Island Class Dock Landing Ship. This ship class marked the first time human factors engineering requirements were included in a Navy ship's contract design requirements. According to Williams (1980), a key criterion in the selection of the Lockheed design was the engineering room layout in which the designers applied established human engineering principles and practices to improve engineering room operator and maintainer performance.

Additional incidents occurred throughout the next several decades that required the USN to strengthen their position on human-centered design, as these accidents pointed to severe design deficiencies. One such accident occurred during 1982, when five sailors drowned in a diving hangar on the *USS Grayback* (U.S. Naval Safety Center, 1982). The diving hangar was designed to have a "dry side" which accessed the rest of the submarine and a "wet side" that could be opened while underwater to launch a vehicle.

The "wet side" could be drained of water to allow the divers to reenter the "dry side" (and the rest of the submarine). As detailed in the accident investigation findings, the primary cause of the accident was that the main vent valve, which vents the space to help the water drain, was not properly positioned. This caused a vacuum condition on the "wet side" of the diving hangar when the water was being drained from that side. The sailors drowned when they lost consciousness in this vacuum. There were several human-centered design issues that contributed to this accident. First, the main vent valve was normally actuated within the "wet side" of the hangar. However, to actuate it, a diver had to go underwater to turn the valve and check its positioning. The valve was not well maintained and was difficult to actuate. This design was not consistent with the remainder of the "wet side" controls, which were accessible to an operator positioned in a pressurized "bubble" so they were out of the water. In addition, although the "dry side" safety observers had the ability to control the main vent valve, they had no indication of its position, so they were unaware that it was misaligned. Similarly, there was no indication of vacuum pressure on either the wet or the dry side of the hangar. These human-centered design issues, along with a lack of approved procedures and a lack of recent training, combined to result in these avoidable deaths (U.S. Naval Safety Center, 1982).

A second accident occurred in 1988, after the USN began a permanent presence into the Arabian Gulf to protect Kuwaiti oil tankers from Iranian attack (Zatarain, 2008). On May 17, 1987, the *USS Stark* was sailing in the central Gulf, where, to date, there had been no attacks by either Iran or Iraq (Zatarain, 2008). An airborne warning and control system (AWACS) aircraft in the area first detected an Iraqi Mirage F-1 and alerted the *USS Coontz*, who fed the information to the *USS Stark*. The *USS Stark* was able to pick up the F-1 on air search radar when it was about 70 miles away, only after switching to a shorter-range mode. The AWACS then noted that the F-1 was moving in the *USS Stark*'s direction and expected to pass within 11 nautical miles (Levinson & Edwards, 1997). Another ship in the area, the *USS LaSalle*, contacted the *USS Stark* to ensure they were aware of the contact. The F-1 then turned directly toward the *USS Stark*, although it appears no one in the *USS Stark*'s Combat Information Center (CIC) noticed this (Levinson & Edwards, 1997; Zatarain, 2008). The F-1 fired its first Exocet missile at a range of about 22 nautical miles. A second missile was fired about one minute later, which was about the same time the *USS Stark* first warned the F-1 (Zatarain, 2008). The crew did turn on the close-in weapons system (CIWS), but they put it in "Standby" mode instead of "Automatic," so the radar was not activated (Zatarain, 2008). The *USS Stark* was struck by both Exocet missiles, resulting in significant injuries and 37 deaths (Zatarain, 2008). In the end, the missiles struck without the *USS Stark* firing any weapons, ordering General Quarters, or taking any defensive measures (Levinson & Edwards, 1997; Zatarain, 2008).

Amidst these heightened tensions, the Aegis cruiser *USS Vincennes* was called into the Persian Gulf to assist in the protection of another damaged ship. On July 3, 1988, *USS Vincennes* misidentified an Iranian commercial airliner as a tactical military aircraft, an F-14 fighter (Zatarain, 2008). The airliner took off after a ground delay from a combined military-civilian airport about 47 miles away from the *USS Vincennes*. The Aegis radar on the ship picked up this contact almost immediately after takeoff. After several unsuccessful attempts to warn the aircraft on both civilian and military frequencies, the *USS Vincennes* shot down that aircraft killing all 290 crew and passengers (Zatarain, 2008). Extensive analysis following the incident examined how a crew of arguably the most advanced warship at the time could misidentify and shoot down a commercial airliner. There were several reasons why such an incident occurred. One of the most obvious reasons for the error was the complex threat environment. At the time of the accident, *USS Vincennes* was engaged in a gun battle with Iranian small boats and conducting high-speed maneuvers (Zatarain, 2008). This, combined with the short time frame (3 minutes and 40 seconds) to make a decision, prevented the *USS Vincennes* from devoting full attention to the contact (Zatarain, 2008). This high-complexity environment caused the crew to feel stressed and defensive, impacting their decision making (Klein, 1989).

However, it was not only the environment that contributed to the incident; it was also the design of the Aegis Combat System. Though the Aegis Combat System is arguably the premier naval weapons system in the world, it is also one of the most complex combat systems ever created, and it had substantial limitations in terms of human-centered design. Because of its complexity, operators in the CIC require months of training to learn how to operate the system and its many control sequences. At the time of the accident, the radar system had characteristics which made it difficult for the crew to integrate information about the flight path of the airliner and whether the airliner was climbing or descending, leading them to mischaracterize the contact as a hostile fighter that was descending and approaching them (Wickens, Gordon, & Liu, 1998). In addition, one of the officers, who was responsible for antiair warfare coordination, was not sufficiently trained on the console use, so he was unable to independently verify the contact's information (Zatarain, 2008). Similarly, the captain of the *USS Vincennes*, who had given that officer responsibility that he was not trained for, had not completed Aegis training school (Zatarain, 2008). Additionally, Klein found that although the "disconfirming" evidence was available to (and sought out by) the operators on the *USS Vincennes*, the combat system displays were so poorly organized the operators could not find the information (Klein, 1989). Therefore, a combination of the hostile environment, crew expectations, misidentification of the airliner, and breakdowns in communication led to this accident (Wickens, Gordon, & Liu, 1998).

The tragic incidents aboard *USS Stark* and *USS Vincennes*, while each unique, involve two common entities: an operator and a command and control (C2) system. Lintern and Naikar (2002) point out that one of the major problems with military C2 systems is that the wealth of information available to operators is poorly represented and organized. In the case of *USS Stark*, a better designed C2 system might have afforded the operator better situational awareness (SA), which potentially may have led to a quicker detection (and potential evasion) of the incoming missiles. The *USS Vincennes* incident showed how even a better C2 system, if not designed with the user and environment in mind, could still result in errors. The operating environments the USN expects its operators to perform in are demanding, complex, and dangerous. Therefore, the systems supporting the operators need to facilitate the decision making process, and not create an additional degree of complexity.

LESSONS LEARNED FOR BETTER DESIGN

Following these accidents, the USN began to recognize that unnecessarily complex systems requiring human interpretation or input oftentimes foster a more error-prone environment. One of the means to mitigate the level of complexity was to introduce more automation. Efficiently designing systems and introducing automation has the ability to reduce manpower and associated training requirements.

The first effort to identify where manpower reductions could be afforded through additional automation was conducted in 1995 by the Naval Research Advisory Committee (NRAC). The NRAC is a committee developed after WWII that is dedicated to providing objective analysis in the areas of science, research, and development to the Secretary of the Navy, the Chief of Naval Operations, Commandant of the Marine Corps, and the Chief of Naval Research. This panel identified that over 60 percent of the USN's budget was tied to manpower, and the clearest means to achieve manpower reductions while maintaining current capabilities and readiness was through automation (NRAC, 1995).

In response to the NRAC report, the "Smart Ship" program office was established in 1995, and *USS Yorktown* was selected as the prototype ship. The Smart Ship effort aboard *USS Yorktown* provided an integrated bridge, voyage management, wireless communication, damage control, and engineering systems. The effort also automated many routine tasks, providing the crew the opportunity to focus on their warfighting skills. The initial Smart Ship effort netted a 15 percent reduction in maintenance workload; a 10 percent manpower reduction, reflecting an estimated manpower savings of $1.75 million; and an estimated $2.76 million per year reduction in life cycle costs (U.S. Navy, 2008a). The amphibious Navy also employed Smart Ship aboard *USS Mount Rushmore*, a program known as Gator 17 (U.S. Navy, 2008b).

Between 1996 and 2001, the Office of Naval Research (ONR) executed the Manning Affordability Initiative (MAI) acting upon the lessons learned from the computing systems aboard Smart Ship. MAI explored the use of computing systems to further reduce the crew size of future naval surface combatants; MAI's focus, unlike Smart Ship's, was on the combat systems. It investigated using human performance modeling to more rapidly conduct design trade-off activities in a more cost-effective manner than humans-in-the-loop studies (Pharmer, 2007). The use of computer systems that afford optimal SA while reducing the number of personnel required to develop a comprehensive command and control picture was groundbreaking. One of the key outcomes of MAI was the development of the multimodal watch station (MMWS). The primary purpose of the MMWS was a risk-reduction effort to develop conceptual command and control designs to support the USN in their objective of reducing the crew size (Booher, 2003). Effectively, the warfighting functions of the MMWS are the "same as current command and control centers, but offer reduced workload and workload distribution capabilities among team members that may enable crew size optimization" (Booher, 2003, p. 744).

Further, MAI provided extensive modeling tools to support the development of new organizational structures and job allocations. The goal was a 50 percent reduction in watchstanders, from eight to four. This was specifically modeled using the traditional Aegis CIC as the baseline organization and job allocation for Air Defense. The result of the modeling, when coupled with the use of the MMWS, was the redesign of the CIC's organization and job allocation to support the efforts of reduced crew size without the loss of critical functionality. The development of modeling and human-centered design tools continue to be used.

Although there were human-centered design improvements from MAI, there were still many issues associated with training. In 1999, the NRAC published a series of recommendations related to training technologies. The overwhelming NRAC finding was that new distributed learning technologies have the potential to revolutionize the delivery of training and education (NRAC, 1999). There were several recommendations from the NRAC study. The most critical was to develop a coherent training organization. NRAC observed that often training systems are the first items to be cut during budget and schedule overruns. Also, poor design, coupled with ineffective training systems, almost always results in increased life cycle costs. Lastly, NRAC recommended the establishment of a standardized process for training product development. This would prevent the development of proprietary training systems that would become obsolete, potentially leading to increased total life cycle costs (NRAC, 1999).

The emphasis by NRAC to integrate training across the acquisition program was not an exclusive observation. In 2001, the USN conducted an extensive review of training in a review entitled "Revolution in Training."

This review, which further validated the recommendations provided by NRAC, emphasized that human performance should be included as a requirement. Specifically, training should be included as a key performance parameter (KPP) to ensure that it is included throughout the life cycle of the system. Finally, the review recommended the inclusion of human performance parameters during evaluations by the test community (NRAC, 2002).

MAKING HUMAN-CENTERED DESIGN THE NORM: ESTABLISHING A HUMAN SYSTEM INTEGRATION POLICY

This history has shaped much of the recent direction of human-centered design in the USN. Within the Department of Defense (DoD), the formal process of assimilating human-centered requirements across the systems engineering process is referred to as Human System Integration (HSI). As such, HSI will be used when discussing the Navy's policy for human-centered design. In 2002, the Systems Engineering, Acquisition and PeRsonnel INTegration (SEAPRINT) program was started in response to a Congressional plus-up that required the USN to establish a program similar to the Army's model of human-centered design. The U.S. Army took the lead in requiring human considerations in their system design in 1984, with the establishment of the Manpower and Personnel Integration (MANPRINT) program as part of their systems acquisition process (U.S. Army PEO STRI, 2008). MANPRINT focuses on the integration of seven key domains: Manpower, Personnel, Training, Human Factors Engineering, System Safety, Health Hazards, and Soldier Survivability. MANPRINT continues to stress the equal weight of human performance and equipment performance, which collectively determine overall system performance. Before a system can begin its acquisition process, developers must determine initial MANPRINT requirements and show how they plan to address these requirements through design and development (Chapanis, 1996). Mandating this requirement for all Army systems ensures the Army acquisition process will continue to "equip the man, not man the equipment" (U.S. Army PEO STRI, 2008).

Under SEAPRINT, the USN established their seven domains of Manpower, Personnel, Training, Human Factors Engineering, Environmental Safety and Health, Personnel Survivability, and Habitability. It was designed to facilitate a sailor-centered approach throughout the Navy. SEAPRINT aimed to identify the tools and processes necessary to facilitate effective application of HSI. There are seven tenets of the SEAPRINT process (Narkevicius, Stark, & Owen, 2006):

1. Initiate HSI early

2. Identify Issues—Plan Analysis

3. Document/Crosswalk HSI Requirements

4. Make HSI a Factor in Source Selection

5. Execute Integrated Technical Process

6. Conduct Proactive Trade-Offs

7. Conduct HSI Milestone Assessments.

Although the term "SEAPRINT" is officially no longer used in the USN, the program facilitated the development of policy and discussion about commonality between the "Navies" or Systems Commands (SYSCOMs): Naval Air Systems Command (NAVAIR), Naval Sea Systems Command (NAVSEA), Naval Supply Systems Command (NAVSUP), Naval Facilities Command (NAVFAC), and Space and Naval Warfare Systems Command (SPAWAR). The road to implementation of HSI in the USN continues. As a note, the U.S. Air Force (USAF) has also established a HSI effort, directed by the Air Force HSI Office (AFHSIO), which reports to the Air Force Vice Chief of Staff.

Challenges in Implementing the Policy

Despite SEAPRINT's efforts to develop HSI policy for the USN, the individual SYSCOMs differed in their means of applying HSI. The divergent implementation was likely due to not having a clear "lead" for U.S. Navy HSI, as there is in the U.S. Army (and the USAF). This led to the establishment of the U.S. Navy HSI virtual SYSCOM (vSYSCOM), which was designed to bolster coordination and cooperation between the "Navies" on HSI efforts.

The vSYSCOM was designed to be a forum to ensure commonality between various groups within the USN. The vSYSCOM began by developing common guidance for Program Managers to explain how to do HSI (in terms of types of tasks and types of expertise required) and the benefits HSI would add to their program. This vSYSCOM HSI working group effort continues today to provide a common forum to develop U.S. Navy HSI processes, tools, and educational opportunities.

Another solution to the lack of coordination in U.S. Navy HSI was the establishment of the Human Systems Performance Assessment Capability (HSPAC). HSPAC was established in 2005 by the Office of Chief of Naval Operations (OPNAV) as a way to help the U.S. Navy HSI community (i.e., the vSYSCOM, Fleet Forces Command, Human Performance Center, OPTEVFOR, and the OPNAV) understand each other's capabilities, what tools were available, and connect to each other's facilities. The goal of HSPAC was to provide a consistent, repeatable set of human performance metrics and a means to collect them. The objectives also included documenting human performance analysis definitions (focused early on in the acquisition cycle) and human performance requirements, identifying common HSI tools and upgrading several of them, identifying a common

HSI simulation environment, and creating a human performance metrics data repository (HSPAC, 2005).

Although the formal HSPAC program was disestablished in 2006, many of the products and efforts have been carried on by the vSYSCOM. In addition, many of these products were shared with the rest of the DoD HSI community, as part of the JPRINT (Joint HSI Working Group). The JPRINT, similar to the vSYSCOM, is a forum to collaborate on HSI; however, this forum is across the Army, Navy, and Air Force rather than just across the Navy. JPRINT was established in response to a Congressional request for a Joint HSI report in 2004. The U.S. Army took the lead to write the Congressional Report and to establish the JPRINT working group. This group has continued to support the development of Congressional Reports and led the development of HSI documentation for the International Council of Systems Engineering (INCOSE; Kimm & Knapp, 2008).

As mentioned above, one of the key issues for U.S. Navy HSI was the lack of a "lead" organization. In 2008, OPNAV N15 (Total Force Training and Education Division) was established as the human system integration and human performance advocate, as well as the U.S. Navy HSI requirements organization. This role was agreed to by both the SYSCOMs and the research communities, ensuring OPNAV N15 is the official voice for U.S. Navy HSI and is responsible for HSI policy and requirements. However, the SYSCOMs will continue to play an active role in the direction of U.S. Navy HSI, as they employ much of the technical expertise.

Another challenge faced in the implementation of HSI within the Navy was the lack of skilled practitioners. By working with both internal experts and the academic community, several educational opportunities have emerged in recent years. As these programs mature (and additional programs are added), the HSI workforce can become more standardized and skilled in its field.

A third challenge for U.S. Navy HSI was the integration into the rest of the systems engineering community. Prior to the SEAPRINT policy, several of the functions of HSI (e.g., manpower, personnel, and training) were carried out by logisticians, who are typically not brought into an acquisition program early. Because of this, the Navy community believed that HSI did not need to be addressed until late in the design cycle. Thus, the U.S. Navy HSI community had to educate systems engineers about the benefits of employing HSI early in a design (e.g., reduced rework of designs, reduced training, reduced manpower requirements, increased quality of life, and improved safety). With this education came a realization that HSI is indeed part of systems engineering. This was formalized recently with a change in the way engineering reviews are executed. The rest of the USN followed NAVAIR's lead by instituting HSI measures within a common Systems Engineering Technical Review (SETR) process (Pharmer, 2007). To execute these reviews, HSI practitioners developed review and certification criteria to ensure programs understand the required activities necessary for them to "pass" the review. Overall, this will help ensure HSI is a consideration on USN programs and that HSI practitioners are members of the systems engineering teams.

Success Stories

HSI has already resulted in safety improvements, performance enhancements, increased quality of life, and reductions in manpower. For instance, HSI personnel identified a safety issue when doing a structured, low-fidelity usability assessment of the helicopter control station on the *DDG 1000* using representative operators. The shipboard helicopter control station requires two egress (evacuation) paths. When interacting with the mock-up, it was discovered the secondary egress path was out of a window, over the side of the ship, and into the water. This was an issue for two reasons. The obvious reason is the safety of the operator who goes into the water. However, the second reason for concern is the additional workload associated with a man overboard recovery while also dealing with a fire on the flight deck (which likely necessitated the egress). By catching this issue early in the acquisition process, HSI personnel were able to work with the ship design team to add an additional egress path.

Similarly, a mock-up of the *DDG 1000* bridge was used to investigate operator performance of representative tasks given the designed layout. The cost of the mock-up was $20,000 for materials and construction. When reviewing the design with operators, the HSI team identified 19 discrepancies with the design, 5 of which were identified to have structural impact. Because it was early enough in the design process, these discrepancies could be corrected. If the mock-up had not been done, it was estimated by industry that the cost of changes would have been $20 million.

In terms of improved performance, HSI personnel were able to identify a five-second reduction in operator reaction time on the Aegis SPY-1 radar system by redesigning the user interface to utilize color coding of friendly and enemy tracks. The changes would obviously be a substantial improvement in performance during combat operations (recall that the complete *USS Vincennes* mishap took 3 minutes and 40 seconds). When trying to match this five-second time reduction by using improvements to the radar, the designers of the radar estimated it would require at least $250 million, whereas the cost of implementing the user interface changes was approximately $200,000.

The mitigation of safety issues and increasing personnel productivity are not the only objectives of HSI; the LPD-17- and LCS-class warships are excellent examples of ships with significant quality of life improvements. These quality of life improvements can lead to better morale and retention, as well as performance improvements. In the case of the LPD-17, HSI personnel designed berths which allow the sailors to sit up in their beds (for reading or relaxing). Historical berths are flat and do not allow sailors to sit up, whereas these berths are shaped like an "L." Additionally, LCS has improved quality of life by providing a bathroom and shower in each berthing space and limiting the number of occupants in a berthing space to eight, with many compartments having only four personnel. Sailors on both platforms have reacted favorably to these improvements.

Additionally, in terms of HSI successes, many USN platforms have reduced the number of people on them through additional automation, job consolidation, and job elimination. Examples of this include *CVN 78* (the next-generation aircraft carrier) and *DDG 1000* (the next-generation destroyer). On *CVN 78*, these reductions are expected to equal 538 people total from the air wing, mission systems, and the ship's crew. The challenge in identifying these reductions is weighing the expected areas of automation, coupled with the paradigm shift in operations and maintenance philosophies, and then selecting areas of personnel consolidation, all the while achieving an increase in overall mission effectiveness.

EXPANDING HSI

The history of HSI in the USN (and the rest of the DoD) was met by varying degrees of success. However, as it is with so many things, the lessons of yesterday lay a foundation for the success of tomorrow. HSI is now well defined in the systems acquisitions process, but there are still areas that could be improved. First, there is a push in the DoD to establish additional HSI requirements that we can use to ensure programs consider the human as a key part of the system from the onset. For instance, *DDG 1000* used manning levels as a KPP (Pharmer, 2007). This will likely require additional HSI education for the contractor community.

As HSI continues to demonstrate successes, other government, industry, and academic organizations have begun to establish human-centered design programs. In order to do this, they have leveraged heavily off the lessons learned within the DoD. As these programs continue to grow, there will be increasing need for common tools, processes, standards, and education. The HSI community is also working to develop these, but it is an iterative process where additional capabilities are continuously added as additional needs are discovered. It will likely be several years before the HSI tools, processes, and standards are considered "mature." However, with the highly collaborative nature of the community, we can ensure the community is investing in complimentary products. In addition, the research community needs to invest in research that addresses the HSI tools required; this synergy is increasing of late. Some needs that are currently being discussed include improved human performance models, improved predictions of human performance under environmental stressors, common task analysis tools, function allocation tools, and research into the life cycle cost impacts of various decision designs. There is also a drive to better integrate with the systems engineering community, in terms of common tool sets, processes, and standards.

In summary, the concepts of HSI and human-centered design have relevance in any environment, but they are especially crucial in high-risk environments, such as military, aviation, medical, nuclear power plant, or space applications. By focusing on the human as part of the system, HSI has led the way for human performance improvements in DoD systems. However, many of the tools and data collected are useful to other applications of human-centered design. For instance, a manpower assessment tool could be used to look at the staffing in a hospital emergency room (i.e., do they have the right skills on hand for treatment, are there sufficient numbers of medical personnel for the expected workload, and how fatigued are the medical personnel?). By collaborating with these other communities, HSI personnel can begin to share lessons learned, as well as leverage the other work to reduce funding requirements. This collaborative process will continue to grow and mature the field of human-centered design, so system performance, regardless of the system type, can be improved.

REFERENCES

Booher, H. R. (2003). *The handbook of human systems integration.* Hoboken, NJ: John Wiley & Sons, Inc.

Chapanis, A. (1996). *Human factors in systems engineering.* New York: John Wiley & Sons, Inc.

Human Systems Performance Assessment Capability. (2005). Retrieved August 8, 2008 from http://www.nswc.navy.mil/ET/HSI/HSPAC_Brief_Sheet_10June05.pdf.

Kimm, L., & Knapp, B. A. (2008). Joint HSI Working Group MANPRINT Practitioner's Workshop Update. Retrieved August 15, 2008 from http://www.manprint.army.mil/presentations/COL%20Larry%20Kimm.pdf.

Klein, G. A. (1989). Do decision biases explain too much? *Human Factors Society Bulletin, 22,* 1–3.

Levinson, J. L., & Edwards, R. L. (1997). *Missile inbound: The attack on the Stark in the Persian Gulf.* Annapolis, MD: Naval Institute Press.

Lintern, G., & Naikar, N. (2002). A virtual information-action workspace for command and control. Available at http://www.dsto.defence.gov.au/attachments/10.pdf.

Narkevicius, J. M., Stark, J. M., & Owen, J. (2006). Human systems integration enhancing performance in network centric warfare: The SEAPRINT perspective. Retrieved August 15, 2008 from http://www.dsto.defence.gov.au/attachments/Narkevicius,%20Stark%20&%20Owen_Pending%20Official%20Release_Human%20Systems%20Integration%20Enhancing%20Performance%20in%20Network%20Centric%20Warfare.pdf.

Naval Research Advisory Committee. (1995). Reduced ship manning. Retrieved September 5, 2008 from http://www.onr.navy.mil/nrac/docs/1995_es_reduced_ship_manning.pdf.

————. (1999). Training technologies. Retrieved September 5, 2008 from http://www.onr.navy.mil/nrac/docs/1999_es_training_technologies.pdf.

————. (2002). Life cycle technology insertion. Retrieved August 23, 2008 from https://www.onr.navy.mil/nrac/docs/2002_rpt_life_cycle_technology_insertion.pdf.

Naval Sea Systems Command. (1997). *Navy weapon system safety program*, Instruction 8020.6D. Washington, D.C.: Naval Sea Systems Command.

Pharmer, J. A. (2007). The challenges and opportunities of implementing human systems integration into the navy acquisition process. *Defense Acquisition Review Journal*, 278–291.

Sanders, M. S., & McCormick, E. J. (1993). *Human factors and engineering and design*. New York: McGraw-Hill, Inc.

The Ordnance Shop. (2008). *Historical mishaps*. Retrieved August 15, 2008 from http://www.ordnance.org/mishaps.htm.

U.S. Army PEO STRI. (2008). *Manpower and personnel integration*. Orlando, FL: U.S. Army PEO STRI.

U.S. Naval Safety Center. (1982). *USS Grayback accident findings*. Norfolk, VA: U.S. Naval Safety Center.

U.S. Navy. (2008a). *"Smart Ship" initiatives successful*. Retrieved August 6, 2008 from http://www.chinfo.navy.mil/navpalib/ships/cruisers/yorktown/smrtship.html.

————. (2008b). *USS Rushmore (LSD-47)*. Retrieved August 6, 2008 from http://navysite.de/ships/lsd47.htm.

Wickens, C. D., Gordon, S. E., & Liu, Y. (1998). *An introduction to human factors engineering*. New York: Addison Wesley Longman, Inc.

Williams, H. L. (1980). *Analysis of LSD-41 machinery room layout*, Defense Technical Information Center Rep. No. A477401. San Diego: Naval Personnel Research and Development.

Zatarain, L. A. (2008). *Tanker war: America's first conflict with Iran, 1987–1988*. Drexel Hill, PA: Casemate Publishers.

Chapter 14

USER-CENTERED INTERACTIVE SYSTEM DESIGN

Kay M. Stanney

Designing interactive systems for high-risk environments requires careful consideration of the target user population. Specifically, user-centered design principles should be used to develop designs that are perceptually and cognitively suitable for the users they support (Righi & James, 2007). This approach aims to ensure ease of learning, ease of use, and subjective satisfaction through a careful match between users' capabilities/limitations and the system design. In recent years, user-centered design has even been promoted as a risk management tool (Skelton & Thamhain, 2005). User-centered design is informed by a deep understanding of the tasks to be supported by the system under design. In terms of risk management, such task knowledge can be used to identify possible deviations in expected performance (e.g., due to past work practices and exceeding users' capabilities) for each design alternative. These deviations are areas where potential human error can occur. By estimating the frequency and severity of such errors (e.g., through Failure Modes and Effects Analysis [FMEA; Israelski & Muto, 2006] or Fault Tree Analysis [FTA; Israelski & Muto, 2004]), a system can be designed to minimize the overall probability of error. Thus, by bringing users' capabilities, limitations, and expectations into consideration, user-centered design can be used to systematically identify the potential for human error and mitigate with error-reducing design strategies, such as by using exclusion strategies to "mistake proof" designs, prevention strategies to avoid errors (e.g., checklists), or fail-safe techniques to reduce or mitigate the consequences of human error (e.g., preventative maintenance; Glendon, Clarke, & McKenna, 2006). This chapter focuses on user-centered interactive system design techniques that can be used to effectively design systems for high-risk environments. In general, such design efforts are guided by user needs analysis, task analysis, usability goal setting, and user-centered requirements analysis, which result from an intrinsic understanding gained from the target work environment.

Although these activities are listed and presented in this order, they are conducted iteratively throughout the system development life cycle.

USER NEEDS ANALYSIS

User-centered design should commence with a user needs analysis, in which an opportunity to improve operations or training within an organization or a deficiency related to an operational or training need is identified and validated. Based on the stated need, alternative concepts and methods to satisfy the need can be explored. The goal of the user needs analysis should be to articulate the needs of target users by identifying and validating an opportunity to improve operations or training within an organization, or a deficiency related to an operational or training need, and recommending the exploration of alternative concepts and methods to satisfy the need. Inadequacies in user needs analysis will lead to designs that do not support user goals, needs, and objectives (see Figure 14.1).

TASK ANALYSIS

Once a need has been identified, background contextual data must be collected to guide user-centered design. These data are gathered via task analysis techniques. The objective of task analysis is to achieve a user-centered model of current work practices (Mayhew, 1999). It is important to determine how users currently carry out their tasks, which individuals they interact with, which tools support the accomplishment of their job goals, and the resulting products of their efforts. This deep understanding of the task context can lead to a design that best fits current work practices or provides solid transitions to new practices in order to minimize the risk of human error (Skelton & Thamhain, 2005) or, as Wiegmann and Shappell (2003) coin them, "unsafe acts," in their Human Factors Analysis and Classification System (HFACS; see Chapter 12 of this book for a detailed discussion of HFACS). Specifically, in the HFACS there are both unsafe acts (i.e., decision errors, skill-based errors, perceptual errors, and routine and exceptional violations) and latent failures (e.g., preconditions for unsafe acts [substandard contextual conditions and substandard user practices], unsafe supervision, and organizational influences) that should be avoided through effective user-centered design. For example, during system interaction, human errors often involve wrong responses (i.e., dysfunctional interactions) or poor decisions due to interactive complexity, where a system interaction is difficult to learn, or exceptional conditions, which could potentially be avoided if the task analysis examined all relevant context under which the system will be used (Woods & Cook, 2002). In addition, mismatches between a user's mental model and the designer's conceptual model (i.e., the complete and accurate model of a

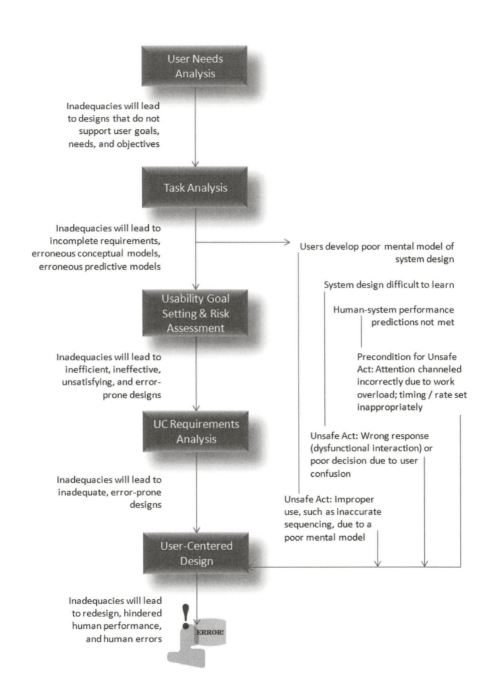

Figure 14.1. Impact of inadequate user-centered design.

system from an engineering perspective) can lead to improper use (e.g., inaccurate sequencing of actions; Wiegmann & Shappell, 2003). A thorough task analysis can direct the design of concise conceptual models and feed predictive models (e.g., Goals, Operators, Methods, and Selection Rules [GOMS—Card, Moran, & Newell, 1983], and FMEA), which can in turn be used to estimate learning and identify mismatches. If these predictive models are accurate, then preconditions for unsafe acts, such as mischanneled attention due to work overload or timing or rate errors due to exceeding human capabilities, can be identified and addressed in the requirements and design. As Figure 14.1 demonstrates, an inadequate task analysis can lead to such issues as incomplete requirements, erroneous conceptual models, and erroneous predictive models, which can in turn result in serious problems such as unsafe acts or latent failures.

The results of a task analysis include work environment and task data, from which mental models can be identified and user scenarios and task organization models (e.g., use sequences, use flow diagrams, and use work flows) can be derived (Mayhew, 1999). These models and scenarios can then help guide the design of a fail-safe system. Task analysis consists of three main steps: gather background information, user profiling, and construction of work practice models.

Gather Background Information

It is important when planning a task analysis for designers to first become familiar with the work environment. Task analysis should thus commence with a review of documentation concerning the practices and terminology utilized in the target environment. This provides a foundation of knowledge from which to reason about the processes or practices to be investigated. If designers do not understand work practices, tools, and jargon prior to commencing a task analysis, they can easily get confused and become unable to follow the task flow. Further, if designers have clipboard and pen in hand the first time users see them, users are likely to resist being observed or change their behaviors during observation. Once users are familiar and comfortable with designers, and designers are likewise versed on work practices, data collection can commence.

User Profiling

It is ultimately the user who will determine if a system is adopted into their lives. Designs that frustrate, stress, or annoy users are not likely to be embraced. The objective of designers should thus be to develop a system that can meet specified user goals, functions, and objectives; all of which should have been identified via a user needs analysis. This can be accomplished through an early and continual focus on the target user population (Gould, Boies, & Ukelson, 1997). It is inconceivable that design efforts would bring products to market without thoroughly determining "Who is the user?" Yet developers are often reluctant to devote resources to characterizing users' needs, capabilities, and desires, as they expedite system development to rush products to market. In doing so they may fail to recognize the amount of time they spend speculating upon what users "might" need, like, or want in a product (Nielsen, 1993). Ascertaining this information directly, by querying representative users, can be both more efficient and more accurate.

Information about users should provide insights into differences in their computer experience, domain knowledge, and amount of training on similar systems (Wixon & Wilson, 1997). The results can be summarized in a narrative format that provides a user profile of each intended user group (e.g., primary users, secondary users, technicians, and support personnel). No system design, however, will meet the needs of all types of users. Thus, it is essential to identify, define, and characterize target users. Separate user profiles should be developed for each target user group.

Mayhew (1999) presents a step-by-step process for developing user profiles. First, a determination of user categories is made by identifying the intended user groups for the target system. When developing a system for an organization, this information may come directly from preexisting job categories but should be augmented by the results of ethnographic studies (Hughes, King, Rodden, & Anderson, 1995). Where user profiles do not exist, marketing organizations often have target user populations identified for a given system or product. Next, the relevant user characteristics must be identified. User profiles should be specified in terms of psychological (e.g., attitudes and motivation), knowledge and experience (e.g., educational background and years on job), job and task (e.g., frequency of use), and physical (e.g., stature and visual impairments) characteristics (Mayhew, 1999; Nielsen, 1993; Wixon & Wilson, 1997). While many of these user attributes can be obtained via user profile questionnaires or interviews, psychological characteristics may be best identified via ethnographic evaluation, where a sense of the work environment temperament can be obtained. Once this information is obtained, a summary of the key characteristics for each target user group can be developed, highlighting their implications to the system design. By understanding these characteristics, developers can better anticipate such issues as learning difficulties and specify appropriate levels of interface complexity. Thus, user profiling involves an assessment of the required levels of such factors as ease of learning, ease of use, level of satisfaction and workload for each target user group (see Table 14.1). Getting these levels "right" is essential in achieving a fail-safe system design.

Individual differences within a user population should also be acknowledged (Hackos & Redish, 1998). While users differ along many dimensions, key areas of user differences have been identified that significantly influence

Table 14.1.   Example of a User Profile

User characteristic	Questionnaire response	System design requirement
Attitude	Fearful	System should be supportive and avoid condescending remarks
Motivation	Generally medium	Emotional impact of system should encourage user interaction
Education level	High school	Simplicity important; training requirements should be minimal
Computer experience	Low	High ease of learning required
Frequency of computer use	Discretionary	High ease of use required; system workload should be minimized
Typing skills	Poor	Minimize typing; use icons and visual displays
Gender	Mostly males	Consider color blindness
Age	Average = 64.5 (s.d. = 3.6)	Text and symbol size should be readily legible

their experience with interactive systems. Users may differ in such attributes as personality, physical or cognitive capacity, motivation, cultural background, education, and training. Users also change over time (e.g., transitioning from novice to expert). By acknowledging these differences, developers can make informed decisions on whether or not to support them in their system designs. For example, marketing could determine which group of individuals it would be most profitable to target with a given system design.

Construction of Work Practice Models

The results of user profiling can be fed directly into task analysis by identifying the user groups for which tasks must be characterized (Mayhew, 1999). Task analysis focuses on behavioral aspects of a task, resulting in an understanding of the general structure and flow of task activities (Nielsen, 1993; Wixon & Wilson, 1997). Beyond providing an understanding of tasks and work flow patterns, task analysis should also identify the primary objects or artifacts that support tasks, information needs (both inputs and outputs), work-arounds that have been adopted, and exceptions to normal work activities. The result of this analysis is a set of work practice models with supporting narrative depicting user-centered task activities and the associated context-of-use.

As there are both formal (e.g., GOMS—Card, Moran, & Newell, 1983; Task Analysis for Knowledge Description [TAKD—Diaper, 1989; Kirwan & Ainsworth, 1992]) and informal (e.g., interviews, observation, shadowing, and surveys) techniques for task analysis, it is important to determine the level of task analysis required for informed design (see Table 14.2). In general, in domains where it is feasible, observational task analysis is recommended. Design based on direct observation of users in their work environments rather than assumptions about users or observations of their activities in contrived laboratory settings can enhance system effectiveness and reduce the risk of human error or unsafe acts (Hackos & Redish, 1998). Observation techniques can also provide information about the environment in which tasks are performed, such as tacit behaviors, social interactions, and physical demands, which are difficult to capture with other techniques (Kirwan & Ainsworth, 1992). In most cases, observation and interview of a small set of diverse users can provide critical insights that lead to effective and acceptable system designs. For usability evaluations, Nielsen (1993) found that the greatest payoff occurs with just three to five users (about one-third of variation is captured with the first user, about one-half with the second, and 70 percent by the fourth). With all of these methods, typically a few domain experts are queried about their task knowledge. It is important to select individuals that can readily verbalize how a task is carried out to serve as informants (Eberts, 1994).

When a very detailed task analysis is required, formal techniques such as TAKD (Diaper, 1989; Kirwan & Ainsworth, 1992) or GOMS (Card, Moran, & Newell, 1983) can be used to delineate task activities. This detailed knowledge, however, comes at a great cost in terms of time to conduct the analysis. Thus, it is important to determine the level of task analysis required for informed design. While formal techniques such as GOMS can lead to very detailed analyses (i.e., at the perceive, think, and act level), often such detail is not required for effective design. Jeffries (1997) suggests that one can

Table 14.2. Task Analysis Techniques for Interactive System Design

Design objective	Task analysis technique
Detailed description of task	TAKD, GOMS, Interviews
Detailed description of task (when difficult to verbalize task knowledge)	Observation, Shadowing
Task description for tasks with significant performance variation; determine specific task characteristics (e.g., frequency)	Surveys, Observation, Shadowing
Clarify task areas	Surveys, Observation, Shadowing, Retrospectives, and Diaries

loosely determine the right level of detail by determining when further decomposition of the task would not reveal any "interesting" new subtasks that would enlighten the design. If detailed task knowledge is not deemed requisite, informal task analysis techniques should be adopted.

Interviews are the most common informal technique to gather task information (Jeffries, 1997; Kirwan & Ainsworth, 1992). In this technique, informants are asked to verbalize their strategies, rationale, and knowledge used to accomplish task goals and subgoals (Ericsson & Simon, 1980). As each informant's mental model of the tasks they verbalize is likely to differ, it is advantageous to interview at least two to three informants to identify the common flow of task activities. Placing the informant in the context of the task domain and having him or her verbalize while conducting tasks afford more complete task descriptions while providing insights into the environment the task is performed within. It can sometimes be difficult for informants to verbalize their task performance because much of it may be automatized (Eberts, 1994). When conducting interviews it is important to use appropriate sampling techniques (i.e., sample at the right time with enough individuals), avoid leading questions, and follow up with appropriate probe questions (Nardi, 1997). While the interviewer should generally abstain from interfering with task performance, it is sometimes necessary to probe for more detail when it appears that steps or subgoals are not being communicated. Eberts (1994) suggests that the human information processing model can be used to structure verbal protocols, determine what information is needed, and determine what is likely being left out.

Surveys are a particularly useful task analysis tools when there are significant variations in the manner in which tasks are performed or when it is important to determine specific task characteristics, such as task timing and frequency of task occurrence (Jeffries, 1997; Nielsen, 1993). Surveys can also be used as a follow-on to further clarify task areas described via an interview. Focused observation, shadowing, retrospectives, and diaries are also useful for clarifying task areas. With retrospectives and diaries, an informant is asked to provide a retrospective soon after completing a task or to document their activities after several task events, the latter being a diary.

Whether formal or informal techniques are used, the objective of the task analysis is to identify the goals of users and determine the techniques they use to accomplish these goals. Norman (1988) provided a general model of the stages users go through when accomplishing goals (see Figure 14.2). Stanton (1998) suggests that there are three main ways in which this process can go awry (see Figure 14.1): by users forming an incorrect goal (perhaps due to a poor mental model), specifying and executing an errant action (perhaps due to user confusion of an ill-learned system), or misperceiving or misinterpreting the current state of the system (perhaps due to incorrectly channeled attention due to high-workload conditions). In observing users of a vending machine, Verhoef (1988) indeed found that these types of errors

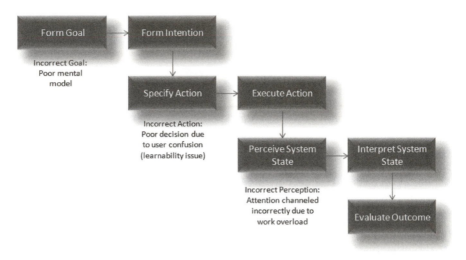

Figure 14.2.   Stages of goal accomplishment and some associated errors. Adapted from Norman (1988).

occur during system interaction. In this case study, users of the vending machine failed to perceive information presented by the machine (precondition for an unsafe act), performed actions in the wrong order (unsafe act), and misinterpreted tasks when they were not clearly explained or when incomplete information was provided (unsafe act).

By understanding the stages of goal accomplishment and the related errors that can occur, designers can more effectively design interactive systems. For example, by knowing that users perceive and interpret the system state once an action has been executed, designers can understand why it is essential to provide feedback (Nielsen, 1993) to the executed action. Knowing that users often specify alternative methods to achieve a goal or change methods during the course of goal seeking, designers can aim to support selection between diverse approaches. Further, recognizing that users commit errors emphasizes the need for undo functionality.

The results from a task analysis should provide insights into the optimal structuring of task activities and the key attributes of the work environment that will directly affect interactive system design (Mayhew, 1999). The analysis enumerates the tasks that users may want to accomplish to achieve stated goals through the preparation of a task list or task inventory (Hackos & Redish, 1998; Jeffries, 1997). A model of task activities, including how users currently think about, discuss, and perform their work, can then be devised based on the task analysis. To develop task flow models, it is important to consider the timing, frequency, criticality, difficulty, and responsible individual of each task on the list. In seeking to conduct the analysis at the appropriate level of detail, it may be beneficial to initially limit the task list and associated model to the primary 10–20 tasks that users perform. Once developed, task models can be used to determine the functionality necessary to support in the system design. Further, once the task models and desired functionality are characterized, use scenarios (i.e., concrete task instances, with related contextual [i.e., situational] elements and stated resolutions) can be developed that can be used to drive both the system design and the evaluation (Jeffries, 1997).

Contextual Variables

Beyond task models, task analysis should focus on developing a thorough understanding of how a system or product will be used in the target context-of-use. Contextual variables include the context itself, both as a global and as a comprehensive factor, and the separate component variables that collectively comprise the context: artifacts, cooperative task activities, organizational structure, situational factors, and interpersonal characteristics (Stanney & Champney, 2005; see Table 14.3).

Table 14.3.   Contextual Design Variables

Design variables	Information to inform design
Context	Description of user, environmental, cultural, and development contexts in which an activity is performed, including physical and social elements that develop over time.
Artifacts	Description of the designed and created objects or systems that humans apply and use to influence the world around them, including "border" or noncentral uses.
Cooperative task activities	Description of the degree to which effective group performance depends on both the transmission of information about task activities and the transmission of information about the values, interests, and personal commitments of group members.
Organizational structure	Description of the norms, power relationships, status relationships, cohesiveness, and group density of an organization or group.
Situational factors	Description of the social networks and relationships that exist among group members, as well as their maturity and cultural differences.
Interpersonal characteristics	Description of the attitudes, behaviors, and motivations of individual group members.

Mental Models

Developers must recognize that users will both come to the system interaction with preconceived mental models of the process being automated and develop models of automated system interaction. Designers should thus seek to identify how users represent their existing knowledge about a process and how this knowledge fits together in learning and performance so that they can design systems that engender the development of an accurate mental model of the system interaction (Young, 2008). By developing an understanding of user mental models, including potential misconceptions and mismatches between the system design and users' mental models, developers can determine how users currently think and act, how these behaviors can be supported by the interactive system design when advantageous, and how they can be modified and improved upon via system automation. This understanding can then be used in the risk management process by addressing any misconceptions and mismatches between a user's mental model and the designer's conceptual model, which, if left unresolved, can lead to improper use and human error (see Figure 14.1).

USABILITY GOAL SETTING AND RISK ASSESSMENT

In designing systems, usability engineering is used to evaluate the resulting design. Usability objectives generally focus around effectiveness (i.e., the extent to which tasks can be achieved), intuitiveness (i.e., how learnable and memorable the system is), and user satisfaction (i.e., how comfortable and satisfied users are with the system; Rubin, Chisnell, & Spool, 2008). In setting such objectives, one should ensure that the usability attributes evaluated are those that are important for meeting project goals, that these attributes are translated into operational measures, that the attributes are generally holistic (i.e., relating to overall system/task performance), and that the attributes relate to specific usability objectives. For systems targeted for high-risk environments, risk assessment becomes an important aspect of usability evaluation.

Failure Modes and Effects Analysis, a bottom-up analysis tool, and FTA, a top-down analysis tool, are commonly used for risk assessment in user-centered design (see Chapter 10 of this book for a particular risk assessment technique; for others see Powers, 2006). FMEA is a design evaluation technique that focuses on defining, identifying, and eliminating potential "failure modes" that are uncovered through the task analysis process (Israelski & Muto, 2006) and, if metaphoric design is used (see Cognitive Approach below), through an analysis of potential misconceptions and mismatches between a user's mental model and the user interface design. With FMEA, each failure mode is defined and prioritized based on two criteria (or sometimes three—including likelihood of detection—but the latter is not recommended; see Schmidt, 2004):

1. Probability of occurrence (estimated frequency of failure on scale from 1—not likely to 10—inevitable).

2. Severity (estimated impact if failure occurs, e.g., injury to operator and degraded performance, on a scale from 1—no effect to 10—very severe with failure affecting user safety and/or system operation without warning; see also MIL-STD 1629A [1980] for an alternative rating scheme).

These criteria can then be used to compute a Risk Priority Number (RPN), which is used as a single measure to assess priorities.

$$RPN = (Probability) \times (Severity)$$

The list of potential failure modes can then be sorted by descending criticality (i.e., RPN) and represented in a Pareto chart.

Fault Tree Analysis is an analytical tool used to evaluate risk at the overall system level through cumulative probabilities of logically combined fault events (Israelski & Muto, 2004). It provides a graphical tree representation that starts with a single undesired event (e.g., user injury and system failure) at the top, and then branches down to show the faults that can lead to the top-level undesired event, with root causes shown at the bottom of the tree. The resulting tree provides a visualization of how individual faults (e.g., user errors and system deficiencies) can combine together and cause the top-level undesired event. In terms of quantifying risks, the nodes of the tree provide a means of representing events in a symbolic logic form to which Boolean logic can be applied. Through the resulting algebraic expression, probabilities can be assigned to each of the individual faults, which can then be combined to determine the probability of the top-level undesired event. FTA thus provides an assessment of overall system-level failures and characterizes the contributing factors to these failure states.

For each of the high-priority failure modes identified through FMEA and FTA, error-reducing design strategies can be implemented (see Table 14.4) and the system can be reassessed in terms of risk. This iterative design process can continue until all higher-priority risks are eliminated and any residual risk is as low as reasonably practicable (ALARP).

Since usability is assessed via a multitude of potentially conflicting measures, oftentimes equal weights cannot be given to every usability criterion. For example, to minimize risk one might have to sacrifice task efficiency. Developers should specify usability criteria of interest and provide operational goals for each metric. These metrics can be expressed as absolute goals (i.e., in terms of an absolute quantification) or as relative goals (i.e., in comparison to a benchmark system or process). Such metrics provide system developers with concrete goals to meet and a means to measure usability. This information can be documented in the form of a usability attribute table and usability specification matrix (see Mayhew, 1999). As demonstrated in Figure 14.1, inadequacies in usability goal setting and

Table 14.4.   Error-Reducing Design Strategies

Resolving issues with poor user interface design:
- Poor support of tasks and/or task flows (i.e., logic of operation).
- Mismatches between users' capabilities and limitations and the user interface design.
- Mismatches or misconceptions in users' mental models.
- Poor feedback, which does not support goal accomplishment.
- Poor support of alternative methods to achieve a goal or a change in methods during the course of goal seeking.
- Lack of undo functionality or other such error-reducing strategies that support users in recognizing, diagnosing, and recovering from errors once they occur.
- Poor labeling or other such directives.
- Poor support of individual differences in experience and task performance.

Resolving organizational issues:
- Inadequate training.
- Individual differences in incentives and motivation.

Resolving environmental issues:
- Issues associated with the context-of-use.

Adapted from Pew and Mavor (2007).

risk assessment will lead to inefficient, ineffective, unsatisfying, and error-prone designs.

USER-CENTERED REQUIREMENTS ANALYSIS

The intent of user needs and task analyses is to achieve a set of requirements that specify what a system should be capable of doing, the functions that must be available to users to achieve stated goals, and the requisite level of usability. Inadequacies in user-centered requirements analysis can lead to costly, inadequate, and error-prone designs (see Figure 14.1). Karat and Dayton (1995) suggest that developing a careful understanding of system requirements leads to more effective conceptual and detailed designs that require less redesign. In general, user-centered requirements analysis involves the specification of the necessary goals, functions, and objectives to be met by a detailed system design (Eberts, 1994).

- Goals specify the desired system characteristics. These are generally qualitatively stated (e.g., automate functions, maximize use, accommodate user types, and minimize risk) and can be met in a number of ways.

- Functions define what the system should be capable of doing, without specifying the specifics of how the functions should be achieved.

- Objectives are the activities that the system must be able to accomplish in support of the specified functions. Note that the system requirements, as stated in terms of goals, functions, and objectives, can be achieved by a number of design alternatives.

Thus, user-centered requirements analysis specifies what the system should be able to accomplish without specifying how this should be realized. It can be used to guide the overall conceptual and detailed design efforts that round out the design specification process.

USER INTERFACE DESIGN

Readied with requisite background information from the user needs and task analysis to feed design, usability goals to meet (see Table 14.5), and a set of user-centered requirements, interactive system design generally commences with an initial conceptual design and evolves into a detailed design specification, from which iterative cycles of evaluation and improvement transpire (Sharp, Rogers, & Preece, 2007). Figure 14.1 demonstrates how inadequacies in design will lead to redesign, hindered human performance, and human errors. Thus, it is essential to use the knowledge from user needs and task analyses to drive requirements specifications that lead to effective, efficient, and fail-safe designs.

Conceptual Design

Conceptual design transitions the identified user needs and task analysis information into potential design concepts. Once a design concept(s) has been selected, it is followed by defining the requirements and developing the

Table 14.5.   Checklist of Information Items (iterative process)

Have the following been achieved:
- Identified necessary goals, functions, and objectives to be met by system design.
- Became familiar with practices, tools, and vernacular of work environment.
- Characterized user profiles in terms of physical characteristics, psychological characteristics, knowledge and skills, and job characteristics.
- Acknowledged individual differences within target user population.
- Developed user models that are relevant, accurate, adaptable to changes in user behavior, and generalizable.
- Developed a user-centered model of current work practices via task analysis and contextual variable and mental model characterization.
- Defined extent of user involvement versus computer automation in system interaction, as well as required support resources (e.g., manuals, online help, and customer support).
- Set usability goals.

system specification for the selected design solution(s) prior to moving into detailed design. To generate a multitude of conceptual design ideas, it is beneficial to use a parallel design strategy (Nielsen, 1993), where multiple designers set out in isolation to generate design concepts. A low level of effort (e.g., a few hours to a few days) is generally devoted to this idea generation stage. Storyboarding via paper prototypes is often used at this stage, as it is easy to generate, readily modified, and cost-effective (Synder, 2003). Typically, conceptual design is a brainstorming process, driven by creativity. While creativity is advantageous, and even essential to conceptual design, there is a need for more systematic techniques to guide conceptual design. Specifically, when designers sit down and commence the conceptual design process, knowledge gained from user needs and task analyses can be used to develop conceptual designs, which can be guided by four main user-centered design approaches: anthropomorphic, cognitive, predictive, and empirical.

Anthropomorphic Approach

The anthropomorphic approach seeks to build elements of human–human communication into the interactive system, which brings to light consideration of advanced interfaces such as voice-based and gesture interaction (Eberts, 1994). This approach factors in world knowledge (how target users currently interact within their operational context-of-use) in order to build in expectations based on users' current mental models and work practices and avoid mismatches between the user's mental model and the designer's conceptual model.

One strategy within the anthropomorphic approach is to design natural affordances and constraints from the real world into user interaction (Gibson, 1977; Norman, 1988). With this technique, designers seek to develop designs that afford desired actions or control user actions through constraints. As an example, a park pathway affords locomotion along its trail in the terrain, just as a runway in a flight simulator scenario affords direction of takeoff. These systems have also incorporated constraints, such as flight modes that restrict interaction (e.g., automatic pilot). Taken together, affordances and constraints aim to enhance the naturalness of interaction by mapping real-world interaction techniques onto human–system interaction. The incorporation of such techniques should lead to interactive systems that are natural and user-friendly (i.e., a system will interact with a user much the way a human interacts with another human, supporting the basic turn-taking structure of human conversation; McFarlane, 1997). Eberts (1994) suggested that naturalness exists if (1) human and system act as supportive partners, (2) interaction between human and system flows easily, (3) the system has some capacity to critique a user's plans, and (4) the system somehow reveals its intentions to the user. Norman (1988) developed several guiding principles for incorporating "naturalness" into design, including visibility, strong conceptual model, good mappings, and effective feedback. There are also several technology forms of "naturalness" that have been adopted, including natural language processing, voice communication, advanced interaction modes (e.g., gesture, facial expressions, and eye gaze), and adaptive systems (e.g., use of automated reasoning, probability and utility theory, user models, automated error diagnosis, decision support, augmented cognition, etc., for custom-tailoring interactive systems to better meet users' capabilities and preferences). These technologies are getting integrated into multimodal solutions that allow users to interact with computers using multiple modes of communication much as they would interact with other humans (Hale, Stanney, Milham, Bell, & Jones, 2009).

While the anthropomorphic approach offers many advantages in terms of user-friendliness, naturalness, and the fostering of innovative design solutions, it is best to couple this approach with others to achieve a robust solution.

Cognitive Approach

The cognitive approach brings cognitive science to the conceptual design process by leveraging models of human information processing, attention, and workload (Eberts, 1994). This approach focuses on developing designs that are within human information processing capabilities and limitations. It seeks to identify potential metaphors and scripts that could guide interactive system design, including those for directing manipulation and navigation, conversing, and instruction. The overall goal of the cognitive approach is to design a system such that the information conveyed through the user interface enables users to develop a mental model (i.e., the model a user forms of how a system works, which evolves through inference as the user interacts with the system) that is as close to the designer's conceptual model as possible. The cognitive approach thus aims to design interactive systems to be as predictable as possible (i.e., respond to the way users perceive, think, and act).

Through the application of the cognitive approach, human–system interaction has evolved into a relatively standard set of interaction paradigms, including windows, icons, menus, and pointing devices. This "standard" is evolving, with a transition from graphical user interfaces to perceptual user interfaces that seek to more naturally interact with the users (i.e., the anthropomorphic approach) through multimodal and multimedia interaction (Turk & Robertson, 2000). In either case, however, these interfaces are characterized by interaction paradigms that try to match users' human information processing capabilities, attentional resources, and workload limitations to the interface design while providing metaphors that guide user interaction.

1. *Models of human information processing*: Current understanding of human information processing suggests that information is perceived through multiple sensory processors (Baddeley, 2000). This information is then perceptually encoded (i.e., stimulus is identified and recognized), processed by a working

memory (WM) subsystem (spatial versus verbal), which is regulated and controlled by attention via the executive function and may be supported by long-term memory, which in turn triggers a human response. Wickens's (1984) multiple resource theory (MRT) addresses the idea that given separable WM subsystem components, alternate resources can be strategically utilized at different points in user interaction to streamline a user's cognitive load (e.g., direct information to the visuospatial sketchpad versus the phonological loop). In such case, the idea of central processing capacity is replaced with limits for specific types of percepts, with total WM capacity depending on how dissimilar streams of information are in terms of modality. Thus, the cognitive approach aims to achieve designs that allocate WM resources in such a way as to allow attention to be time-shared among various modalities, thereby implementing modalities according to predicted available WM stores, as well as considering potential wanted or undesirable cross-modal sensory integration effects. For example, haptic interaction could be added to support spatial processing, as it is an effective modality for spatial processing and could off-load the visual sensory channel (Hale, Axelsson, Samman, & Stanney, 2005).

2. *Attentional resources*: Three general categories of attention theories can be found in the literature, including "cause" theories, in which attention is suggested to modulate information processing (e.g., via a spotlight that functions as a serial scanning mechanism or via limited resource pools); "effect" theories, in which attention is suggested to be a by-product of information processing among multiple systems (e.g., stimulus representations compete for neuronal activation); and hybrids that combine cause and effect theories (Fernandez-Duque & Johnson, 2002). In general, attention is suggested to be a selective process, via which stimulus representations are transferred between sensory memory and WM, which contributes to the processing of information once in WM. Attention improves human performance on a wide range of tasks, minimizes distractions, and facilitates access to awareness (i.e., focused attention). In the best case, attention helps to filter out irrelevant multimodal stimuli. In the worst case, critical information is lost due to overload of incoming information, stimulus competition, or distractions, which are preconditions for unsafe acts (see Figure 14.1). Thus, if one were to try to enhance WM via multimodal interaction, such stimulation would impose a trade-off between the benefits of incorporating additional sensory systems and the costs associated with dividing attention between various sensory modalities. Thus, the cognitive approach aims to achieve designs that judiciously moderate the allocation of attention to enhance human–system interaction.

3. *Workload*: There are many forms of workload, such as mental demands, physical demands, temporal demands, own performance, effort, and frustration (Hart & Staveland, 1988). Cognitive workload is often of central importance to interactive system designers, as it relates to the mental demands a user must expend when interacting with a system. It can serve as a useful diagnostic by identifying points in human–system interaction where users have to expend excessive mental effort to achieve acceptable performance levels. Such diagnostic information can be obtained by a number of metrics, including subjective survey techniques (e.g., Cooper & Harper's [1969] Measure of Perceived Mental Workload,

Subjective Mental Effort Questionnaire [SMEQ; Zijlstra, 1993], and NASA TLX [Hart & Staveland, 1988]), as well as physiological indicators (see Chapter 15 of this book for a comprehensive review). Measures of cognitive workload are particularly useful when users are expected to be over- or underloaded. A system that demands low levels of mental effort may hamper efficiency due to issues of boredom or lack of vigilance. On the other hand, excessive cognitive workload may also lower efficiency as it can cause loss of information due to information overload, and thus result in errors, unsafe acts, and degraded performance. The cognitive approach thus aims to assess the cognitive workload imposed by a system to predict and avoid through effective design problems of overload or underload.

4. *Metaphors*: When using the cognitive approach, designers often try to ease the complexity of system interaction by grounding interface actions and objects and related tasks and goals in a familiar framework known as a metaphor (Neale & Carroll, 1997). A metaphor is a conceptual set of familiar terms and associations. If designed into a user interface, it can be used to encourage users to relate what they already know about the metaphoric concept to the system interaction, thereby enhancing the learnability of the system (Carroll & Thomas, 1982). Metaphors thus provide users with a useful orienting framework to guide system interaction. For example, a visual metaphor often provides insights into the spatial properties of a user interface (Carroll & Mack, 1985), thereby enhancing a user's ability to tie together a configural representation (or mental model) of the system to guide interaction (Kay, 1990). If effective, such a metaphor would both orient and situate users within the system interaction, helping users focus on critical cues and drawing attention away from irrelevant distractions (i.e., enhance visual access; Kim & Hirtle, 1995). Parunak (1989) accomplished this in a hypertext environment (i.e., applications that allow nonlinear, associative linking between text, ideas, images, and sounds, such as the World Wide Web) by providing between-path mechanisms (e.g., backtracking capability and guided tours), annotation capabilities that allowed users to designate locations that could be accessed directly (e.g., bookmarks in hypertext), and links and filtering techniques that simplified a given topology. The cognitive approach thus aims to achieve coherent, well-structured metaphoric designs that guide user interaction through the development of accurate mental models. Poor mental models, on the other hand, can lead to unsafe acts through improper use (see Figure 14.1).

A primary advantage of the cognitive approach is that it treats users as flexible, adaptive information processors with limited resources who are actively trying to solve problems when interacting with a computer. It then leverages this knowledge to achieve designs that are a good "cognitive fit" for users. However, just as with the anthropomorphic approach, it is best to couple this approach with others to achieve a robust solution.

Predictive Approach

The predictive approach seeks to model interaction with a system in order to predict human performance with different design alternatives. The value of this approach is that predictions can be made concerning different design concepts prior to the software prototyping of a system. One predictive approach is TAKD (Diaper, 1989; Kirwan & Ainsworth, 1992), which uses knowledge representation grammars (i.e., sets of statements used to describe system inter-action) to represent task knowledge in a task descriptive hierarchy. This tech-nique is useful for characterizing complex tasks that lack fine-detail cognitive activities (Eberts, 1994). GOMS (Card, Moran, & Newell, 1983) is a predictive modeling technique that has been used to characterize how humans interact with computers. Through a GOMS analysis, task goals are identified, along with the operators (i.e., perceptual, cognitive, or motor acts) and methods (i.e., series of operators) to achieve those goals and the selection rules used to elect between alternative methods. Card, Moran, and Newell (1983) developed the Model Human Processor (MHP) to provide a means for fine-grained analy-sis of design alternatives. Hale et al. (2009) have recently extended this model for multimodal interaction. The multimodal MHP can be used to predict several dimensions of user performance (i.e., capacity, decay, and processing time).

The advantage of the predictive approach is that it can provide an in-depth understanding of task characteristics, which can be used to quantify the benefits in terms of consistency (TAKD) or performance time gains (GOMS) of one design versus another (cf. Gray, John, & Atwood, 1993; McLeod & Sherwood-Jones, 1993). It is useful in developing error and time estimates. While the specific quantitative outcomes from such analysis may be off by an order of magnitude (i.e., Design A is x percent faster than Design B), the rela-tivity of the prediction (i.e., Design A is better than Design B) tends to be accu-rate. The predictive approach, however, is very labor-intensive to apply and different analysts may come up with different predictions due to biases in their task analyses (thus the same analyst should evaluate all alternatives in a compa-rative analysis). Further, poor task analysis can lead to erroneous predictive models, which in turn can lead to inaccurate human performance predictions, thereby resulting in designs that do not match human capabilities—a precondi-tion for unsafe acts (see Figure 14.1). The predictive approach is thus best used for small-scale analyses, such as a comparative evaluation of a particular menu design, rather than a comprehensive design comparison.

Empirical Approach

The empirical approach allows for direct comparison of design alternatives, as well as specification of human and task performance measures that can be used to assess system effectiveness. With the empirical approach, the correct choice between design options is the one that fairs the best during experimenta-tion (Eberts, 1994). A primary advantage of this approach is that it provides an alternative to designer's intuition (which is often proven wrong) about the efficacy of a given design alternative. This approach, however, requires: (1) careful control of testing conditions, which can reduce the validity of the findings by removing real-world implications; (2) a narrow focus, which can limit generalizability; and (3) use of select groups of participants, which again can limit generalizability. In addition, such studies can be costly and time-intensive and they oftentimes lack any theoretical guidance in the generation of the designs evaluated (designs tend to be needs—rather than theory—driven). The latter issue can be resolved by complementing this approach with the cognitive approach.

Each of the four approaches has different strengths and weaknesses. The anthropomorphic approach seeks naturalness, the cognitive approach seeks to identify optimal means of displaying and conveying information so as to support human capabilities and limitations, the predictive approach seeks to predict how effective a design will be, while the empirical approach seeks to measure how effective a design will be. By incorporating a combination of these approaches into the conceptual design process, more robust design concepts can be passed forward to detailed design.

Detailed Design

Detailed design brings the conceptual design into a completed form. The level of detail necessary to finalize a design specification can be realized through the use of several techniques, including specification of nouns and verbs that represent interface objects and actions, use scenarios, use sequences, use flow diagrams, and use work flows. Storyboards and rough interface sketches can support each stage in the evolution of the detailed design.

Objects and Actions

During detailed design, workplace artifacts, identified via the task analysis, become the objects in the interface design (Hackos & Redish, 1998). Nouns in the task flow also become interface objects, while verbs become interface actions (Young, 2008). Through paper prototyping, artifacts, nouns, and verbs represented in the task flows can each be specified on sticky notes and posted to a working storyboard. Desired attributes for each object or action can be delineated on the notes. The objects and actions should be categorized and any redundancies eliminated. Narratives and categories can generate ideas on how interface objects should look, interface actions should feel, and how these might be structurally organized around identified categories.

Use Scenarios, Use Sequences, Use Flow Diagrams, and Use Work Flows

These task-related techniques can all be used to support detailed design (Hackos & Redish, 1998). Use scenarios are narrative descriptions of how the goals and subgoals identified via the task analysis will be realized via the interface design. Beyond the main flow of task activities, they should address task exceptions, individual differences, and anticipated user errors. If detailed designs are robust, they should be able to withstand the interactions demanded by a variety of use scenarios with only modest modifications required. Once the "running" of use scenarios fails to generate any required design modifications, their use can be terminated.

If parts of a use scenario are difficult for users to achieve or designers to conceptualize, use sequences can be used. Use sequences delineate the sequence of steps required for a scenario subsection. They specify the actions and decisions required of the user and the interactive system, the objects needed to achieve task goals, and the required outputs of the system interaction. Task work-arounds and exceptions can be addressed with use sequences to determine if the design should support these activities. Providing detailed sequence specifications highlights steps that are not appropriately supported by the design and thus require redesign.

When there are several use sequences supported by a design, it can be helpful to develop use flow diagrams for a defined subsection of the task activities. These diagrams delineate the alternative paths and related intersections (i.e., decision points) users encounter during system interaction. The representative entities that users "encounter" throughout the use flow diagram become the required objects and actions for the interface design. If these are coherently represented in the design, then this will help guide users in their selection among alternatives and reduce the chance for human error.

When interactive systems are intended to yield savings in the required level of information exchange, use work flows can be used. These flows provide a visualization of the movement of users or information objects throughout the work environment. They can clearly denote if a design concept will improve information flow. Designers can first develop use work flows for the existing system interaction, and then eliminate, combine, resequence, and simplify steps to streamline the flow of information.

Storyboards and Prototypes

The efforts devoted to the development of use scenarios, use sequences, use flow diagrams, and use work flows result in a plethora of design ideas. Designers can brainstorm over design concepts, generating storyboards of potential ideas for the detailed design (Synder, 2003). Storyboards should be at the level of detail provided by use scenarios and work flow diagrams (Hackos & Redish, 1998). Prototypes, or working models, of the favored storyboard designs are then developed (Arnowitz, Arent, & Berger, 2006). They are generally developed with easy-to-use tool kits (e.g., Macromedia Director, ToolBook, SmallTalk, or Visual Basic) or simpler tools (e.g., hypercard scenarios, drawing programs, even paper or plastic mock-ups) rather than high-level programming languages. Whether high- or low-end techniques are used, prototypes provide means to provide cost-effective, concrete design concepts that can be evaluated with target users (usually three to six users per iteration) and readily modified until usability goals are met. They prevent developers from exhausting extensive resources in formal development of products that will not be adopted by users.

Evaluating Error-Reducing Designs

Error-reducing, performance-enhancing design specifications should result from conceptual and detailed design processes that are grounded in user needs and task analyses (see Figure 14.1). But how can a designer determine if the result is an error-reducing design? Predictive Human Error Analysis (PHEA) can be used to determine if an error-reducing design has been achieved (Stanton & Young, 1999). Specifically, PHEA first classifies each goal, operation, or task step identified through the task analysis into a potential error using a human error taxonomy with five types of errors: action, retrieval, checking, selection, and information communication. An error description (see Table 14.6), associated consequences to user interaction, and recovery possibilities are noted for each possible error, along with its probability (e.g., from FTA)

Table 14.6. Predictive Human Error Analysis

Error type	Error description
Action errors	Step too long/too short Step too early/too late Step too fast/too slow Step omitted Step occurred in wrong sequence Step execution incomplete
Information retrieval errors	Information not retrieved Wrong information retrieved Information retrieval incomplete Too much information retrieved
Checking errors	No check performed Check incomplete Wrong check performed Check performed on wrong operation Check too early/too late
Selection errors	Selection omitted Incorrect selection made Selection made in wrong sequence
Information communication errors	Information not communicated Information communication incomplete Wrong information communicated

and criticality (RPN from FMEA; or low, medium, high). Finally, possible error-reducing design strategies are proposed (see Table 14.4). Thus, PHEA provides a systematic process by which to use the results of a task analysis and identify and investigate potential user errors and their connection to design (e.g., design omits steps, takes too long, and leads to wrong information retrieval choices). With this knowledge in hand, error-reducing design strategies can be incorporated to reduce risks. For example, for high-criticality errors exclusion strategies can be incorporated that design the possibility for these errors out of the system (Glendon, Clarke, & McKenna, 2006). Prevention strategies can be used to make it difficult to make information retrieval errors by providing very detailed instructions on the type and amount of information to be retrieved. Finally, fail-safe techniques can be used to make designs error tolerant and reduce the consequences of human error. For example, using confirmations to ensure users want to execute selected actions, thereby reducing errors in selection. Thus, techniques such as PHEA can be used to identify predictable ways in which user interaction is anticipated to lead to errors and use error-reducing design strategies to remedy these shortcomings. Successful application of such evaluation techniques will lead to designs that reduce or eliminate opportunities for human error and provide the strategies necessary to address any that do occur, thereby reducing the risks of system interaction.

CONCLUSIONS

User-centered design of interactive systems is meant to make user interaction more effective, efficient, intuitive, safe, and enjoyable. The consideration of various design techniques discussed in this chapter must be recognized as an iterative design process. By considering these factors in an iterative manner, system designs can evolve until the desired level of performance and safety is achieved. This allows valuable resources to be saved or applied to other endeavors. Further, a multidisciplinary team should be involved in the development process. The team must be supported by ergonomists who understand physical requirements, human factors engineers who understand cognitive requirements, industrial designers who understand aesthetic requirements, systems engineers who understand functional requirements, and a management who believe in the competitive edge that can be gained by developing user-centered interactive systems. Close collaboration between these team members can lead to the development of remarkably effective, highly usable, and fail-proof systems that are readily adopted by users.

REFERENCES

Arnowitz, J., Arent, M., & Berger, N. (2006). *Effective prototyping for software makers*. San Francisco, CA: Morgan Kaufmann.

Baddeley, A. D. (2000). The episodic buffer: A new component of working memory? *Trends in Cognitive Science*, 4, 417–423.

Card, S. K., Moran, T. P., & Newell, A. L. (1983). *The psychology of human-computer interaction*. Hillsdale, NJ: Lawrence Erlbaum Associates.

Carroll, J. M., & Mack, R. L. (1985). Metaphor, computing systems, and active learning. *International Journal of Man-Machine Studies*, 22, 39–57.

Carroll, J. M., & Thomas, J. C. (1982). Metaphor and the cognitive representation of computing systems. *IEEE Transactions on Systems, Man and Cybernetics*, 12, 107–116.

Cooper, G. E., & Harper. R. P. (1969). The use of pilot rating in the evaluation of aircraft handling qualities. NASA TN D-5153.

Diaper, D. (1989). *Task analysis for human computer interaction*. Chichester: Ellis Horwood.

Eberts, R. E. (1994). *User interface design*. Englewood Cliffs, NJ: Prentice Hall.

Ericsson, K. A., & Simon, H. A. (1980). Verbal reports as data. *Psychological Review*, 87, 215–251.

Fernandez-Duque, D., & Johnson, M. L. (2002). Cause and effect theories of attention: The role of conceptual metaphors. *Review of General Psychology*, 6 (2), 153–165.

Gibson, J. J. (1977). The theory of affordances. In R. E. Shaw & J. Bransford (Eds.), *Perceiving, acting, and knowing*. Hillsdale, NJ: Lawrence Erlbaum Associates.

Glendon, I. A., Clarke, A., & McKenna, E. F. (2006). *Human safety and risk management*. Boca Raton, FL: CRC Press.

Gould, J. D., Boies, S. J., & Ukelson, J. (1997). How to design usable systems. In M. Helander, T. K. Landauer, and P. V. Prabhu (Eds.), *Handbook of human-computer interaction* (2nd ed., pp. 231–254). Amsterdam: North-Holland.

Gray, W. D., John, B. E., & Atwood, M. E. (1993). Project Ernestine: Validating a GOMS analysis for predicting real-world task performance. *Human-Computer Interaction*, 6, 287–309.

Hackos, J. T., & Redish, J. C. (1998). *User and task analysis for interface design*. New York: John Wiley & Sons.

Hale, K., Axelsson, P., Samman, S., & Stanney, K. M. (2005). Validation of predictive workload component of the Multimodal Information Design Support (MIDS) system. *The 49th Annual Human Factors and Ergonomics Society Meeting*, Orlando, FL, September 26–30, 2005.

Hale, K. S., Stanney, K. M., Milham, L. M., Bell, M. A., & Jones, D. L. (2009). Multimodal sensory information requirements for enhancing situation awareness and training effectiveness. *Theoretical Issues in Ergonomics Science*, 10, 245–266.

Hart, S. G., & Staveland, L. E. (1988). Development of a multi-dimensional workload rating scale: Results of empirical and theoretical research. In P. A. Hancock & N. Meshkati (Eds.), *Human mental workload* (pp. 139–183). Amsterdam, The Netherlands: Elsevier.

Hughes, J., King, V., Rodden, T., & Anderson, H. (1995). The role of ethnography in interactive systems design. *Interactions*, 2 (2), 56–65.

Israelski, E. W., & Muto, W. H. (2004). Human factors risk management as a way to improve medical device safety: A case study of the Therac 25 Radiation Therapy System. *Joint Commission Journal on Quality and Safety*, 30 (12), 689–695.

————. (2006). Human factors engineering and the design risk management in medical devices. In P. Carayon (Ed.), *Handbook of human factors and ergonomics in healthcare and patient safety* (Part V, Technology). Mahwah, NJ: Erlbaum.

Jeffries, R. (1997). The role of task analysis in the design of software. In M. G. Helander, T. K. Landauer, & P. V. Prabhu (Eds.), *Handbook of human-computer interaction* (pp. 347–359). Amsterdam: North-Holland.

Karat, J., & Dayton, T. (1995). Practical education for improving software usability (pp. 162–169). *CHI '95 Proceedings*.

Kay, A. (1990). User interface: A personal view. In B. Laurel (Ed.), *The art of human-computer interaction* (pp. 191–207). Reading, MA: Addison-Wesley.

Kim, H., & Hirtle, S. C. (1995). Spatial metaphors and disorientation in hypertext browsing. *Behaviour & Information Technology*, 14 (4), 239–250.

Kirwan, B., & Ainsworth, L. K. (Eds.). (1992). *A guide to task analysis*. London: Taylor & Francis.

Mayhew, D. J. (1999). *The usability engineering lifecycle: A practitioner's handbook for user interface design*. San Francisco, CA: Morgan Kaufmann.

McFarlane, D. C. (1997). *Interruption of people in human-computer interaction: A general unifying definition of human interruption and taxonomy*. Technical Report No. NRL/FR/5510—97-9870. Naval Research Laboratory, Washington, D.C. [Online] http://interruptions.net/literature/McFarlane-NRL-97.pdf.

McLeod, R. W., & Sherwood-Jones, B. M. (1993). Simulation to predict operator workload in a command system. In B. Kirwan & L. K. Ainsworth (Eds.), *A guide to task analysis* (pp. 301–310). London: Taylor & Francis.

MIL-STD 1629A. (1980). Procedures for performing a failure mode, effects and criticality analysis. http://www.sre.org/pubs/Mil-Std-1629A.pdf (accessed March 11, 2008).

Nardi, B. A. (1997). The use of ethnographic methods in design and evaluation. In M. Helander, T. K. Landauer, & P. V. Prabhu (Eds.), *Handbook of human-computer interaction* (2nd ed., pp. 361–366). Amsterdam: North-Holland.

Neale, D. C., & Carroll, J. M. (1997). The role of metaphors in user interface design. In M. Helander, T. K. Landauer, & P. V. Prabhu (Eds.), *Handbook of human-computer interaction* (2nd ed., pp. 441–462). Amsterdam: North-Holland.

Nielsen, J. (1993). *Usability engineering*. Boston: Academic Press Professional.

Norman, D. A. (1988). *The psychology of everyday things*. New York: Basic Books.

Parunak, H. V. (1989). Hypermedia topologies and user navigation. In *Hypertext '89 Proceedings* (pp. 43–50). New York: ACM Press.

Pew, R. W., & Mavor, A. S. (2007). *Human-system integration in the system development process: A new look*. Washington, D.C.: National Academies Press.

Powers, D. M. (April 2006). Risk management for IVDs: Part 2: Assessing risks to patients from incorrect test results. *IVD Technology*, 12 (3), 24–31.

Righi, C., & James, J. (2007). *Design stories: Real-world UCD case studies*. San Francisco, CA: Morgan Kaufmann.

Rubin, J., Chisnell, D., & Spool, J. (2008). *Handbook of usability testing: How to plan, design, and conduct effective tests*. Indianapolis, IN: Wiley Publishing.

Schmidt, M. W. (March 2004). The use and misuse of FMEA in risk analysis. *Medical Device and Diagnostic Industry*, 26 (3), 56–61.

Sharp, H., Rogers, Y., & Preece, J. (2007). *Interaction design: Beyond human-computer interaction*. New York: Wiley.

Skelton, T. M., & Thamhain, H. J. (2005). User-centered design as a risk management tool in new technology product development. *Proceedings of the 2005 IEEE International Engineering Management Conference* (vol. 2, pp. 690–694), St. John's, Newfoundland & Labrador, Canada, September 11–13, 2005.

Stanney, K. M., & Champney, R. (2005). Social centered design. In W. Karwowski (Ed.), *International encyclopedia of ergonomics and human factors* (2nd ed., pp. 1708–1712). New York, NY: Taylor and Francis.

Stanton, N. (1998). Product design with people in mind. In N. Stanton (Ed.), *Human factors in consumer products* (pp. 1–17). London: Taylor & Francis.

Stanton, N., & Young, M. S. (1999). *A guide to methodology in ergonomics*. Boca Raton, FL: CRC Press.

Synder, C. (2003). Paper prototyping: The fast and easy way to design and refine user interfaces. San Francisco, CA: Morgan Kaufmann.

Turk, M., & Robertson, G. (2000). Perceptual user interfaces. *Communications of the ACM*, 43 (3), 33–34.

Verhoef, L. W. M. (1988). Decision making of vending machine users. *Applied Ergonomics*, 19, 103–109.

Wickens, C. D. (1984). Processing resources in attention. In R. Parasuraman & D. R. Davies (Eds.), *Varieties of attention* (pp. 63–102). New York, NY: Academic Press.

Wiegmann, D., & Shappell, S. (2003). *A human error approach to aviation accident analysis: The human factors analysis and classification system*. Aldershot, Hampshire: Ashgate Publishing.

Wixon, D., & Wilson, C. (1997). The usability engineering framework for product design and evaluation. In M. Helander, T. K. Landauer, & P. V. Prabhu (Eds.), *Handbook of human-computer interaction* (2nd ed., pp. 653–688). Amsterdam: North-Holland.

Woods, D. D., & Cook, R. I. (2002). Nine steps to move forward from error. *Cognition, Technology, and Work*, 4 (2), 137–144.

Young, I. (2008). *Mental models: Aligning design strategy with human behavior*. Brooklyn, NY: Rosenfeld Media, LLC.

Zijlstra, F. R. H. (1993). *Efficiency in work behaviour: A design approach for modern tools*. Delft: Delft University Press.

Chapter 15

WORKLOAD, SITUATION AWARENESS, AND THE RIGHT STUFF FOR ASSESSING COCKPIT DESIGN

Jefferson D. Grubb

INFORMATION MANAGEMENT AND THE WARFIGHTER

In Book I of *On War* (originally published in 1832), Clausewitz (2008) noted that information management was an essential task for warfighters of his era. To make informed decisions, military leaders needed an accurate picture of the overall situation. The only way to form such a picture was to integrate bits of incomplete and often contradictory information. However, collecting and processing this information took time, during which events on the battlefield continued to unfold. Thus, the quality of a leader's decisions was limited by the continuous outcome of a race between events in the real world and his ability to collect and process information about those events.

In the nearly two centuries since Clausewitz made those observations, engineers have attempted to develop technological solutions to many of the problems that faced Napoleonic armies. For example, the menagerie of sensor systems that a modern military unit brings into battle allows that unit to collect vastly more information than its Napoleonic counterpart could. Modern data links allow that information to be distributed in real time to other units across large distances. Together, these two technological advances are supposed to yield a Nirvana of information processing called network-centric warfare, in which decision makers at all levels of the military have access to all of the information that they need, when they need it (Cebrowski & Garstka, 1998; Department of Defense, 2005).

Our current ability to collect and distribute vast quantities of data is a great technological achievement. However, by itself this does not fix the fundamental problem of information processing that Clausewitz identified. To use such networked information, warfighters must still be able to integrate the various bits into a unified picture of what is going on around them (Perry, Crisp, McKneely, & Wallace, 2000). Ultimately, a successful network-centric system is one that has not only the hardware to access to vast quantities of information but also the interface to present that information to its operator in such a way that it can be readily used (Miller & Shattuck, 2006).

Information Management in Tactical Aircraft

The importance of such cognitive human factors to the design of modern weapon systems is particularly evident in the development of aircraft that are popularly described as "fifth-generation fighters." One of the defining characteristics of fifth-generation fighters is information *integration and fusion* (Houston, 2004; Lockheed Martin Aeronautics Company, 2006; Wosje, 2007). Essentially, the avionics suites of such aircraft are designed to automatically combine data from separate sources, correlate that data where possible, and present the results in a way that is easy for the pilot to understand. There are two important points to this statement. First, the emphasis here is not simply on increasing the volume of information that the aircraft can access but also on improving the way in which that information is presented to the pilot. Second, modern fighters are in part actually *defined* by their cognitive human factors characteristics. In other words, the next generation of fighters is designed to defeat threats specifically through superior human factors. By comparison, "modern fighters" of the late 1950s were designed to defeat the threats of that era through superior speed and altitude capabilities (Thomason, 2008). Consequently, the 1950s' fighters were defined by engine and aerodynamic improvements that enabled supersonic flight. In effect, cockpit design has become the modern equivalent of "coke-bottle"-shaped fuselages and afterburners. Do human factors engineers have the "Right Stuff" to meet the challenges of this newfound importance?

The specific challenge that human factors engineers now face is to ensure that new cockpit designs will truly provide aviators with a generational leap in information management ability before those designs go into full production. No one has ever strived to build a mediocre cockpit, but program managers must allocate limited development resources across the numerous subsystems that make up the aircraft. Those subsystems that are essential to how the aircraft is intended to perform naturally receive more programmatic attention and funding than subsystems that are seen as secondary to the aircraft's mission capability. When speed was the defining feature of fighters, engineers focused on achieving ever greater supersonic speeds and devoted less effort into cockpit design. They developed analytic and test techniques that allowed them to iteratively correct and improve aerodynamic designs before any actual airplanes were built. This emphasis on aerodynamics enabled the Douglas F4D, Vought F8U, and McDonnell F4H to all set speed records during their test programs (Thomason, 2008). However, it also left the F4D with a radar scope that was obscured by the control stick and led to cockpit visibility limitations in the F8U and F4H (Naval Air Systems Command, 1969). With cockpit design now identified as a defining feature of modern fighters, human factors engineers are no longer charged with providing cockpits that are merely usable. Instead, they must design cockpits that are themselves central to the aircraft's mission capability.

The cockpit of a modern tactical aircraft is fundamentally the interface of a network-centric system. As such, the design and production of modern cockpits should conform to basic guidelines for user-centered design (Perry et al., 2000). As Stanney (Chapter 14 of this volume) outlines, this process begins with a thorough analysis of the tasks that users will be asked to perform and of the skill sets that the user population is likely to have. This information is used to produce conceptual and prototype designs of the interface. Test users are then brought in to test the prototype system's performance. The objective of these assessments is to gauge how well the interface supports the users' information management demands.

METRICS OF INFORMATION MANAGEMENT

One of the biggest challenges to measuring how well cockpits support the pilots' information needs is to select operational measures of information management that are both sufficiently inclusive and reliable to support engineering decisions. There are two broad categories of measures that are commonly used in modern cockpit assessments.

Measures of Mission Performance

One way to measure whether a cockpit meets the pilot's information management needs is to measure the performance outcomes of simulated missions that are flown by test users. For example, if an aircraft is designed to attack ground vehicles, the cockpit must allow the pilot to search for, target, and attack the vehicles while also maintaining airspeed, altitude, and other basic flight parameters. If test users were unable to use the cockpit interfaces to successfully find targets, or were unable to maintain required flight parameters while searching for targets, this would suggest that the design was not meeting the aviator's information management needs.

The problem with mission performance measures is that there are often many ways to achieve the same performance outcome. For example, in a test mission that is designed to measure whether the cockpit provides the aviators with sufficient threat information, an aviator may avoid getting shot down by a surface-to-air missile by recognizing its existence and actively flying around the missile's engagement envelope. However, the aviator could also fly around the missile's envelope by chance without knowing that the missile was there. By the law of large numbers, the more test scenarios that are flown, the more likely the latter pilot is to enter the missile envelope and get shot down. However, limited testing budgets and schedules preclude running enough trail missions to base design decisions on performance outcomes alone. Engineers must therefore be able to measure those cognitive human factors that lead to the performance outcome.

Cognitive Metrics

Engineers commonly assess the cognitive load a device places on the users in terms of the situation awareness (SA) provided by the device and the cognitive workload that the user experiences while using the device. SA is a very broad term that refers to the extent to which one knows all task-relevant information (Endsley, 2000). Essentially, it refers to the completeness of the mental picture that Clausewitz identified as the basis of informed decisions.

In one of the more widely accepted models, Endsley (1995) emphasizes that there are three levels of SA. The first level, perception, entails accessing raw information about the operational environment. The second level, comprehension, involves synthesizing the raw information in order to understand what is presently happening. The third level, projection, involves using the understanding of the current situation to predict how the situation is likely to evolve. Devices that better support the user's information needs should provide the user with a more complete and higher level of SA.

SA is a particularly attractive metric for cockpit design because the term originated with aviators (Watts, 1996, p. 94). Consequently, the term not only encapsulates most of what human factors engineers seek to measure, but the user population instinctively understands its meaning and importance. On the other hand, SA is such a broad and widely used concept that measuring or even defining it in a universally accepted way is difficult.

In contrast, cognitive workload is a much narrower concept that refers to the extent to which tasks absorb a person's available mental resources (Sammer, 2006). As such, this metric draws on the extensive resource allocation literature within cognitive psychology. While under high cognitive loading, the user is less able to cope with additional tasks and may even shed part of the current task load in an attempt to preserve performance on a particular task. This limits mission performance in two important ways. Most obviously, if the aviator is forced to shed a task that is critical to overall mission performance, mission performance will be compromised. More subtly, in dynamic environments, the maintenance of SA itself can be thought of as a necessary task. In an analysis of 376 general aviation mishaps in which loss of SA was deemed a causal factor, Jones and Endsley (1996) found in 22 percent of the cases that high workload levels led to the lack of SA. Although it is important to recognize the workload and SA are independent constructs, designs that impose high workloads on the user are likely to reduce overall SA (Wickens, 2001, 2002). Thus, the design that allows users to perform a given set of tasks with the least workload should be the one that better supports their overall information management needs.

METHODS OF ASSESSMENT

Subjective Methods

The most common way that engineers have measured workload and SA is via subjective questionnaires (Charlton, 2002). After using a mock-up or prototype of a new device to perform mission representative tasks, test users answer questions about how task saturated or informed they felt. Questionnaires such as the Bedford Workload Scale, NASA Task Load Index (NASA TLX), and Situation Awareness Rating Technique (SART) have been validated against user performance and experimental manipulations of workload (Gawron, 2000). Moreover, because they have been standardized and used in many different domains, measurements obtained with these questionnaires have an apparent degree of cross-design comparability. Logistically, questionnaires are relatively inexpensive and easy to administer. They do not necessarily require modification to the prototype or mock-up. For cockpit evaluation, simple questionnaires such as the Bedford Scale can be included in the test pilot's knee board cards, permitting human factors data to be collected between events during a test flight. More involved questionnaires can be administered during debrief sessions.

Although their cost and simplicity are real advantages, subjective questionnaires have a number of features that limit their ability to assess SA and workload. First, answers to questionnaires are necessarily retrospective. The quality of the data therefore depends on how well the test users remember what happened in the test session. Human memory being fallible, the more time that elapses between an event and when the test user is asked about the event, the more likely it is that his or her memory for the event will be faulty (Ward, 2001). This problem can be partially mitigated by administering questionnaires more frequently during a testing session. However, if the task does not naturally contain break periods during which the questionnaire can be administered, this may not be possible.

The problems with relying on memory exacerbate a more fundamental limitation of subjective questionnaires. They are subjective. One obvious problem that this entails is that the resulting data are vulnerable to the test user's mood and biases. In aviation, test users (i.e., test aviators) pride themselves on their emotional stability and integrity (Wolf, 1979). Also, they have a heavy incentive to provide accurate data because their own lives and those of their colleagues depend on the quality of the product that they are testing. However, for multibillion dollar government acquisition contracts, even the perception that design decisions were based on biased data can prove costly. Thus, subjective ratings would seem a rather weak basis on which to build an essential component of a modern weapon system.

More importantly, even with a completely unbiased test user, subjective questionnaires are not able to fully assess workload and SA. Rather than measuring how task saturated or well-informed the user is, questionnaires measure how task saturated or informed the user feels. This is particularly problematic for measuring SA because as one pilot that the author has worked with observed, "You don't know that you don't have SA until you get some." That is, for users to rate their SA as low, they have to have enough knowledge of the situation (i.e., SA) to understand that their mental picture of what is going on is incomplete.

Objective Measures

Human factors researchers have developed some techniques to address the limitations that are inherent in subjective questionnaires. In particular, researchers have used various probe techniques to measure both workload and SA with more temporal precision and objectivity (Gawron, 2000). Because workload refers to the extent to which a task absorbs the user's cognitive resources, engineers can theoretically measure the workload that is required to perform a given task by measuring how well a user is able to simultaneously perform an additional probe task. As the user's cognitive resources are absorbed by the primary task, he or she will have fewer resources available to perform the secondary probe task. Consequently, his or her performance on the secondary task will tend to decline (Kahneman & Treisman, 1984). A probe task can be one that the user would likely also have to simultaneously do in the real world. For example, engineers might measure the workload required to use the navigation system by measuring changes in the precision with which the pilot flies the plane while entering waypoint data. Alternatively, the probe task could be an arbitrary and artificial task, such as a cursor tracking task. Although an artificial probe task decreases the face validity of the assessment, it enhances the comparability of the results. For example, if workload is measured in terms of the precision with which a pilot maintains an assigned heading and altitude, then that workload measurement is implicitly dependent on the stability of the airplane. The same task performed in an airplane with different control characteristics would yield a different estimate of the workload required to perform the task. Because an arbitrary task can be introduced into different cockpits more or less equally, it is less vulnerable to this limitation.

The equivalent of the probe technique for measuring SA is the Situation Awareness Global Assessment Technique (SAGAT; Endsley, 1990). With the

SAGAT, users perform mission representative tasks in a simulator. At unpredictable intervals, the simulation is stopped, critical displays are blanked, and the users are asked specific questions about the current situation. For example, pilots might be asked what their current altitude and airspeed are.

Though these techniques yield objective data, they have limitations of their own. First, they are often difficult to implement in a naturalistic way. Obviously, one cannot pause a real airplane in mid-flight and blank out its displays, so the SAGAT is limited to use in laboratory simulators. Likewise, by definition, artificial probes require the user to do something that he or she would not typically be doing during a real mission. Even naturalistic probes may not be truly naturalistic. For example, pilots are famously indoctrinated to "aviate, navigate, and communicate," in that order. By using aircraft control precision as the probe task, engineers are effectively counting on the test pilot to invert that order.

More importantly, probe techniques may themselves impact workload and SA. As Clausewitz noted, information flow in the real world is dynamic and the challenge is to stay abreast of the situation as it changes. Halting a scenario to ask questions disrupts the natural flow of information. It may give the test user a moment to compose his or her thoughts and thereby yield an artificially high estimate of SA. Alternatively, it could disrupt the user's train of thought and yield an artificially low estimate of SA.

For estimates of workload, the probe technique assumes that there is no interaction between the baseline amount of workload that is required to do the task of interest and the workload that is required to perform the probe task. If the goal is to measure the relative amounts of workload that are imposed by different designs and the same probe task is used in all assessments, then the effects of this should be negligible. However, if the purpose is to determine the extent to which a single design imposes workload on the user, then interaction effects become significant.

Thus, the tools in our current repertoire of workload and SA assessment techniques either yield subjective measures or measures that are contaminated by the assessment techniques themselves. To date, these limitations have been acceptable because cockpit design has been seen as secondary to the overall success of the aircraft design. Combinations of these measurements, on top of more general comments by expert test users, have allowed engineers to sort bad designs from those that are acceptable. What they have not been able to do is objectively tell which acceptable designs are better and by how much.

Psychophysiological Measures

Theoretically, psychophysiological measurements could provide a way to objectively assess workload and SA without interfering with how the user performs the task (Kramer & Parasuraman, 2007). Fundamentally, workload and SA are cognitive states of the user. Historically, there have been a number of philosophical paradigms for explaining such psychological phenomena (Churchland, 1996), but by far the most dominant and successful paradigm within the scientific community posits that psychological phenomena are the products of physical processes in the nervous system (Churchland & Sejnowski, 1992). In other words, cognitive states are brain states. Since cognitive states are ultimately brain states, and psychophysiological techniques measure brain states, it may be possible to use those psychophysiological techniques to assess workload and SA. If reliable psychophysiological markers for SA and workload can be found and the requisite recordings can be made unobtrusively, it should be possible to reliably tell the difference between an acceptable cockpit design and one that is outstanding.

In research settings, a wide variety of psychophysiological variables have been found to correlate with elements of workload and SA. People tend to experience task saturation as stressful, so it is not surprising that many of the classic psychophysiological indexes of stress have been used to measure workload. Experimental manipulations of cognitive workload have been reported to affect blink rate (Stern, Walrath, & Goldstein, 1984), pupil diameter (Van Orden, Limbert, Makeig, & Jung, 2001), visual scan pattern (Ephrath, Tole, Stephens, & Young, 1980), heart rate variability (HRV; Nickel & Nachreiner, 2003), galvanic skin response (GSR; Lindholm & Cheatham, 1983), spectral power of the electroencephalogram (EEG; Wilson & Russell, 2003), amplitude of certain event-related brain potentials (ERPs; Prinzel, Freeman, Scerbo, Mikulka, & Pope, 2003), and regional cerebral hemodynamic response (Jansma, Ramsey, Coppola, & Kahn, 2000).

Although many psychophysiological techniques appear to be sensitive to workload, actually using the techniques to assess cockpit and other device designs is not straightforward. For example, the most precise technique for measuring regional cerebral activity, functional magnetic resonance imaging (fMRI), requires the participant to lie motionless in a large scanner that generates extremely strong magnetic fields. These constraints preclude fMRI from being used in naturalistic human factors assessments. Like fMRI, functional near-infrared spectroscopy (fNIRS) can infer regional brain activity from changes in cerebral blood flow (Toronov, Zhang, & Webb, 2007). However, it does so with much less spatial specificity than fMRI and is unable to assess activity of brain structures that are more than a few millimeters from the scalp. Consequently, human factors engineers may not be able to take advantage of many of the correlations that laboratory neuroscientists report between regional brain activity and workload or SA.

Other techniques may be logistically feasible, but susceptible to recording artifacts that would be commonly generated in the environments in which engineers would want to perform assessments. EEG is sensitive to ambient electromagnetic fields, vibration, and muscle activity. Cockpits are often characterized by vibration and strong electromagnetic fields, and the normal movements that pilots make would generate significant muscle artifacts. These factors do not rule out the use of EEG for human factors assessments. Several groups of researchers have successfully collected EEG-based measurements of pilot workload in real aircraft (e.g., Wilson & Russell, 2003; Schnell, Keller, & Macuda, 2008). Thus, with proper filtering and artifact correction techniques, it is possible to obtain good EEG recordings in naturalistic test environments. However, engineers must be mindful of the impact that artifacts and artifact correction techniques have on recordings. For example, to combat electromagnetic noise that is generated by the AC power grid in North America, researchers there commonly use 60-Hz notch filters when recording EEG (Davidson, Jackson, & Larson, 2000). Unfortunately, this also eliminates EEG components in the 60-Hz range and thus could affect measurements dependent on spectral power in the Gamma band of the EEG.

Finally, many of the psychophysiological measures that have been found to be sensitive to workload and SA are not specific to these metrics. For example, a number of researchers have reported that changes in pupil diameter can be used as an index of cognitive workload (Lindholm & Cheatham, 1983; Van Orden et al., 2001). However, similar pupil changes have been reported in response to a variety of emotionally arousing stimuli (Bradley, Miccoli, Escrig, & Lang, 2008). Likewise, in addition to psychological factors, pupil diameter is better known to change with changes in the amount of ambient light. Thus, change in pupil diameter alone does not necessarily indicate a change in cognitive workload. One way that engineers can mitigate this lack of specificity is through the simultaneous use of multiple physiological measures. Indeed, most recent attempts to classify user's cognitive state via psychophysiological recordings have involved the simultaneous use of multiple recording techniques (Schnell et al., 2008; Van Orden et al., 2001; Wilson & Russell, 2003). If separate techniques each yield indications of high workload, it is more likely that the user is truly experiencing high workload as opposed to merely a change in ambient lighting conditions. Thus, the lack of specificity that psychophysiological measures have to workload or SA is not an insurmountable problem, but human factors engineers must simply take care in designing assessments and interpreting the results.

To summarize, there are many obstacles to using psychophysiological techniques for cockpit assessment. However, in most cases there are also ways to mitigate these obstacles. Given the length of time that many of these techniques have been in use in laboratory settings, it naturally raises the question of why psychophysiological measures are not more widely used in human factors assessments.

PSYCHOPHYSIOLOGY IN THE REAL WORLD

Costs versus Benefits

The vast majority of engineering decisions involve cost-benefit trade-offs. For program managers to endorse the use of psychophysiological techniques, the additional benefits of using those techniques would need to clearly outweigh any additional costs that the techniques entail. From a program manager's perspective, the cost of performing typical subjective assessments is extraordinarily low. The vast majority of current human factors engineers have some familiarity with questionnaires, so it is not difficult to find personnel to staff assessments and analyze the resulting data. The necessary equipment for subjective assessments essentially consists of a pencil and photocopies of questionnaires. The expert users' time and dedicated time in mock-ups, simulators, or test aircraft can be expensive, but because the users can answer questionnaires between events or in debrief sessions, it is often possible to piggyback subjective human factors assessments on simulation and flight test events that are primarily geared toward other purposes. In contrast, psychophysiological techniques require special equipment that is often quite expensive. The engineers who operate that equipment and analyze the resulting data need specialized training that is not common in human factors degree programs. Lastly, the additional preparation time, recording constraints, and other factors make it difficult to piggyback psychophysiological assessments on other events. Thus, psychophysiological techniques are much more costly to use than traditional techniques.

Unfortunately, current psychophysiological techniques do not provide sufficient engineering benefits to justify these increased costs. When researchers report that a psychophysiological technique is sensitive to manipulations of workload, what they typically mean is that they observe different patterns of psychophysiological data during different portions of a task that imposes different levels of workload on the participant. For example, Nickel and Nachreiner (2003) examined the sensitivity of HRV to different levels of workload on a variety of tasks. Confirming previous findings, these researchers were able to discriminate between periods of rest and work based on decreases in the 0.1-Hz component of the HRV. Likewise, Wilson and Russell (2003) collected EEG, oculomotor, heart, and respiration data from participants who performed a standardized cognitive workload task at two levels of difficulty. For each participant, recordings made at each difficulty level were submitted to a neural network analysis to identify which psychophysiological variables best discriminated between the two levels of workload. The results of these analyses were used to create participant-specific calibration files, which were then used to classify whether subsequent recordings from the participants were made under low, medium, or high workload conditions. Wilson and Russell (2003) report that such subsequent classifications were 85 percent accurate on average.

In both of these examples, the researchers were able to discriminate between discrete task phases that required different levels of mental effort, so they can arguably claim that their techniques index workload. However, this level of workload analysis is of limited use in an engineering context. Program managers care about workload only in so far as it reduces the user's ability to perform necessary tasks. Although the physiological techniques could be used to determine whether a task imposed a cognitive load on the user, they do not speak to what impact that load would have on the user's performance. To be truly useful, the physiological techniques would either need to measure how close a user's workload level was to a hypothetical maximum or need to measure the user's spare cognitive capacity.

By comparison, many existing subjective and objective techniques are constructed to deliver measures of workload in exactly these terms. With workload questionnaires such as the Bedford Workload Scale, test users generate workload ratings by answering a series of questions about how well they were able to do the task (Gawron, 2000). In assessments using probe techniques, the users' workload levels are explicitly measured in terms of their ability to process extra information. Despite their limitations, these techniques at least measure workload in terms of the impact on the user's ability to perform a task. In contrast, most current psychophysiological techniques effectively measure workload in terms of how "stressed" the user appears and then would require the engineer to infer what this stress level would mean for information processing.

Building a Better Measure

To make psychophysiological techniques more useful for human factors assessments, researchers essentially need to better link their workload measurements to actual information processing. If psychophysiologists could show that the information processing necessary to perform a given task was impossible when users displayed a certain pattern of psychophysiology data, program managers would be much more interested in psychophysiological techniques. Such techniques would be truly useful if psychophysiologists could tell how close to that hypothetical cognitive red line any given pattern of data indicated that the user was. However, to achieve such capabilities, psychophysiologists must first be able to reliably map patterns of psychophysiological data onto reliable and relatively fine-grained measures of user information processing. Since part of the motivation to develop psychophysiological measures of workload is that the alternative methods of measuring workload are not sufficiently reliable or fine-grained in the first place. Thus, validating psychophysiological measures is a nontrivial problem.

In part, previous researchers have begun to solve this problem by attempting to correlate psychophysiological measurements of workload with corresponding subjective data (e.g., Van Orden et al., 2001; Wilson & Russell 2003). The success of many of these efforts indicates that the development of psychophysiology-based objective measures of workload is at least plausible. However, such attempts at validation are not wholly satisfying because the result is an "objective" workload measure that is built to match subjective ratings. Since subjective assessment techniques are cheaper, it is difficult to justify the additional expense and logistical difficulties that psychophysiological techniques entail.

Another way that psychophysiological researchers have approached the circular reference problem is by comparing physiological estimates of workload to predicted workload levels that have been generated by computational workload models. For example, Tremoulet and colleagues (2006) measured the EEG of sailors who performed a cruise missile strike exercise in a ship combat information center simulator. The EEG recordings were classified as indicating high or low workload based on an algorithm that had previously been validated against performance on simple cognitive tasks and subjective workload ratings. These EEG-derived workload estimates were then compared to workload estimates that were generated by the Multimodal Interface Design Support (MIDS). MIDS is a computational model that predicts when during an extended task that a user will experience excessively high workload. Tremoulet and colleagues reported high correlations between the EEG-derived estimates of workload and those predicted by MIDS. This is a significant improvement over correlations with subjective workload data because the MIDS workload estimates were generated based on the number and kind of cognitive tasks that the sailors would have to do at any moment to successfully complete the strike.

Given that the sailors were able to successfully complete the task, it is likely that the EEG-derived workload estimate indexed actual task-related information processing. However, we cannot know this for certain. For example, the EEG-derived measure could actually be indexing anxiety or stress that is related to information overload. If so, future EEG-based workload estimates could be vulnerable to stress or anxiety that is not related to workload. Alternatively, if operators habituate to the stress of a given workload, such a measure would indicate decreasing workload despite the user still being required to process the same amount of information in the same amount of time. Also, if the EEG indicated low workload levels, it could mean that the necessary subtasks did not impose a substantial load on the user or it could mean that the user did not do all of the subtasks. If the task can at least sometimes be successfully completed without accomplishing all of the subtasks, we cannot be sure which of these possibilities the EEG-derived estimate indicates.

What psychophysiologists need is a direct link between objective measures of information processing and candidate measures of workload. One such link may be provided by video eye tracking. As the name implies, eye trackers monitor eye and head movements to determine where a person is looking. Because vision is the primary sense by which people explore their environment (Previc, 2004), monitoring where they have looked gives some indication of what information they can know. If a user has not looked at a display since the display was last updated, the user is unlikely to know the new information that is presented on that display. Visual scan pattern may also provide insights into what kind of additional information the user thinks is important given the current situation. For example, fighter pilots who were preparing for beyond-visual-range engagements would likely spend more time looking at their air-to-air radar displays than they would at other times. Pilots in such a scenario who did not look at the radar could alternatively already have acquired all of the necessary information from another source or may have insufficient SA to know that they should be looking at the radar. In either case, knowing when (or whether) a pilot looks at the radar display provides insight into his or her SA.

In addition to measures of SA, eye tracking can also provide measures of workload. Changes in pupil diameter and the randomness of a person's scan pattern (Di Nocera, Camilli, & Terenzi, 2007; Ephrath et al., 1980; Hilburn, Jorna, Byrne, & Parasuraman, 1997) have both already been reported to be sensitive to workload. Thus, eye tracking provides the potential to simultaneously assess both the user's level of workload and the potential consequences of that workload on information gathering. Hypothetically, one could use such a double measure to say not only that performing a specific cockpit function increased the pilot's workload but that it slowed his or her instrument scan by X percent and decreased its spatial extent by Y percent. Such combined data would be much more compelling than saying only that performing the function increased pilot workload.

Outlook for Physiological Measures

The factors that have led to this new emphasis on cognitive human factors in tactical aircraft are not specific to fighter cockpits. Most obviously, under network-centric warfare, all units of a force, regardless of type, are to be connected by robust data links so that they can share information and more readily operate in concert (Cebrowski & Garstka, 1998). The same need for information integration and fusion that drives the design of tactical cockpits will therefore also drive the design of interfaces of ships and ground vehicles. Likewise, civilian jobs are increasingly characterized by information synthesis and management. The interfaces that a civilian employee uses to perform those jobs must therefore support his or her information management needs in the same way that tactical cockpits must support the needs of the aviator. Consequently, the benefits of developing robust physiological methods for assessing workload and SA would extend far beyond tactical aviation.

As outlined above, some recent research efforts have made progress toward the development of such methods. Recent advances in sensor technology and recording techniques have made it possible to measure a wide variety of psychophysiological variables under operational conditions. To take advantage of this opportunity, psychophysiologists need to better tailor their research to the logistical and programmatic needs of human factors engineers. In particular, future research in this area should focus more on linking physiological data to objective measures of information processing than on merely correlating physiological data with subjective workload reports. Without this, psychophysiologists may be left out of the cognitive human factors revolution.

REFERENCES

Bradley, M. M., Miccoli, L., Escrig, M. A., & Lang, P. J. (2008). The pupil as a measure of emotional arousal and autonomic activation. *Psychophysiology*, 45 (5), 602–607.

Cebrowski, A. K., & Garstka, J. J. (1998). Network-centric warfare: Its origin and future. *United States Naval Institute Proceedings*, 124 (1), 28–36.

Charlton, S. G. (2002). Measurements of cognitive state in test and evaluation. In S. G. Charlton & T. G. O'Brien (Eds.), *Handbook of human factors testing and evaluation* (pp. 97–126). Mahwah, NJ: Erlbaum.

Churchland, P. M. (1996). *Matter and consciousness* (7th ed.). Cambridge, MA: MIT Press.

Churchland, P. S., & Sejnowski, T. J. (1992). *The computational brain*. Cambridge, MA: MIT Press.

Clausewitz, C. (2008). *On war*, trans. J. J. Graham. Radford, VA: Wilder. (Orig. pub. 1832.)

Davidson, R. J., Jackson, D. C., & Larson, C. L. (2000). Human electroencephalography. In J. T. Cacioppo, L. G. Tassinary, & G. G. Berntson (Eds.), *Handbook of psychophysiology* (pp. 27–52). New York: Cambridge.

Department of Defense. (2005). *The implementation of network-centric warfare*. Washington, D.C.: Department of Defense.

Di Nocera, F., Camilli, M., & Terenzi, M. (2007). A random glance at the flight deck: Pilot's scanning strategies and the real-time assessment of mental workload. *Journal of Cognitive Engineering and Decision Making*, 1, 271–285.

Endsley, M. R. (1990). A method for the objective assessment of situational awareness. In *Situational awareness in aerospace operations (AGARD-CP-478)* (pp. 1/1–1/9). Neiully Sur Seine, France: NATO-AGARD.

———. (1995). Toward a theory of situation awareness in dynamic systems. *Human Factors*, 37 (1), 32–64.

———. (2000). Theoretical underpinnings of situation awareness: A critical review. In M. R. Endsley & D. J. Garland (Eds.), *Situation awareness analysis and measurement* (pp. 4–32). Mahwah, NJ: LEA.

Ephrath, A. R., Tole, J. R., Stephens, A. T., & Young, L. R. (1980). Instrument scan—Is it an indicator of the pilot's workload? *Proceedings of the Human Factors Society 24th Annual Meeting* (pp. 257–258). Santa Monica, CA: Human Factors and Ergonomics Society.

Gawron, V. J. (2000). *Human performance measures handbook*. Mahwah, NJ: LEA.

Hilburn, B., Jorna, P. G., Byrne, E. A., & Parasuraman, R. (1997). The effect of adaptive air traffic control (ATC) decision aiding on controller mental workload. In M. Mouloua & J. Koonce (Eds.), *Human–automation interaction: Research and practice* (pp. 84–91). Mahwah, NJ: Erlbaum.

Houston, M. S. (2004). *Is the JSF good enough? Can Australia's air defense requirements be met by the F-35, or do we need the F/A-22 (Strategic Insight Paper 9)?* Barton, ACT: Australian Strategic Policy Institute.

Jansma, J. M., Ramsey, N. F., Coppola, R., & Kahn, R. S. (2000). Specific versus nonspecific brain activity in a parametric N-back task. *Neuroimage*, 12 (6), 688–697.

Jones, D. G., & Endsley, M. R. (1996). Sources of situation awareness errors in aviation. *Aviation, Space, and Environmental Medicine*, 67 (6), 507–512.

Kahneman, D., & Treisman, A. (1984). Changing views of attention and automaticity. In R. Parasuraman & D. R. Davies (Eds.), *Varieties of attention* (pp. 29–61). New York: Academic Press.

Kramer, A. F., & Parasuraman, R. (2007). Neuroergonomics: Application of neuroscience to human factors. In J. T. Cacioppo, L. G. Tasinary, & G. G. Berntson (Eds.), *The Handbook of psychophysiology* (pp. 704–722). New York, NY: Cambridge.

Lindholm, E., & Cheatham, C. M. (1983). Autonomic activity and workload during learning of a simulated aircraft carrier landing task. *Aviation, Space, & Environmental Medicine*, 54 (5), 435–439.

Lockheed Martin Aeronautics Company. (2006). *5th generation fighters: The future has clearly arrived* [Brochure]. Fort Worth, TX: Lockheed Martin Aeronautics Company.

Miller, N. L., & Shattuck, L. G. (June 2006). A dynamic process model for the design and assessment of network centric systems. Paper presented at the 2006 Command and Control Research and Technology Symposium, San Diego, CA.

Naval Air Systems Command. (1969). Report of the air-to-air missile system capability review (U). NAVAIR Publication No. A241559. Washington, D.C.: Naval Air Systems Command.

Nickel, P., & Nachreiner, F. (2003). Sensitivity and diagnosticity of the 0.1-Hz component of heart rate variability as an indicator of mental workload. *Human Factors*, 45 (4), 575–590.

Perry, A. A., Crisp, H. E., McKneely, J. A., & Wallace, D. F. (2000). The solution for future command and control: Human-centered design. In P. Hamburger (Ed.) *Proceedings of the Society of Photo-Optical Instrumentation Engineers: Vol. 4126. Integrated Command Environments* (pp. 42–53). Bellingham, WA: SPIE.

Previc, F. H. (2004). Visual illusions in flight. In F. H. Previc & W. R. Ercoline (Eds.), *Spatial disorientation in aviation* (pp. 283–317). Reston, VA: AIAA.

Prinzel, L. J., III, Freeman, F. G., Scerbo, M. W., Mikulka, P. J., & Pope, A. T. (2003). Effects of a psychophysiological system for adaptive automation on performance, workload, and the event-related potential P300 component. *Human Factors*, 45 (4), 601–613.

Sammer, G. (2006). Workload and electro-encephalography dynamics. In W. Karwowski (Ed.), *International encyclopedia of ergonomics and human factors* (pp. 561–567). Boca Raton, FL: Taylor & Francis.

Schnell, T., Keller, B. M., & Macuda, T. J. (2008). Sensor integration to characterize operator state. In. D. D. Schmorrow & K. M. Stanney (Eds.), *Augmented cognition: A practitioner's guide* (pp. 41–74). Santa Monica, CA: Human Factors and Ergonomics Society.

Stern, J. A., Walrath, L. C., & Goldstein, R. (1984). The indigenous eyeblink. *Psychophysiology*, 21 (1), 22–23.

Thomason, T. H. (2008). *U.S. Naval air superiority: Development of shipborne jet fighters 1943–1962*. North Branch, MN: Specialty.

Toronov, V. Y., Zhang, X., & Webb, A. G. (2007). A spatial and temporal comparison of hemodynamic signals measured using optical and functional magnetic resonance imaging during activation in the human primary visual cortex. *Neuroimage*, 34 (3), 1136–1148.

Tremoulet, P., Craven, P., Poythress, M., Russell, C., Siegel, S., Berka, C., et al. (October 2006). Correlation between expected workload and EEG indices of cognitive workload and task engagement. Paper presented at the 50th Annual Meeting of the Human Factors and Ergonomics Society (HFES 2006), San Francisco, CA.

Van Orden, K. F., Limbert, W., Makeig, S., & Jung, T. P. (2001). Eye activity correlates of workload during a visuospatial memory task. *Human Factors*, 43 (1), 111–121.

Ward, G. (2001). A critique of the working memory model. In J. Andrade (Ed.), *Working memory in perspective* (pp. 219–239). New York: Taylor & Francis.

Watts, B. D. (1996). *Clausewitzian friction and future war (McNair Paper 52)*. Washington, D.C.: Institute for National and Strategic Studies, National Defense University.

Wickens, C. D. (2001). Workload and situation awareness. In P. A. Hancock & P. A. Desmond (Eds.), *Stress, workload, and fatigue* (pp. 443–455). Mahwah, NJ: Erlbaum.

———. (2002). Situation awareness and workload in aviation. *Current Directions in Psychological Science*, 11 (4), 128–133.

Wilson, G. F., & Russell, C. A. (2003). Real-time assessment of mental workload using psychophysiological measures and artificial neural networks. *Human Factors*, 45, 635–644.

Wolf, T. (1979). *The right stuff*. New York, Bantam.

Wosje, M. (September 2007). Fifth generation fighters. Presentation at the 51st Annual Meeting of the Tailhook Association, Reno, NV.

Part VI: Future Directions in Enhancing Human Performance

Chapter 16

HUMAN PERFORMANCE ENHANCEMENT: USE-INSPIRED SCIENCE AND THE PROMISE OF HUMAN–TECHNOLOGY INTERACTION AND INTEGRATION

Stephen M. Fiore, Eduardo Salas, and Davin Pavlas

Research blending basic and applied approaches has been productive in providing enhancements to human performance, largely because of its interdisciplinary nature and willingness to examine the human, system, and task in context. Future advances in the science will need to continue this inclusive approach when investigating and developing new technologies and strategies for improving human performance. But we submit that they will also need to be more strategic in their integration of such approaches. Taking a strategic approach to research requires an explicit articulation of how to develop, at a policy level, a portfolio of research projects with each targeting particular needs and gaps. Questions appropriate for a program on human performance must focus on developing a better understanding of how it is that technology can support an operator when humans and systems interact in modern systems—not hinder and not replace him or her.

From a programmatic standpoint, engaging in such a human-centered effort requires research that is firmly grounded epistemologically *and* ecologically. Only then can we develop the foundational understanding of the underlying learning and performance processes that are involved in hybrid tasks. In the next section, so as to guide researchers in applying the lessons of the past to the problems of the future, some promising avenues for human performance research are provided. We describe a set of interrelated areas of research that are changing our conceptions of human performance in complex environments: (1) unmanned systems such as unmanned ground and aerial vehicles, (2) intelligent agent technology, and (3) augmented cognition. We conclude with a brief discussion on how to think strategically about these developing areas so that the field can explicitly and systematically pursue a more programmatic use-inspired basic science in human performance research.

UNMANNED SYSTEMS

Here we consider training and performance issues surrounding the operation of unmanned systems as an example of how a use-inspired approach can be implemented. Key objectives for a programmatic scientific effort studying human performance in unmanned systems must include (1) issues of transfer across environments, (2) the degree to which Unmanned Aerial Vehicles (UAVs) and Unmanned Ground Vehicles (UGVs) differentially require human intervention, and (3) at which times and which contexts intervention is critical. From this we see that research must address multilevel interaction factors involving training for individuals and teams and, increasingly, in working with other services as well as coalition partners. Addressing this effectively is challenging from both the technology and the human standpoint. For example, issues of human performance are complicated by the fact that unmanned systems are not completely autonomous and act both as a "teammate" (cf. Hoeft, Kochan, & Jentsch, 2005) and as a system requiring supervision. This leads to a need to understand how to balance their use with a more sophisticated understanding of how human-agent teams can work together. Further, simultaneously studying similarities and differences across varieties of hybrid systems (e.g., UAVs and UGVs), while considering the range of issues associated with training, selection, and safety, and across the multilevel factors described previously, would benefit from a strategic integration.

INTELLIGENT AGENTS

The intersection of computer science, simulation, and psychology has produced an interesting tool in the quest for improving human performance: the intelligent agent. Intelligent agents are automated, socially able artificial intelligence programs that, depending on their purpose, may reflect aspects of human cognition (e.g., Wooldridge & Jennings, 1995). Their potential for use is broad, as they can be useful in applications ranging from simulation (Harbers, Bosch, & Meyer, 2008; Stacy, Freeman, Lackey, & Merket, 2004; Tambe et al., 1995) to on-time decision support (Bul & Lee, 1999; Taylor, Stensrud, Eitelman, Dunham, & Harger, 2007). The former application is particularly meaningful for training, while the latter has obvious implications for the ability of technology to support humans in high-stress environments (Petrox & Stoyen, 2000). While agents are a very promising avenue for enhancing human performance, much remains to be understood about how to design and employ such systems. For a strategic research agenda, an interdisciplinary approach must work toward an understanding of the following. First, the utility of intelligent agents mirroring or emulating human cognition or emotion is a subject of great debate (Wooldridge & Jennings, 1995), and the costs and benefits of including more and more human elements to agents must be better understood. For example, the issue of how to present agents and how interactions with them should take place is largely driven by the context in which they are to appear. Thus, research crossing modalities with interaction contexts is a necessary precursor to the effective use of agents to enhance performance. But the field does not need to wait for full emulation. Through the use of "man behind the curtain" studies, where confederates play the role of agents, we can gain important insights into human behavior when agent intelligence and emotion are implemented. In this way, research on intelligent agents can be conducted with the future in mind—once agents are sophisticated enough to enhance human performance, the scientific base should already contain useful practices for integrating them with task performers.

AUGMENTED COGNITION

While intelligent agents are a form of instantiated cognition, augmented cognition takes a different approach to enhancing human performance. Instead of providing an individual with an automated assistant, augmented cognition works to amplify the advantages, and ameliorate the drawbacks, of human cognition. Much is known about cognitive biases, memory capacities, and other cognitive limitations of humans (Baddeley, 1986; Kleinmutz, 1985). Similarly, the capabilities of computer systems grow day by day. The confluence of these developments represents a tremendous opportunity for enhancing human performance. For example, the allocation of attention is particularly difficult for humans to manage properly and a visual search task can be aided by an automated system tagging potential matches and allowing the user to decide which presented stimuli are relevant (Pavel, Wang, & Li, 2003). While computer image recognition is still relatively nascent, it can be used to reduce the cognitive burden on individuals. In this way, computerized systems can be used as cognitive prostheses, performing work that an individual is less able (or less apt) to attend to. Merging the science of cognition with applied technologies has numerous potential applications, from assisting decision making in a war zone (Muth, Kruse, Hoover, & Schmorrow, 2005) to providing contextually based memory aids for the elderly (Adams & Gill, 2007). The role science must take in applying augmented cognition is to take the known shortcomings of the human and find ways to remove their impact on high-risk situations while simultaneously enhancing and harnessing those skills at which humans excel.

DEVELOPING A USE-INSPIRED AND MULTIDISCIPLINARY HUMAN-CENTERED FRAMEWORK

Conceptually, what we can see from these somewhat disparate fields are important developments in human performance that would greatly benefit from a tighter integration of theory and method. In particular, if we reflect upon these we can see the human connecting with the physical world, the human connecting with the networked world, and the human enhanced through, and with, the physical and networked world. But it is not enough to see this conceptual linkage. Perhaps nowhere is the need for melding ecological relevance and epistemological validity more apparent than within, and across, these domains. From this standpoint, what is required is a grounded set of theories capable of integrating each of these in such a way that design, training, and selection can proceed more systematically. Further, from a policy standpoint, the field and the funders must work more closely so as to strategically plan for research portfolios producing a tighter integration and understanding of theory, technology, and context, which can make great strides in improving human performance. In the final section we offer one such approach to illustrate how it is possible to link systems composed of humans and technology.

UNDERSTANDING LINKAGES BETWEEN BRAIN–BODY–ENVIRONMENT

The inherent interdisciplinary nature of human performance research requires an inclusive approach to understanding the brain–body–environment intersection. Traditionally, the human component of a system is examined piecemeal: information processing theory concerns itself with the cognitive actions of an individual, ergonomic science considers physical limitations, tasks are only examined within the context of performance, etc. While such approaches have undoubtedly provided useful advances in how humans are understood, they do little to provide a full view of the nature of performance in high-risk environments. A full understanding of the brain–body–environment linkage requires consideration of both the internal and the external processes exhibited by an individual within the specific context of their task performance. As already discussed, human performance research has benefited from a merging of cognitive and human factors science to produce the knowledge necessary to understand the brain–body–environment in complex, high-risk situations. But, from a theory development standpoint, it has yet to make significant strides in developing a complex theoretical account capable of guiding research and development in human performance. We next describe how this can be accomplished by integrating a more strategic approach to science policy with a richer theoretical grounding of human performance as it unfolds in the real world.

First, from the theoretical standpoint, a promising development coming out of cognitive science in the last decade may provide the necessary theoretical grounding along epistemological and ecological lines. In particular, the interrelated concepts of *embodied*, *enactive*, and *embedded* cognition have arisen as a way to describe cognition emerging and unfolding beyond just the skull and highly situated within particular contexts. Traditional cognitive psychology has focused on cognition as computational rules, treating the mind as an information processing system which acts on and manipulates formal symbols. The computer metaphor and the resulting "information processing" revolution brought the mind back to studies of *cognition* in the face of behaviorism. But, by emphasizing an abstract, algorithmic, and logical characterization of mind, it ignored the role of the body and the body's interaction with the environment in our understanding of cognition (Newell & Simon, 1972). Embodied cognition views cognition as being contained within a greater system—the human body—and has its roots in the philosophy of Merleau-Ponty (1962). To view cognition without considering its purpose and context within the body is to needlessly ignore a key component thereof (e.g., Fiore, Elias, Gallagher, & Jentsch, 2008; Gallagher, 2005; Wilson, 2002). Similarly, enactive cognition examines cognition not only within the context of body and task but also in light of the goals and beliefs of an individual (McGee, 2005). The enactive component emphasizes the more dynamical nature of cognition. It espouses self-organization in real time where the cognitive system reconstitutes itself continually in a form of "mutual system-environment interaction and co-determination, particularly over extended timescales in both the past and future" (Vernon, 2004, p. 1). Such views are being used to argue for a more ecologically based view of artificial intelligence (see Froese & Ziemke, 2009). Finally, such a system is obviously embedded in the environment with which it is coupled. Thus, embedded cognition moves a step further and views cognition within the context of an interaction taking place. Cognition does not occur in a vacuum, but rather within a task or behavior (see also Clark, 2001; Clark & Chalmers, 1998; Hutchins, 1995; Rowlands, 1999). Across these views is an emphasis on the *practice* of cognition "by which internal representations are incomplete contributors in a context-sensitive system rather than fixed determinants of output: and they too focus on the ongoing interactive dance between brain and world" (Sutton, 2006, p. 282). Clark (1997) refers to the collaboration between brain, body, and technology as a *continuous reciprocal causation.* As he later explained:

> Much of what matters about human intelligence is hidden not in the brain, nor in the technology, but in the complex and iterated interactions and collaborations between the two ... The study of these interaction spaces is not easy, and depends both on new multidisciplinary alliances and new forms of modeling and analysis. The pay-off, however, could be spectacular: nothing less than a new kind of cognitive scientific collaboration involving neuroscience, physiology, and social, cultural, and technological studies in about equal measure (Clark, 2001, p. 154).

When adapted to human performance research, these distinctions provide a meaningful taxonomy for classifying the various contexts in which performance is examined. Embodied human performance describes the cognitive and physical manifestations of performance, recognizing that cognition arises not just in the head, but through the body. Enactive performance considers the higher-level purpose and intended implication of behavior, seeing it as an emergent phenomenon between a tightly coupled brain–body–task context. Embedded performance describes this performance beyond the brain–body–task context, recognizing that the human acts and interacts within a social-cultural space that both contributes to and helps shape cognitive processes. We suggest that using these concepts as lenses through which to consider performance in high-risk environments will provide richer epistemological validity, finer granularity, greater ecological relevance, and, last, consistency across research efforts when human performance is to be enhanced by technology and highly situated.

Second, from the policy standpoint, as we have noted, human performance system paradigms exemplify the need to better merge basic and applied research in order to address national goals and increase the practical and theoretical value of such line of research. We have just briefly outlined a theoretical approach to cognition and performance that moves beyond the standard views of information processing. For such an approach to take hold, though, what is required is support from the policy community. Like small pieces of a large puzzle, the complex factors involved in our understanding of human performance need to carefully be integrated and viewed from a variety of angles to allow for a theoretically coherent and practical picture to emerge. In turn, by allowing research to explore different angles of this given research area, we can obtain a comprehensive understanding of interdisciplinary processes. Such collaborative research is key to building consistent strategies that would implement training and design for optimal operational efficiency.

But combining research efforts from a variety of disciplines must allow for researchers and policymakers alike to concur on the ecological and societal importance of such work. This crucial assumption is best suggested by Stokes (1997) who argued that a "system for appraising scientific promise and social value at the project level should enlist the insight of the working scientist into the nature of the social goals on which his or her research bears" (p. 116). A similar argument was brought about by Hoffman and Deffenbacher (1992) who suggested that it is up to the research community to persuade that high epistemological research is also high in ecological consequence. When relating this view to human performance systems, the result is a research agenda that underlines both the scientific and the operational worthiness of related goals and projects. From this, funding would be "allocated among alternative projects through peer review by panels capable of judging scientific promise and the societal benefits from the resulting scientific knowledge" (Stokes, 1997, p. 121).

In short, perhaps there is no better place to catch a glimpse of the potential benefits of closer integration between the basic and applied sciences, and of a more human-centered focus, as the development, testing, and fielding of human performance-based systems. Researchers need to consider how

Table 16.1.   Technology-Centered versus Human-Centered Approaches to Human Performance Research

	Technology-centered approach to human performance research (misguided model)	Human-centered approach to human performance research (appropriate model)
Focus	What can technology do	How can performance of the human be augmented via embodied and enactive-based technologies
Starting point	Power of technology	Personnel and/or system capabilities and limits
Goal	Improve technological capabilities	Improve personnel's capabilities embedded in particular contexts
Theory of hybrid systems	More technology with less humans	Better operational effectiveness by linking embodied, enactive, and embedded views of human performance
Role of technology	Replace operators	Cognition and performance enhancer

Adapted from Mayer (1999).

technological innovation is construed from a scientific standpoint so as to be ever mindful of the problems that can arise when research related to human performance is centered too much on technology. Specifically, it is misguided to only be concerned with what technology can do, without also considering the role of the human in the process. Table 16.1 (adapted from Mayer, 1999) juxtaposes a more technology-centered approach with a more human-centered approach to human performance systems based upon the embodied, enactive, and embedded theoretical approach. This point is underscored by statements made by the Deputy Under Secretary of Defense for S&T. Specifically, when discussing Cognitive Readiness for Transformational Knowledge Systems and the implementation of new technologies, it was noted that the "human is the prime resource and key enabler in all warfighting systems . . . and forces must be manned, trained, and equipped to respond to an array of contingencies" (www.dodsbir.net/current/word/osd022.doc). When viewing the human performance research in the context of this statement, it is apparent that the complexity of issues surrounding such a goal requires both a fundamental and an operational understanding.

CONCLUSIONS

When it comes to enhancing performance, high-risk situations are one of the most salient examples of the usefulness of a multidisciplinary approach to human behavior that reaches beyond the lens of psychology. The complex tasks that are part of nuclear power plant control, open heart surgery, or combat aviation provide many opportunities for catastrophic failure. To date, research efforts have provided many means, including training, selection, and design, by which to improve the way such tasks are conducted. However, the need to investigate human performance in high-risk environments is far from over. While the history of applied psychology has many examples of effective interdisciplinary work being performed with the goal of enhancing performance, there are many more contributions to be made to the field. Researchers targeting high-risk tasks and situations will meet success by continuing the inclusive practices that have led to the successes achieved thus far. This is not to say that it is enough to merely follow the path set by past research. Rather, science must move forward with a focus on interdisciplinary, use-inspired research while continuing to challenge and refine new ideas. By drawing on the lessons that have led to the past successes in the field of human performance research, it will be possible for science to continue to meet the needs of individuals in high-risk situations.

We trust that the arguments illustrated above underline the importance of finding the right equilibrium in research that is not based on the traditional basic versus applied dichotomy, nor capitalizes on either the technology-centered or the human-centered approaches. Rather, the balance in research and funding for human performance should be based on fundamental research that supports operational needs in order to more readily apply human learning and performance findings to technology development and implementation. Our overall goal was to demonstrate how human performance research can be based on existing theories that are epistemologically valid and, at the same time, support ecologically grounded research in order to develop the knowledge that can contribute to solving relevant societal issues.

ACKNOWLEDGMENTS

The writing of this paper was partially supported by Grant N000140610118 and Grant N0001408C0186 from the Office of Naval Research. The views, opinions, and findings contained in this article are the authors' and should not be construed as official or as reflecting the views of the University of Central Florida or the Department of Defense.

REFERENCES

Adams, R., & Gill, S. (2007). Augmented cognition, universal access and social intelligence in the information society. In D. D. Schmorrow & L. M. Reeves (Eds.), *Augmented cognition* (pp. 231–240). Heidelberg: Springer-Verlag.

Baddeley, A. (1986). *Working memory*. Oxford, England: Clarendon.

Bul, T., & Lee, J. (1999). An agent-based framework for building decision support systems. *Decision Support Systems*, 3, 225–237.

Clark, A. (1997). *Being there: Putting brain, body, and world together again.* Cambridge, MA: MIT Press.

———. (2001). *Mindware.* Oxford, England: Oxford University Press.

Clark, A., & Chalmers, D. (1998). The extended mind. *Analysis*, 58, 7–19.

Fiore, S. M., Elias, J., Gallagher, S., & Jentsch, F. (2008). Cognition and coordination: Applying cognitive science to understand macrocognition in human-agent teams. *Proceedings of the 8th Annual Symposium on Human Interaction with Complex Systems*, Norfolk, Virginia.

Froese, T., & Ziemke, T. (2009). Enactive artificial intelligence: Investigating the systemic organization of life and mind. *Journal of Artificial Intelligence*, 173 (3–4), 466–500.

Gallagher, S. (2005). *How the body shapes the mind.* Oxford: Oxford University Press.

Harbers, M., Bosch, K. van den, & Meyer, J.-J. (2008). Self-explaining agents in virtual training. In *CEUR Workshop Proceedings of 3rd EC-TEL 2008 PROLEARN*, Maastricht, The Netherlands.

Hoeft, R. M., Kochan, J. A., & Jentsch, F. (2005). Automated systems in the cockpit: Is the autopilot, "George," a team member? In C. A. Bowers, E. Salas, & F. Jentsch (Eds.), *Creating high-tech teams: Practical guidance on work performance and technology* (pp. 243–259). Washington, D.C.: American Psychological Association.

Hoffman, R. R., & Deffenbacher, K. A. (1992). A brief history of applied cognitive psychology. *Applied Cognitive Psychology*, 6, 1–48.

Hutchins, E. (1995). *Cognition in the wild.* Cambridge, MA: MIT Press.

Kleinmutz, D. N. (1985). Cognitive heuristics and feedback in a dynamic decision environment. *Management Science*, 31, 680–702.

Mayer, R. E. (1999). Instructional technology. In F. T. Durso, R. S. Nickerson, R. W. Schvaneveldt, S. T. Dumais, D. S. Lindsay, & M. T. H. Chi (Eds.), *Handbook of applied cognition* (pp. 551–569). Chichester, England: John Wiley & Sons.

McGee, K. (2005). Enactive cognitive science. Part 1: Background and research themes. *Constructivist Foundations*, 1 (1), 19–34.

Merleau-Ponty, M. (1962). *Phenomenology of perception*, trans. C. Smith. London: Routledge Press.

Muth, E. R., Kruse, A. A., Hoover, A., & Schmorrow, D. (2005). Augmented cognition: Aiding the soldier in high and low workload environments through closed-loop human-machine interactions. In T. W. Britt, C. A. Castro, & A. B. Adler (Eds.), *Military life: The psychology of serving in peace and combat* (vol. 1, pp. 108–128). Westport, CT: Greenwood Publishing Group.

Newell, A., & Simon, H. A. (1972). *Human problem solving.* Englewood Cliffs, NJ: Prentice-Hall.

Pavel, M., Wang, G., & Li, K. (2003). Augmented cognition: Allocation of attention. In *Proceedings of the 36th Annual Hawaii International Conference on System Sciences*.

Petrox, P. V., & Stoyen, A. D. (2000). An intelligent-agent based decision support system for a complex command and control application. In *Proceedings of the Sixth IEEE International Conference on Engineering of Complex Computer Systems*, 94–104.

Rowlands, M. (1999). *The body in mind: Understanding cognitive processes.* Cambridge, England: Cambridge University Press.

Stacy, W., Freeman, J., Lackey, S., & Merket, D. (2004). Enhancing simulation-based training with performance measurement objects. *Proceedings of the Interservice/ Industry Training, Simulation and Education Conference (I/ITSEC).* Arlington, VA: NDIA.

Stokes, D. E. (1997). *Pasteur's quadrant: Basic science and technological innovation.* Washington, D.C.: Brookings Institution Press.

Sutton, J. (2006). Introduction: Memory, embodied cognition, and the extended mind. *Philosophical Psychology*, 19 (3), 281–289.

Tambe, M., Johnson, W. L., Jones, R. M., Koss, F., Laird, J. E., Rosenbloom, P. S., & Schwamb, K. (1995). Intelligent agents for interactive simulation environments. *AI Magazine*, 16 (1), 15–39.

Taylor, G., Stensrud, B., Eitelman, S., Dunham, C., & Harger, E. (2007). Toward automating airspace management. In *Computational Intelligence for Security and Defense Applications (CISDA).* Honolulu, HI. IEEE Press.

Vernon, D. (2004). Accelerated social evolution of enactive cognitive systems. In *New directions for ICTs in FP7: Grand challenges for basic research,* a FET workshop for preparing for FP7, Brussels.

Wilson, M. (2002). Six views of embodied cognition. *Psychonomic Bulletin & Review*, 9 (4), 625–636.

Wooldridge, M., & Jennings, N. (1995). Intelligent agents: Theory and practice. *Knowledge Engineering Review*, 10 (2), 115–152.

INDEX

ABOUT THE
EDITORS AND CONTRIBUTORS

Alison America is the Research Associate for the SUBSCREEN program at the Naval Submarine Medical Research Laboratory. Additionally, she is an adjunct professor at the University of Hartford, where she teaches graduate and undergraduate courses for the Psychology Department.

Andrew Bellenkes, CDR, USN, is military Assistant Professor and former Director of the Aviation Psychology/Human Factors programs at the United States Air Force Academy. A specialist in human factors and performance in aviation safety, CDR Bellenkes has written and lectured extensively on mishap investigation and prevention. He maintains ongoing flight safety efforts with military and civilian counterparts throughout Europe and the Americas.

Chris Berka, CEO/Co-Founder, Advanced Brain Monitoring, has 25 years' experience managing research, development, and commercialization of new technologies. She coinvented 15 patented/patent-pending systems, served as the Principal Investigator for $17 million National Institutes of Health/Department of Defense awards, authored 50 EEG/cognition papers, received her BA with distinction in Psychology/Biology at Ohio State University, and completed graduate studies in Neuroscience at UCSD.

Mark N. Bing, Ph.D., served as the SUBSCREEN Principal Investigator for the Submarine Force and is currently an Assistant Professor of Management at the University of Mississippi. He serves on the editorial boards of the *Journal of Applied Psychology* and *Organizational Research Methods*, and has over 25 publications on personnel selection and other human resource topics.

Justin S. Campbell, Ph.D., is an Adjunct Assistant Professor at Embry-Riddle University and has served as a Naval Aerospace Experimental Psychologist. He is interested in applying neuropsychological-informed theories of personality to investigate how coping styles affect performance in applied settings.

Regan H. Campbell, Ph.D., is the Human Systems Integration Technical Director for the Naval Sea Systems Command. She recently completed the elite Commander's Development Program (CDP), where she worked for the Pearl Harbor Naval Shipyard, the LPD 17 program office, the CVN 78 program office, and the Deputy Assistant Secretary of the Navy for Ships. She has published over 19 articles and book chapters.

Ralph E. Chatham has been a submariner, laser-building physicist, small-business corporate officer, and DARPA program manager. He remains a professional storyteller, an all-purpose curmudgeon, and a private insultant, selling questionable advice on technology and training. He chaired two task forces of the Defense Science Board, herding DoD elephants to explore issues of training superiority and training surprise.

Joseph V. Cohn, Ph.D., is a recognized leader in developing and evaluating human performance-enhancing technologies. He is a Lieutenant Commander in the U.S. Navy, is a Fellow of the American Psychological Association and the Society for Military Psychology, and is the Inaugural President of the U.S. Naval Aerospace Experimental Psychology Society.

Geoffrey Eaton provides program acquisition support to the Human Systems Integration Requirements Division Director at the Washington Navy Yard. He is a former Surface Warfare Officer with over 10 years of operational experience. He has an extensive background in human performance, training, and personnel development. He has previously published professional journal articles.

Cali Fidopiastis, Ph.D., is the Associate Director for Applied Cognition for the ACTIVE Lab at the University of Central Florida's IST. Cali holds bachelor's degrees in Biology and Psychology and a master's degree in Experimental Psychology from UC Irvine, CA. Her Ph.D. is in Modeling and Simulation-Human Factors from the University of Central Florida.

Stephen M. Fiore, Ph.D., is faculty with the University of Central Florida's Cognitive Sciences Program in the Department of Philosophy and Director of the Cognitive Sciences Laboratory at UCF's Institute for Simulation and Training. He maintains a multidisciplinary research interest that incorporates aspects of cognitive, social, and computational sciences in the investigation of learning and performance in individuals and teams.

J. D. Fletcher is a research staff member at the Institute for Defense Analyses. He has held university positions in psychology, computer science, and systems engineering and government positions in DoD Laboratories, DARPA, and the Office of Science and Technology Policy. His research interests include design and evaluation of instruction and analyses of human performance.

Jefferson D. Grubb is an Aerospace Experimental Psychologist who currently works at the Naval Aerospace Medical Institute. His research interests include the development of noncognitive metrics for aviation selection and the assessment of information processing in naturalistic settings.

Robert G. Hahn is an instructor and associate director at the U.S. Navy's School of Aviation Safety. He flew the aircraft carrier-based S-3 Viking during his previous career with the U.S. Navy. He also teaches for Embry-Riddle University and is currently working toward his Ph.D. in education.

Jerry C. Lamb, Ph.D., is Technical Director of the Naval Submarine Medical Research Laboratory (NSMRL) and has been involved for many years with submarine technology, simulator development, training systems, and human performance research. He has also held management positions in government as a Senior Executive, academia as Dean, and industry as CEO.

Corinna Lathan, Ph.D., PE, is the Co-Founder, CEO, and Board Chair of AnthroTronix, Inc. and has been involved in research related to advanced human–technology interfaces for over 10 years. Dr. Lathan received a BA in Biopsychology and Mathematics, an SM in Aeronautics/Astronautics, and a Ph.D. in Neuroscience from MIT.

Paul E. O'Connor, Ph.D., is an Aerospace Experimental Psychologist working as an Assistant Professor at the Naval Postgraduate School. His research is concerned with identifying the human factors that cause accidents and with designing, implementing, and evaluating methods to address the human factors that cause accidents.

Tatana M. Olson, LT, USN, received her Ph.D. in Industrial/Organizational Psychology from Purdue University in 2004. Serving as an Aerospace Experimental Psychologist in the Navy, she currently works as a Strategic Analyst for the Chief of Naval Personnel. Her research interests include personnel selection, training, and aviation human factors.

Davin Pavlas is an Applied Experimental/Human Factors doctoral student at the University of Central Florida. His research focuses on serious games, the interaction of aesthetics and usability, simulation, and flow state.

Henry L. Phillips IV, LCDR, USN, was awarded his Ph.D. in Industrial/ Organizational Psychology from the University of Houston in 2001 and winged as a Navy Aerospace Experimental Psychologist in 2002. He currently serves as Head of the Operational Psychology Department at the Naval Aerospace Medical Institute. His research interests include personnel selection, training, and quantitative methods.

Eduardo Salas, Ph.D., is Trustee Chair and Professor of Psychology at the University of Central Florida. He also holds an appointment as Program Director for Human Systems Integration Research Department at the Institute for Simulation and Training. Previously, he was a senior research psychologist and Head of the Training Technology Development Branch of NAVAIR-Orlando for 15 years.

Marc Sebrechts is Professor of Psychology and Department Chair at the Catholic University of America (CUA). His research examines the role of technology in perception and learning. He is founding director of the Cognition and Virtual Reality Laboratory, where he investigates how virtual environments can improve our understanding of spatial cognition.

Scott Shappell, Ph.D., is Professor of Industrial Engineering at Clemson University. Before joining the faculty at Clemson, he spent 6 years with the FAA's Civil Aerospace Medical Institute and over 16 years in the U.S. Navy as an Aerospace Experimental Psychologist. He has published extensively in the fields of accident investigation, system safety, and fatigue.

Anna Skinner is a Senior Biomedical Engineer at AnthroTronix, Inc. She specializes in human–computer interaction, human–robot interaction, human factors design, and augmented cognition. Anna holds a bachelor's degree in Biomedical Engineering from the CUA and is currently completing her graduate studies in Human Factors Psychology at the CUA.

Kay M. Stanney is President of Design Interactive, Inc., a woman-owned small business dedicated to enhancing the human–machine interface. Her research and development efforts focus on next-generation human–systems interaction paradigms, including virtual environment training systems, augmented cognition, and multimodal interaction. She received her master's and Ph.D. in Industrial Engineering from Purdue University.

Jack Vice is the Co-Founder, President, and CTO of AnthroTronix and is responsible for management of the company's DoD research and oversight of all technical resources. Prior to ATinc, Mr. Vice served in the U.S. Marine Corps and received his BS in Computer Science from the University of Maryland.

Peter B. Walker, LT, USN, received his Ph.D. in Cognitive Psychology from the University at Albany, State University of New York. He currently serves as a Navy Aerospace Experimental Psychologist, teaching at the School of Aviation Safety in Pensacola, Florida.

Steve Watson is an Engineering Psychologist currently serving as the Head of Navy Selection and Classification in Washington, D.C. His research interests vary from the practical application of human performance models to basic research in timesharing ability, mental rotation, problem solving, and personnel testing.

Sandra K. Wetzel-Smith is currently a Senior Research Psychologist at the Space and Naval Warfare Systems Center Pacific in San Diego, CA, and also serves as the Director, Tactical Systems (N6), at the Naval Mine and Anti-Submarine Warfare Command, San Diego. She specializes in the development of training and C4I systems for antisubmarine warfare.

James C. Whanger has managed the SUBSCREEN testing program at the Naval Submarine Medical Research Laboratory since 2005, including a large-scale validation study of a slightly revised version (NAVSCREEN) for the larger Navy population. He was also a member of the SEAL Selection Working Group tasked by Rear Admiral Gary Jones, then Commanding Officer of Naval Service Training Command.

Douglas A. Wiegmann is an Associate Professor of Industrial and Systems Engineering at the University of Wisconsin. In addition, he has held research, investigative, and academic appointments at the Mayo Clinic College of Medicine, the University of Illinois at Urbana-Champaign, the National Transportation Safety Board, and the U.S. Navy.

Wallace H. Wulfeck II is a Senior Research Psychologist at the Space and Naval Warfare Systems Center Pacific in San Diego, CA. During 2004–2007 he served as Science and Technology Officer for the Capable Manpower Future Naval Capability program at the Office of Naval Research. He conducts training research, technology development, and transition to operational use.